Interpreting Greek Tragedy

Also by Charles Segal

Landscape in Ovid's Metamorphoses: A Study in the Transformation of a Literary Symbol. Hermes Einzelschriften 23

The Theme of the Mutilation of the Corpse in the Iliad. Mnemosyne Supplement 17

Tragedy and Civilization: An Interpretation of Sophocles. Martin Classical Lectures, vol. 26

Poetry and Myth in Ancient Pastoral: Essays on Theocritus and Virgil

Dionysiac Poetics and Euripides' Bacchae

Pindar's Mythmaking: The Fourth Pythian Ode

Language and Desire in Seneca's Phaedra

As Editor:

Cedric H. Whitman, *The Heroic Paradox: Essays on Homer, Sophocles, and Aristophanes*

G. B. Conte, *The Rhetoric of Imitation: Genre and Poetic Memory in Virgil and Other Latin Poets*

Interpreting Greek Tragedy

MYTH, POETRY, TEXT

Charles Segal

Cornell University Press

ITHACA AND LONDON

Open access edition funded by the National Endowment for the Humanities/Andrew W. Mellon Foundation Humanities Open Book Program.

Cornell University gratefully acknowledges a grant from the Andrew W. Mellon Foundation that aided in bringing this book to publication.

Second paperback printing 2019

ISBN 978-0-8014-1890-7 (cloth: alk. paper)
ISBN 978-1-5017-4669-7 (pbk.: alk. paper)
ISBN 978-1-5017-4670-3 (pdf)
ISBN 978-1-5017-4671-0 (epub/mobi)

Librarians: A CIP catalog record for this book is available from the Library of Congress

Cover photo: Tragic actor. Terracotta figure, probably late third century B. C. Agora excavations. Athens, T862. Photograph Vincent. Used by permission of the Agora Excavations, American School of Classical Studies at Athens, courtesy of Mrs. Dorothy Burr Thompson.

For Bernard Knox

Contents

Contents

Preface

The essays collected in this volume were published over a period of some twenty years. They reflect some of the changes in the modes and concerns of the study of Greek tragedy in the United States during this period, from the New Critical approach of the essay on Euripides' *Hippolytus* to the increasing concern with myth, psychoanalytic interpretation, structuralism, and language and writing in the recent pieces. They illustrate, I believe, the contention that the many-faceted poetic dramas created by the geniuses of Greek culture at its apogee are, and will probably remain, open to many different modes of interpretation.

That these dramas cannot be circumscribed by a single interpretive discourse may disturb positivistically minded scholars who would like to have one final meaning for each surviving play, but it augurs well for the survival of these works into whatever uncertain future awaits our descendants. These are complex meditations on mortality, on the inevitability of our confrontation with death, suffering, and the unpredictable in human life, on the force of the passions and the irrational behind our actions, on justice and retribution, and on the question of what larger power, if any, is responsible for the shape that our world and our lives take. They will, we may expect, continue to intrigue, attract, disturb, puzzle, and in their own mysterious way help us make sense of the strange and precarious thing that life often seems to be.

The essays were chosen to illustrate particular methodologies and to present Greek tragedy in a perspective that would interest the general reader as well as the classical specialist. The arrangement is by topic rather than by date of publication, proceeding from the more general to the more particular and then back to the general. I begin with three recent pieces, all concerned with tragedy in relation to myth and language. There follow two essays on Sophocles and four on Euripides. In some cases the pairing of essays on the same play (as with the *Hippolytus* and the *Bacchae*) shows how a shift in one's critical viewpoint and terminology may illuminate quite different facets of the same work. Essays 10 and 11 are paired because each in a different way explores the partial dependence of the tragic effect on our basic sense of physicality, on our consciousness of the mortal vulnerability of our bodies. The final essay, though not directly concerned with drama, I have included because it articulates some of the problems and assumptions underlying the interpretation of literature now. It thus places the study of the tragic drama of the Greeks in the larger framework of the humanities in general.

In selecting these pieces, I have tried to avoid overlap with my other books on ancient drama and to present material that could stand on its own. Although the temptation to revise, add, subtract, and annotate was strong, I have resisted the temptation and let these pieces, with some excisions and additions noted below, stand as published. The collection, I felt, should indicate the shifting critical stances, developments, and varied points of view that one student of these works has experienced over many years rather than the imposed uniformity of a single moment.

The changes from the original form of publication are as follows. From the first essay, "Greek Tragedy and Society," I have deleted a few pages discussing Euripides' *Hippolytus* and *Bacchae* to avoid overlap with material in part III of this book. For the same reason I have deleted a few sentences of essay 8. To the third essay, "Greek Tragedy: Writing, Truth, and the Representation of the Self," I have added a paragraph on the *Oedipus Tyrannus* and incorporated (in revised form) three pages on the *Iphigeneia in Tauris* from another essay that is absent from this volume. Considerations of space and scale made it necessary to abbreviate the long essay on Euripides' *Helen,* with accompanying changes in the notes. The footnotes to essay 6, "The Tragedy of the *Hippolytus,*" have been slightly curtailed. In a few cases the notes have been slightly recast for the sake of uniformity of reference. There are also minor stylistic revisions throughout. Translations are my own unless otherwise noted.

In looking back at work done over so many years, I am made aware of how much I owe to former teachers and to friends and colleagues. I cannot render all those thanks here, but they are nonetheless deeply felt. I also express my gratitude to the students with whom I have read and discussed these plays, both in Greek and in English, over the last quarter century. Their intense questioning of what these works had to say to them about the meaning of life often taught me as much as I taught them. I renew, with pleasure, the expressions of thanks in the individual essays. I warmly thank my colleagues in classics and in comparative literature at Brown University for many years of friendship, encouragement, and advice. I am sensible of the great debt of gratitude that I owe to numerous other friends and colleagues on both sides of the Atlantic, and in some cases on the other side of the Pacific, who discussed these works with me, generously sent copies of publications, and gave me the benefit of their insight, acumen, and learning.

Fellowships from the American Academy in Rome, the Center for Hellenic Studies in Washington, the American Council of Learned Societies, the John Simon Guggenheim Memorial Foundation, and the National Endowment for the Humanities provided the leisure and freedom in which many of these essays were developed and written. I thank all of these institutions for their trust and support. The task of typing and retyping the manuscripts over the years was undertaken with ever-cheerful efficiency by Frances Eisenhauer and Ruthann Whitten. Mrs. Whitten also retyped the notes for several of the essays. Karen Bassi helped with editorial details. Two anonymous readers of Cornell University Press provided helpful advice about selecting the essays. Bernhard Kendler of the Press, who conceived and encouraged this project, displayed exemplary patience toward my changing views of what to include. The staff of the Press, as in the past, proved courteously and efficiently helpful at all stages of production. In particular, I thank Roger Haydon, whose incisive copy editing consistently improved the readability of the text.

My dedication expresses my gratitude for all that I, like so many others, have learned about Greek drama from Bernard Knox and for his broader, if less tangible, contributions to the classics in his quarter century as director of the Center for Hellenic Studies in Washington.

CHARLES SEGAL

Providence, Rhode Island

Acknowledgments

The essays in this volume originally appeared in the publications listed below. I am grateful to the editors, journals, and publishers for permission to reprint them here.

1. "Griechische Tragödie und Gesellschaft," in *Propyläen Geschichte der Literatur*, vol. 1, *1200 BC–600 AD* (Propyläen Verlag, Berlin 1981) I.198–217 and 546–47. Reprinted by permission of Propyläen Verlag and Ullstein Verlag.

2. "Greek Myth as a Semiotic and Structural System and the Problem of Tragedy," *Arethusa* 16 (1983) 173–98.

3. "Greek Tragedy: Writing, Truth, and the Representation of the Self," *Mnemai: Classical Studies in Memory of Karl K. Hulley*, ed. Harold J. Evjen (Scholars Press, Chico, Calif. 1984) 41–67. In addition, I have incorporated pages 149–51, in revised form, from "Tragédie, oralité, écriture," *Poétique* 50 (1982) 131–54.

4. "Visual Symbolism and Visual Effects in Sophocles," *Classical World* 74 (1980/81) 124–42.

5. "Sophocles' Praise of Man and the Conflicts of the *Antigone*," *Arion* 3, no. 2 (1964) 46–66.

6. "The Tragedy of the *Hippolytus:* The Waters of Ocean and the Untouched Meadow," *Harvard Studies in Classical Philology* 70 (1965) 117–69. Copyright © 1965 by The President and Fellows of Harvard College. Reprinted by permission of Harvard University Press.

7. "The Two Worlds of Euripides' *Helen*," *Transactions of the American Philological Association* 102 (1971) 553–614.

8. "Pentheus and Hippolytus on the Couch and on the Grid: Psy-

choanalytic and Structuralist Readings of Greek Tragedy," *Classical World* 72 (1978/79) 129–48.

9. "Euripides' *Bacchae:* The Language of the Self and the Language of the Mysteries," *Die wilde Seele,* Festschrift for George Devereux, ed. Hans Peter Dürr (Suhrkamp Verlag, Frankfurt forthcoming).

10. "Boundary Violation and the Landscape of the Self in Senecan Tragedy," *Antike und Abendland* 29 (1983) 172–87. Reprinted by permission of *Antike und Abendland* and Walter de Gruyter & Co., Berlin.

11. "Tragedy, Corporeality, and the Texture of Language: Matricide in the Three Electra Plays," *Classical World* 79 (1985–86) 7–23.

12. "Literature and Interpretation: Conventions, History, and Universals," *Classical and Modern Literature* 5, no. 2 (Winter 1985) 71–85.

Abbreviations

AC   *L'Antiquité Classique*
AJP   *American Journal of Philology*
C & M   *Classica et Mediaevalia*
CJ   *Classical Journal*
CP   *Classical Philology*
CQ   *Classical Quarterly*
CR   *Classical Review*
CW   *Classical World*
D, Diehl   Ernest Diehl, ed., *Anthologia Lyrica Graeca* (Leipzig 1925)
D-K   Hermann Diels and Walter Kranz, eds., *Die Fragmente der Vorsokratiker*, 6th ed. (Berlin 1952), 3 vols.
G & R   *Greece and Rome*
GRBS   *Greek, Roman and Byzantine Studies*
HSCP   *Harvard Studies in Classical Philology*
ICS   *Illinois Classical Studies*
Jacoby   Felix Jacoby, ed., *Die Fragmente der griechischen Historiker* (Berlin 1923–30 and Leiden 1940–   )
JHS   *Journal of Hellenic Studies*
K   Theodor Koch, ed., *Comicorum Atticorum Fragmenta* (Leipzig 1880–88)
Lobel-Page   Edgar Lobel and Denys Page, eds., *Poetarum Lesbiorum Fragmenta* (Oxford 1955)
MH   *Museum Helveticum*
Nauck   Augustus Nauck, ed., *Tragicorum Graecorum Fragmenta*, 2d ed. (Leipzig 1889), with Supplement, ed. B. Snell (Hildesheim 1964)
Page, *PMG*   D. L. Page, ed., *Poetae Melici Graeci* (Oxford 1962)
PCPS   *Proceedings of the Cambridge Philological Society*
PP   *La Parola del Passato*
QUCC   *Quaderni Urbinati di Cultura Classica*
RE   Pauly-Wissowa-Kroll, eds., *Real-Encyclopädie der classischen Altertumswissenschaft* (Munich and Stuttgart 1894–   )

Abbreviations

REG   *Revue des Etudes Grecques*
RhM   *Rheinisches Museum für Philologie*
SB Berlin   *Sitzungsberichte der Preussischen Akademie der Wissenschaften zu*
Berlin, Philosophisch-historische Klasse
SB Vienna   *Sitzungsberichte der Österreichischen Akademie der Wissenschaften*
in Wien, Philosophisch-historische Klasse
SSR   *Studi Storici-Religiosi*
TAPA   *Transactions of the American Philological Association*
Tüb. Beitr.   *Tübinger Beiträge*
YCS   *Yale Classical Studies*

Greek and Roman authors are cited from the Oxford Classical Texts where available. Abbreviations follow standard usage. The following list is provided for the nonclassicist.

Aeschyl.   Aeschylus
  Ag.   *Agamemnon*
  Cho.   *Choephoroe, Libation Bearers*
  Eum.   *Eumenides*
  Pers.   *Persians*
  PV   *Prometheus Bound*
  Sept.   *Seven against Thebes*
Ar.   Aristophanes
  Lys.   *Lysistrata*
  Thesm.   *Thesmophoriazusae*
Eur.   Euripides
  Alc.   *Alcestis*
  Ba.   *Bacchae*
  Cycl.   *Cyclops*
  El.   *Electra*
  Hec.   *Hecuba*
  Hel.   *Helen*
  HF   *Heracles, Heracles Mad*
  Hipp.   *Hippolytus*
  IA   *Iphigeneia in Aulis*
  IT   *Iphigeneia in Tauris*
  Med.   *Medea*
  Or.   *Orestes*
  Phoen.   *Phoenissae, Phoenician Women*
  Tro.   *Troades, Trojan Women*
Hom.   Homer
  h. Cer.   *Homeric Hymn to Demeter*
  h. Ven.   *Homeric Hymn to Aphrodite*

Il.	*Iliad*
Od.	*Odyssey*
Seneca	
Ag.	*Agamemnon*
HF	*Hercules Furens*
HO	*Hercules Oetaeus*
Med.	*Medea*
Oed.	*Oedipus*
Pha.	*Phaedra*
Phoen.	*Phoenissae*
Thy.	*Thyestes*
Soph.	Sophocles
Antig.	*Antigone*
El.	*Electra*
OC	*Oedipus Coloneus*
OT	*Oedipus Tyrannus, Oedipus Rex*
Phil.	*Philoctetes*
Trach.	*Trachiniae, Trachinian Women*

I/

GREEK TRAGEDY:
MYTH AND STRUCTURE

CHAPTER I /

Greek Tragedy and Society:
A Structuralist Perspective

I

Over the past two or three decades, students of Greek tragedy have shown an increasing concern with conceptual patterns, with structures of thought, action, and language. A greater circumspection about the nature of character in ancient drama has lessened the tendency to view the plays in terms of psychological realism. Earlier in the century the Cambridge School of Harrison, Murray, and Cornford stimulated interest in the social and ritual structures reflected in the plays and pointed students to underlying patterns rather than to surface literalism. At about the same time Freud and Jung were setting the foundation for the recovery of underlying patterns of a different nature. From the 1930s on, especially in Germany, scholars devoted special attention to tragedy's formal and dramatic structure: dialogue and monologue, the patterning of the odes, the messenger's speech, patterns of intrigue and deception.

In America the New Criticism of the fifties focused on patterns latent in the poetic language of the plays. Such studies as R. F. Goheen's of the *Antigone* and Bernard Knox's of the *Oedipus Tyrannus* tried to discern the relation between the poetic texture and the intellectual armature of the work.[1] Repeated images, clustered about certain characters or the attitudes embodied by those characters, could

---

1. R. F. Goheen, *The Imagery of Sophocles' Antigone* (Princeton 1951); B. M. W. Knox, *Oedipus at Thebes* (New Haven 1957).

help articulate the main concerns of the play and relate them to patterns of language and action.

Anthropologically or psychologically oriented scholars, among them Dodds, Adkins, Vernant, Gouldner, and Slater, have also viewed Greek tragedy as the battleground for conflicting value systems and latent tensions within society.[2] J.-P. Vernant especially, concerned with the question of how the social order deals with the antinomies that it contains, has stressed tragedy as the field of the problematical where the familiar institutions are called into question and the moral vocabulary, no longer adequate, becomes ambiguous or self-contradictory.

Society, from this approach, appears not a crystalline, coherent entity inherited by each of its members but rather an ongoing process of constructing, abandoning, and readjusting systems of analogies and interlocking relations. Interaction and continuous development of individual institutions in their relations to one another rather than the unity of a centralized entity emerges as the dominant subject for scrutiny. This view of the ancient Greek city stresses, in the words of A. Momigliano and S. C. Humphreys, "the study of relations of complementarity or conflict between the behavioral norms associated with different contexts of interaction."[3]

The structuralist's position has some similarities to that of the sociologist. "Reality" has its existence in its relation to the mental, social, and linguistic constructions of the thinking subject. The social system resembles the literary work in being viewed, as Roland Barthes would say, in the present rather than the perfective tense. Social man is not a being secure in the given nexus of familial, ritual, and political ties that hold his life together but rather a being continually engaged in creating that nexus.[4]

The structuralist emphasis falls not so much upon the dominant, ideal values at the surface of the culture as on the subsurface tensions within the system, the dynamic pulls that the culture has to allow,

2. E. R. Dodds, *The Greeks and the Irrational* (Berkeley and Los Angeles 1951); A. W. H. Adkins, *Merit and Responsibility* (Oxford 1960); J.-P. Vernant and P. Vidal-Naquet, *Mythe et tragédie* (Paris 1972); Alvin Gouldner, *Enter Plato* (New York and London 1965); Philip Slater, *The Glory of Hera* (Boston 1968).

3. A Momigliano and S. C. Humphreys, "The Social Structure of the Ancient City," *Annali della Scuola Normale Superiore di Pisa* 43 (1974) 366.

4. See Roland Barthes, "The Structuralist Activity," in R. and F. DeGeorge, eds., *The Structuralists from Marx to Lévi-Strauss* (Garden City, N.Y. 1972) 153.

resist, and contain in order to exist. The achievement of classical Athens, then, appears less the crystallization of a marmoreal harmony than the open equilibrium between competing values and unresolvable polarities.

Such a view gives us a tragedy that reflects the anxieties rather than the confident verities of its audience. Robert Browning's Balaustion may have found "those Greek qualities of goodness and beauty" in "that strangest, saddest, sweetest song" of Euripides, but recent critics find themselves attuned more to the disonances, contradictions, and harsh archaic residues that the tragic poet's reworking of myth heaves back to the surface.

The rationality of the form of Greek tragedy only sets off the irrationality that it reveals just below the surface of myth, cult, and other social forms. Literary critics influenced by both the Freudians and the Frazerians have increasingly probed for these latent, often darker, meanings which bear promise of revealing the hidden patterns and unquestioned assumptions of the society or the knowledge that the conscious mind is unwilling or unable to face. In this way the darker side of Greek civilization, as expressed in its creation of tragedy, has enabled modern man in his turn to confront the darker side of existence and explore what lies beneath the surface of his own highly rationalized, desacralized, excessively technologized culture.

From Nietzsche onward, Greek tragedy has appeared to hold the key to that darker vision of existence, the irrational and the violent in man and the world. Tragedy's rediscovery and popularity since World War II have filled a need for that vision in modern life, a need for an alternative to the Judaeo-Christian view of a world order based on divine benignity and love.

II

Because it approaches myth as a system of tensions and oppositions, the methodology of Claude Lévi-Strauss is especially suited to explore the conflictual aspect of tragedy. For Lévi-Strauss, mythic thought operates in terms of bipolar oppositions. The function of myth is to mediate fundamental contradictions in human existence, man's relation to man in society and to nature in the external world. Recognizing that our perception and representation of experience are structured by coded patterns of language, gesture, ritual, and so on, structuralism provides a frame in which we can formulate precisely and thoroughly the interrelation between the political, the linguistic, the religious, the psychological—all the many levels of dramatic action.

In a structuralist analysis the details of kinship, dress, architecture, eating, and ritual are not merely isolated data or *Realien* but elements of a structured message, a "code." Each code expressed in its own terms—the "languages" of ritual, kinship, diet—a microcosm of the social order. In the analysis of a myth or a literary work it is not the surface details in themselves which are important but the relational patterns, the configurations, of these details in the various codes, the "analogy of functions" rather than the "analogy of substances."

Whereas the New Criticism tends to isolate a work in a cultural vacuum and to limit itself to the internal coherence of verbal structures, structuralism seeks to relate the value structures of the society to the aesthetic structures of the literary work. Its concern, however, is not so much with the internal logic and coherence of the codes per se as with the cognitive patterns of the culture which they imply and the correspondence between the semantic structures of the literary work and the social structures of the culture as a whole.

When we turn from structures of society to structures of literary texts, however, we encounter a fundamental difficulty. The literary work imposes a secondary structure of language and meanings upon the given structures of the society. Unavoidably, it uses the codes that constitute the mental patterns of the society; and it could be analyzed, at one level, solely in terms of those accepted, normative codes. But at the same time it deliberately manipulates, distorts, or otherwise transforms those patterns in the special self-conscious structures—linguistic, psychological, societal—superimposed by its own internal, aesthetic coherence. To put it differently, the work of literature overlays the codified contiguity of *signifiant* and *signifié* with a new internal coding wherein the relationships between sound and sense, between overt and latent meaning, between literal and figurative significance of words, change from the familiar (that is, the precoded) to the unexpected, the novel, and the striking.

Tragedy's relation to the expression of the social order encoded in myths is particularly complex. As part of a public festival, a ritual in honor of the god Dionysus, tragedy validates the social order. It demonstrates the dangers of excess, impiety, or overconfidence within a coherent system of symbols representative of the divine, political, and social order. The presence of the gods, the palace of the king, the altars and shrines, the oracles, the house create a microcosm of the totality of that order. At the same time the violence of the action, the radical questioning of justice both human and divine, the searching explorations of the failure or the betrayal of public and private morality take us outside that order. In the magical circle of the orchestra the normal coherence that distinguishes and balances good and evil, love and hate, kin and stranger breaks down. The world order is stretched to its limits; its intelligibility is suspended.

So tragedy, while affirming the interrelatedness of all parts of the human and divine order, also has the peculiarity of calling into question the normative codes themselves. Both in language and in its enacted narrative, tragedy effects a violent derangement of the codes, a deliberate destructuring of the familiar patterns of order. In tragedy, as to some degree in all literature, the "message" of the specific text not only brings to life something that was not in the code but can threaten to destroy the code itself.

The parallels between strained diction, violent metaphors, perverted rituals, and inverted sexual roles in the *Oresteia* show the violence done to the linguistic, ritual, and familiar codes. The *Oedipus Tyrannus* develops an elaborate correspondence between the confusion of language in the riddles of the Sphinx and in the oracles of the gods (the two polar forms of utterance have a disconcerting unity), the social inversions of king and scapegoat, the ritual inversions of pollution and purification, and the domestic confusion of father and husband, father and brother, wife and mother. Here, as in the *Oresteia,* the linguistic, political, ritual, and familial codes are all involved simultaneously in the unstable situation from which tragic suffering arises. Confused intermingling, inversions, troubling identifications replace reassuring demarcation or differentiation. The original structures are suspended, forcing the mind to reach beyond those structures in the painful search for other principles of order or in the even more painful admission that there are no principles of order. Here men must face the chaos that their mental structures— social, linguistic, political, sexual, spatial—deliberately shut out.

III

A Greek tragedy is a special kind of mythical narration. We cannot approach it exactly as Lévi-Strauss approaches a given myth, reconstructing an underlying pattern by comparing the corresponding terms ("mythemes") in a large number of variants.[5] The structuralist analysis of the coding processes of language can trace the relation between aesthetic patterns and patterns of order in the society as a whole. The literary critic, on the other hand, is concerned not with the core structure of the myth as revealed and realized in its variants but with the particular variant that is the literary work.

To take a specific example, to which we shall return later, Sophocles' *Trachiniae* uses a system of analogies based on an underlying opposition of god and beast, civilization and savagery. The play opens with Deianeira anxious about the long absence of Heracles, her husband. She laments the cares of her life and tells how the monstrous river-god, Achelous, and Heracles fought to win her hand, a battle described in a later choral ode (497–530). A messenger announces Heracles' return. Deianeira sees the young and beautiful Iole in the entourage and soon learns that Iole is destined for Heracles' bed. At first calm and forgiving, she later returns to the stage resolved to try a love charm given to her in another violent wooing, the attempted rape long ago by the Centaur Nessus. Fatally wounded by Heracles' arrow, poisoned with the Hydra's venom, Nessus instructed Deianeira to save the blood clotted around his wound. All these years she has kept it stored in the inner chambers of the house. Now she anoints a robe with it and sends it to Heracles for his sacrificial celebration at Cape Cenaeum, across the water from Trachis. Her son Hyllus arrives soon after with the news of the robe's effect: Heracles, in the midst of slaughtering bulls at the sacrificial fires, was suddenly seized by terrible agony, and he is now coming to Trachis to exact vengeance from Deinaeira. Realizing what she has done, she exits in silence; soon her suicide in the bedchamber is described. Ferocious in his pain, Heracles arrives, ready to kill De-

---

5. For example, Claude Lévi-Strauss, "The Structural Study of Myth" (1955), in DeGeorge and DeGeorge (note 4) 169–94; *The Raw and the Cooked: Introduction to a Science of Mythology*, trans. J. and D. Weightman (New York 1970); and subsequent volumes of *Mythologiques*.

ianeira with his own hands. When he learns the details of the poison
and hears the name of Nessus, he realizes that he is doomed in accordance with an old oracle from Zeus. He forces the reluctant Hyllus to
marry Iole and makes him promise to take him to Mount Oeta where
he is to be burned on a funeral pyre. In a last speech he checks his cries
of pain with heroic endurance and exits with son and followers for
Oeta. Hyllus (or the chorus) closes the play with a lament about the
remoteness and indifference of the gods.

From this rather complicated action emerges a symmetrical relation between Nessus, the beast-man, and Heracles, the man who
stands in a special proximity to the gods. Structurally, the success of
Nessus' revenge and the deaths of Heracles and Deianeira can be
described as a series of failed mediations between the poles of bestiality and divinity. Heracles acts out the anomalous role of a beast-
god insofar as he, the son of Zeus, repeats the violence of the Centaur. Sacrifice in the ritual code, marriage in the sexual code, the safe
interior of the house in the spatial and familial codes—all are isomorphic expressions of this basic failure of mediation, the destruction
of the mean where civilization is possible. Normal communication
between man and god is destroyed, and with it collapse the hierarchical relation between beast, man, and god, the equilibrium between the violent sexual instincts which links man with beast, and the
coherent social and cosmic order that links man with gods. The
triumph of the "beast" Nessus through his poisoned blood, a spec-
ious love charm that reaches back to the destructive monstrosity of
the Hydra, the resultant perversion of the sacrificial rite into the
killing of the god-man by the beast-man, and the destruction of the
house and marriage are not only elements in a causal sequence but
also simultaneous manifestations of an underlying structure—or
rather, the disintegration of structure. Achelous and Hydra, for example, are agents within a causal series that culminates in Heracles'
death, but they are also forces ever present in the action, existing
simultaneously with and parallel to Nessus and the bestial aspect of
Heracles.

Sacrifice, which plays a central role in this and other tragedies, is
the mediating vehicle within the system of relations and communica-
tions that link gods and men. Sacrifice validates the world order by
affirming the hierarchical relation of god-man-beast. The immortal
gods receive the airy smoke that mounts from the durable bones

Mortal men sustain themselves with the roasted meat of the perishable flesh. The human celebrant who offers the victim to the gods is as far above the beast as he is below the god who receives the offering.[6] The ritual stylization of killing during the sacrifice and the roasting of the flesh to be consumed by the celebrants after the sacrifice separate the structured world of "culture" from the savagery of wild "nature." By establishing a system of conjunctions and disjunctions, sacrifice makes manifest the implicit logic of the world order. It separates gods from men and men from beasts, but it also opens a way of access from men to gods. In tragedy that system of logical relations is confused or overthrown, sometimes to be recreated on a new basis. The centrality of sacrifice as a symbolic expression of system explains, in part, why sacrifice and its distortions or perversions play such an important role in tragedy: one thinks of the stories of Thyestes, Iphigeneia at Taurus and at Aulis, Medea, Ajax—all recurrent subjects of tragedy and all characterized by perverted sacrifice.[7]

Kingship, like sacrifice, is not merely a one-dimensional social category, political in the case of kingship, religious in the case of sacrifice. In tragedy, as in early Greek myth and literature more generally, the king occupies the symbolic point where the human and the divine, the natural and supernatural worlds intersect. His sufferings represent the efforts of the society to maintain those relations with the cosmic order on which its physical and spiritual life depends. In the *Oresteia,* by illustration, Aeschylus takes great pains to establish the spatial coordinates of this kingship. The point at which the king suffers and dies is a point of crossing between elemental opposites: sea and fire (*Ag.* 281ff., 650f., 958), winter and summer (966–72), upper and lower limits (cf. *hyper-, hypo-,* "above," "below," in *Ag.* 786), divine honor and bestial degradation. It is not just the suffering of Agamemnon as an individual which moves us but the cosmic, religious, and social vibrations in the drastic reversal and fearful collapse of polarities that define both the ordered structure of the society and the natural and supernatural order. Hence Agamemnon's walk-

---

6. For this view of sacrifice see M. Detienne, J.-P. Vernant, et al., *La cuisine du sacrifice en pays grec* (Paris 1979); M. Detienne, *Les jardins d'Adonis* (Paris 1972); and J.-P. Vernant, *Mythe et société en Grèce ancienne* (Paris 1974).

7. See Walter Burkert, "Greek Tragedy and Sacrificial Ritual," *GRBS* 7 (1966) 87–121; also his *Homo Necans* (1972; Berkeley and Los Angeles 1983).

ing on the carpet is not merely an act of individual pride which provokes the "envy" of gods and men (cf. *Ag.* 921–25, 947) but a terrifying confusion of boundaries in the figure who is charged with the sacred task of linking human and divine, making visible in his mortal person the numinous order of the gods.

The Greek tragic hero, then, is not a "character" quite as the hero of a modern fiction is a character, an individual with a three-dimensional, idiosyncratic personality. He is, rather, both an individual caught in a moral conflict and a symbolic element within a complex socioreligious structure. He carries the linear flow of the action and is a constellation of patterns present simultaneously in all parts of the action. Alongside the individualized personalities of Aeschylus' Agamemnon, Sophocles' Oedipus, or Euripides' Pentheus, that is to say, stands the role of sacral kingship; and in that role each of these figures concentrates in himself the crisis in relations between the human, natural, and supernatural worlds which forms the starting point for the tragic action.

In the *Oedipus Tyrannus,* for example, the plague, manifestation of a disturbance in the relation between man and god, both reveals and engages the hero at the point of maximum exposure to the unknown. It forces him to take responsibility for the troubled cosmic order and propels him into reversals of power and helplessness, knowledge and ignorance, divine and bestial in the ensuing dramatic action. The king supplicated with nearly divine honor in the prologue (*OT* 31–54) proves to be the beastlike pollution wandering "in the savage woodland, the bull of the rocks" (477ff.). The spatial coordinates of this reversal in the ritual and biological codes are clearly demarcated in the fall of the "tyrant" from rooftop to ground in the third stasimon (863–79). A horizontal axis from palace to wild, city to mountain, man to beast, intersects a vertical axis from highest to lowest, king to scapegoat. At the point of intersection stands Oedipus, whose identity consists of this intersection of contradictions, this simultaneous presence of polarities.

To describe these structural and spatial coordinates of Oedipus' tragic situation is to supplement, not to deny, our affective reactions of pity and fear to the undeserved agonies of a great-souled man as they unfold before us. A structuralist approach to Oedipus' tragedy reinforces its connections with the patterns of sacral kingship, linking him with Aeschylus' Agamemnon, with Euripides' Heracles and

Pentheus, or even with Shakespeare's Lear and Hamlet. Within the limits of the play itself, the approach helps us appreciate the cosmic implications of Oedipus' ruin and hence the underlying seriousness—*spoudaiotēs* is Aristotle's term—of our involvement in that ruin. It is no ordinary individual who undergoes this suffering but a paradigmatic figure. His fate must deeply concern us because it involves a fundamental issue—the order or chaos of our world and the capacity of our social and intellectual constructs to contain that chaos.

Like psychological analysis, a structuralist reading seeks to uncover latent, subsurface meanings, to reveal implicit rather than explicit structures; and so a structuralist view of sacrifice focuses on the nexus of logical relations described above. From a psychological point of view, however, sacrifice expresses the violence beneath the surface of the social order and the need to expel that violence. René Girard, who has approached tragedy from this point of view, portrays the tragic action as sacralizing violence by the choice of an arbitrary victim, a *pharmakos* or scapegoat whose death or suffering removes violence from the realm of men and gives it back to the gods.[8] In the sacrificial action of tragedy, the hero doubles with his bestial opposite—Heracles with Nessus in the *Trachiniae,* Pentheus with Dionysus in the *Bacchae*—only to be separated from him in the sacrificial death that reestablishes distinctions and gradations and thereby prevents a further collapse into chaos.

The cultural meaning that certain symbols possess does not, of course, preclude their psychological significance. To the cultural historian, for example, the opening of the *Oedipus Coloneus* reflects the Greeks' religious concern with pollution and purification and the rites of supplication. To the Freudian critic, Oedipus' blind entrance to an inviolate grove of hallowed female goddesses is not only the ritual frame for the ensuing drama but also the reenactment of a prior pattern in Oedipus' life: it recapitulates at a new level the hero's transgressive entrance into a dark forbidden place of the mother, a place connected with her mysterious power of creating life. Entrance to the grove is a movement from the Bad Mother who cast him into the wild to the nurturing mother who receives and shelters him. The response to cruel expulsion from the womb, from Jocasta's body to

8. René Girard, *Violence and the Sacred,* trans. P. Gregory (1972; Baltimore 1977).

Cithaeron (symbol of the Bad Mother), is acceptance back into the womblike earth of that generous mother, the pious city of Athens.

In moving from the *Tyrannus* to the *Coloneus,* Sophocles shifts from an infantile world of primary acceptance or rejection to a public realm of civic action. Through the symbolism of the Eumenides and their grove the civic frame of Athens in the *Oedipus Coloneus* seems able, finally, to reconcile the two faces of woman, the generosity and the destructiveness of the mother as perceived by the totally dependent infant to whom her absence or presence means denial or fulfillment.[9]

From a structuralist perspective, the grove is the point of conjunction between the city and the wild, the place of shelter and the exposed world of the polluted outcast. It is also the focus for a vertical spatial axis between upper and lower worlds, gods and men. It unites the two poles of Oedipus' status: *below* the human as the despised, impure, exiled parricide and incestuous criminal and *above* the human as a hero mysteriously called by divine voices that come from both above and below.

Mother, womb, mother earth, and city are all parts of a single symbolic complex. Oedipus' acceptance by Athens in the *Oedipus Coloneus* is thus a shift from the unmediated swing of the polluted and exiled king between godhead and bestiality so dangerous in the *Tyrannus* to the king's restoration to a civic frame. He becomes the mediator between chthonic and Olympian powers and stands in a privileged relation to the goddesses who embody both the destructive and the creative forces of nature. His marginal status thus parallels that of the Eumenides themselves. Like them he is an ambiguous figure whose place is at the fringes of the city, the liminal space at the borders of the land. Like them he dispenses both curses and blessings. Received back into the city, he has a place of honor as a hero, but he is still in a sense outside, for his tomb is unknown to all but Theseus. His end is hidden in mystery, associated with places of mysterious transition between worlds, the "brazen-footed road" with its "bronze steps" into the earth (*OC* 57, 1590ff.).

9. Helen Bacon, "Women's Two Faces: Sophocles' View of the Tragedy of Oedipus and His Family," in *Science and Psychoanalysis,* American Academy of Psychoanalysis Decennial Memorial Volume (New York 1966) 10–27.

IV

Lévi-Strauss's view of myth as exploring and validating the opposition between nature and culture, the "raw" and the "cooked," is
substantiated by a great deal of Greek tragedy. Here the tension
between *nomos* and *physis,* culture and nature, often takes the form of
a tension between the spheres of confident human authority and
divine autonomy. On the one hand lies the polis and its Olympian-
sponsored, male-oriented institutions, the area where man imposes
structure and the ordering conventions of nomos upon the potentially
threatening impulses of physis. On the other hand lies the power of
the gods in its elusive, unknown aspects, the chthonic divinities and
the areas of human life under their supervision, the stain of impurity,
the threatening realm of women, the biological processes of birth and
death, the demands of nurture (*trophē*) and blood ties, and the curses
produced or transmitted in the area of such blood ties.

The origins and development of civilization, the emergence of law
(nomos) and justice (*dikē*), the mastery over the savagery both in
nature and in man himself are important themes in all the surviving
tragedians as well as in the thought of their contemporaries, Herodotus, Protagoras, Hippias, Hippocrates, Democritus, and others.
Aeschylus' Prometheus trilogy (of which only the *Prometheus Bound*
survives) deals with the origins of civilized technology. In his *Oresteia*
the juridical resolution of homocide in the city evolves from primitive blood vengeance in the family. Sophocles won his first victory
with a play about a culture hero, the *Triptolemus* of 468 B.C. His lost
Palamedes, Nauplius, and probably *Daedalus* seem to have been based
on similar subjects. The first stasimon of the *Antigone* (332–75) is one
of the great texts of the fifth century on man's conquest of nature; it
brings this broad evolutionary perspective to the play's conflicts between political authority and the ties of blood, between the rationalism and Olympian religion supposedly governing the state and
the emotional bonds among kin and the chthonic deities whose
sphere is burial and respect for the dead. Sophocles' *Philoctetes,* whose
hero has been described as an ancient Robinson Crusoe, draws heavily on Sophistic theories about the origins of culture to explore the
paradox that the miserable outcast on a desert island may embody a
more valid and humane vision of civilized order than the goal-ori-

ented, unscrupulous, manipulative leaders of the Greek army at Troy.

Aeschylus sets these issues in a religious framework that implicates the entire cosmic order; Sophocles tends to embody them in deeply involving personalities. Sophocles' richness of characterization sometimes distracts attention from questions of social order and justice, but those questions are always strongly present nonetheless. In his *Electra,* for example, the heroine's personal suffering and endurance seem to occupy the foreground. Yet they derive much of their impact and importance from the fact that she is the sole champion of justice in the corrupt land of Mycenae. The king has long ago been murdered by the selfish and licentious queen Clytaemnestra, his death symbolizing the corruption in both the political and the moral order. Rituals too are violated; family ties are turned from love to hate; the natural order is inverted. Orestes, coming from outside, bent on the practical fulfilment of the deed (*ergon*) of revenge in a male world of efficient action and a logically defined background of space and time, stands in stark contrast to an Electra confined to the house, involved in an inner, female realm of static words (logoi), uttering Niobe-like lamentations in a petrified timelessness (145–52). Electra's tragedy of sheer spirit, force of will, and feeling turned to hatred and killing, though relieved in part by the joyful reunion with her brother in the moving recognition scene of the play, remains defined by a larger, suprapersonal field of reversals. In that field, life has become death, the king's palace is a locus of corruption rather than order, and justice, recoverable only at the cost of matricide, becomes confused and problematical.

The scale and violence of the Peloponnesian War, with its atrocities of Corcyra, Melos, and Mytilene, made men more keenly aware of how precarious are the ordered forms of civilized life. Euripides depicted the breakdown and disintegration of those forms in such tragedies as the *Medea, Hecuba, Trojan Women, Phoenissae,* and *Bacchae.* The *Medea,* produced in the year that the Peloponnesian War began (431 B.C.), shows the unleashed violence of love turned to hatred, passion to ferocity. In its heroine the traditional passivity of woman is changed to a murderous revenge that destroys maternal love and leaves the male antagonist impotent and shattered. In the *Hippolytus* and the *Bacchae* too, the potential destructiveness of the emotional life

33

centers on woman as the symbol and the focal point for the irrationality that the polis must suppress. In the *Bacchae* the destructive power of the irrational annihilates the city itself. Dionysus, god of wine, religious ecstasy, madness, and illusion, retaliates against the Theban king, Pentheus, who has rejected his worship, by maddening the women of the city and driving them to the mountain with the king's mother, Agave, at their head. The hierarchical separation of god, man, and beast breaks down as the god appears in the form of bull, snake, or lion and is present to his worshipers in the holy thiasos, the ecstatic band of Maenads. Pentheus, the substitute victim of the god, becomes a fearsome human sacrifice, torn apart as a beast-victim in a sacrifice where the mother is the "priestess of the murder" (1114). The king's death in the Dionysiac *sparagmos* or ritual "rending apart" is a symbolic rending of the city itself, no longer able to integrate emotionality and religious ecstacy into the order of civic institution and law. That order collapses with the centrifugal movement that ends the play, the exile of the queen mother Agave after she kills her son and the bestial metamorphosis of the old king, Cadmus, the culture hero who had founded Thebes.

Throughout Greek tragedy, systems of linked polarity—mortal and divine, male and female, man and beast, city and wild—operate within the dense fabric of the language and the plot. They encompass not just the emotional, interior world of the individual character or spectator but the whole of society in its multiple relationships to the natural and supernatural order.

V

The hero of Greek tragedy stands at the point where the boundaries of opposing identities meet, where identity itself becomes the paradoxical conjunction of opposites. To return to the example of Aeschylus' Agamemnon, the king, trying in vain to avoid the doom to which, inexorably, his own nature, his past actions, and the violent passions of his wife are pulling him, asks, "Revere me as a man, not as a god" (λέγω κατ᾿ ἄνδρα, μὴ θεόν, σέβειν ἐμέ, *Ag.* 925). By walking upon the carpet, however, he overreaches to a godlike status, only to plummet suddenly, in a dramatic reversal from god to beast, sacrificed like a bull in an unholy and perverted rite.

Heracles in the *Trachiniae* follows a similar pattern. Son of Zeus and conqueror of monsters, he fuses with the bestial victims that he sacrifices, burned and devoured by the Hydra's poison. His pyre on Mount Oeta is the place of both his triumph and his defeat. It hints at his immortalization as a god, but it also marks his subjection to the bestiality inside him which is still unconquered and which is symbolized by the monsters of his past. The Hydra and Nessus have, in a sense, vanquished him.

The perverted ritual, a recurrent feature of Greek tragedy, itself indicates the destruction of the mediations between god and beast which the forms of civilized life assert. Civilization separates man from the "beastlike life" (*thēriōdēs bios*) on the one hand and places him in a subordinate but propitious relation to the gods on the other. The tragic hero, however, is polarized at the opposite extremes: either he is involved in bestial actions (incest, matricide, and parricide fall within this category), or else he aspires to some form of godlike power or autonomy.

Tragedy differs from ritual. Tragedy stresses not the orderly process of transition from one stage of life to another but the in-betweenness, the marginality, and the ambiguity in the juxtaposition of the two stages. In the cultic background of the *Trachiniae*, the pyre on Mount Oeta was important in a ritual that rewarded Heracles for his life of labors, which freed the earth of monsters and made it safe for civilized life. A shrine on Oeta where burnt offerings were made from early archaic times attests to this cult of the apotheosized hero. In Sophocles' play, however, the pyre is part of the ambiguity between god and beast which surrounds Heracles. In stressing the pyre in the promises that Heracles exacts from his son Hyllus at the end, Sophocles raises the issue of the hero's apotheosis. Yet he gives no clear, unambiguous reference to Heracles' future immortality on Olympus, only dark and uncertain hints. In cult the pyre and the rituals around it affirm the mediation between god and man; in tragedy that focal point in the ritual becomes the center of the most problematical part of the hero's existence, the mystery of his suspension between the highest and lowest extremes.

In Euripides' *Electra* the death of Aegisthus, though just, is a kind of human sacrifice. In the grim justice of the play that quasi-sacrificial act has a spatial analogue; it is located outside the polis, performed in honor of the Nymphs, divinities of forest and mountain who are also (ironically in the context of the *Electra*), divinities connected with marriage. Marriage and sacrifice are here combined, as they are throughout a play whose series of perverted rites weave together familial, sexual, spatial, biological, and political codes in its violated cosmic and social order. Likewise in the *Heracles Mad* the hero who ostensibly defends the civilized order comes to embody its destruction. After saving his family from the cruel tyrant Lycus, Heracles is afflicted with a homicidal madness in the throes of which he performs a perverted ritual: he sacrifices his children to the accompaniment of an insane inner dancing and song. Coming from the Underworld, he would purify himself from that dark realm and thus reestablish order. But then he plunges into the even darker Hell of his own violence, from ritual purification to the most horrible pollutions.

The order affirmed by ritual is both literal and symbolic. The ritual represented as part of the tragic action is therefore a symbol within a symbol. It is a literal recreation of the cosmic order in the regular succession of stylized acts performed just as they were *in illo tempore,* to use Mircea Eliade's terminology—the magical time of creation reenacted by myth, when order emerges from chaos. It is at the same time a symbolic expression of the order that the rite reasserts through the symbolic or metaphorical meaning acquired by these acts in constant repetition over centuries.

The perverted ritual of tragedy can for these reasons serve as the most intense and inclusive focus of the disrupted cosmic order. It enacts the disruptions of that order in one particular code among many, but at the same time the particular code, itself the fullest symbolic expression of the harmonies between man and god and between man and nature, includes all other codes. Ritual's special symbolic and expressive function in the society, in other words, gives it a privileged status within the secondary, superimposed structure of the literary work. Here it is both a code among codes and the code that expresses the harmonious interlocking of all codes in the order of the whole.

In the literary work, whose medium is words, language has a similarly privileged function. The powerful effect of the Cassandra scene of the *Agamemnon* derives in part from the close interlocking of ritual and linguistic codes. There is a parallel breakdown of the two most expressive, synoptic focuses of the civilized and aesthetic order; each code functions in the work as a metaphor virtually interchangeable with the other code, and each functions as a code that sums up all other codes.

To return to Sophocles, the entity "Oedipus" in the *Tyrannus* similarly renders problematical the familiar configurations by which civilized man keeps chaos at bay. There is a reciprocal relation and interaction between Oedipus as individual character and Oedipus as king, the focal point for the cosmic order. On the one hand Oedipus polarizes the universe into unmediated extremes: overdetermination by the gods and utter chaos; gods who are providential and intelligent and gods who "leap" upon their victims like beasts of prey (*O T* 469, 1311; cf. 263); the riddles of the bestial Sphinx and the oracles of Olympian Apollo. On the other hand this ambiguous world order simultaneously polarizes the unstable configuration of personal traits that make up the character we call Oedipus. It leaves him precariously oscillating between the two opposite fields of his identity: quasi-divine power and bestial rage, strength and weakness, self-affirmation and utter helplessness, confident knowledge and abysmal ignorance, proud rationality and uncontrolled passion. As his world splits into two increasingly disparate halves, so Oedipus splits into the antithetical halves of a self that can no longer hold together on the old terms. He can no longer exist (or rather coexist) as both murderer and ruler, both destroyer and savior; he has to confront the identity-in-polarity of himself as both king and scapegoat. Whatever new unity and strength of self Oedipus possesses at the end rests on a new set of balances between authority and weakness, autonomy and subjection.

In the poetry of the plays, metaphor facilitates the interconnection of the codes and the convertibility of one code into another. In the *Bacchae* the wild Maenads who will destroy the king-victim Pentheus, are "foals which have left their yokes" (1056). The king, "in the power of" this ambiguous god, allows himself to be dressed as a bacchant and speaks of "being dedicated" to him (*anakeisthai,* 934). Yet the god is also the beast in bull, serpent, and lion form (1016f.) and the hunter whose "noose" will hurl the prey beneath the "herd" of Maenads that will destroy him (1020–23). This metaphorical interlocking, as in the *Oedipus Tyrannus,* is compounded by the ironies of double vision, madness, and ecstatic transport; so there are actually two levels of interlocking codes, one through metaphor and another through the ironic interchange of appearance and reality. Through the peculiar nature and powers of Dionysus as god of madness and illusion, the trope becomes the reality. That blurring on the level of language corresponds to analogous blurring on the levels of perception (madness and sanity, illusion and truth) and ritual (celebrant and deity, sacrificer and sacrificed). Pentheus, figuratively savage (*agrios*) and the offspring of a lioness (cf. 542, 988–90), is seen as an actual lion by the maddened Agave (1174, 1215, 1278, etc.). He himself sees the god in the form of the beast (e.g. 617ff., 922; cf. 1159).

Like the *Oedipus Tyrannus*, the *Bacchae* is in a sense a paradigm of tragedy itself, simultaneously telescoping polarity and identity. The tragic king is the figure who must occupy both extremes at the same time. Kingship is located at the isolated point of exposure to elemental forces and their abrupt reversal, the point where order crosses over into disorder, where apparent chaos harbors a coherence hitherto unseen.

VI

Just as the king, standing at the summit of happiness and power, can suddenly move from highest to lowest through chance event or the "envy of the gods" (Herodotus 1.207), so the tragic hero, through accident or inner nature or some combination, finds his strength turned to weakness, his prosperity to misery. It is through his suffering and integrity of spirit that he creates new definitions of these values.

Sophocles, in particular, depicts tragic figures who are more exposed than other men to the extremes of the human condition as they appear in the world and their own natures. "Such natures," as Creon says in the *Oedipus Tyrannus*, "are justly most difficult for themselves to bear" (674–75). These figures, in their intense reactions to these extremes, become paradigms of the precarious status of honor, power, happiness. They have affinities with the savage world outside the limits of the city, but they also possess qualitites indispensable to their societies. Ajax, Antigone, Oedipus, Philoctetes are or become outlaws, and yet they are also champions of values essential to civilized life: personal integrity, devotion to kinship ties, energy, and intelligence. The course of the tragic action takes these heroes through a sharp reversal of status, thereby requiring a redefinition of basic values. In the *Ajax* the trusty warrior becomes a hated criminal. In the *Oedipus Tyrannus* the king who has saved the city becomes the source of its pollution. In the *Philoctetes* and the *Oedipus Coloneus,* by contrast, the helpless outcast becomes the true hero, the source of an inner strength invisible to others. Within the boundary situations created by tragedy, truth and illusion undergo paradoxical shifts. Fragility may prove to be the source of another form of power.

Anthropologists, Victor Turner among them, have called attention to the importance of these liminal situations and to the liminal status of such figures as the outcast and the suppliant.[10] These liminal situations threaten and confuse the old order, but they also create a kind of free space in which the old elements can be reshuffled in new combinations, where new alternatives to the old conditions can be imagined. We have already noted how Aeschylus brings together the opposites of sea and fire, upper and lower, man and sacrificial victim for the suffering of Agamemnon. The first ode of the *Trachiniae* brings together death and life, birth and destruction, in a cosmic frame for Heracles' imminent doom. This universe is characterized by a disturbing violence and a sexual quality in its basic processes (*Trach.* 94–96):

> ὃν αἰόλα νὺξ ἐναριζομένα
> τίκτει κατευνάζει τε φλογιζόμενον,
> Ἅλιον, Ἅλιον, αἰτῶ . . .

You whom shimmering Night, as she is slain, brings to birth and then lays to bed as you blaze in flames, Helios, Helios, I call upon you. . .

The alternation of day and night reflects not a stable, regular natural order (as in *Ajax* 672–73) but the violent death of the mother, the female Night who, as she "is slain" (the verb ἐναρίζειν describes violent death in Homer and the killing of Agamemnon in Aeschylus), "gives birth" to the "blazing" light of the new sun at dawn. We need not go into the elaborate inversions of light and darkness, birth and death, which run beneath the action of the play to realize that the

---

10. E.g. Victor Turner, *The Ritual Process* (London 1969), and *The Forest of Symbols* (Ithaca 1973).

heavenly bodies' involvement through metaphor in the pain of the human life cycle provides a cosmic analogue to the sufferings of the protagonists. Their involvement links the human action to the great rhythms of the universe. Deianeira, like Night here, is a *mater dolorosa* whose births are all pain (cf. *Trach.* 28–31, 41–42). Like Night, too, she will be violently "slain" (indeed, ἐναριζομένα could be read as a reflexive middle, "slaying herself," as Deianeira does); and shortly before, she is closely linked with night and night's rhythms in her statement of her unhappy life: "For night leads in pain and night in succession drives it away" (28–29). Heracles, the far-wandering hero whose journeys, like those of the sun, span continents (100f.), ends his mortal life ablaze in his fiery death on the pyre where he has been "put to rest" (note the repeated εὐνάσαι, εὔνασον in 1005–6, 1041) through the agency of a female figure connected with birth and with darkness (cf. 573, 579, 685–92).

Scholars such as Knox and Cedric Whitman have sensitively interpreted this isolated, asocial aspect of the tragic hero.[11] A structuralist approach supplements their reading. It emphasizes not the hero's affective responses to his world and that world's rejection or acceptance of him but social and moral structures themselves as they define the hero and are expanded, redefined, or confused by him.

To dwell again on the Heracles of the *Trachiniae,* the issue for a structuralist reading is not the worth or worthlessness of Heracles vis-à-vis Deianeira or the assessment of her generosity against his brutality, important as judgments on these matters are for a full evaluation of the play. Rather, the issue is the polarization of values as each figure reaches outside the civilized world to a destructive, bestial violence from his or her past. The play thus appears not just the domestic tragedy of a doomed house, nor the personal tragedy of a man and woman whose lives have carried them in opposite directions, but the tragedy of civilized values disintegrating under the impact of powerful forces which always threaten life from without and within.

The structural paradox of the tragic hero revealed by such an approach runs parallel to the paradox of the performance of which he is

11. Cedric Whitman, *Sophocles: A Study in Heroic Humanism* (Cambridge, Mass. 1951), and *The Tragic Paradox,* ed. C. Segal (Ithaca 1982); B. M. W. Knox, *The Heroic Temper* (Berkeley and Los Angeles 1964).

the center. The social context of the performance presupposes a safe, limited world hedged about by the order of rituals and stable community and communication, but the action of the performance explores what transgresses that order. As a communal act, a part of the Dionysiac or Lenaean festival, tragedy affirms the solidity of social forms and celebrates the gods of the polis. But the content stands in tension with the ritual and social context. The tragedies contain the most terrible pollutions, the most feared crimes, the most puzzling and disturbing cruelties of the gods, the killing of parents by children and of children by parents (*Agamemnon, Heracles Mad, Medea*), incest (*Oedipus Tyrannus*), the death or prolonged suffering of the innocent (*Hippolytus, Philoctetes*), the triumph of the wicked and unscrupulous (*Hecuba, Trojan Women*).

VII

The ritual and social situation of the drama thus sets up a powerful tension between the fictional and the actual rite and between character and audience. This tension is essential to Greek tragedy, possibly to all tragedy. A festival at the very heart of the city shows the social and ritual order of the city inverted and turned against itself in conflict and division. Yet it is part of the deeper social effect of tragedy that the citizens who behold this negation of their civic and religious order therein experience what that order signifies, what its limitations may be, what stands below or above it in the realm of the incomprehensible, the mysterious, and the irrational.

This heightened sense of the preciousness and precariousness of that order, this intensified cosmological consciousness, is at least as probable a social effect of tragedy as Aristotle's "cleansing" of violent emotions. Plato, appreciating the subversive implications of Greek tragedy, was in this respect the more sensitive critic. As Brian Vickers has put it recently, "Reading the *Oresteia* makes one afraid for one's life."[12]

The metaphorical and symbolic language of the plays functions as we suggested above, in part to interweave the multiple codes of this

12. Brian Vickers, *Towards Greek Tragedy* (London 1972) 425.

order. *Agamemnon* 1384–98 provides a good illustration of the process:

παίω δέ νιν δίς, κἀν δυοῖν οἰμώγμασιν
μεθῆκεν αὑτοῦ κῶλα καὶ πεπτωκότι
τρίτην ἐπενδίδωμι, τοῦ κατὰ χθονὸς
Διὸς νεκρῶν σωτῆρος εὐκταίαν χάριν.
οὕτω τὸν αὑτοῦ θυμὸν ὁρμαίνει πεσὼν
κἀκφυσιῶν ὀξεῖαν αἵματος σφαγὴν
βάλλει μ' ἐρεμνῆι ψακάδι φοινίας δρόσου,
χαίρουσαν οὐδὲν ἧσσον ἢ διοσδότωι
γάνει σπορητὸς κάλυκος ἐν λοχεύμασιν.
ὡς ὧδ' ἐχόντων, πρέσβος 'Αργείων τόδε,
χαίροιτ' ἄν, εἰ χαίροιτ', ἐγὼ δ' ἐπεύχομαι·
εἰ δ' ἦν πρεπόντως ὥστ' ἐπισπένδειν νεκρῶι,
τάδ' ἂν δικαίως ἦν, ὑπερδίκως μὲν οὖν·
τοσῶνδε κρατῆρ' ἐν δόμοις κακῶν ὅδε
πλήσας ἀραίων αὐτὸς ἐκπίνει μολών.

I strike him twice; and with two cries there on the spot he let his limbs go slack: and then, when he is down, I add a third stroke, a welcome prayer-offering to the Zeus beneath the earth, the savior of the dead. So he belches out his own life as he lies there, and blowing forth the sharp slaughter of his blood, he strikes me with a darksome shower of gory dew; and I rejoiced no less than the crop rejoices in the rich blessing of the rain of Zeus when the sheath is in labor with the ear.

So stands the case, noble elders of Argus here: be glad, if ye will be glad; for me, I glory in it. And were it possible to pour libations over the dead body in a manner that would suit the circumstances, this [my doing] would be just, yea, more than just: so many are the curseful evils wherewith this man in his house has filled a bowl, a bowl which he now drains himself on his return. (E. Fraenkel's translation, slightly modified)

This passage interconnects the ritual, familial, biological, and sexual codes. The very density of the closely packed metaphors creates a special language in which the various codes of the civilized order can come together to express a synoptic vision of the totality of that order—political, religious, and domestic, natural and supernatural— at a moment of crisis when that order is pushed to its extreme limits and questioned in its most fundamental values. The *Oresteia* is probably the richest development of this technique, and it may be that this deliberate interlocking of the various codes through repeated, expanded, and interwoven sequences of metaphor is the creation of Aeschylus, stamped upon Attic tragedy by his genius as one of its basic techniques.

Interlocking metaphor is also important in Sophoclean tragedy. The wound of the *Philoctetes,* for example, is the focal symbol of an ambiguous divine order, a corrupt social order, and an inward sickness and savagery (*agriotēs*) that parallels the physical sickness and the savage, beastlike state of Philoctetes' life. Clytaemnestra's dream of Agamemnon's "scepter by the hearth" "blooming" and "shadowing over" the land of the Mycenaeans (Soph., *El.* 417ff.) interconnects the familial, civic, biological, and cosmic orders. Deianeira's comparison of Heracles to a farmer plowing an outlying field that he visits only at the time of sowing and the time of harvest (*Trach.* 31–33) brackets the familial order of the house with the biological order implicit in agriculture. As the *Trachiniae* continues, an increasingly ironical discrepancy cracks open between fertility and destruction. Sophocles draws on the interweaving of marriage and agriculture as the two basic civilizing acts. In the Athenian marriage ceremony the father bestows the bride on her husband "for the *sowing* of legitimate children" (ἐπὶ παίδων γνησίων ἀρότῳ). What is probably a rather inert metaphor or a vaguely felt parallelism in the social structure becomes active as part of a system of signs, metaphors, and values within the secondary structure of the literary work. By this process the literary work exercises what Roman Jakobson and others term the "metalingual" function of language: language calls attention to its own coding of experience.[13] In the wider, social structure the conscious interweaving of codes by metaphor also calls attention to the unconscious coding processes that are part of society's unification of the various human activities and roles, to the interdependence of society's various parts, and to the interaction of various codes in homologous areas.

The tragic force of the *Trachiniae* lies in the twisting together of the multiple codes of the civilized order to their complete destruction. Both models of the civilized life, the domestic wife who faithfully

13. Roman Jakobson, "Linguistics and Poetics" (1960) in DeGeorge and DeGeorge (note 4) 85–122, especially 111ff.

keeps house and hearth and the beast-taming hero, come to embody what their model social roles have most resisted. The faithful wife destroys house and husband with the poison of the Hydra and the blood of the lustful beast-man; the hero famous for his civilizing triumphs reenacts the part of his bestial double, Nessus, sacking a city and annihilating a house (cf. 257, 351–65) for the sake of lust, raging with subhuman cries and carried away by a blind thirst for bloody revenge (1066ff., 1133). The maiden Iole, taken within the house as if in legitimate marriage, is "yoked" (536); this metaphor, which usually indicates the domestication of the "unyoked" virgin who is part of the wild until she is tamed by marriage, points here to the beast world of the mythic background. In the ode immediately preceding, Deianeira is the "heifer" fought over by two "bulls," Heracles and the river-god Achelous. Everything about the pseudo-marriage with Iole is awry. Coming as a kind of second wife into an established ménage, as Deianeira bitterly complains (543–51), this bride destroys rather than unites the two houses in question. Rather than producing legitimate children in a fruitful marriage, she can only "give birth to a great Fury for this house" (893–95).

The homology between the familial and agricultural codes which Deianeira suggests in the prologue has its negative aspect too, for agricultural images describe the deadly effects of the love charm, effects that Deianeira discovers too late (701–4). The inverted fertility of the agriculture parallels the inverted significance of the love gift. What was intended to unite the house dissolves it; what was meant to bring love brings deadly hate; what should have asserted the unifying bonds of civilized institutions manifests the vengeful power of a monstrous nightmare world of Centaurs and Hydras.

Greek tragedy, while interlocking the various codes of civilization through its metaphorical language, also makes language itself a sufferer, as it were, in the inversions or disintegrations that threaten all civilized norms. The tragic situation distorts normal speech, producing such paradoxes or oxymora as Ajax's "darkness by light, dimness most brilliant" (*Ajax* 393–95), or Antigone's "holy impiety" (*Antig.* 74, 924, 943), or Oedipus' "wedless wedlock" (*OT* 1214; cf. 1256). Like ritual, language is both a code among codes and also the special mode by which the different codes relate to one another. The disintegration of language into ambiguity or paradox, or the celebrated Sophoclean irony, signifies both a loss of coherence in the world and a loss of human ability to grasp and communicate coherence. The verbal ironies of the *Oedipus Tyrannus* reflect both the ultimate failure of Oedipus to solve the true riddle of the play—the riddle of the meaning of life in a universe governed by chance or by distant and mysterious gods—and the very incoherence of a universe that *logos,* reason-as-language, cannot make intelligible. The "bridling" of Iphigeneia's mouth in the human sacrifice at the beginning of the *Oresteia* (*Ag.* 228–47) likewise couples the literally unspeakable that is being done with the perverted communication between man and god: verbal communication and ritual communication are isomorphic. Heracles' bestial roaring at Cenaeum in the *Trachiniae* reflects, as we have seen, the distorted communication between man and god in the rite. But it also stems from noncommunication between husband and wife; the deceptive gift of the robe passes between them in lieu of words that, in fact, they never address to each other.

Language itself, therefore, is a major concern of Greek tragedy. Its dissolution parallels the shedding of kindred blood or incest in the familial code and the perversion of man/god communication in the ritual code. All three codes, language, family, and ritual, meet in the sacrifice of Iphigeneia or the misunderstood prophecies of Cassandra in the *Agamemnon.* Indeed, the whole *Oresteia* can be read in terms of a dissolution and gradual reconstruction of language which runs parallel to a destruction and reconstitution of ritual forms. Language is a central theme in Sophocles' *Electra, Philoctetes,* and two Oedipus plays. Instead of clarity, tragic language creates ambiguity (*Oedipus Tyrannus*). Instead of communication, it enforces deception, even on the part of those whose natures incline to heroic truth and straight speaking (*Electra, Philoctetes,* the "Trugrede" of *Ajax* 646ff.). Instead of separating man from beast, it obscures the boundary between them as the heroes roar, bark, or wail.

VIII

Greek tragedy is remarkable for its ability to face the disintegration of the cosmic, social, or psychological order without losing all sense of coherence. Tragedy in Greece was rooted in mythical paradigms. Those paradigms gave a certain unity and shared intelligibility to experience, but they still remained open to radical questioning and undogmatic speculation. Tragedy could thus combine a sense of the sacred, the numinous, and the mysterious entering into human life with a belief in the power of human intelligence to plumb the deepest questions of existence. For this reason, perhaps, it could step beyond conventional morality to confront the unjust suffering of an Oedipus, a Hippolytus, or a Philoctetes without losing touch with its own imaginative abilities to shape new forms of order—the power of the city to create law in the *Oresteia;* man's capacity for spiritual strength, compassion, friendship, and loyalty in the midst of chaos and destruction in Sophocles' Oedipus plays and *Philoctetes,* Euripides' *Heracles* and *Hippolytus;* the restorative vitality of language and myth in tragedy itself, implicit in Euripides' *Helen* and the finales of Sophocles' *Philoctetes* and *Oedipus Coloneus.*

From a structuralist perspective, the complexity of Greek tragedy lies both in its full use of the highly coded structures of the social order and in its dissolution of those structures. For these reasons, any structuralist analysis of tragedy is engaged in the paradoxical activity of elucidating structures that are deliberated, questioned, negated, inverted, or on the verge of dissolving into chaos. The structural analysis of myth can be normative and descriptive, viewing the infrastructure of a society's values through the relationships composed and varied in the metaphorical and symbolic equivalents of values, in the language of the myths. The structural analysis of tragedy, however, is forced in just the opposite direction. It highlights the infrastructure of a society's values only to see them strained to the breaking point or beyond.

At some point, therefore, the analytic rigidity of constructing parallel sequences of homologies must pass into the flexibilities of ironic deconstruction. The structuralist literary critic, at least the critic of tragedy, may begin as the reassembler of *bricolage* ("structural man takes the real, decomposes it and then recomposes it . . .") but is soon confronted with the systematic disassembling that is going on beneath the logical structures, a *basso ostinato* moving ever farther away from the dominant. Like the tragic work itself, he is continually forced away from the logic of noncontradiction into the area of paradox and the coexistence of opposites.

Barthes has defined structuralism as an activity as opposed to a subject-matter, concerned with reconstructing the mental processes through which man makes his world intelligible:

Creation or reflection are not, here, an original "impression" of the world, but a veritable fabrication of a world which resembles the first one, not in order to copy it but to render it intelligible. Hence one might say that structuralism is essentially an *activity of imitation,* which is also why there is, strictly speaking, no *technical* difference between structuralism as an intellectual activity on the one hand and literature in particular, art in general on the other: both derive from a *mimesis,* based not on the analogy of substances (as in so-called realist art), but on the analogy of functions (what Lévi-Strauss calls *homology*).[14]

Yet the structuralist study of tragedy must take special account of the structured deconstruction of those patterns, for that process is part of the uniqueness of the tragic form. Tragedy maintains and even intensifies the systems of homologies and the analogies of functions on which the social order, like the aesthetic order of a work of art, depends. But even as it uses and, through its interlocking metaphors, clarifies the codes of normative values, it is always and simultaneously pulling in tension against the normative, the mediated realm of social life, toward the abnormal, and unmediated, the liminal.

14. Barthes (note 4) 150.

CHAPTER 2

Greek Myth as a Semiotic and Structural System and the Problem of Tragedy

In the infancy of society every author is necessarily a poet because language itself is poetry. . . . Every original language near to its source is in itself the chaos of a cyclic poem: the copiousness of lexicography and the distinctions of grammar are the works of a later age, and are merely the catalogue and the form of the creations of poetry.
                    —P. B. Shelley, "A Defence of Poetry"

I

The structuralist controversy of the seventies, as Marc-Eli Blanchard suggests, has gradually been replaced by a semiotic controversy.[1] From the point of view of semiotics, culture depends on manipulating complex sign systems; and the activities of culture, in large part, consist of the continuous transformation and translation from one communicative system to another. Language obviously occupies a privileged place in the semiotics of culture, not only because of its unique communicative power but also because of its unique ability to reflect explicitly on the nature of the semiotic process and the interrelation of the various semiotic networks that make up the totality of a given culture. At the same time semioticians have

I thank Nancy Rubin for many helpful comments and suggestions. I gratefully acknowledge a fellowship from the John Simon Guggenheim Memorial Foundation (1981–82), during which this essay was put into final form.
    1. Marc-Eli Blanchard, *Description: Sign, Self, Desire. Critical Theory in the Wake of Semiotics* (The Hague 1980).

called attention to the fact—hard to acknowledge for those of us trained as philologists—that language does not have an exclusive monopoly on signification. The question of the relations between verbal and nonverbal sign systems becomes particularly interesting and important in the study of myth. As a form of *mythos,* a spoken tale or account, myth is obviously inseparable from language, but it is, some would argue, at least partially independent of language or even transcends language.[2]

The study of myth is both important and difficult for semiotics because myth stands at an intersection of different sign systems. Myth comprises a system of symbols, verbal, visual, and religious. Each myth is built up of already existing symbols and forms and, like all narrative, reforms and reorganizes those symbols into its own structures. Myth, as Roland Barthes suggests, is a "second-order semiotic system," which creates its own language, its own system of relations between signifier and signified, from the primary significations of cultural values and narrative forms.[3] At one level, myth provides a body of stories and symbols that validate cultural norms. A society's myths are the imaginative distillation of its descriptions and prescriptions about what life is and should be. We can easily think of Greek myths that warn about violating taboos or marrying within certain degrees of kinship or, more positively, set forth the ideal mode of behavior for husband or wife, son or daughter, old or young.

Viewed with an eye to structure rather than content, myths form a body of interrelated narratives that reveal an implicit system of logical relations. These relations become particularly striking when a large body of myths is examined at once, as Claude Lévi-Strauss has done for the Indians of the Amazon Basin. The totality of a corpus of myths may be read as a single text that possesses the internal coherence, autonomy, and coding processes of Barthes's second-order

2. See Albert Cook, *Myth and Language* (Bloomington, Ind. 1980), Introduction and chaps. 2 and 11. For the question of narrative discourse in myth and other forms of discourse see also J.-P. Vernant, *Mythe et société* (Paris 1974) 214ff.

3. Roland Barthes, *Mythologies,* trans. A. Levers (London 1972) 113ff.; see also Terrence Hawkes, *Structuralism and Semiotics* (Berkeley and Los Angeles 1973) 131ff. Juri Lotman, *The Structure of the Artistic Text,* trans. R. Vroon, Michigan Slavic Contributions 7 (Ann Arbor 1977) 9ff. speaks of "secondary modeling systems," and see also his remarks on "recoding," 35ff.

semiotic system. In reading the whole body of a society's myths in this way, we are constructing the "megatext" of its mythic material (I shall explain the term more fully later). This megatext is an artificial construct, necessarily invisible and unconscious to the society whose exemplary narratives and symbolic projections of what reality is are located within that system.

The first section of this essay attempts to show how Greek myth may be described in terms of a megatext, or in other words how the inherent systematicity of Greek myth operates in specific texts and narratives. Section II focuses on tragedy as a special form of mythical narration. Tragedy, I shall argue, simultaneously validates and disintegrates the mythic system both as a form of narrative representation and as a reflection of a coherent world order whose stable, hierarchical interrelation of parts is encoded into the myths.

Myth, though operating primarily through language, also shares common boundaries of content, formal organization, and expression with the visual arts, ritual, music, and in ancient Greece architecture also, for the plastic expressions of the myths frequently occur on the friezes and metopes of temples and other sacred buildings. Because of this overlap, no single brief definition of myth can encompass all its many functions and aspects. From a semiotic point of view, however, we may say that myth is a narrative structure whose sign- and symbol-systems are closely correlated with the central values of the culture, especially those values which express a supernatural validation, extension, or explanation of the cultural norms. Myth is also a more or less coherent system of symbols that express relationships between the human world and the forces of nature and the various forms of the unknown: the gods, the dead, the afterlife.

Greek myth is especially interesting from a semiotic point of view for two reasons. First, the presentation of myth in Greek literature shows a high degree of what we may call the metaliterary or metalingual consciousness. Even in Homer the poet is clearly conscious of shaping his work by structuring language and narrative elements. Within the mythic corpus the creative power of language, art, and poetry is itself often a subject of narrative: we may recall the pervasive details of weaving and crafting; the interest in the poet as an actor, a figure in the narrative (particularly in the *Odyssey*); the inclusion of comprehensive symbolic artifacts, such as the Shield of

Achilles in the *Iliad*,[4] and the frequent representation of the heroic warrior himself as a bard, whether literally or metaphorically or, as in the *Odyssey*, both simultaneously;[5] and the magic of poet figures like Orpheus, Musaeus, Amphion, and Zethus.[6]

A conscious awareness of sign systems, furthermore, pervades early classical myth in its literary expression. In Aeschylus, for example, the devices on the shields of the seven warriors who attack and defend Thebes, the attention to the beacons in the *Agamemnon* as a coded form of communication apart from language,[7] the concern with names and naming as in the famous ode on the name of Helen (*Ag.* 681–98), the interest in omens and prophecies, and in Sophocles and Euripides the puns on names such as Oedipus and Pentheus—all are indications of an advanced, if not explicit, semiotic consciousness.[8] At a later date this awareness of the signifying power of language, or metalingual consciousness, receives theoretical formulation in the work of some of the early Sophists, among them Protagoras, Prodicus, and Gorgias, who are among the first philosophers of language and literature in the West, and in their immediate successors, Cratylus and Democritus. The latter, the most systematic of the fifth-century materialistic philosophers, speculated on whether language existed by convention (*nom*os) or by nature (*physis*), that is, as a secondary invention or as an instinctive capacity of man.[9] This highly

---

4. See K. J. Atchity, *Homer's Iliad: The Shield of Memory* (Carbondale, Ill. 1978).

5. E.g. *Od.* 11.368 and 21.405ff.; also *Il.* 9.186ff. See Klaus Rüter, *Odysseeinterpretation*, ed. K. Matthiessen, Hypomnemata 19 (Göttingen 1969) 237ff.; C. Segal, "*Kleos* and Its Ironies in the *Odyssey*," *AC* 52 (1983) 22–47.

6. See C. Segal, "The Magic of Orpheus and the Ambiguities of Language," *Ramus* 7 (1978) 106–42, especially 114–21.

7. See J. J. Peradotto, "Cledonomancy in the *Oresteia*," *AJP* 90 (1969) 1–21, and "The Omen of the Eagles and the *Ethos* of Agamemnon," *Phoenix* 23 (1969) 237–63; Froma Zeitlin, "Language, Structure and the Son of Oedipus in Aeschylus' *Seven against Thebes*," in *Contemporary Literary Hermeneutics and Interpretation of Classical Texts*, ed. Stephanus Kresic (Ottawa 1981) 235–52, and *Under the Sign of the Shield: Semiotics and Aeschylus' Seven against Thebes* (Rome 1982); Pierre Vidal-Naquet, "The Shields of the Heroes," in J.-P. Vernant and Vidal-Naquet, *Tragedy and Myth in Ancient Greece*, trans. Janet Lloyd (Brighton, Sussex 1981) 129ff.

8. See H. Van Looy, "Παρετυμολογεῖ ὁ Εὐριπίδης," in *Zetesis*, Festschrift for E. De Strijcker (Antwerp and Utrecht 1973) 345–66; C. Segal, "Etymologies and Double Meanings in Euripides' *Bacchae*," *Glotta* 60 (1982) 81–93; J. H. Quincey, "Etymologica," *RhM* 106 (1963) 142–48, on Aeschylus and Pindar.

9. E.g. Democritus D-K 68 B9 and 125. See in general U. von Wilamowitz-

sophisticated metalingual consciousness plays an important part in the later phase of Greek tragedy, especially the late works of Sophocles and Euripides; but it is, I believe, implicit in all of Greek literature.

The second reason for semiotic interest in Greek myth is that myth functions as a complex network of interrelated symbols, patterns, and structures that encode the values of the culture into an extensive and comprehensive system. The total corpus of myths, read synchronically, can be regarded as a megatext within which the specific literary narrations of particular myths (the Homeric epics, Hesiod's *Theogony*, the *Homeric Hymns,* the narrative portions of choral poetry, and tragedy) operate as subtexts, exploiting particular aspects of the megatext, commenting on it, and sometimes making explicit networks of interconnection implied but not openly stated in the megatext. By megatext I mean not merely the totality of themes or songs that the poets of an oral culture would have had available in their repertoires but also the network of more or less subconscious patterns, or deep structures, or undisplaced forms, which tales of a given type share with one another.[10] The term thus includes the Greeks' own consciousness of the thematic affinities among the privileged narratives that we call myths (e.g., the perception of the common sequence of events in tales of the young hunter studied by Nancy Rubin and William Sale). It also includes the subconscious patterning from which these myths are generated, visible to us through comparative analysis of a large body of myths but not overtly perceived by the Greeks themselves as a pattern (e.g., the ambivalence surrounding the mature female figure studied by Slater, or the *pharmakos* pattern in the Oedipus myth pointed out by Vernant, or the initiation patterns in legends about the returning heroes of the Trojan War discussed by Bremmer).[11]

Moellendorff, *Euripides, Herakles* (Berlin 1907) on line 56; Felix Heinimann, *Nomos und Physis* (Basel 1945) 156–62; W. K. C. Guthrie, *A History of Greek Philosophy* 3 (Cambridge 1969) 204ff.

10. On displaced and undisplaced narrative forms see Northrop Frye, *The Secular Scripture: A Study of the Structure of Romance* (Cambridge, Mass. 1976) 36ff.

11. See Nancy Rubin and William Sale, "Meleager and Odysseus: A Structural and Cultural Study of the Greek Hunting-Maturation Myth," *Arethusa* 16 (1983) 137–71; Philip Slater, *The Glory of Hera* (Boston 1968) passim; J.-P. Vernant and Pierre Vidal-

The megatext of Greek myth is remarkably coherent. It owes that coherence in part to the way that the literary forms in which all extant Greek mythic narrative occurs have already done some of the work of laying bare and developing the implicit logic of the system. Oral narrative in monumental epic, and particularly Homer and Hesiod (as Herodotus pointed out, *Histories* 2.53), further refined and regularized the megatext.[12] Indeed, Homer seems to lay particular stress on the internal coherence of the mythic corpus by linking myths from different parts of the corpus to one another for illustration and paradigmatic analogy:[13] the references to the Theban cycle, the tale of Meleager in *Iliad* 9, the songs of Demodocus in *Odyssey* 8, and the cosmogonic myths (whether or not overtly marked as such) in both epics. Even if we allow for the originality of an individual genius, Homer is probably developing a systematic coherence already present in the mythic material.

In Greek culture, in any case, the myths come down to us filtered through the nascent semiotic consciousness, or what I have called the metalingual consciousness, of the authors on whom we depend for the narratives of these myths. We have no other access to mythic material. The visual representation of the myths on painted vases and in sculpture presents exactly the same situation. Even the mythological compilations and handbooks of Apollodorus and the mythographers are not innocent of this literary restructuring, for they are themselves drawing upon literary or artistic versions of the myths. To use a linguistic analogy, analysis can reveal some aspects of the *langue,* the synchronic structure of myth as a megatext, beneath the *parole* of the individual works of verbal or visual art which have

---

Naquet, *Mythe et tragédie* (Paris 1972) 101–31 (or *Tragedy and Myth* [note 7] 87–119); and Jan Bremmer, "Heroes, Rituals, and the Trojan War," *SSR* 2 (1978) 5–38.

12. See Walter Burkert, *Structure and History in Greek Mythology and Ritual,* Sather Classical Lectures 47 (Berkeley and Los Angeles 1979) 141. For indications of the mythic corpus prior to Homer, see T. B. L. Webster, *From Mycenae to Homer,* 2d ed. (London 1964) chap. 6; also B. C. Dietrich, *The Origins of Greek Religion* (Berlin 1974), with the bibliography. For some scholars, Hesiod already represents an intermediate stage between oral myth and the systematizing of written narrative: see Eric A. Havelock, *The Greek Conception of Justice* (Cambridge, Mass. 1978) 193ff., and Vernant, *Mythe et société* (note 2) 208ff.

13. See M. M. Willcock, "Mythological Paradeigma in the *Iliad,*" *CQ* 14 (1964) 141–54; B. K. Braswell, "Mythological Innovation in the *Iliad,*" *CQ* 21 (1971) 16–26.

imposed their secondary aesthetic structure on mythic narrative, or to put it differently, have recoded these structures into their particular idiolect of artistic expression.[14]

In the classical period, with which I am chiefly concerned, Greek myth operates with a set of more or less uniform symbols, culturally defined, whose syntagmatic relations are predominant. The paradigmatic axis remains overlaid by the logical coherence of the syntagmatic. The expression that these myths take in art and literature stays very close to naturalistic representation, wherein the paradigmatic relations are only implicit, rarely explicit. In the balance between the paradigmatic and the syntagmatic axes which operates in all narrative, Greek art forms privilege the syntagmatic axis.[15] The narrative or the visual depiction, that is to say, stresses temporal and spatial continuity and a well defined series of cause-effect relations among the parts. This logic of syntagmatic relations has, of course, dominated Western art and literature and until recently formed the basis of its naturalistic representation of the world, both in verbal and in visual expression.[16] The balance is just the reverse of the iconic form of, say, Byzantine art where, as Boris Uspensky shows in his semiotic study of the Russian icon, the paradigmatic relation forces itself through the syntagmatic.[17]

The success of the Greeks in promoting the continuous frame of their syntagmatic axis is such that classicists have tended to accept that axis, the naturalistic surface of forward-moving plot, as the only legitimate object of study (how many titles like "Plot Coherence in X" or "Narrative Inconsistency in Y" recur in our bibliographies!). Only gradually and recently, partly as a result of structuralist and

14. Some scholars prefer Noam Chomsky's terms competence and performance to Saussure's langue and parole, but the latter remain serviceable. For discussion see Victor Turner, "Symbolic Studies," *Annual Review of Anthropology* 4 (1975) 149–50, and J. J. Peradotto, "Originality and Intentionality," in *Arktouros: Hellenic Studies Presented to B. M. W. Knox,* ed. G. W. Bowersock, W. Burkert, and M. C. J. Putnam (Berlin and New York 1979) 5–6.

15. For a lucid account of syntagmatic and paradigmatic in a classical context see J. J. Peradotto, "*Odyssey* 8.564–71: Verisimilitude, Narrative Analysis, and Bricolage," *Texas Studies in Language and Literature* 15 (1974) 818ff.

16. For the bias toward realistic conventions of narrative see Frye (note 10) 44ff. A propos of Shakespeare's *Pericles* he remarks (44): "The play shows us nothing at all about the relation of fiction to reality: what it shows us is that some conventions of storytelling are more obsessive than others."

17. Boris Uspensky, *The Semiotics of the Russian Icon* (Lisse 1976) chap. 1.

semiotic analysis, have we begun to stress the paradigmatic level that operates through and beneath the syntagmatic axis. J.-P. Vernant's study of the *Oedipus Tyrannus* and Froma Zeitlin's of the *Seven against Thebes* are good examples of this recovery of the paradigmatic axis.[18] Reluctantly, we have acknowledged that metaphor, image, and symbol constitute meaning just as much as does the linear progression of the plot.

The special place given to the art of the fifth century B.C., partly as a result of historical and intellectual movements in the eighteenth and early nineteenth centuries (e.g., classicism), has also had its share in our collaboration with the Greeks in the assumption of the "naturalness" and inherently logical nature of the syntagmatic axis. Archaic art, however, gives a fuller role to the iconic aspect of the image and to the paradigmatic relations that accompany it.[19] It relies more heavily than classical art on a system of relations that are not explained or clarified in the linear or spatial unfolding of the work but become intelligible only through a cross-section of many such works. In some early vase paintings, for example, the hieratic symbol of the goddess of animals, surrounded by her pair of heraldic lions, has been abstracted to a column with a scroll on either side.[20] Or the apotropaic function of the Gorgon-mask in a fairly naturalistic representation of a human face gives way to the eyes alone, represented on the vase with no attempt at subordination into that syntagmatic order of lineaments which would integrate them into a clearly recognized total image of a human face.

I suggest two ways of approaching a semiotic analysis of Greek myth: first, through a reconstitution of its symbolic network as a

18. See above, note 7; Vernant and Vidal-Naquet, *Mythe et tragédie* (note 11) 101–31 (or *Tragedy and Myth* [note 7] 87–119).

19. The shift of emphasis from classical to archaic art forms, which may be discerned, for example, in Nietzsche's influential *Birth of Tragedy* (1872), ushers in a new, "modern" phase of critical values: see M. S. Silk and J. P. Stern, *Nietzsche on Tragedy* (Cambridge 1981) 33–37.

20. In Max Hirmer and P. E. Arias, *A History of Greek Vase Painting* (London 1962), for example, compare the Boeotian "Potnia Theron" (plate 11) or the figure on the neck of the François Vase (plate 46, top) with the lions on the neck of the late geometric Cycladic amphora, color plate V. Cf. the suggestive remarks on the symbolic interchangeability of human form and architectural column by Guido von Kaschnitz-Weinberg, *Die mittelmeerischen Grundlagen der antiken Kunst* (Frankfurt a.M. 1944) 22ff., with figs. 15–16.

whole; second, through an analysis of certain logical relations in a few characteristic myths.

To take a relatively simple instance of this network, the youth at the transitional point between adolescence and manhood is a recurrent figure in Greek myth: Theseus, Perseus, Telemachus, Orestes, Phaethon, Hippolytus, and Actaeon are familiar examples. Their importance reflects concern with the socialization of adolescent energies. These myths have been analyzed anthropologically in terms of rites of passage and psychologically in terms of dependency on a powerful maternal figure (Erich Neumann's "Great Mother").[21] From a semiotic point of view, however, what is interesting is the process of coding which interrelates all of these myths as common parts of the megatext. In all or most of these myths the youth is a hunter (Hippolytus, Actaeon), or ends up in the wild (Pentheus) or as hunted victim (Orestes), or undertakes a journey from home into the unknown, monster-plagued wilderness (Telemachus, Theseus, Oedipus, Perseus). Structural analysis enables us to decode the form of sequential (diachronic) biographical narrative into a synchronic structure of polarities which underlies the cultural values, an opposition between nature and culture, wild and civilized, bestial and human. The figure of adult male warrior, citizen, and farmer occupies the civilized realm as the norm of cultural values, and the not fully socialized figures of adolescent youth, child, and unmarried woman occupy the opposite pole of the uncivilized or wild. Thus the myth of the young man cannot be viewed in isolation. It is homologous with the myths that treat the child as a beast or view the young girl as an unyoked heifer (an animal not yet fully brought into the realm of domesticated usefulness), or a faun, or a filly that has not yet been ridden. These relations, in turn, parallel the marginal political, religious, and military status of the adolescent figure. In other words,

21. Erich Neumann, *The Origins and History of Consciousness*, trans. R. F. C. Hull (Princeton 1954) chap. 2. For a "decoding" of these myths in terms of cultural, narrative, and historical patterns see P. Vidal-Naquet, "The Black Hunter and the Origin of the Athenian Ephebeia," in *PCPS* n.s. 14 (1968) 49–64; Joseph Fontenrose, *Orion: The Myth of the Hunter and the Huntress*, University of California Publications in Classical Studies 23 (Berkeley and Los Angeles 1980). For a good survey of modern approaches and cross-cultural comparisons see A. Brelich, *Paides e Parthenoi*, Incunabula Graeca 36 (Rome 1969) 13–112.

the myths encode that marginality into a number of homologous narrative forms to express its various aspects in differing but parallel symbols: wilderness rather than city, virginity rather than sexual maturity, adherence to the mother rather than the father, wandering rather than stability, and so on.

Particularly interesting from a semiotic perspective is the way in which any one of these figures may serve as a paradigm for another. We are dealing here with a coded system of virtually interchangeable symbols. In the story of Pentheus as told by Euripides in the *Bacchae,* for instance, the young man undergoes a failed rite of passage: instead of defending the walls of his city as a stable, disciplined hoplite warrior and proving his rightful place within the city in a patrilinear inheritance, he is made female in his disguise as a female worshiper of the god of madness, brought outside the city walls into the wilderness of the mountains, treated as a hunted beast, defeated by women, reduced to the stage of infancy, and even symbolically devoured by his own mother.[22] Not only is there a systematic logical reversal of the positive paradigm of the megatext here, but there is a consciousness of the interrelated wholeness of that text through the example of Actaeon, cited no fewer than four times as a parallel to Pentheus. Likewise, the *Odyssey* repeatedly draws elaborate and explicit parallels between Telemachus, who proves his maturity by defending his right to his patrimony, and Orestes, who has defended his patrimony and reestablished the honor of the male line at Mycenae by killing his mother, Clytaemnestra, and her paramour, Aegisthus.

All these youthful figures on the threshold of manhood have a common structural relation that the poets regularly exploit. The parallels between them can be explicit and hortatory (anagogical) as in the *Odyssey;* more or less implicit, as in Aeschylus' *Eumenides* or Euripides' *Hippolytus* and *Bacchae;* or entirely implicit. The last type is perhaps the most interesting for semiotic analysis, for it reveals the operation of a subverbal pattern of narrative structures only.

In Sophocles' *Trachiniae,* for example, the poet is able to draw on the megatext in order to present the action of the play as suspended between two simultaneous and opposing paradigms, the myths of the

22. See C. Segal, *Dionysiac Poetics and Euripides' Bacchae* (Princeton 1982) chap. 6.

Odyssey and the myth of the *Oresteia*. We may present their relation to the action diagrammatically:

Telemachus	←———————	Hyllus	——————→	Orestes
Odysseus	←———————	Heracles	——————→	Agamemnon
Penelope	←———————	Deianeira	——————→	Clytaemnestra

Deianeira begins as a Penelope-figure, the patiently waiting, faithful wife, but ends up a Clytaemnestra, the murderous wife who destroys her husband at his homecoming. Heracles seems an Odysseus, off in remote places in the execution of heroic deeds, but he returns an Agamemnon, a proud and violent man who has destroyed a city and brings back a captive princess as his prize with little regard for the sanctities of his house or his marriage. (Note that Odysseus leaves Nausicaa, a potential Cassandra or Iole, on Scheria and returns unaccompanied, his arrival marked by a meeting with the nonsexual, nonseductive virgin Athena, disguised, in fact, as a male.) Hyllus too is strung between the two sets of paradigms. He begins as Telemachus, going off in search of his father as the first step in leaving his mother and the female-dominated household. But he ends up playing the role of Orestes, having to choose between father and mother and in fact asked to collaborate in the killing of his mother in vengeance for his father.

Noteworthy here is that neither Telemachus nor Orestes is ever explicitly mentioned in the *Trachiniae;* nor are Agamemnon and Clytaemnestra, Odysseus and Penelope. The tragedian can count on the implicit systematicity of the mythic corpus as megatext. Or, to put it differently, he can expect that his audience will be able to reencode the relations of the characters of his play into the parallel and homologous configurations in the megatext, and he can count on both the interchangeability and the polysemicity of these figures in the megatext. Any individual mythic figure can function as the starting point for a whole nexus of logical relations and subtle modulations between paradigms.

To turn to another set of such relations, a large body of myths deal with sacrifice and especially with perverted or distorted sacrifice (e.g., the myths of Atreus and Thyestes or Agamemnon). These myths do not merely justify rituals or explain their origins, after the manner of so-called charter myths or etiological myths. They must be viewed as part of the same semiotic system, an intricate web of logical relations having to do with the hierarchical ordering of the world biologically (god, man, beast), spatially (Olympus, earth, underworld), eschatologically (immortal, mortal, dead), and through diet (ambrosia as the food of the gods, grain and the cooked and perishable flesh of animals for mortal men, raw food on which wild beasts live). In such a system an element such as ambrosia is not just a food but a symbol with multiple interconnections to other codes, most strikingly to the poles of mortality and immortality, since etymologically it is exactly cognate with immortal.[23]

The dynamics of the system, by which an individual mythic figure generates parallels with analogous forms of the same relation elsewhere in the megatext, can be seen from two myths where ambrosia is especially important, the story of Tithonus, husband of Eos, and the story of Ganymede, cupbearer of the gods on Olympus. These two myths are correlated as complementary paradigms to the god-mortal union of Anchises and Aphrodite in the *Homeric Hymn to Aphrodite*. This early text tells the story of the siring of Aeneas from the union of mortal Anchises and the goddess of love. Both Tithonus and Ganymede are paradigms for mortal-immortal unions. Taken together with the story of Anchises and Aphrodite, they give that model a further level of meaning and thereby illustrate the overdetermination or redundancy characteristic of the encoding of cultural values within this megatext. To put it differently, they encode the message of the subtext (the union of immortal and mortal) into several other sets of terms.

In the narrative of the *Hymn* the interlocking parallels between Ganymede and Zeus, Tithonus and Eos, and Anchises and Aphrodite validate the symmetry between men's separation from the gods by age and death and their approximation to the gods through beauty and the power of eros (a point that Plato will develop in a very different way some three centuries later). Ganymede reaches Olympus and enjoys an eternity of unchanging youth. Tithonus gains an immortality of increasing old age; he is placed not on Olympus but "by Ocean's streams at the limits of earth" (227). Anchises meets his immortal lover, Aphrodite, on the earth, Mount Ida. He remains mortal but obtains the equivalent of immortality allowed to mortals,

23. For a systematic exposition of these homologies, see Marcel Detienne, *Les jardins d'Adonis* (Paris 1972).

a son who will perpetuate his race from generation to generation, ruling over the Trojans (196–99).[24]

The graduation in the biological code from immortal youth to mortality, heterosexual reproduction, and old age is also present in the parallel codes of space and food. Ganymede, on Olympus, pours out the gods' immortalizing beverage, "rosy nectar from a golden jar" (206). Tithonus, who gains immortality but not eternal youth, has as his diet an anomalous mixture of "both grain and ambrosia" (*sitōi t' ambrosiēi te*, 232). His abode is neither earth nor Olympus but a place distanced from both, "Ocean's streams at the limits of earth" (226). The anomalous plus in the dietary code (both grain and ambrosia) is symmetrical with the minus implicit in the spatial code (neither earth nor Olympus).

A similar spatial anomaly characterizes the offspring of the union between mortal Anchises and immortal Aphrodite. As the heir to a mortal patrimony, Anchises and his descendants will rule over a city of men. But as the child of a goddess, conceived not in a civilized house but in a shepherd's steading on the wild mountainside, Aeneas spends his first years of life in the forest, between city and wild, nurtured by Nymphs who live on earth but eat "immortal food" (*ambroton eidar*) and have their long life-span (260) measured by the life of trees in the forest (264–72). Mediating between gods and men as between passionate erotic union and incorporation in regularized civic life, the Nymphs "follow neither mortals nor immortals" (259) but have as their sexual partners the silenoi (262), who combine the features of gods and beasts, and Hermes, the god of mediation between gods and mortals, Olympus and Hades. Aphrodite's union with Anchises hovers ambiguously between the pure lust of seduction and the sanctions of marriage (cf. 117–42, 150). Luring him by talk of marriage, she makes even legitimate union serve her end of seduction. So too the child born of this union hovers ambiguously between recognition by his parents and concealment by his parents. The mother refuses to allow public recognition of her union with the father, Anchises, and yet like a true mother provides for the child's nurture (*trophē*: cf. 273) and describes prophetically his early years of

24. For further details, see C. Segal, "The Homeric Hymn to Aphrodite: A Structuralist Approach," *CW* 67 (1973/4) 205–12, and *Tragedy and Civilization: An Interpretation of Sophocles*, Martin Classical Lectures 26 (Cambridge, Mass. 1982) 22–24.

dependency on her maternal surrogates (273–79). Spatial, sexual, marital, dietary, and biological codes are all correlated in homologies that create a concrete, nonabstract systematicity organizing both natural and supernatural worlds.

The mythical structures of Pindar's Odes lend themselves to similar analysis. In the first *Olympian* the love relations of Ganymede-Zeus and Pelops-Poseidon in the sexual code are symmetrical with the god-mortal relations violated in the dietary code. Ganymede's successful attainment of Olympus parallels Pelops' dismissal from Olympus. The symmetrical mediations between god and mortal effected by both Ganymede and Pelops (though to different degrees) contrast with the failed mediation of Tantalus. Ganymede is a mortal youth taken up to Olympus by the gods. Pelops is sent from Olympus down to earth and later, allowed to reach the gods through the mortal mediatory forms of eros, ritual, and heroic honors. But Tantalus is sent from Olympus to Hades, beneath the earth, for attempting to bestow the gods' nectar upon his mortal companions. This violation of the god-man boundary in the dietary code is correlated also with the other crime to which the ode alludes, Tantalus' serving of his son Pelops as meat to the gods, an act whereby they would be reduced to the subhuman level of cannibals feasting on human flesh (*Ol.* 1.48–54). Stealing and distributing to men the divine prerogative of the immortalizing liquid (*Ol.* 1.55–67), Tantalus evokes another mediating figure in the megatext, the arch-mediator Prometheus (cf. Hesiod, *Theogony* 535ff.), whose mixture of theft and generosity also involves the establishment of boundaries and passages between gods and men. Pindar's dense interweaving of paradigmatic analogies both uses and exemplifies the generative order contained in the megatext of these myths. He correlates the aesthetic and moral order of truth, poetry, and art with the sexual, dietary, and spatial order in the proper relations between gods and mortals.

In the first *Pythian Ode* that correlation of poetic, spatial, and moral order is made visually concrete in the image of Mount Aetna as a mythical locus of coinciding opposites, land and sea, fire and water, light and darkness, gentleness and power (cf. *Pyth.* 1.19–26).[25] Con-

---

25. On *Pythian* 1 see Gilbert Norwood, *Pindar*, Sather Classical Lectures 19 (Berkeley and Los Angeles 1945) 101–5; S. D. Skulsky, "*Pollōn peirata syntanysais:* Language and Meaning in *Pythian* 1," *CP* 70 (1975) 8–31.

stituted as a mythic place, it is a "heavenly column," *kiōn ourania* (19b), a form of the familiar cosmic pillar or *axis mundi,* holding the monster Typhos down under the earth but also extending upward from Hades through the mortal world of middle earth to Olympus.[26] Here Apollo's golden lyre, "beginning of radiance" (2a), creates song as a unifying symbol of divine order among men. Drawing probably on the Hesiodic depiction of Typhos as a creature of confused and dissonant voices (*Theogony* 830–35),[27] Pindar sets up an elaborate correlation of cosmic and musical order whose validation and present realization are the musical performance of the Ode itself. In what we may call an auditory or acoustic code, harmony reigns on Olympus through the "beginning of radiance," emanating from Apollo's golden lyre to the voice of the singers and the steps of the dancers (1–4). On earth the song of the poet, Pindar himself, contrasts the praise of lawful rulers with the just blame of bad kings such as Phalaris, who tortured his victims by making them roar in a bull of bronze which he had heated by fire (94–98). In the natural order the heavenly column of Aetna has its own cacophonous roar as it sends its fiery streams and rocks crashing down into the sea, a sound appropriate to the monster that it keeps down in Tartarus (15, 20–24) but a source of wonder to those who see and hear it (26), for presumably they have been taught through the ode's ordering of the meaning of sounds to perceive the moral coherence behind such a monster and prodigy (*teras,* 26).

Pindar's elaborate correlation of song with the hierarchical cosmic order brings the poet's very act of artistic creation into the mythic structure: the frame is itself included in the content, the sender in the message. The poet thereby calls attention to his own role as a maker of hierarchies. He consciously draws his own aesthetic ordering of the world into parallelism with the cosmic ordering of Zeus, just as his lyre, the earthly and specific manifestation of Apollo's golden lyre, brings to mortal men the order-bringing, beauty-creating

26. On the cosmic pillar see Mircea Eliade, *Patterns in Comparative Religion* (New York 1958) 265ff.; on its place in *Pythian* 1 see Segal, *Tragedy and Civilization* (note 24) 22. In Aeschylus, *PV* 363–69, too, the monster's subjection to Zeus' order spans the "roots" and "highest crown" of Aetna.

27. A. von Mess, "Der Typhonmythus bei Pindar und Aeschylus," *RhM* 56 (1901) 167–74 notes the Hesiodic parallels but is not interested in their implications. See J.-P. Vernant and Marcel Detienne, *Les ruses de l'intelligence* (Paris 1974) 90f., 115f.

power of the divine lyre on Olympus and makes the festal celebration of the moment transparent to the eternally reenacted harmony among the gods (cf. 97f. and 1ff.).

Here a strong caveat is necessary. To separate the logical armature of the myth from its function in the literary work is to risk giving us a thin and partial reading of the text, the skeleton rather than the living flesh. A full analysis of the *Homeric Hymn to Aphrodite,* for example, would also demand our saying something about the play of deception which forms the essential nature of the love goddess as she appears to mortals and acts among mortals. We should say something about the way in which the constellation of lies, mountains, wild beasts, and seduction or rape not only forms a part of the cultural codes dealing with marriage and civic life but also enters into the language of the poem and creates Aphrodite's characteristic tone of playfulness. We should consider how the seductiveness and artful wiles of the goddess are also the seductiveness and artfulness of the poem itself, how the goddess' skillful telling of tales parallels the poet's skillful telling of tales: both use a mixture of truth and deception to accomplish their ends and to make of the passing pleasure of the moment something that, perhaps unintentionally, endures within the city and among its descendants. We should also have to pay attention to how these matters impinge upon the formulaic language of early hexameter poetry. We should study the poet's use of and modification of the formulaic attributes and traditional roles of the goddess of love as she appears in her various manifestations in the culture and in earlier poetry, an area where work by Gregory Nagy and Paul Friedrich has made important contributions.[28]

II

Greek tragedy is a peculiar form of the megatext, the extended text of Greek myth regarded as a unified corpus. It is simultaneously a commentary on the megatext of the mythic system and the final text of the system, simultaneously the culmination of the system and its dissolution. Tragedy, like epic, correlates paradigms from different

28. Gregory Nagy, "Phaethon, Sappho, Phaon and the White Rock of Leukas," *HSCP* 77 (1973) 137–78; Paul Friedrich, *The Meaning of Aphrodite* (Chicago 1978).

parts of the text in the way we have examined in the first part of this essay. Tragedy specializes in a complicated running together of homologous codes through metaphor and parallel narrative structures (we need think only of the *Oresteia*). More distinctively still, it plays with the logic of the system by working through elaborate reversals of the expected patterns. It prefaces the dynamic syntax of the archaic myths, as it were, with a negative sign. Its semiotic function in the culture may be compared with the concept of the carnivalesque in the work of Bakhtin, Kristeva, and Toporov or with the liminal and liminoid in work of Victor Turner.[29]

The god of the carnivalesque in Greek culture is also the god of tragedy and comedy: Dionysus. The peculiar relation of Greek tragedy to its mythical material has undoubtedly much to do with the god at whose festival and under whose aegis the plays were performed. Greek tragedy, one might say, places the megatext of myth in the liminal, carnivalesque space occupied by its god. The mediations of opposites which occur in the myths are collapsed together in multiple paradoxes and ironies in the realm of the god whose very nature is a constellation of coexisting contradictions: male and female, young and adult, chthonic and Olympian, human and bestial, Asian and Greek, creative and destructive. In tragedy the firm polarities and the clear expression of values in the social order are dissolved in ambiguity, complex inversions, and conflicts. The basic moral terms of civilized life become fluid and uncertain or tense with contradictions: wisdom and nature in the *Bacchae,* justice in the *Oresteia* or *Antigone,* knowledge in the *Oedipus Tyrannus,* purity in the *Hippolytus,* and so on.

One reason for this peculiar relation of Greek tragedy to the megatext of myth is the fact that tragedy itself seems to arise when social, political, and moral systems are in crisis or at a crossroads. At such junctures not only are value systems in flux but so, necessarily, are the modes of discourse that convey, describe, and encode those value systems. Language and the narrative forms dependent on language

29. See M. Bakhtin, *Rabelais and His World,* trans. Helene Iswolsky (Cambridge, Mass. 1968); Julia Kristeva, *Sēmeiōtikē: Recherches pour une sémanalyse* (1969; Paris 1978) 99ff.; V. N. Toponov, "On Dostoevsky's Poetics and Archaic Patterns of Mythical Thought," trans. S. Knight, *New Literary History* 9 (1978) 333–52; Jean-Claude Carrière, *Le carnaval et la politique* (Paris 1979) 29ff., 127ff.; Victor Turner, *The Forest of Symbols* (Ithaca 1973) and *Dramas, Fields, and Metaphors* (Ithaca 1974).

inevitably participate in the crisis and the transition. As Timothy Reiss comments, "In Western history tragedy seems to have appeared at moments that, retrospectively, are marked by a kind of 'hole' in the passage from one dominant discourse to another."[30] The seventy-year period (just two generations) spanned by extant Greek tragedy, which represents its mature creative phase, is clearly such a moment. The passage from one mode of social discourse to another includes the development of a language of conceptual thought, the languages of history and philosophy which the Greeks shaped for the rest of Western culture, and also a new narrative language of myth: tragedy.

Tragedy pulls the verbal ordering of language and the narrative ordering of myth in two different directions simultaneously: it validates, even if covertly, the established social, political, and religious values of the community, and it also enacts and releases the tensions within and among those values. Because of this double pull inherent in the critical and transitional nature of the mythic discourse in tragedy, it is possible to have a Marxist reading of Greek tragedy as the justification of the Establishment, like that of Peter Rose, and a more deconstructive reading of tragedy as reflecting breaches in the Establishment, like that of Jean-Pierre Vernant.[31]

There is another factor in this transitional moment of Greek tragedy: tragedy develops in Greece at the point of intersection between oral and literate modes of narration and representation. Although writing existed in Greece in early times, earlier narration was primarily oral and audience-controlled.[32] With tragedy, I believe, the role of writing becomes decisive in composition, for tragedy implies a written text, necessary to organize its dense, compact, multimedia

30. T. J. Reiss, *Tragedy and Truth* (New Haven 1980) 284.

31. Peter W. Rose, "A Dialectical View of Greek Tragic Form," *Radical History Review* 18 (1978) 77–94; Vernant and Vidal-Naquet, *Mythe et tragédie* (note 11) 13–17, 21–40 and *Mythe et société* (note 2) 205ff. On the danger of viewing Greek tragedy as reflecting the ideas and values of a ruling class or dominant elite see S. Said, "Travaux récents sur la poésie grecque, (1960–80)," *Information Littéraire* 33 (1981) 73. From a different point of view, it is possible that tragedy can be viewed in this double perspective because of its own never fully resolved tension between a wisdom of limits (*sōphrosynē*) and an admiration for the unlimited aspirations of heroism: see A. Terzakis, *Homage to the Tragic Muse,* trans. A. Anagnostopoulos (Boston 1978) 189.

32. See Havelock (note 12) passim; Cook (note 2) 6ff.; Vernant, *Mythe et société* (note 2) 196–200.

performance (dance, music, dialogue, recitation, etc.). Indeed, it is possible that the increasing importance of writing in the still largely oral culture of the early fifth century B.C. may have been one of the determinants in the origin of tragedy. The intersection of a literate and an oral culture results in the crossing between two semantic systems and a resultant complexity in the nature of mythic representation.

By the very fact of writing—and I have in mind also *écriture* in Jacques Derrida's sense—the poet of a hitherto oral culture is implicated in a system of abstractions which poses a barrier between his text and the univocal "truth" of an oral performance. Where the oral poet speaks as a voice of tradition and gives assurance of the validity of that tradition by his authoritative presence as the visible and present speaker or singer, the author of the oral performance of tragedy is absent, hidden behind his text. There is no single voice of truth. Instead, there is a plurality of voices, each with its claim to truth, justice, right, and piety; and no authoritative voice can pronounce unambiguously for any one of these voices, not even the chorus.

As dramatic performance, tragedy represents myth in its most solid, concrete, three-dimensional form, enacted on the stage before us. Yet at every moment there is a potential division between this surface tangibility and the abyss of illusion, appearances, deception. Tragedy presents a world characterized by a perpetual tension between deceptive surface and hidden truth, between appearance and reality. Poised between full representation and self-conscious fictionality, tragedy simultaneously culminates and dissolves the semiotic system behind the mythical material it uses.

This division between a surface world of illusion and a truth that lies beneath rests in part on the crossing between the two sign systems in its background, a verbal and a visual, a hidden text of written signs and a public, open, oral performance. The poet himself is operating in two different semantic systems, two different modes of communication, one (the oral) involving a social transaction of participation and exchange and the other (written) involving the abstractive distancing of écriture. "Writing is the grand symbol of the far," wrote Oswald Spengler.[33] Hence the representation of myth in trag-

---

33. Quoted and discussed by Jack Goody and Ian Watt, "The Consequences of Literacy," in Goody, ed., *Literacy in Traditional Societies* (Cambridge 1968) 55.

edy hovers between distance and closeness at the same time.[34] In the *Trachiniae,* for example, Sophocles brings on the stage a woman endowed with the civilized sensibilities of fifth-century Athens, someone whom the audience would have no trouble identifying as a contemporary. Yet she lives in a world where river-gods, Hydras, and Centaurs, the primordial monsters subdued by Heracles, are still recent and fresh.

Sophocles' *Oedipus Tyrannus* is simultaneously the most powerful instance of tragedy's divided world of appearance and reality, illusion and truth, and also the most elaborate example of tragedy's inversions of the coded systems in the megatext of Greek myths. It involves not only the reversal of king and scapegoat, as Vernant has pointed out, but a kind of rite of passage in reverse.[35] The king, recovering the origins of his life, finds his place not within the palace as the legitimate king's son—the usual pattern for the foundling hero, Theseus, Perseus, Cyrus, Ion—but in the wilderness as the polluted murderer, parricide, and incestuous husband of his mother, the total negation of the ordering power that should attach to the role of sacred kingship. These reversals are correlated with complex reversals in the nature of language and syntax, including the interchangeability of divine oracle and bestial shrieking of the monstrous Sphinx and the intricate double meanings of riddling speech in the celebrated tragic irony of Sophocles.

The *Oedipus'* self-consciousness about the logical patterning and its reversibility inherent in the syntax of language is paralleled by an analogous self-consciousness of reversibility in the syntax of the narrative structure, which Freud extrapolated as a universal life-plot of the human condition.[36] The coincidences that seem to guide the plot, accidentally, to its necessary conclusion also image the "coincidences," the coming together of disparate elements (*syntychia*) through which the poet shapes his work, interweaves and interconnects the separate elements of the narrative, the isolated incidents,

---

34. For a somewhat different view of this relation of closeness and distance in the relation of tragedy to myth, see Vernant, *Mythe et société* (note 2) 205f.; also Wolfgang Rösler, "Die Entdeckung der Fiktionalität in der Antike," *Poetica* 12 (1980) 312ff. For a fuller discussion of these questions in relation to tragedy and literature, see C. Segal, Tragédie, oralité, écriture," *Poétique* 50 (1982) 131–54 and "Greek Tragedy: Writing, Truth, and the Representation of the Self" in this volume.

35. Vernant, *Mythe et tragédie* (note 11) 117ff.

36. Peter Brooks, "Freud's Masterplot," *Yale French Studies* 55/56 (1977) 280–300.

into a unified design. In the story of Oedipus, then, Sophocles projects upon heroic myth the syntax of tragedy, the coincidental coming together of accidents into a fully bound and integrated form that conveys a sense of necessity and inevitability. Here again tragedy constitutes at the same time both the fullest exemplification of the interlocking system of the megatext of myth and the deepest questioning of its coherence.

The very subject of the *Oedipus Tyrannus* is polysemicity. Few works of classical literature pay so much attention to their own semiotic system. The *Oedipus Tyrannus* pursues the logic of its inversions with the inexorability that Aristotle, founder of logical systematization, could never admire enough. Like the *Bacchae,* which it resembles in this conscious exploitation of logical reversal, it treats kinship as a system of logical relation and logical relation as a form of kinship. It explores the sexual roots of knowledge, the sexualization of knowledge, and the intellectualization of sexuality. Oedipus' search for himself is both man's emotional needs to grasp origins and man's intellectual need for orientation in the otherness of the world through such systems of relational logic as kinship. Confusion in the generational code (incest) is parallel to confusion in the linguistic code (riddle and oracle coming together, the multiple ambiguities of Oedipus' name and its origins as *oidi-pous* [swell-foot], *oida-pous* [know-foot], *oida-pou* [know-where], *oi-dipous* [alas, two-footed]). Incestuous marriage, a denial of the father, denies the hierarchizing and differentiating processes that operate both in language and in the social order to create personal identity and personal responsibility. Brought back to his origins by replacing his father, "sowing where he was sown," Oedipus questions the whole enterprise of culture, in which men mark the otherness of the phenomenal world and separate themselves from the nameless, random life of nature.

At the center of a semiotic system that is both too full and yet always threatening to disintegrate into emptiness, Oedipus is a constellation of opposites where the ambiguity of the individual's primal word, his name, implicates the entire denotational, differentiating system of language itself.[37] As a focal point for the equivalence of the

37. See Segal, *Tragedy and Civilization* (note 24) 241–44; also C. Segal, "The Music of the Sphinx: The Problem of Language in *Oedipus Tyrannus,*" in Kresic (note 7) 151–63.

codes (familial, sexual, cognitional, biological, spatial, ritual), the myth exhibits and explores its own polysemicity with particular transparency; concurrently it explores its own a-semicity, the precariousness of signification, and the possibility that language may point to meaninglessness or deceive by the false appearances of meaning.

It is partly for this reason that Oedipus can be and has been interpreted with equal validity in so many different systems: psychoanalytical, linguistic, political, historical, religious, structuralist. The very problem of his existence, as posed in the myth is the problem of language: language crystallizes self and world into static forms, yet these forms have the changing aspect of things always in flux. Oedipus himself can be defined by his name only when the play has taken us through a powerful and painful experience that reveals the deceptiveness of language as an interpreter of reality and as a mediator between apparently steady surface and ever-shifting depths, between truth and appearance. Myths like this, which reflect (literally "bend back") upon themselves, on their own narrative syntax and its reversibility, seem to have the remarkable quality of deconstructing themselves. Certain myths, at least—I would put here those of Oedipus and Pentheus—reveal and explore the mechanisms for the deconstruction of the system of myth and the system of language out of which they themselves grow. The simultaneous use and questioning of these systems constitute perhaps the most distinctive feature of the recasting of myth in tragedy, carried to its furthest point in the *Oedipus Tyrannus*.

The *Tyrannus* shows how tragedy, as a secondary elaboration of myth, can tell its story while deliberately calling into question one of the most fundamental elements of mythic narration, the representation of time. Sophocles' play virtually deconstructs the myth by revealing the illusoriness of temporal progression in the story. The forward movement of the hero, driven like the audience by a curiosity both intellectual and sexual, both public and intimate, takes a path that is linear (because it marks an advance into the future) and simultaneously circular (because it reveals the present only as a repetition of the past, gripped at every point by the domination of past events that it cannot transcend). The push toward solution and closure becomes, at every point, an increasingly intense involvement in origins, opening wider gaps and larger spaces of the past. Each of the hero's conquests in the forward movement of his life, like each movement of the plot to a new episode, is only a clearer revelation of a hidden past, secrets of birth that prove more elusive the closer he gets. When Oedipus recovers his city and his mother by ignorantly solving the riddle of the Sphinx, he is blind to the real truth of himself. Beneath his alien status as victor and foreign husband he conceals the truth of his origins as legitimate son and heir. The remote past, with the blood ties that should assure him an intimate place in both house and city, cancels out the present, in which he possesses wife and kingdom after fulfilling the role of the young conquering hero (like Perseus or Theseus) who arrives from a distant land.

As Oedipus uncovers his hidden origins, so the tale of the birth of a child is also the discovery of a hushed attempt to murder a child.[38] The discovery of a father is also the discovery of killing a father. Finding his mother becomes the finding of himself as the husband of his mother, father of her children. Each discovery of origins opens upon something that must be immediately closed; the recovery of lost knowledge demands a closing up and concealment of that knowledge. Oedipus becomes the reader of a tale who discovers at its end that he is the missing piece which alone can bring the tale to its conclusion. Yet only the delay, by refusal of that discovery (a refusal that sometimes seems blind and perverse), allows the tale to unfold at all.[39]

At the peripety, blinding himself with the brooches that he takes from Jocasta's robe, Oedipus reenacts the unraveling and unconcealing that pull every forward progress back to dark origins. His act of self-blinding brings with it the implication of baring (again) his mother's body, but now it gives him an inner vision that previously he had lacked. This penetration, by both feet and eyes, to places that should have remained hidden from him reveals to him the truth of his equivocal status as both the insider and the outsider, and it also

---

38. Shoshana Felman, "Turning the Screw of Interpretation," *Yale French Studies* 55/56 (1977) 161ff. quotes an interesting passage from Serge Leclair, *On tue un enfant* (Paris 1975): "Insupportable est la mort de l'enfant: elle réalise le plus secret et le plus profond de nos voeux. . . ."

39. Felman (note 38) 175 has some interesting remarks on the parallelism of the *Oedipus Tyrannus* as a detective story and Henry James's *The Turn of the Screw*.

reveals the transgressive status of his amgibuously legitimate place within the house and within the city.[40]

The paradoxes surrounding the hero's discoveries parallel the paradoxes surrounding the kind of truth that the tragic poet reveals: this is a truth that intertwines darkness and clarity in our knowledge of ourselves and our place in the world. Spinning a web of pleasant deceptions, *apatai* in Gorgias' sense (82 B 23 D-K), the tragic poet reveals behind the delightful surface, the *terpsis* or *hēdonē*, of myth the ugly, painful, or shameful things that we know but cannot or will not speak. In the *Tyrannus* both the hero in his life story and language in the permutations that it undergoes in the course of the play have their *pathē*, their sufferings. In both an ultimately sexual mechanism of allure and seduction, the curiosity to see and experience, is transformed into the recognition of a horror that is simultaneously repulsive and fascinating. With the hero we, the audience, are drawn on in increasing desire to see and to know, even as we recognize more and more certainly that there will be pain, not pleasure, in what we will see. Uncovering the body of Jocasta in the intimate inner chambers of the palace near the end is the prelude not to a night of nuptial pleasure but to a perpetual night of guilty, tormenting knowledge.

In the *Bacchae,* as in the *Oedipus,* tragedy emerges as the form able to encompass its own contradiction, able to hold a delicate counterpoise between the creative and destructive energies of life and the centripetal and centrifugal forces of all (mythical) narrative. The god of tragedy asks the protagonist of the *Bacchae,* also deluded by appearances and fascinated by secrets that a mother would keep concealed, "Would you then see with pleasure what is bitter to you?" (ὅμως δ' ἴδοις ἂν ἡδέως ἅ σοι πικρά; 815). Here Euripides explores not only the systematic inversions made possible by the reversible syntax of the myth of Pentheus—shifts of active to passive, god to beast, highest to lowest, and so on—but also the relation of these reversals to the form that myth assumes in tragedy, that is, myth in the liminal, carnivalesque space of Dionysus.

The structure here is not a static antithesis but a tensely maintained

---

40. See John Hay, *Oedipus Tyrannus: Lame Knowledge and the Homosporic Womb* (Washington, D.C. 1978) 104ff., 119, 125; P. Pucci, "On the 'Eye' and the 'Phallos' and Other Permutabilities in *Oedipus Rex*," in *Arktouros* (note 14) 130–33.

harmony of opposites like that described in the celebrated fragment of Heraclitus (22 B 51 D-K): "They do not understand how being drawn apart from itself it agress with itself; a back-stretched harmonious fitting, as of a bow and lyre." The inner dynamics of the play show the capacity of the aesthetic form to absorb the destructiveness of the contents and the power of those contents to call into question and to disturb the beauty of the aesthetic form.

The *Bacchae* maintains this "back-stretched harmony" between the life-giving and the life-destroying power in Dionysus and the myths about Dionysus. There is a just and an unjust Pentheus, a just and an unjust Dionysus, a terrible and a gentle god, a lyrically mystical and a savagely murderous band (thiasos) of bacchants, a play that calls to the remote beauty of ecstatic worship of the life energies in the world and in ourselves and a play that makes us recoil with revulsion from the release of those energies. Euripides' tragic art makes both sides visible in their simultaneity, complementarity, and inseparability.

The play, by its very existence, marks the place where the destructive side of the Dionysiac energies of both god and storyteller have been overcome by the creative, the place where those energies have resisted desublimation and have been transformed into implements of civilization, into a token of personal reflection on the god and his rites. Coming at the end of the creative phase of Greek tragedy, the *Bacchae* reflects on the origin and nature of tragedy, on the point where art separates from ritual. The *Bacchae* also reflects on the destructiveness of the rite and dramatizes the emergence of self-conscious suffering and remorse out of group participation in the Dionysiac omophagy, the emergence of the individual from the group, and with that the emergence of tragedy from myth.

The vicarious representation of the Dionysiac ritual within the city limits at the Greater Dionysia replaces the celebration of the rites in the ecstatic thiasos on Cithaeron. Were those rites celebrated with full exuberance on the mountain and in the forest, without resistance, without reflection or hesitation, there would be no tragedy, perhaps no civilization. In the participation in the rites of the god in the *oreibasia*, the nocturnal revel on the mountain, there is no residue; everything is used up, joyously, in the moment of fusion with the god and in participation in nature's vital energies. In the performance of the rite in its symbolic and vicarious form in the theater of Dionysus, there remains the tragedy, which survives for future ages to ponder. In this celebration the participants sit immobile in their seats; and the action is entirely mental and inward, a complex, many-sided reflection on the rites that were or might be performed with the fullest, most energetic action on the mountains outside.

Tragedy is a form of myth which not only uses, illustrates, and interweaves the codes but also reflects on the logic implicit in the whole mythical system. In the *Bacchae*, Euripides has tragedy act out, in the visual form of dramatic representation, its own illusion-creating processes of masking, robing, and fiction making. The great scene where Dionysus, god of dramatic illusion as well as of wine, madness, and religious ecstasy, dresses the young king as a Maenad on the stage, visually enacts that process of fictional representation which the poet practices. The scene mirrors back to the audience their own willingness to endow an actor on the stage with the personage of a mythical being merely by virtue of the mask and robes with which the poet clothes him.

At the end of the *Bacchae*, Agave enters in her madness carrying the bloody head of Pentheus. Cadmus asks, "Whose *prosōpon* do you carry in arms?" (1277). His word *prosōpon* can mean "face" or "visage," but it can also mean "mask." It calls attention to the illusionistic process of the play itself, the use of masks to represent faces. It also marks a certain progression in the mimetic representation of the fiction being acted out on the stage before us. There is the face of Pentheus, which is really a mask (the double meaning of prosōpon), over which Dionysus has placed the wig and cap of a Maenad, in which Agave sees the head of a savage lion— "Do you see that cloud that's almost in shape like a camel?—By the mass, and it's like a camel indeed.—Methinks it's like a weasel.—It is back'd like a weasel.—Or like a whale?—Very like a whale" (*Hamlet* III.iii. 393ff.). After playing a number of mutually contradictory roles—king and scapegoat, hunter and hunted, antagonist of the god and sacrificed victim-surrogate of the god, authoritarian monarch and ambiguously female bacchant—Pentheus is finally reduced to being an empty mask, carried by his mother who thinks that she is carrying the head of a lion.

Tragedy, then, develops the deconstructive potential inherent, perhaps, in all myth and indeed in all narrative. Emerging at a unique historical moment when the traditional values of an oral culture are increasingly subjected to the critical spirit fostered by literacy and when the relatively secure hierarchies of the archaic world order are tested and reexamined, tragedy experiments with the reversal or violent interweaving of the codes of the social order and deconstructs the system to show the hidden logic of its workings. It can even represent the zero-degree of signification, when the relations are so densely interwoven, the description so thick (to use Clifford Geertz's term)[41] that signification itself is called into question, as in the scene of Cassandra's prophecy in the *Agamemnon* (1072–1177). Unlike more static cultures, the Greeks of the classical period were able to incorporate into their narrative systems this process of reflexivity and its ambiguous potential for negating the logic of those narrative systems. It is one of the most remarkable qualities of the megatext of the mythical narratives that it could expand to assimilate its own negations and reversals.

Tragedy stands at the intersection of two opposing relations to its mythical material: the further expansion of the mythic megatext as it generates fresh narratives from the old matrices and the continual questioning, analyzing, and even negating of the mythical models. This elasticity of the myths is perhaps latent in the dynamic potential of the system from the beginning, that quality which could generate the kind of paradigmatic relation so characteristic of Greek mythic literature from its earliest times.

For this metalingual and metaliterary functioning of myth in tragedy, structural and semiotic analysis has much to contribute. It can reveal the interlocking of relations in the symbolic systems formed by the myths. It can also help analyze the clash of value systems, the functioning of the sign systems, and particularly those metaliterary levels where the text calls attention to its own fragility and artificiality as a construct of signs and symbols. Tragedy is a form of mythical narrative which makes overt its own deliberateness as a device of the human intellect to keep out chaos or, in other terms, to resist entropy and its symbolic equivalent in language: disorder, incoherence, unintelligibility, nonmeaning, meaninglessness. It thereby reinscribes that potential disorder and chaos into the structured nature of human life with that safe danger whose paradox is the paradox of tragedy.

---

41. T. Clifford Geertz, "Thick Description: Toward an Interpretive Theory of Culture," in his *The Interpretation of Culture* (New York 1973) 3–30; also "Deep Play: Notes on the Balinese Cockfight," in the same volume, 412–53.

CHAPTER 3 /

Greek Tragedy: Writing, Truth, and the Representation of the Self

I

When tragedy is born in Athens around 500 B.C., the city creates in its midst the civic space in which it can look at itself in the mirror of the ancient myths. *Theatron,* "theater," is a space for beholding, derived from the verb *theaomai,* to behold with wonder. This narrative form is the most vivid possible representation of myth in Greek culture. It is also a form of mythic representation which highlights all the tensions, contradictions, and problems that arise when the Athenians adapt to their new democracy the aristocratic legends of the past: tales about kings and heroes, about ancient families that claim descent from the gods, and about the hereditary curses handed down in the bloodlines of these families.[1] But throughout Greece in the course of the sixth and fifth centuries, social changes (including the increasing use of writing) and consequent changes in the role of the poet bring concomitant changes in the character and function of mythic narration.[2]

A French version of some parts of this essay, in a different form and with a different emphasis, appears as the introduction to my *La musique du Sphinx: Structure, mythe, langage dans la tragédie grecque* (La Découverte, Paris, forthcoming). I thank the John Simon Guggenheim Memorial Foundation for a fellowship in 1981–82, which supported the research for this study. I am grateful to Froma Zeitlin of Princeton University for friendly criticism and advice.

1. See Jean-Pierre Vernant, "Tensions et ambiguïtés dans la tragédie grecque," in Vernant and P. Vidal-Naquet, *Mythe et tragédie* (Paris 1972) 24ff.; also Vidal-Naquet's chapters on the *Oresteia* and the *Philoctetes* in the same volume, especially 149ff. and 168ff.

2. For the changing role of the poet in the archaic period, see J. Svenbro, *La parole*

In fifth-century Athens, writing enables the democratic polis to see itself in a new perspective and to claim for its contemporary existence, despite its ideology of change and innovation, a patrimony of glorious tradition analogous to the myths of the ancient aristocratic families. The written histories of Herodotus and to a greater degree of Thucydides, as Diego Lanza has argued,[3] are analogous to tragedy in that they create for the democracy a mirror in which Athenians can contemplate the deeds of their city and preserve in memory the words of its leaders. These speeches, now condensed into definitive form and fixed as part of the history's eternal possession, *ktēma es aiei*, are not only the record of what has impelled the city to its actions but also the verbal expression of its elusive consciousness, its essential character.

II

The notion of the unity of Greek culture stretching in a more or less unbroken line from Homer to Aristotle is deeply inbedded in the historical imagination of the modern world, from its early exponents, Lessing, Herder, and Winckelmann, to the historical synthesizing of Wilamowitz. But in the last few decades this unitary structure has suffered multiple fractures. The most recent attack has come from the work of Eric Havelock, whose studies of the implications of literacy and preliteracy over the last twenty years have forced us to reexamine some of the massive changes in concerns, outlook, and expression brought about by the transition from an oral to a literate culture.[4]

Havelock himself has paid remarkably little attention to tragedy and only recently included it within his reexamination of the intellectual history of early Greece.[5] While aware of tragedy's position be-

---

et le marbre (Lund 1976), which references to earlier literature. For archaic poetry in the perspective of an oral culture, see B. Gentili, "Aspetti del rapporto poeta, committente, uditorio nella lirica corale greca," *Studi Urbinati* 39 (1965) 70–88.

3. D. Lanza, *Lingua e discorso nell' Atene delle professioni* (Naples 1979) 56; also 75f.

4. E. A. Havelock, *Preface to Plato* (Cambridge, Mass. 1963), *The Greek Conception of Justice* (Cambridge, Mass. 1978), and essays collected as *The Literate Revolution in Greece and Its Consequences* (Princeton 1982).

5. Havelock, "The Oral Composition of Greek Drama," *QUCC* n.s. 6 (1980) 61–113 (or *Literate Revolution* [note 4] 261–313).

tween the oral and literate phases of Greek culture, he emphasizes the continuities of tragedy with the attitudes and style of oral poetry. The tragedian, according to his view, is a late manifestation of the oral poet, conveying communal and traditional wisdom. My purpose is to give more importance to the tensions inherent in tragedy as a literary form and to allow more importance to the radical departures from an oral tradition which are implicit in tragedy.

Tragedy is an oral performance, but one controlled by a written text.[6] It is performed in the agonistic and ritual setting that characterizes most of early Greek literature. Unlike oral epic, however, tragedy is not recreated afresh on each occasion by the improvisatory art of the aoidos, the oral singer. If the plays were acted again after initial performance at the Dionysiac festival of the Lenaea or the Dionysia (a privilege allowed only to the plays of Aeschylus), they were not re-creations requiring a fresh inspiration and a new composition for that occasion, as in oral poetry, but the replication of a fixed text.[7] In the fifth century the text serves primarily as the script for a performance. Tragedians do not seem to think of their work as intended for a reading public until the fourth century.[8]

As the creator of a written text destined for oral performance, the tragic poet, unlike the oral singer, stands in a deferred relation to his work. Composition and performance no longer coincide; instead, there is an intermediate stage when the work is complete but unrealized. Indeed, a tragedian may have composed plays that were not

6. On tragedy and the development of writing see U. von Wilamowitz-Moellendorff, Einleitung in die griechische Tragödie, vol. 1 of his Euripides, Herakles (Berlin 1907) 120–27; see in general Walter Ong, S. J., Orality and Literacy (London and New York 1982) 148f. Comedy, though it allows for more improvisation in performance, also depends on a fixed text, and the development of comedy as a literary form postdates that of tragedy in fifth-century Athens.

7. For the difference between oral recreation and exact reproduction see A. B. Lord, The Singer of Tales (Cambridge, Mass. 1960) chap. 6. He has reiterated how foreign is the notion of a fixed text in an oral culture in "The Influence of Fixed Text," To Honor Roman Jakobson 2 (The Hague and Paris 1967) 1196–1206, especially 1206. See also J. Goody, "Mémoire et apprentissage dans les sociétés avec et sans écriture," L'Homme 17 (1977) 29–52, especially 44. For recent discussion, with ample bibliography, see Bruno Gentili, "Oralità e scrittura in Grecia," in M. Vegetti, ed., Oralità scrittura spettacolo (Turin 1983) 30–52.

8. Aristotle, Rhetoric 3.12,1413b12ff.; also Albin Lesky, Greek Tragedy, 3d ed., trans. H. A. Frankfort (London and New York 1967) 204. See also Aristotle, Poetics 26, 1462a11–17 and G. F. Else, Aristotle's Poetics: The Argument (Cambridge, Mass. 1957) 635f., 640f.

presented until months or years later. Tragedians might revise a play already presented, as Euripides did with his *Hippolytus Veiled*—a procedure that itself implies heavy reliance on writing in the mode of composition—or might revise a play that would then exist only as a written text, as seems to have happened in the case of Aristophanes' *Clouds*.[9] Admittedly, a choral poet like Alcman composed songs that others would perform later; but such works were far shorter and less complex than a tragedy. The long compositions of Stesichorus that have recently come to light—the Jocasta fragment and the *Geryoneis*—are not certainly choral and seem much closer to oral epic in the smooth narrative flow, the simple and linear movement of the plot, and the elaboration of surface detail.[10]

This division between the two stages in the production of a tragedy—text and performance—may have contributed to the distance from the mythical subject that the conflictual, open-ended, and questioning spirit of Greek tragedy demands. Instead of one-sidedly celebrating a local hero, as choral lyric tends to do, tragedy combines sympathetic participation with the presentation of different points of view, attitudes, and perspectives, no one of which is necessarily final or right.[11] Hence Aeschylus can movingly depict the suffering of his audience's mortal enemies in the *Persians*, and Euripides can portray with compassion the defeated enemies of the Greeks in the *Andromache, Hecuba,* and *Trojan Women*.

It is also possible—though here we are in a realm of pure speculation—that this two-stage mode of production sensitizes the tragic poet to the two systems of communication and representation, verbal and visual, that his art involves: the power of visualization inherent in the image-making power of the word itself and the concrete act of visualization on the theatrical stage. The coexistence of verbal and visual representation unique to the theater involves, at nearly every point, dichotomy, contradiction, or paradox in the existence of truth.

9. It is widely agreed that the version of the *Clouds* handed down to us is the revised text of a play that may never have been performed: see K. J. Dover, *Aristophanes, Clouds* (Oxford 1968) lxxxff.

10. On formulaic elements in Stesichorus see G. Vognone, "Aspetti formulari in Stesicoro," *QUCC* n.s. 12 (1982) 35–42, who sees in the style an intermediate stage between the oral, rhapsodic tradition and literate poetry. I should say that the former predominates.

11. On this point see Alvin Gouldner, *Enter Plato: Classical Greece and the Origins of Social Theory* (New York and London 1965) 114; also Vernant's "Tensions" (note 1).

The conflict between appearance and reality, what is seen and what is said, is of course a recurrent theme of Greek literature from its earliest beginning: the external, visual attractions of women's beauty are already dangerous in Hesiod's Pandora, and Homer's Odysseus is a master of lies and disguises. These tensions between the surface world that we see and the hidden truths that we do not are also explored by the philosophers, from Thales and Anaximander to Parmenides and the Atomists. Yet in tragedy the rift between seen and unseen truth acquires a more vivid representation through being enacted before our eyes, in the gestures and movements of living men in real space.

In early Greek society the poet is a "master of truth," the speaker of a discourse that derives validity from a set of culturally privileged narratives.[12] Homer invokes the Muses as his source of knowledge about the past (*Il.* 2.484–87). Hesiod relates how the Muses on Helicon give him a *skēptron*, a staff, emblem of authority, and breathed into him the power of song along with the knowledge of its capacity for both truth and falsehood (*Theogony* 26–34).[13] By the late sixth century, however, that authority for truth has been secularized and internalized. Oral poetry—and I have in mind the Homeric poems in particular—gives us the sensation of the full presence of events: we feel that we have all the necessary details and that we possess that immediacy of foreground eioquently described by Erich Auerbach in the famous first chapter of *Mimesis*. Tragedy, based as it is on a written text, is full of elusive details, missing pieces, unexplained motives, puzzling changes of mood, decision, or attitude. Instead of the oral poet who tells us in person of the will of Zeus, we have the absent poet who has plotted out every detail in advance. And we have the feeling, at times, that we have been plotted against, that we are the victims of a calculated counterpoint between surface and depth, appearance and reality, seeming and being.

As the basis for bardic authority is reexamined in the critical spirit fostered by writing, authors need to shape another kind of narrative in order to lay claim to a discourse of truth. They need to tell a

12. M. Detienne, *Maîtres de vérité dans la Grèce archaïque* (Paris 1967).

13. For recent discussion of the Muses in Homer and Hesiod, see W. Rösler, "Die Entdeckung der Fiktionalität in der Antike," *Poetica* 12 (1980) 294–98, with further bibliography; also P. Pucci, *Hesiod and the Language of Poetry* (Baltimore and London 1977) 8–44.

different kind of story about themselves in order to support the truth that they claim to speak. Such, for instance is the journey of Parmenides, cast in the traditional form of a Homeric narrative and studded with phrases borrowed from the epic vocabulary.[14] But Parmenides' traditional language serves only to set off the unique, mysterious quality of his journey and his destination. This poet is going not to a mythical land of Laestrygonians but to a realm of philosophical concepts, being and nonbeing. Such too is Thucydides' new story about himself, a story not about gods and Muses but about a "journey" of investigation, inquiry, strenuous examination, *zētēsis tēs alētheias,* "a searching out of truth" (Thucyd. 1.20.3 and in general 1.20–22).

The increasing literacy of the late fifth century, at least in Athens,[15] is one of several interrelated influences that tend to cut the discourse of truth loose from the communal, performative, and agonistic context of the archaic period and thereby to require the poet to reflect consciously on the source of truth or, in other words, on the kind of story that he has, implicitly, to tell about himself. Later poets, Callimachus and Theocritus, for example, do this almost as a matter of course and in the spirit of a self-conscious literary *topos,* to distinguish their art from that of their predecessors and contemporaries.[16]

What is the implicit story of the tragic poet? It is no longer a tale of meeting Muses of gods (such as even Pindar still could tell).[17] The tragedian's story resembles perhaps that of Oedipus or Teiresias; it is the story of a double vision or a double language (*dissai phōnai*), of a

---

14. Parmenides frag. 28 B1 (D-K).

15. For the growing importance of literacy in the last quarter of the fifth century see F. D. Harvey, "Literacy in the Athenian Democracy," *REG* 79 (1966) 585–635; E. G. Turner, *Athenian Books in the Fifth and Fourth Centuries* B.C. (London 1952); A. R. Burns, "Athenian Literacy in the Fifth Century," *Journal of the History of Ideas* 42 (1981) 371–87; Lanza, *Lingua e discorso* (note 3) 52–84, with the bibliography, 85–87; Giovanni Cerri, *Legislazione orale e tragedia greca* (Naples 1979) 33–45, 65–74. On the upper limits of literacy among the Athenians, despite the number of inscriptions in the city, see Oddone Longo, *Tecniche della comunicazione nella Grecia antica* (Naples 1981) 120, with 125 n.20. It is part of Havelock's "oral" thesis that literacy be placed as late as possible in the fifth century, though he admits, rather reluctantly, the high literacy at the end of the century: *Literate Revolution* 199ff., especially 203f.

16. Cf. Theocritus 7.123–30, especially 128ff.; Callimachus, *Aitia* I, frag. 1, 21ff., where the status of the fully literate poet is signaled by the presence of the writing tablet on his knees; also frag. 2.

17. For example, Pindar, *Pyth.* 8.56–60; *Pyth.* 3.77–79, with scholion 137b (Drachmann).

backstage, of something hidden behind or beneath.[18] For Aristophanes, the verse by Euripides that reads "My tongue has sworn, but
unsworn is my mind" (*Hipp.* 612) became almost a motto of that
poet's form of tragedy, the ironic emblem of his defeat in the *Frogs*
(1471). In representing the visually concrete and physical exterior of
the mythical character, tragedy heightens the mystery of his interior
life. A self-conscious tragedian like Euripides repeatedly calls attention to the problem of representing, realizing, and verifying this
interior realm.

In the fifth century the "graphic space" of alphabetic writing becomes a convenient metaphor for making visible the hidden realm of
the emotional life. As the concretization into solid, stable, and visual
form the fluid, invisible breath of the voice's "winged words," writing can represent the process of revealing what lies unseen within the
mind. The most common of these graphic metaphors is that of the
tablets of the mind, frequent in the tragedians, with the concomitant
figure of unrolling or unfolding the interior secrets of the heart.[19] We
may include here Gorgias' figure of persuasion's "stamp" or "impression" upon the soul (*tēn psuchēn etupōsato*) and his image of *logoi*
that make things to be seen by "the eyes of opinion" (*tois tēs doxēs
ommasin, Helen* 13). Immediately afterward he speaks of the persuasive power of a *logos* that is "*written* with art" (*technēi grapheis*).
Then a few paragraphs later, describing the power of vision to arouse
fear and desire, he uses another metaphor of writing: "So has vision
inscribed [*enegrapse*] on thought the images [*eikonas*] of actual things
seen" (*Helen* 17). He goes on to speak of painters (*grapheis*) and
sculptors whose work brings pleasure and pain to the eyes. These
visual metaphors, in turn, are intended as analogies for the force of
eros as a quasi-corporeal power that enters the soul through the eyes.

At least two factors aid this association of writing and emotional
interiority: the tendency in an oral culture to connect writing with
private, secret, or deceitful communication (particularly of an erotic
nature) and the importance that writing gives to vision, for the
Greeks the most powerful stimulus to eros.[20] Gorgias' theory of

18. Eur., *Hipp.* 925–31; *Med.* 516–19; *HF* 655–72. For the hidden in human life see
Hipp. 191–97 and the echoes later in Artemis' speech to Theseus, 1287ff.

19. E.g., Eur., *Hipp.* 985; cf. IT 793.

20. See, for example, R. C. Jebb, *Sophocles, The Plays and Fragments*, Part III, *The
Antigone* (Cambridge 1891) on 795ff.

desire depends on this four-way association of writing, emotional life, eros, and vision. This graphic space, I shall suggest later, corresponds to the tragedians' new self-consciousness about what is going on behind and beneath, about what cannot be shown visually in the scenic action (the self as inner and hidden) and in the scenic language (the written text).

It would, of course, be a mistaken exaggeration to attribute to writing alone massive shifts of emphasis in Greek society which resulted from the interaction of many complex factors, economic, social, political, religious, and so on. The growing individualism of the fifth century, aided by the rationalism of the philosophers and the Sophists, the questioning of traditional values in the various crises of the Peloponnesian War, the gradual evolution of moral speculation over the previous century which included an increasing shift from "shame-culture" to "guilt-culture," all contribute to this concern with the inner self and the real nature of what we are.[21] Nevertheless, the movement away from the face-to-face exchange of information in a small, village-type society, where everyone is familiar and defined by multiple nexuses of relationships, to the more abstractive, intellectual, and less personal mode of communicating information and ideas inherent in a literate culture accentuates the problem of self-knowledge and self-definition.[22] Writing accompanies that increasing acknowledgement of complexity in the vision of self and world which marks the fifth century. The self defined by the physical externals of health, beauty, strength, and the opinion of others[23] is no longer adequate to a world view aware of irrational, invisible, mysterious forces within the individual and the governance of the universe.

Along with civic cult, epic and rhapsodic recitation, choral performances, and such other rituals of a dramatic nature as the Mysteries, drama depends upon a system of symbols and conventions to effect its mimesis of reality. The audiences that came to the first tragedies had long been schooled in a mode of thought that could "see" the Troad or Lemnos or Egypt in the circular orchestra of the theater or could accept the figure moving and speaking behind the mask as

---

21. For some speculation on these social changes see Gouldner (note 11) 113f., 133f.
22. For the face-to-face mentality of village-type, oral societies see Longo, *Tecniche della comunicazione* (note 15) 13ff.
23. See Gouldner (note 11) 98ff., 105ff.

Theseus, Heracles, or Agamemnon. But phonetic writing gives new force and simplicity of expression in everyday life to this process of conventionalized, symbolic representation. The increasing alphabetization of Athens as tragedy is developing, along with the critical spirit fostered in a literate society, sharpens awareness of the discrepancy between the imagined and the actual objects, just as phonetic writing sharpens awareness of the discrepancy between the alphabetic conventions and the tactile reality.[24] Hence the tragedians are interested not only in creating spectacles but in calling attention to their own *power* to create spectacles, to the system of conventions with which the form itself operates. We are familiar with such self-consciousness about the symbolic system of representation in late Euripidean plays, in the *Helen* and the *Bacchae*,[25] but the tendency is there even as early as Sophocles' *Ajax,* where the prologue seems to allude to the poet's illusionistic power as a kind of divine *technē* (86), enabling us the audience to be present as if unseen at events acted out before our eyes (83–86):[26]

> *Athena.* He could not see you, do not fear, even if you stand next to him.
> *Odysseus.* How, if he sees with the same eyes?
> *Ath.* I will darken his eyes, even though they see.
> *Od.* Everything may come about with a god's devising craft.

III

Writing provides a fixed point of orientation and organization around which are focused the mental energies that are in an oral culture more diffused. The new skill appears not merely an intellec-

24. On the importance of phonetic writing as the source of a conventionalized symbol-system for tragedy see D. de Kerckhove, "Synthèse sensorielle et tragédie: L'espace dans *Les Perses* d'Eschyle," in *Tragique et tragédie dans la tradition occidentale,* ed. P. Gravel and T. J. Reiss (Montreal 1983) 69–83, especially 75ff., who seems to me to have isolated and exaggerated the importance of writing. Writing may have contributed to self-consciousness about the conventions, but the conventions themselves have older, deeper, and more diverse origins. See also his 1979 essay (note 28).
25. See below, notes 75 and 76.
26. The discovery of Ajax's body at the climax of the play may also be calling attention to the technique of using the eccyclema to make visually powerful what would otherwise remain hidden: cf. 976–78 and 890 with 915–17.

tual technique but the sheer power of mind and eye (often closely associated by the Greeks, for whom to know is to see, as the two verbs have the same root, *vid-*). Simonides' new "art of memory" at the end of the sixth or beginning of the fifth century seems to have used visualization as its main component.[27] Thus the power of memory, instead of being attached to hearing and speech and therefore being oriented externally, toward others, is made part of visual experience and is oriented inwardly, toward oneself, toward silence and privacy. The metaphor, frequent in tragedy, of writing on the tablets of the mind identifies memory with something both visual and interior, a kind of interiorized writing (see below, section VIII). The literate revolution probably played an important role both in emphasizing visualization and in celebrating the power of mind, a recurrent theme in the classical period, from about 460 B.C. to the end of the century.

One of the most famous celebrations of this intellectual power is the *Prometheus Bound* of Aeschylus. Here, I think, we find an important indirect reflection of the new mode of mental organization implied in writing. The Titan, imprisoned and immobilized on his rock in the Caucasus in punishment for teaching the arts of civilization to mortals—including the arts of writing and counting—holds the center of the stage, an object of magnetic vision to all who approach him.[28] Like the organizing force of a written text, this figure at the center of the spectacle is the source from which all the mental energy

27. See Cicero, *De Orat.* 2.86.354 and 2.87.357. See Gentili in Vegetti (note 7) 32. See also Kerckhove (note 28) 359–61 on Simonides and the "interiorization of a visual space" (361).

28. After I had written this section, Professor Froma Zeitlin pointed out to me that a similar point had been made about the *Prometheus* by D. de Kerckhove, "Sur la fonction du théâtre comme agent d'intériorisation des effets de l'alphabet phonétique à Athènes au V siècle," *Les imaginaries, II, Cause commune*, 1979, no. 1, "10/18" (Paris 1979) 345–68, especially 351–56. Although we both stress the importance of Prometheus' immobility, Kerckhove emphasizes the effect of sensory deprivation. In his view this is central to the reorganization of perceptual reality, for it creates a mode of thinking that is now directed by the repression of the body and shifts away from oral-aural participation to the more abstractive processes that he connects with phonetic writing: "Or c'est la tension entre la répression sensorielle et l'impossibilité de réagir physiquement qui permet à l'énergie de Prométhée de se concentrer dans une intériorité d'où s'échappe interminablement sa parole" (353f.). Stimulating as this approach is, it suffers from isolating only one factor in what is a complex movement toward the conception of an interiorized self in late archaic and classical Greece. If theatrical space, moreover, is in one sense analogous to the symbolic conventionality

in the play seems to radiate. He imposes order and limit by means of his intellectual power—power that consists in the ordering, presenting, and withholding of knowledge.

At roughly the midpoint of the action, after Prometheus has enumerated at length his civilizing gifts to mankind, the cow-maiden Io enters. Zeus' lustful pursuit has driven her over the earth in confused wanderings. A figure of total disorientation, she utters inarticulate cries, does not know where she is, and is amazed that Prometheus knows her name. Their meeting is like the confrontation of oral and written mentalities. Io is immersed entirely in an immediate present beyond which she cannot see. She is surrounded by mysterious voices that drive her onward, and she is pursued by vague, dreamlike visions of the night that she can only partially discern and cannot understand. Following a journey that seems to hold neither end nor goal, she lacks the kind of centering and focusing of experience which Prometheus embodies in the play.

When Prometheus urges Io to "write down on the remembering tablets of her mind" the extent of her future travels (789), he provides her with both the temporal and the spatial organization that the ordering of reality by writing makes possible. In clear and well articulated order he indicates the definite stages in her journey. He orients her according to the directional marks of north and south, sunrise and sunset (cf. 790f., 796f.), just as he had oriented mortals by giving them the knowledge of seasonal limits and by teaching them how to read the signs and omens of the future from the birds (484–99). The verb "set on a path," *hodoun,* occurs in both passages (498, 813) and marks the directional, orienting nature of the kind of knowledge which Prometheus gives to mortals.

Prometheus' spatial ordering of Io's movements by explaining the route of her wanderings has a temporal equivalent in the future of the places that she traverses. These nameless points, Prometheus says, will become famous in later times, fixed markers in a strange territory, because of her passage (e.g. 732–34, 839–45). He tells her also of the remoter end of her sufferings when she reaches her goal in the land of Egypt and of another kind of relief in the fact that one of her descendants will be his liberator. In the dimensions of both space and

---

of phonetic script, the Greek theatrical performance, with its multimedia and multisensory effects, is far from the abstractive result of sensory deprivation.

time, then, Prometheus gives her formless world a shape and a form, just as he gives her journey and her experiences a direction and a coherence. He makes available to her the organizing intelligence that comes with writing, coordinating past and future, tracing patterns in the shapeless mass of both space and time, and making patterns visible in the midst of a chaotic mass of unordered detail. He creates for the inarticulate half-human creature of suffering what is virtually a map of where she has been and where she is to go (we recall again that verb of orienting direction, "set on a path," *hodoun,* in 813).

IV

Another exemplary text of this period has as its central theme the problem of organizing experience into knowledge and moving between different communicative and signifying systems, namely the *Oedipus Tyrannus* of Sophocles. Here even more sharply than in the *Prometheus* the problem of truth has to do with the crossing over between aural and visual modes of sorting and preserving information. It is commonplace to observe the importance of sight in the play. But less commonly observed is the interlocking of sight and hearing in many of Oedipus' statements about knowledge. When the primary object of inquiry arises in the prologue, namely the question of the death of Laius, Oedipus describes his knowledge of Laius as follows: "I *know* [of him] by *hearing;* for never have I *seen* him" (105). Since *oida,* "I know," is the first syllable of Oedipus' name, the line immediately associates Oedipus' knowing with seeing.

When Oedipus, near the end, blinds himself and returns to the stage, it is as a man returned to the one-dimensional knowledge of an oral/aural culture, reborn into a world dominated by the presence of sound as the primary mode of knowledge (1309f.): "Where in the earth am I borne, miserable? How does my voice fly around me, borne aloft?" (*diapotatai phoradēn*). The voice, *phthonga,* becomes something concrete and solid, a separate entity that has a quasi-corporeal reality, a locomotive power, like the Sphinx or like the magical, incantatory winged word in an oral culture. When he asks to close off the channels of hearing as of sight (1386–90), Oedipus restates in negative form the double sensory power that constituted the basis of knowledge in the prologue. In his anger and ignorance he

Writing, Truth, and the Self

accused the inwardly seeing Teiresias of being *"blind* in his *ears"* as well as in his "mind and eyes" (*OT* 371). But Oedipus himself is exemplary of tragedy in his determined exploration of the interlocking of visual and auditory knowledge and in his awareness of the doubleness of verbal meanings in man's difficult search for truth. One thinks here too of Sophocles' contemporary, Empedocles, and his concern with the multiple avenues of knowledge through the senses.[29]

V

The ambiguity of language as a medium of truthful discourse implied in the *Oedipus* receives perhaps its most pregnant formulation in prose from the rhetorician and Sophist Gorgias near the end of the fifth century. In the *Helen* (c. 13) he evokes the power of language in the oral tradition to give pleasure (*terpein*) and persuade (*peithein*).[30] He distinguishes, however, between the "word written with artful skill," *technēi grapheis,* and the word "spoken with truth," *aletheiāi lechtheis.* A fragment of his *Epitaphios* contrasts the "freshness" and "vitality" of actions with the "paleness" and "trembling" feebleness of letters (*tremonta kai ōchra*).[31] Gorgias can still play upon *alētheia* as the truth communicated in the living interaction of the oral exchange, but with a major difference: he is conscious of being a scriptor who has written the logos of Helen (*grapsai, Helen* c. 21) and therefore made a plaything or a fiction, a *paignion* (the last word of the *Encomium on Helen*) not a piece of "truth." "I wished to write my discourse," he concludes, "as an encomium for Helen and as a plaything of my own." His work, then, falls into the category of what is "written with art, not spoken with truth" (*Helen* c. 13); he is no longer a "master of truth." As a writer, he has a special consciousness of himself as the shaper of his own discourse, with the element of play that it can exemplify.

29. Empedocles 31 B3, 9ff. (D-K); also B2.7f.
30. See C. Segal, "Gorgias and the Psychology of the *Logos,*" *HSCP* 65 (1962) 99–155, especially 106f., 110f., 122ff.; W. J. Verdenius, "Gorgias' Doctrine of Deception," in G. B. Kerferd, ed., *The Sophists and Their Legacy,* Hermes Einzelschrift 44 (Wiesbaden 1981) 121f.
31. For the text, see Friedrich Solmsen in *Hermes* 66 (1931) 249 n.2 (or his *Kleine Schriften* [Hildesheim 1968] 2.159 n.2).

Play is also freedom, the new freedom of the writer, detached from the public context of the oral performance, free of the responsibility of transmitting and recording the traditions of his people, able to develop ideas because they interest him alone.[32] He can follow his own path of words and thoughts with an independence not possible for the oral bard subject to the audience's control of the performance. This kind of author makes no claim to a transpersonal truth beyond himself. Unlike the oral poet, he knows the moment of his words' origin; he knows that they arise from within himself, that they are an object that he himself has fashioned and sees materialized as a text.

We may contrast with Gorgias' self-consciousness of writing the powerful affirmation of the truth of oral as against written statement a generation earlier in the Argive King's decree in Aeschylus' *Suppliants* (946–49), where spoken words have the solidity and tangible presence conveyed in the metaphor of the firmly fastened "peg" or "bolt" of his decree (*gomphos*, 945).[33] "These things are not written down on tablets," says the King, "nor sealed up in the foldings of scrolls: you hear the clear words of a tongue and a mouth that speak in freedom." But for Gorgias' younger contemporary, Thucydides, the relation between the spoken and the written word is just the other way around. The spoken word deceives and misleads and its seductive promise of pleasure (*terpsis*) in the agonistic context of recitation (Thucyd. 1.22.1), whereas the written word is the result of effort (*ponos*) and investigation (*zētēsis*) and yields accuracy (*akribeia*). Writing is surer than speaking in revealing what is hidden (*to aphanes*) behind surface appearances (*phanera opsis*, 1.10.2; cf. 1.23.3–6).[34]

The division in the philosophers, historians, and the tragic poets between surface and depth, appearance and reality, is encouraged by the special status of the written text in a hitherto oral culture. These authors have before them two models of mental organization. Oral

32. This play element has a notable role in Euripides' *Bacchae*. See C. Segal, *Dionysiac Poetics and Euripides' Bacchae* (Princeton 1982) 266ff.

33. On this passage and the solidification of speech as inscribed document see Turner, *Athenian Books* (note 15) 9; also Longo, *Tecniche della comunicazione* (note 15) 122f.

34. On these passages see C. Segal, "*Logos and Mythos*: Language, Reality, and Appearance in Greek Tragedy and Plato," in *Tragique et tragédie* (note 24) 25–27; also B. Gentili and G. Cerri, *Le teorie del discorso storico nel pensiero greco e la storiografia romana arcaica* (Rome 1975) 24f.; F. Solmsen, *The Intellectual Experiment of the Greek Enlightenment* (Princeton 1975) 96f.

communication faces outward, to the interactive contextual space between speaker and audience; written communication faces inward, toward the personal relation with the hearer. Its concern is syntactics rather than pragmatics.[35] As Aristotle points out in his discussion of the graphic and the agonistic styles, writing fosters the internal subordination of ideas within the syntax of the sentence.[36] Oral communication, on the other hand, depends less on the internal logic and structuring of the ideas than on the repeated assertions of its message, the fullness and copiousness of its style, qualitites that take account of the needs and limitations of the listener. The written message is far more enclosed in the autonomy of its own internal coherence. Some of the tensions explored by tragedy may be due to this pull between the inner cohesion of the written text and the other-directedness of the oral medium.

VI

The beginnings of such a tension coincide with the critical reflection on the mythic tradition which writing unquestionably aided. Around the middle of the fifth century Hecataeus of Abdera, like Thucydides, designates himself explicitly as a scriptor, the composer of a writing. His new graphic space fragments the prior vision of truth into a plurality of modes of understanding the world.[37] In the few fragments that survive of Protagoras' interpretation of Homer, we can see the same processes of distancing and critical examination: the copious flow, the forward-moving impetus, of the oral epic is interrupted after the first words. The fluid linkage of each phrase to the next is broken up into small, discontinuous fragments of discourse which can be scrutinized and dissected. It is the same technique that Aeschylus applies to the prologues of Euripides in Aristophanes' *Frogs*.[38]

35. See Ong, *Orality and Literacy* (note 6) 37f., who cites T. Givón, "From Discourse to Syntax: Grammar as a Processing Strategy," *Syntax and Semantics* 12 (1979) 81–112.
36. Aristotle, *Rhet.* 3.12, especially 1413b8–14a7.
37. Marcel Detienne, *L'invention de la mythologie* (Paris 1982) 138ff., a propos of Hecataeus frag. 1 (Jacoby); see also Rösler (note 13) 306.
38. Aristoph., *Frogs* 1119–1250; cf. Protagoras 80A28–29 (D-K), and C. Segal,

For Democritus, perhaps at about the same time, even the numinous quality of poetic inspiration is linked to the written word: "Whatever a poet *writes* [*graphēi*] with inspiration and the holy afflatus is indeed beautiful."[39] The power of a divine mind (*theios nous*) lies no longer in the gift of inspiration from the goddesses of memory but in a ratiocinative capacity, something like dialogic reasoning.[40] In the oral tradition it is the Muse and the goddess Mnemosyne who endow the poet with the power of lengthy, continuous utterance, made possible by a ready abundance of words and matter. The written word encourages density, concentration, discontinuity. Tragedy, in an intermediate position between orality and literacy, contains both tendencies: the flow of the long messenger speeches and the staccato effect of the dialogue, often marked by the sharp conflict of arguments in *antilogiai* and stichomythia.[41]

From the late sixth century on, critical reflection about the traditional tales gains momentum with writing. When variant versions can be fixed in a written text, discrepancies and contradictions are more easily detected.[42] The tragic poets—like Pindar, Hecataeus, Herodotus—do not merely repeat or retell the myths but reflect on them in a critical spirit.[43] In the graphic space that opens before the tragic poet as the writer of a fixed text, there opens also the autonomous space of the fictional, the possibility of free invention, though obviously within prescribed limits. Instead of being a master of truth, conveyer of multipersonal norms and values fixed in the conventionalized symbolic system of mythical tales recounted in heavily formulaic language, the poet is on his way to becoming the fabricater of fictions. Younger tragedians, Agathon, for example, even experimented, though rarely, with plots of their own invention.[44] The task

---

"Protagoras' *Orthoepeia* and Aristophanes' 'Battle of the Prologues,'" *RhM* 113 (1970) 158–62.

39. Democritus 68 B18 (D-K).

40. *Dialogizesthai*, Democritus 68 B112 (D-K).

41. See Solmsen, *Intellectual Experiment* (note 34) 17 and 28ff.; also John H. Finley, Jr., "The Origins of Thucydides' Style," in *Three Essays on Thucydides* (Cambridge, Mass. 1967) 74–82, 110–12.

42. See. J. Goody and I. Watt, "The Consequences of Literacy," in *Literacy in Traditional Societies,* ed. Goody (Cambridge 1968) 27–68, especially 44ff.; see also Svenbro (note 2) 15.

43. Detienne, *L'invention* (note 37) chaps. 3 and 4; also Svenbro (note 2) 173–212.

44. Aristotle, *Poetics* 1451b19–26.

of the tragic poet is now not to unveil reality but to create a self-conscious imitation of reality.[45]

The Homeric interpretation of Theagenes of Rhegium at the end of the sixth century is an interesting forerunner of this kind of imitated universe of the art work. Our knowledge of Theagenes is pitifully scanty, but from the extant fragments it seems clear that he wrote a commentary on the Homeric poems, interpreting some of the more troublesome anthropomorphic features of the gods in an allegorical way. In this endeavor he had a predecessor in the Homeric criticism of Xenophanes earlier in the sixth century; but where Xenophanes only criticized, Theagenes seems to have allegorized.[46] To interpret a text, to reflect on it as an object apart from the context of its immediate performance, is to imply a second plane of truth. As a writing, such poetry no longer opens to a public world, fully visible to all and immediately comprehensible in the shared values that it utters and endorses. Instead, as a text, the poem reveals a hidden world that becomes visible only as we scrutinize the words as an object of contemplation. Its surface has to be lifted away or penetrated to reveal the deeper levels; it contains a thought that lies beneath the visible meaning (*hypo-noia*) or, in later terminology, says something other than its overt statement (*all-ēgoria*).[47] With a written text, it becomes possible to distinguish a first level of meaning from a second, and there enters a critical distance that does not exist in a traditional society whose truth is firmly ensconced in the memory of its members. With the practice of writing, the true meaning of the traditional wisdom is hidden and invisible, something to be reached by that effort of intellect and abstraction which writing makes possible.

This is the kind of speech in which Thucydides is also engaged, far

---

45. See Rösler (note 13) 309ff.; J.-P. Vernant, "Le sujet tragique: historicité et transhistoricité," *Belfagor* 34 (1979) 639f., and "Naissance d'images," in *Religions, histoire, raisons* (Paris 1979) 111. Verdenius (note 30) 123f. points out the generally negative attitude toward poetry as fiction in early Greek literature.

46. The little that is handed down about Theagenes can be found in D-K 1.51f. (number 8). If the tradition is reliable, he was a contemporary of Aeschylus and Pindar, and he "wrote" his comments down (*grapsas*, frag. 2 ad fin. and frag. 4). Something at least survived in writing for Hellenistic scholarship to pass on to late antiquity, from which come our only notices of his work. For Theagenes' Homeric interpretation and the implications of literacy see Detienne, *L'invention* (note 37) 130.

47. The term hyponoia is probably pre-Platonic; allēgoria is late; see Svenbro (note 2) 113–15.

more self-consciously. He rejects the fluid surface of Herodotus' discourse, still oriented to the oral context,[48] in favor of the more strenuous examination of evidence, comparison of divergences, abstraction, and inferences that all go along with writing. For the atomists Democritus and Leucippus, the phenomenal world itself is a text, a surface of appearances that has to be analyzed into its permanent but invisible truth of atom and void, the *stoicheia,* "elements," "letters," of its invisible atoms.[49] To reach truth one must distance onself from the "human lifeworld" and plunge beneath this surface into the depths *(buthos).*[50] Such, mutatis mutandis, is also the investigative procedure of Thucydides: he seeks to recover the hidden causes that are *aphanes,* invisible, hidden behind the *phanera opsis,* the "visible appearance" (cf. 1.10, 1.22–23).

VII

In a preliterate society, conflicts are acted out in social situations of encounter and exchange.[51] So too, values are embodied in concrete, externalized objects—solid and visible points of reference for everyone.[52] With its distancing of experience and its removal from the necessity of face-to-face exchange in communication, writing encourages the internalizing of experience and the exploration of the private, the self-consciously personal.[53] The realm of the private, the personal, begins to appear. Conflicts are interiorized, and the whole inner world of the emotional life opens up. Phaedra's refusal to speak of her love, her reluctance to enter into dialogue with the Nurse and the women of Troezen, is symmetrical with the ambiguous silent speaking of the written tablets that she leaves for her husband.

48. For the predominance of the oral code in Herodotus see Longo, *Tecniche della comunicazione* (note 15) 72 n.26.
49. Leucippus 67 A9 (D-K) (or Aristotle, *De gen. et corr.* 1.315b6ff.) and Lucretius, *De rerum natura* 1.197f., 823-29, 2.688–99 are also evidence for the atomists' use of the letters of words as analogous to the atoms of things.
50. Democritus, 68 B117 (D-K). On the notion of truth in things beneath the surface and compounds of buthos in archaic poetry, see Svenbro (note 2) 119–21.
51. See J. Russo and B. Simon, "Homeric Psychology and the Oral Epic Tradition," *Journal of the History of Ideas* 29 (1968) 483–98.
52. See L. Gernet, "La notion mythique de la valeur en Grèce," in *L'anthropologie de la Grèce antique,* ed. J.-P. Vernant (Paris 1968) 93–137.
53. See Ong, *Orality and Literacy* (note 6) 178f.

The further development of writing increases the duplicitous potential of language. The gap between word and thing, logos and ergon, between what one says and what one is, becomes ever more evident and more problematical: compare Theseus' complaint of the deceptive discrepancy between men's voices (what they say) and their characters (what they are) in *Hippolytus* 925ff. Language now is no longer the fullness of ready, serviceable stories that flow from the generous gifts of goddess memory; it becomes an ambiguous series of signs, traces, and absences.[54] Sophocles' Oedipus confronts language as a difficult track (*ichnos*) that he must follow out to the unknown end, like a hunter following the spoor of his prey (*OT* 108–11; cf. *Ajax* 5–10). *Muthoi* and *logoi*, what men say to one another, lead no longer to an open road but to a narrow and difficult path. Parmenides' route is "outside the track of men."[55]

The first reference to writing in Greek literature assigns to it the quality of ominous mystery as a sign. Such are the *sēmata lugra*, baleful markings, what Bellerophon bears in the folded tablets intended to lead him to his doom (*Il.* 6.168ff.). Yet even into the fourth century, writing is the distillation of the deceptiveness of language and the difficulty of communication. It can be a mark of prestige and a guarantor of accuracy and truth.[56] But a culture that still privileges face-to-face contact and immediate sensory experience also regards writing as an object of suspicion, the characteristic tool of guile and treachery. In Thucydides' account of the Spartan Pausanias' illicit dealings with the Persian king, letters are the mark of his secrecy; but the ephors, to whom he is betrayed by letters, are convinced of the man's guilt only when they see and hear for themselves.[57]

Sophocles' *Trachiniae* and Euripides' *Hippolytus* (as well as the latter's lost *Stheneboea*) associate writing, trickery, concealed love, and female desire as all related distortions of truth. In tragedy, writing often serves as a motif or a figure around which the poet can

54. This point becomes explicit à propos of written language in Plato's famous myth about writing in *Phaedrus* 274c–276a. Building on Plato, Derrida works back from writing to all language as a protowriting.

55. Frag. 28 B1.27 (D-K): *ektos patou*.

56. E.g., Herodotus 1.125 or 3.128; Thucyd. 7.8. See Longo, *Tecniche della comunicazione* (note 15) 61f., 66f.

57. Thucyd. 1.133. On this passage see Longo, *Tecniche della comunicazione* (note 15) 62f.

crystallize the ambiguous attitudes of the culture toward the female and especially toward female desire.[58] In the *Hippolytus,* writing appears as a duplicitous silent speaking that can subvert the authority of king and father. As a concentrated form of seduction and persuasion, such "female" writing is doubly a threat to the masculine ideal of straightforward talk and forthright action.[59]

In the *Trachiniae* the letters that Heracles leaves behind for his family serve the father's goal of assuring the disposition of the patrimony after his death (46f., 156ff.; cf. also 1166–72). But there is another kind of writing, the metaphorical bronze tablet that describes Deianeira's memorization of Nessus' instructions about what she believes to be a love charm (680–84). The metaphor deepens the theme of communication and exchange in this portion of the action, for the robe on which she smears the drug is sent to Heracles as her message of fidelity, a sign of faith of words (*logōn pistis,* 623).[60]

This metaphorical writing essential to the transmission of the robe, along with the sexual charm that the robe supposedly contains, is a continuation of the Centaur's deceptive speech. The tablet expresses in a visual metaphor Deianeira's susceptibility to his ambiguous persuasion, with its erotic magic (710; cf. 660–62). It speaks a language of her unknown or unacknowledged self. As a silent remnant and record of the last words that Nessus addressed to her on the banks of his river, it shows Deianeira to herself as the exemplar of destructive female sexuality. It reveals the monstrous power of sexual desire that she can see in Heracles, Nessus, and Achelous but that she cannot recognize in herself.[61]

In the interior space of the *oikos,* the woman's world, the open violence of the Centaur's masculine lust is transformed into feminine guile, persuasion, and seduction; and its murderous force operates through characteristically feminine arts. This baneful and mysterious power of female desire works not on the open, visible surfaces of the

58. We may recall here Gorgias' *Helen,* discussed above, which probably draws on tragic material (cf. frag. B23).

59. On women and writing as a joint object of suspicion, cf. Menander, frag. 702K, on which see Harvey, "Literacy" (note 15) 621; also Susan G. Cole, "Could Greek Women Read and Write?" *Women's Studies* 8 (1981) 137 and 155.

60. For the theme of communication and exchange in the *Trachiniae,* see C. Segal, *Tragedy and Civilization: An Interpretation of Sophocles* (Cambridge, Mass. 1981) 94ff.

61. For some implications of the tablet see Longo, *Tecniche della comunicazione* (note 15) 65f.; Page duBois, *Centaurs and Amazons* (Ann Arbor 1982) 98f.

body but on the inner organs (1053–57). Its effects in these lines are described in metaphors of ingestion and digestion, processes involving the body as interior space, hollow, or vessel. It uses enclosure, enfolding, and immobilization rather than penetration (cf. 1057). Heracles explicitly contrasts the wounds inflicted on him by the robe with the masculine weapons of war, the spear and the sword (1058, 1063).

The metaphorical tablet is not only the negation of the patriarchal order implicit in Heracles' letters, but it is also the dark counterpart of the robe's intended message of wifely fidelity (492–95). It conveys a different message about the nature of women. Its perverted speech utters the feared and suppressed truth that the chaste wife is also a lustful female, that the bride of Heracles is also the woman who yielded to the Centaur's persuasion/seduction and might yield to the more overt sexuality of his animal nature. These themes extend far beyond the implications of the "writing of the brazen tablet" in 683; yet the implicit transformation there from speech to writing, voice to silence, force to guile, male to female desire is a focal point for the inversions of the social codes which tragedy often explores.

It is part of the multiple and shifting meaning that writing can have in this period that men can also send deceitful and death-bearing messages (Agamemnon in *Iphigeneia in Aulis*), and letters by women can bring salvation (Iphigeneia in the Taurian *Iphigeneia;* Andromeda in Euripides' lost play of that name).[62] In the political sphere, written laws are a safeguard against tyranny and the guarantee of fairness and equality under the Athenian democracy (Eur., *Suppliants* 429–37); yet the unwritten laws still enjoy the prestige of ancient tradition and sacral usage (Soph., *Antig.* 450ff.; cf. Thucyd. 2.37.3).[63] The combination of the practical, day-to-day utility of writing with its relative unfamiliarity and perhaps its Near Eastern origins doubtless encouraged such ambiguous, even contradictory meanings.

On the rational side, the practice of writing gradually transforms the invisible, quasi-magical power of the spoken word into a familiar,

62. Euripides is probably more open to these ambiguous associations of writing than Sophocles: see Longo, *Tecniche della comunicazione* (note 15) 66.

63. On the relation of literacy and orality to the debate between written and unwritten law in the fifth century see Cerri, *Legislazione orale* (note 15) especially chaps. 4 and 5; also Fabio Turato, "Seduzioni della parola e dramma dei segni nell' Ippolito di Euripide," *Bollettino dell'Istituto di Filologia Greca,* University of Padua, 3 (1976) 181f.

material object, a well defined, clearly delimited human creation.[64] This concretization of language into writing gives an impulse to the study of language and communication per se.[65] Indeed, one finds a fascination with the origin and nature of language throughout this entire period, in the Sophists, in Thucydides, Herodotus, and the tragedians. All of the tragedians speculate on the origins of language and the origins of writing. A curious fragment of Euripides' lost *Theseus* shows a fascination with the physical form of letters (a character describes the shape of the letters that make up the name Theseus); and the popularity of the passage is indicated by the fact that it was closely imitated by two of Euripides' younger successors, Agathon and Theodectes. All three are interested in the physical form of letters as visual signifiers of the spoken word.[66] Such passages are indications of the new consciousness of the textuality of the work, operating at the microcosmic level of the basic act of composing shapes into language.

Instead of disappearing into the collective memory once the performance is over, being absorbed back into the communal voice, the written word of the poet has an autonomous existence apart from the spoken utterance that realizes it. The literate poet becomes even more aware than the archaic bard that his words are the component parts of an artistic product, a crafted object. His work is no longer a memorial to others' deeds, as in Homeric epic or even the archaic encomium, but a distinctive entity of his own, the guarantor of his own skill, not his patron's eternal fame.[67] Of the extant tragedians, Euripides most frequently uses this metaphorical crystallization of poetry as a monument or an artifact[68]—and also as a text.

---

64. See J. Goody, Introduction, *Literacy in Traditional Societies* (note 42) 1: "Its [writing's] most essential service is to objectify speech, to provide language with a material correlative, a set of visible signs. . . ."

65. See in general Longo, *Tecniche della comunicazione* (note 15) chaps. 2 and 3; Lanza, *Lingua e discorso* (note 15) chap. 1, with the bibliography, 50f.

66. Eur. frag. 382; Agathon, frag. 4; Theodectes, frag. 6 (Nauck); see Harvey, "Literacy" (note 15) 603f.

67. See Svenbro (note 2) 186ff. on Simonides. Contrast passages like Ibycus 282.47f. (Page) or Theognis 237–54 with passages like Pindar, *Ol.* 1.111ff. or *Ol.* 6. 1–4 or *Pyth.* 6.7–18. For recent discussion of the poetics of sixth-century singers see Gentili in Vegetti (note 7) 53–76, especially 62ff., with the bibliography, 75f.

68. See, for example, *Alc.* 962–71; *Med.* 190–203; *Hipp.* 1125ff., 1428–30; *Ion* 1143–65; *HF* 673–95; see in general P. Pucci, "The Monument and the Sacrifice," *Arethusa* 10 (1977) 165–95; also Segal, *Dionysiac Poetics* (note 32) 318ff.

VIII

In tragedy, where the poet never speaks in his own person, this kind of self-conscious textuality can work only implicitly, behind the dramatic spectacle. To show how it may function, even where the play seems relatively unself-conscious about its own poetics, I shall examine briefly the climactic events in Sophocles' *Oedipus Tyrannus* (1237–96). The main actors are absent from the stage, and the dramatic enactment of the events is suppressed in favor of a long narrative account in the third person by an outsider, a new arrival, the second messenger who tells the tale. The Messenger begins by pointing out that he tells of things that were and are not seen: "There is [was] no vision present" (*opsis ou para,* 1238). He thereby sets into relief the distinctive quality of the telling that takes place through the visual representation onstage.[69]

Within the Messenger's narrative, memory itself has a spatial correlative in the penetration to the private, interior parts of the palace: first Jocasta's violent rushing inside the doors (*pylai,* 1244) to the place where she "has memory [makes mention] of the old seeding" from Laius (1246), then Oedipus' breaking through those doors (*pylai,* 1261) to find her body. Here, as in the *Agamemnon* or the *Bacchae,* the most memorable events of the play are revealed to us only in verbal narration: the suicide of Jocasta and the self-blinding of Oedipus. Sophocles is of course following the convention of Greek drama which demands that such violence be enacted offstage. But in calling specific attention to the contrast between dramatic enactment and narration, he also implies a new self-consciousness of the textuality of the work.

The Messenger's tale not only presents the visual contents of memory; it is also an emblematic account of memory's inner vision. Memory here becomes correlative with vision, a kind of nonvisual seeing just as writing is a nonoral speaking. It is also an interiorized seeing, and we may recall here the implications of the metaphorical writing on the tablets of the mind.

This memory of the Messenger conducts us, verbally, inside the

---

69. For a more detailed discussion of this passage, see C. Segal, "Time, Theater, and Knowledge in the Tragedy of Oedipus," *Edipo: Il teatro greco e la cultura Europea,* ed. B. Gentili, forthcoming.

gates of the palace where Oedipus rushes around in wild despair. Then it shows us the interior space of Jocasta's marriage chamber, the scene of her suicide and Oedipus' self-blinding. The narration, however, permits us to glimpse these most important events only in fragments, by significant absence rather than through the full presence of the actors or the enacted events. By calling attention to the fact that he is withholding the visual appearance of his chief protagonists in favor of a purely verbal narration, the poet also reveals his consciousness of the theatrical spectacle as a special form of narrative, mediating between external and interior vision, between visible, physical acts and the emotional world that they reveal.

The Messenger ends his long narrative with the words, "For these gates of the palace are opening; soon you will see a spectacle [*theama*] such that even the one who loathes it will feel pity" (1295f.). The theatrical action, the visible opening of the outer doors of the palace, now mirrors the Messenger's verbal account. That recited narrative, based on a carefully structured *text*—words set down in advance to be delivered exactly as the poet has planned—has its own mode of revealing what is kept hidden. Its climactic moments too are the acts of closing and opening doors (1244, 1261f.; cf. 1287, 1294f.), but these acts take place entirely in the unseen, interior space within the palace.

Sophocles uses the conventional device of the messenger-speech with a new consciousness of the relation between the poet's text and the dramatic (visually enacted) events. He stresses the parallelism and the contrast between verbally describing the unseen events behind the palace and bedchamber doors and theatrically showing Oedipus as a spectacle on the stage (1295f.). Oedipus now emerges through the palace doors as the center of all attention and the object of pitiable *sight* to all. "O suffering fearful for men to *see*" is the immediate response of the chorus (1298). The terms for vision, spectacle, and the opening of gates shift between the narrator and the events he describes, the hideous violence that takes place behind closed doors.[70] Sophocles thus calls attention to the double mode of narration going on before us. He implies thereby the self-consciousness of the text that has plotted out the story in advance of the performance. The spectacle onstage has behind it a narrative of actions in which "there is no vision present" (*opsis ou para*, 1238). The Messenger's purely

70. E.g., 1238, 1253, 1261, 1265, 1287, 1294.

verbal tale is like the stage business before our eyes: it too is a way of opening doors to the hidden events that arouse our terror and our pity.

This textual self-consciousness, I suggest, owes much to the transitional moment of the form between oral and literate. This concern with the hidden, private, inner space, here and elsewhere in Greek tragedy, points to a poet-writer whose frame of reference is *both* the physical, public space of the oral performance in the theater *and* the graphic space of the text. This interior space of house or palace is, by the conventions of Greek drama, not represented on the stage but is always implicit behind the action. The poet composes for a stage that shows only the outside, but that exterior face of the represented world has a depth of meaning which derives in part from its hidden interior scene. That inner scene corresponds both to the emotional life of the characters and to the graphic space of the poet whose act of composition takes place before and apart from the public appearance in the theater where his words are given full realization.

The hiddenness of the tragic poet's text in the performance is the negative sign of something always hidden from view, on the other side of the palace wall, which is also the side of the Other. As poet/writer who manipulates real bodies in real space on the stage, the dramatist becomes sensitized both to the invisible graphic space of his text and to the hidden, interior space of the self. What is concealed behind doors and gates—the gates of the palace, of the mouth, or of the body—becomes the problem of his writerly art.

Greek tragedy has no word for the self. As John Jones, arguing from Aristotle's *Poetics,* maintains, tragedy concentrates on exterior forms and events, on *mythos* as a concatenation of actions, *pragmata*.[71] Yet the sense of a self, of a complex inner life of motives, desires, and fears, is everywhere implicit. How does the tragedian make the inner life of the self visible? It appears not on the stage but in the behind-the-stage implied by the invisible text; something *there* but not representable, or representable only as a tension between the seen and the unseen. This interplay between interior and exterior space parallels

71. *Poetics* 6. 1450a 2ff. John Jones, *On Aristotle and Greek Tragedy* (London 1962), especially 24ff., 35ff., 41ff. I am not advocating return to post-Romantic psychologism but rather suggesting a way of looking at the vexed issue of character in Greek drama through posing the self as problem. Here, as elsewhere, the Greeks raise the fundamental questions of representing reality in art with exceptional clarity.

the increasing awareness of the interior realm of the *psychē,* the individual personality, that develops in late fifth-century thinkers as Socrates and Democritus.

Euripides is more explicit than Sophocles about the operations of this new textual awareness and the interior life that it implies. The *Hippolytus* is perhaps his most interesting work in this respect. This play, so concerned with the dichotomies of visible and invisible, inner and outer purity, tongue and heart, also makes an explicit correlation between what is hidden behind the gates of the mouth and the gates of the palace and, furthermore, connects this movement between inner and outer with writing.[72] The silent speaking of Phaedra's written tablets, left in the interior chamber where she hangs herself, proves to be more persuasive than the spoken utterances of face-to-face confrontation between Theseus and Hippolytus.

When the absent king returns to Athens, the scenic action stresses a double contrast, between interior and exterior space and between the silence of written speech and the sounds of words cried out in pain or anger. Theseus is surprised at the "shouting" and "heavy cry" from within (790f.), and he is indignant that "the house does not deem it worthwhile to open the gates and address me joyfully" (792f.). Told of Phaedra's death, he gives orders to open the "enclosures of the gates, in order that I may *see* the bitter *sight*" (808ff.; cf. 792f.). But when that inner scene is exposed (through the stage machinery of the eccyclema), it reveals the ambiguous speech-in-silence of the woman's tablets inside her chamber. Theseus responds (877–81): "The tablet shouts, shouts things not to be forgotten. How shall I flee the weight of woes? For I am gone, utterly destroyed. Such a song, alas, have I seen crying forth through the writing." His repeated allusions to the barrier of communication between himself and the unspeaking corpse (e.g. 826f., 842) set off this anomalous speaking of the tablet (cf. 856–65). This utterance is something "not endurable, not speakable" (847 and 875).

The spatial movement between inner and outer through the gates of the palace (793, 808) now shifts to a metaphorical movement between oral and written in words that pass or do not pass through

---

72. I have touched on the interior/exterior contrasts in C. Segal, "Shame and Purity in Euripides' Hippolytus," *Hermes* 98 (1970) 278–99, and on possible connections with writing in "Tragédie, oralité, écriture," *Poétique* 50 (1982) 148f.

the gates of the mouth (*stomatos pulai*, 882). As a speech that does not pass through the gates of the mouth, writing is an ambiguous mode of communication; but here that stifled form of utterance does in fact "shout out" (877) with full communicative power. When Theseus first saw the tablet, he described it as "showing" and "saying" (*sē-mēnai*, 857; *lexai*, 865); now its oral force intensifies. In reply, Theseus cannot contain his cry of grief (882–86): "I shall no longer hold down in the gates of the mouth this thing of ill passage outside, a destructive evil. O city! Hippolytus has dared to touch my bed by force, dishonoring the holy eye of Zeus." The passage continues the collocation of visual and oral which pervades the scene (e.g. 865, 879). In contrast to the woman's enclosed chamber of the unspeakable crime stand the speaking out and showing forth of revealed crime to the public space overseen by the eyes of father Theseus and Father Zeus (886). As in the *Oedipus*, the Other Scene, the son's violation of the most sacred and most forbidden of interior spaces, is presented as a series of recessive movements to a closed interior; and here that interior is explicitly identified with the ambiguous graphic space between utterance and silence, concealment and revelation, containment and ejaculation.

Writing is a metaphor, as in the *Trachiniae*, for the deviousness that female sexuality brings into the world. Communication between Phaedra's realm of feverish desire inside the house and the males outside is by indirection. She addresses Hippolytus only by the intermediary of the Nurse,[73] and she addresses Theseus only through the silent speech of her writing. In her famous speech early in the play, resolving to die, she laments the confusion that surrounds the two forms of *aidōs*, shame or modesty, two meanings spelled with "the same letters" (386–88).[74] Here, as in the case of her tablet, writing is the model for the ambiguities of language, because the possibilities of error and deception exist as opposite meanings slide into each other. From this source flows a whole series of confusions in the lives of the characters and in the value systems that impinge upon them. The clearly delineated roles and stable, univocal meanings of a traditional,

73. In the first *Hippolytus*, however, presumably followed in this respect by Seneca in his *Phaedra*, there was a face-to-face interview between the queen and Hippolytus.

74. For the grammata of 387 in relation to the problem of signs and language in the play, see Turato (note 63) pp. 163f. with note 25.

aristocratic society, with its emphasis on face-to-face contact, have been lost; instead, words and modes of behavior become paradoxical, and familiar boundaries no longer hold. Hippolytus is both bastard and well born (cf. 1454f.); Theseus is the source of domestic and political order and also of violence, bloodshed, and impurity (cf. 34f.); Phaedra is both noble in her fame (*eukleia*) and shameless in her passion (cf. 1299ff.; also 715ff.).

The later plays of Euripides show another kind of awareness of tragedy's power as a medium that doubles the mimetic capacity of the word by the physical mimesis of deeds acted out by three-dimensional figures on the stage. The long recognition scene between brother and sister in his *Iphigeneia in Tauris* is especially instructive in this regard. Orestes, after long wanderings, has landed in the remote barbarian land of the Taurians, who sacrifice strangers to Artemis. Iphigeneia, who has been supernaturally transported here at the moment of being sacrificed at Aulis by her father, King Agamemnon, is the priestess of the goddess and as such must prepare the new victims for the sacrifice. In the course of the long three-way dialogue between Iphigeneia, Orestes, and his companion, Pylades (576–826), the long-lost brother and sister come to recognize each other. The medium of recognition is a discourse about messages and about the relative values of writing and speech as secure and accurate modes of communication.[75] The context is also one of domestic ties that shift abruptly between the extremes of distance and nearness. The poet praises the written word, implicitly, for its capacity to span great distances and to communicate the living presence of love between those hopelessly separated. The abstract system of signs which constitutes writing enables even the total stranger to convey a message of intimate emotion. But through the paradoxes of Euripides' brilliant dramatic situation, that impersonal, generalized capacity of the written message is negated unexpectedly by the living, emotional power of the spoken word in a face-to-face, oral/aural encounter.

The written message is something concrete and physical, an object that may be carried, sent, given (584, 589–90, 603, 667). But as Iphigeneia warms to the emotional reality of what this medium of communication can achieve, she begins to endow it with a quasi-

75. The following discussion of the *Iphigeneia in Tauris* is drawn from "Tragédie, oralité, écriture" (note 72) 149–51.

animate life. Instead of a "messenger" who would "announce" her news in Argos (ὅστις ἀγγείλαι μολὼν / ἐς Ἄργος αὖθις, 588–89), she describes the tablet itself as "speaking" and "announcing" (δέλτος . . . / λέγουσα πιστὰς ἡδονὰς ἀπαγγελεῖ, 641–42). This shift suggests the incommensurability between the physically circumscribed nature of the tablet as a tool or a means of conveying information in an impersonal manner and the rich human feelings attaching to the actual words that it contains. In reflecting on this paradoxical relation, Euripides allows Iphigeneia, carried away by emotion, to confuse the two.

That fusion deepens in a further complication that simultaneously affirms and destroys the power of the written word. The destined recipient of the written message in remote Argos proves to be the hearer to whom she is dictating it, standing right beside Iphigeneia in the Taurian land. This message, doubled by its oral, dictated form in order to prevent loss of the contents at sea, is simultaneously complete as both oral and written communication. When its intended bearer, Pylades, raises the problem of the tablet's loss at sea (755–57), Iphigenia replies (762–65):

> ἢν μὲν ἐκσώσῃς γραφήν,
> αὐτὴ φράσει σιγῶσα τἀγγεγραμμένα.
> ἢν δ᾽ ἐν θαλάσσῃ γράμματ᾽ ἀφανισθῇ τάδε,
> τὸ σῶμα σώσας τοὺς λόγους σώσεις ἐμοί.

If you preserve the writing, itself, in silence, will speak what has been written on it. But if the writings are made invisible in the sea, in saving your body you will save my words as well.

These lines play upon the paradoxes of the visible-invisible and the silent speaking which we have noted in the *Hippolytus*. But here Euripides holds these paradoxes up to the shifting lights of his kaleidoscopic art and gives them another turn. The written sign that marks absence turns into the means of recreating presence; now, however, it does so not through the deferred, abstractive, silent medium of writing but through a face-to-face oral/aural interchange. Thus the oral message, the reading aloud of the written text, intervenes to prevent the separation between brother and sister by the sacrifice—the sacrifice that this letter, like Phaedra's, implicitly sanctioned, for its sending meant acquiescing in the sacrifice of one of the two Greek youths captured by the Taurians.

Orestes then dismisses the letters of the tablet, along with their distanced conveyance of communication in far-off lands, for an immediate *hēdonē* of touch and embrace, of tangible acts rather than words (793–94):

> παρεὶς δὲ γραμμάτων διαπτυχὰς
> τὴν ἡδονὴν πρῶτ᾽ οὐ λόγοις αἱρήσομαι.

Letting go the folded letters (of the tablet), I shall take my joy not in words.

Harking back to Iphigeneia's words some seventy lines earlier, Orestes' gesture caps the ambiguity and incompleteness of communication by the written word. As Iphigeneia was about to consign the tablet to Pylades, she spoke of its presence as if it were a mythical being (727–29):

> δέλτου μὲν αἵδε πολύθυροι διαπτυχαί,
> ξένοι, πάρεισιν. ἃ δ᾽ ἐπὶ τοῖσδε βούλομαι,
> ἀκούσατ᾽.

Strangers, the many-doored foldings of the tablet are present here. But as to what I wish in addition, do you hear.

But as the discussion of delivering the tablets at Argos goes on, the written medium wavers between reliability and unreliability (755–65). Both qualities are functions of its tangibility and impersonality. The pull between strong verbs of direct, oral communication like "tell," "announce," "hear" (729, 753, 762, 769) and the giving or losing of letters (745, 756f., 763f.) with their anomalously silent speech (763), underlines that crossing between the two communicatory systems.

Euripides rings one further change on these shifts between written and oral at the end of the scene. Orestes, who receives the written message in an oral form, dismisses the *grammata* in favor of direct, physical gesture, as noted above (793–94). Yet his oral/aural perception and response prove insufficient. Iphigeneia has need of further proofs, *tekmēria* (808–22). These tekmēria (significantly, a word belonging to the rationalistic vocabulary of the Sophistic movement) brings us back from the technology of writing to the remote, quasimythical tales of the house of Atreus, the stories of the golden ram and the sun's stopping in its course, woven, not written, on the tapestries of a young girl in her house (811–17). They are, in fact, stories that Euripides himself artfully tells in the second stasimon of the *Electra* (669–746). Chronological relation between the two plays aside, this movement from letters to weaving bears on Euripides' own self-awareness of his art. He locates his tragic version of the myths between a newer, written technology of communication, indicated in the letters (grammata) of the tablet, and an older, more traditional form, symbolized by the age-old art of weaving, which is itself an ancient and traditional metaphor for the telling of tales in oral culture.

In his last play, the *Bacchae,* Euripides weaves the madness of Pentheus into a complex texture of illusionistic effects and places it in a precarious balance between seeming and being, hallucination and reality, which reflects the paradoxical status of the theater itself. Amid the visible presences and tangible actions, every event is also a form of illusion.[76] The god's visitation of madness upon his mortal victim becomes part of this tension between a subjective, distorted, private view of the world and the objective reality of the god's supernatural power.

The *Bacchae* problematizes the mask as the symbol of the god's power. In so doing it also problematizes the power of the theatrical spectacle to represent the hidden reality of the interior life, the subsurface beneath the mask. Dionysus in the play appears not only as the god of wine and religious ecstasy but also as the god of the mask and of the theatrical illusion embodied in the mask.[77] The crisis of knowledge (and self-knowledge) is now framed as a theatrical crisis, that is, as a form of the question, How much and what kind of reality is contained in the fictional construction of the spectacle? Is there a truth hidden beneath the mask and beneath the act of wearing masks?

76. See my *Dionysiac Poetics* (note 32) 215–71. On this concern with appearance and reality in Greek thinking about art, see Vernant, *Religions, histoires, raisons* (note 45) 128ff.
77. See my *Dionysiac Poetics* (note 32) 215ff., 223ff., 260ff.

Or, yet further back, What kind of truth can be claimed by a discourse whose origins are no longer sacred, no longer derived from the inspiration of the Muses, but lie entirely in the writer himself as the fabricator of a text whose very materiality attests to its human creation? The increasing pressure of these questions follows with that inexorable logic which pervades early Greek culture and is perhaps one of the factors responsible for the demise of tragedy as a creative form.

The *Bacchae* is among the last of these tragedies. A generation earlier, in Sophocles' *Oedipus Tyrannus*, the god, however mysterious, retains his Olympian otherness, the objective reality of his mysterious power. In the *Bacchae* the god enters the subjective play of disguise and role-playing on the tragic stage and is himself a kind of externalized projection of human fantasies, fears, desires.[78] At its most optimistic, the last phase of Greek tragedy celebrates its power to create fictions. This more optimistic mood pervades the *Helen* of Euripides.[79] At its most pessimistic, it calls attention to the airy bubble of its imagination, floating precariously in a world that no longer knows what reality is. In the terms of the *Bacchae,* the mask is an extension of the god's power, the sign of his ambiguous presence among men, forcing them to choose between illusion and ultimate reality; but it is also a human creation, the sign of man's power to shape fictions that may be only an emptiness behind the illusionistic covering.

IX

In a preliterate society, one knows what one can recall. What is useful, appreciated, valued, and therefore relevant is preserved and lives on the lips of men. The winners are remembered; the losers fade

78. For these concerns of late fifth-century drama see Helene Foley, "The Masque of Dionysus," *TAPA* 110 (1980) 107–33; Froma Zeitlin, "The Closet of Masks: Role-playing and Myth-making in the *Orestes* of Euripides," *Ramus* 9 (1980) 62–77, and "Travesties of Gender and Genre in Aristophanes' *Thesmophoriazusae,*" *Critical Inquiry* 8 (1981) 301–27, especially 309ff. I take a rather different view of the mask from Jones, *On Aristotle* (note 71) 43ff., 59f.

79. See below, chapter 7, "The Two Words of Euripides' *Helen,*" ad fin.; also C. Segal, *Dionysiac Poetics* (note 32) 340ff.

away.[80] The effect is what anthropologists have called homeostasis, a tendency to maintain the current values and modes of behavior by a kind of natural selection of what supports them.[81] When Herodotus undertakes to preserve in writing what would otherwise become *exitēla* (1.1), that is, vanish into the detritus of the forgotten, he marks a new stage in Greek culture. When the tales about the past, the myths, genealogies, wise sayings, proverbs, laws, and instructions can be fixed definitively, in the form of writing, they can be scrutinized and criticized for discrepancies or contradictions. In a purely oral culture all the variants are true, that is, all have a claim to be heard simply because they are told, because they are living tales through which the society expresses its consciousness of itself. When men have the unsorted multiplicity of such tales crystallized in writing beneath their eyes, truth or accuracy becomes something to be adjudicated among conflicting or contradictory claims. Hecataeus may smile at the plurality of tales which he sets down in writing (*graphō*, 4F1 Jacoby),[82] but in the more serious mood of tragedy, conflicting claims on truth involve life and death.

While Hecataeus and Herodotus and to a far greater extent Thucydides were fixing in writing, for critical examination, the events of the recent past, the tragedians fixed in writing, for another kind of examination, the myths, the tales of gods and remote heroes, whose overt content is the distant past. Contemporary subjects, such as Phrynichus' *Capture of Miletus* or Aeschylus' *Persians*, are rare; and even such recent events gain a certain aura of mythical remoteness through the elevated language, the close presence of the gods, and the intervention of the supernatural in ghosts, omens, prophecies, and the like. Tragedy resembles the poetic narrative of an oral culture in that its concern is the present relevance of the myths it uses. These tales are remade to fit a homeostatic present with little concern for historical depth. Yet the quality of that mythical narrative is determined by the spirit of criticism fostered by writing. The myths told by tragedy are no longer the myths of an oral society, clear exemplars of a received truth or accepted communal values.

Innovation in mythical narration is the stock-in-trade of Greek

80. See Ong, *Orality and Literacy* (note 6) 47f.
81. Goody and Watt (note 42) 31–34; see Rösler (note 13) 304.
82. See Detienne, *L'invention* (note 37) 138.

poets beginning with Homer. In tragedy, however, that innovation is more drastic, less predictable, and cuts more radically to the heart of the story's meaning. Attending a tragic performance, one could never be certain just how a given myth would be told. The surviving tragedies about Iphigeneia, Electra, and Orestes and what we know of Oedipus or Philoctetes in the three tragedians show how divergently a myth could be handled. And even a single tragedian could present quite different versions of the same subject, as Euripides does with the tales of Hippolytus and Phaedra, Orestes, Iphigeneia, and Helen.

Mythology, Marcel Detienne has argued, comes into being only with the crystallization of oral tales into the written form that fixes them as fictional stories, *muthoi plasthentes,* as Plato calls them.[83] For Plato, whose battle against the mentality of the oral culture Havelock has eloquently traced in *Preface to Plato,* truth should be the property of the philosopher who enunciates the values and norms that had previously been in the hands of the poets. The philosopher is a writer; Plato, with whatever elaboration and malaise, writes down the conversations of Socrates. The philosopher rethinks and rebuilds from the ground up what had been diffused in the scattered tales, maxims, sayings, and paradigms handed down orally from generation to generation without critical examination. From this perspective, which is the perspective that the historical development of Greek culture has bequeathed to us moderns, myth appears as something remote and primitive to which we look with nostalgia and wonder, a mode of expression untampered with by the secondary elaboration of writing.

The oral culture of early Greece is mediated for us by writing, and the search for the preliterate substratum may be another form of Western man's perpetual longing for a primordial world of innocence and simplicity.[84] When writing becomes the major force not only in recording, but also in creating and shaping myth, we may be dealing with "l'illusion mythique" rather than with the genuine, first-degree myth of an oral culture; and access to a realm of pure myth, uncon-

---

83. Plato, *Republic* 2.377b; Detienne, *L'invention* (note 37) 180.
84. D. Wesling, "Difficulties of the Bardic," *Critical Inquiry* 8 (1981) 73 warns against the modern myth of the bardic, which is part of "print culture's nostalgia for oral culture."

taminated by the reflective and distancing processes of recording them, becomes ambiguous, uncertain, and paradoxical.[85]

Our own interpretation of Greek culture curiously recapitulates the experience of the Greeks themselves at the end of their great tragic age. As we take account of the controlling and reshaping power exercised by writing in forming the versions of the myths which come down to us as literature, as letters and by virtue of being preserved in letters, with all the absences that letters imply, we too are inevitably involved in the demystification and demythification of the mythical. We too become not merely hearers or even readers but interpreters, confronted with the paradox of a text that is forever fixed and forever elusive. The tragedians also, as writers, are not only mythicizers but the self-conscious interpreters of myth. It is important to recognize the complexities implied in their textual production and not idealize them, following Nietzsche's myth of tragedy's Dionysiac music and fusion with nature, as participants in the immediacy of oral vitality and the living, spontaneous power of primordial myth.

85. Detienne, *L'invention* (note 37) 226.

II /

SOPHOCLES

CHAPTER 4

Visual Symbolism and
Visual Effects in Sophocles

There was speech in their dumbness, language in their very gesture;
they look'd as they had heard of a world ransom'd, or one destroyed. A
notable passion of wonder appeared in them; but the wisest beholder,
that knew no more but seeing, could not say if th' importance were joy
or sorrow; but in the extremity of the one, it must needs be.
                                    —Shakespeare, *Winter's Tale*, V.ii. 13–21

I

Though less flamboyant in the use of visual effects than Aeschylus
(*Vita Aeschyli* 7 and 9), Sophocles, credited by Aristotle with the
invention of scene painting (*Poetics* 1449a 18f.), also paid considerable
attention to the element of spectacle (*opsis*) in his plays. It is the
purpose of this essay to call attention to the symbolic dimension of
certain of these visual effects and especially to their relation to the
central concerns of the works in which they appear. Not all visual
effects constitute the striking spectacle defined by Aristotle. Nor am I
concerned with all such effects, only with those where a symbolic
significance seems evident. Moreover, because all meaning in the

I presented an earlier version of this essay at a panel entitled "Greek Tragedy on
Stage" at the Annual Meeting of the American Philological Association, Vancouver,
B.C., December 28, 1978. I thank the editor of *Classical World*, Jerry Clack, and the
anonymous reader for a number of helpful suggestions that substantially improved
this paper at several points.

Sophocles

theater is, in a sense, visual,[1] it is not always possible to draw a clear line between symbolic and nonsymbolic; some overlapping is inevitable.

By "visual symbols" I mean specifically details in the scenic enactment of the play which express, in the condensed, evocative way of symbols, the major concerns of the work. By their very nature, symbols are both specific and elusive. Their concreteness focuses meaning in specific and precise detail; but their sensuous qualities, and their shifting relations to other details and acts as different facets emerge in the unfolding of the work, render that meaning manifold and suggestive rather than simplex and denotative.

As an essay of this scope must necessarily be limited, I shall concentrate primarily upon four symbols: the sword in the *Ajax,* the robe in the *Trachiniae,* the urn of the *Electra,* and the bow of the *Philoctetes.* Although I might have studied other visual details obviously of major thematic significance (the cave of the *Philoctetes,* expressive of the hero's ambiguous relation to civilized society;[2] the grove of the Eumenides in the *Coloneus,*[3] which stands at the crucial point of Oedipus' passage between wandering and settledness, pollution and cultic honor as a hero; the corpse in the last act of *Ajax,*[4] the reminder of the polarizing and problematic effect of Ajax even when he is dead), I have selected these four symbols because they are particularly illustrative of how rich, multiple meanings accrue to a single concrete object on the stage. They have the further advantage of focusing their major impact in a single scene while their many-leveled

1. On visual meaning see Oliver Taplin, *The Stagecraft of Aeschylus* (Oxford 1977) 12–28.

2. On the cave in *Phil.* see D. B. Robinson, "Topics in Sophocles' *Philoctetes,*" *CQ* 19 (1969) 34–37; A. M. Dale, "Seen and Unseen on the Greek Stage," *Wiener Studien* 69 (1956) 104–6; W. Jobst, *Die Höhle im griechischen Theater des 5. und 4. Jahrhunderts,* *SB Vienna* 268, fasc. 2 (1970) 41–43; C. Segal, "Philoctetes and the Imperishable Piety," *Hermes* 105 (1977) 156, with further bibliography in n.64.

3. For the symbolic implications of the grove see Helen Bacon, "Women's Two Faces: Sophocles' View of the Tragedy of Oedipus and His Family," in *Science and Psychoanalysis,* American Academy of Psychoanalysis, Decennial Memorial Volume (New York 1966) 17ff.; Barbara Lefcowitz, "The Inviolate Grove," *Literature and Psychology* 17 (1967) 78–86.

4. As commentators since Jebb have pointed out, the burial of that corpse is crucial to the unity of the *Ajax:* see R. C. Jebb, *Sophocles, The Plays and Fragments,* Part 7, *The Ajax* (Cambridge 1907) xxxixff.; B. M. W. Knox, "The *Ajax* of Sophocles," *HSCP* 65 (1961) 25f.

meanings remain diffused over the entire play. Here verbal text and visual action form that unique web of textures and sensations through which a play works on its audience.

Since we have only the words of Sophocles, complete certainty about the dramatic realization is impossible. The cues in the text provide a good deal of evidence, albeit not always as clearly as we would like. Ajax's sword, for example, obviously central to the action, must have been prominently displayed onstage. About the scepter-staff of Oedipus in the *Tyrannus* we can be less confident: it is a case where a modern director would have some latitude in staging the play. The four objects with which I am principally concerned would all, I believe, have had a visible and important place in the stage business. In a few other cases, which I shall touch on more briefly, my remarks may be taken as indications of possibilities inherent in the text which may have been (or might still be) developed in production. In the third and last section of this essay I attempt to distinguish what is characteristically Sophoclean in such visual symbolism and related visual effects.

II

Symbolic implications in verbal texture are sometimes realized in physical presence onstage, verbal and visual action thus reinforcing each other. The *Oedipus Tyrannus* is the most familiar example. Oedipus' blind and wounded eyes, which could be depicted on the mask as he returns to the stage from the sight of Jocasta's body, concentrate the play's paradoxes of sight and blindness in an overpowering and deeply significant visual image.[5] He now begins to possess an inward sight stronger and clearer than the sound eyes with which he failed to see the plain truth. Hurt, he has a health truer than the apparent health of his flourishing kingship. Deformed outwardly, he can recognize that his nobility and beauty of appearance had "festering evils beneath" (*kallos kakôn hypoulon*, 1396).

The sword of Ajax, our first major example, has an analogous

---

5. See most recently John Hay, *Oedipus Tyrannus: Lame Knowledge and the Homosporic Womb* (Washington, D.C. 1978) 76f., with the references cited in 65 n.2; Oliver Taplin, *Greek Tragedy in Action* (Berkeley and Los Angeles 1978) 89 and 110f.

Sophocles

symbolic and dramatic power.⁶ Ostensibly signifying the mutability
of human affairs as a token of exchange between foes, Ajax and
Hector, it is cited at three crucial points, in elaborate and important
rhetoric, as a paradigm of persistency in hatred (661–65, 817–22,
1024–35). It links donor and recipient, Trojan and Greek, in a bond
not of friendship but of battle to the death, the true constant of their
relationship (see especially 1025–33).

The sword is first mentioned indirectly by other characters—Athena, Odysseus, the chorus, Tecmessa—as the instrument of the
bloody, shameful deed of Ajax's dark night of madness (30, 94f., 231,
286f.; cf. also 10, 147, 325). Possibly it accompanied Ajax onstage,
without any particular emphasis, in the prologue, for Athena's question, "That sword—tell me—did you dip it well in the army of
Argives?" (ekeino . . . enchos, 94f.), could easily imply a gesture toward the sword reddened with the blood of the slaughtered cattle.
The sword has an unambiguously prominent place on the stage,
however, appropriately in the two crucial scenes where Ajax asserts
and then executes his rejection of the vicissitudes of the mortal world.
Foil to the relationship of steady loyalty (Tecmessa and Teucer) and
enmity changing to friendship (Odysseus), the sword's visual presence symbolizes the isolated, self-destructive side of the hero's rejection of change.

It is now Ajax himself who calls attention to the sword. A few lines
after delivering a simile, full of ambiguities, about being softened like
"iron in the dipping" (650–652) which figuratively evokes the sword
(cf. "iron" for "sword" in 147 and 325), Ajax puts his hand to the
sword at his side (657–59):

Going to an untrodden place, wherever I may find it, I will hide this
sword of mine here [tod' enchos toumon], burying it in the earth where no
one will see it.

In the follow-up scene, the third and last of Ajax's great speeches,
the sword is unsheathed. A chilling and powerful stage presence, it
massively controls the opening of the scene (815ff.). Ajax's "conceal-

6. See Knox (note 4) passim, especially 15ff.; David Cohen, "The Imagery of
Sophocles: A Study of Ajax's Suicide," G & R 25 (1978) 24–36.

ment" of the sword by "burial" (*krypsô . . . oryxas,* 658f.) now hard-ens to fixity:

> It stands set [*hestêken*], the slayer, in the way in which it would be most cutting. . . (815f.).
> It is fixed fast [*pepêge*] in the Trojan enemy earth. . . . (819).

A few minutes later, after invoking the eternal elements of sun, light, and earth, Ajax hurls himself upon it (with a grim detail, earlier, about the physical pain, 833f.) to seal his commitment to perma-nence. Now become the symbol of a rigidity that refuses the potential for change it embodied as Hector's gift, it is the appropriate instru-ment of his suicide, his means of rejecting the world with which he will not compromise.

Now his body, with the sword embedded in it, becomes the focal point for the rest of the action, symbol of his troubling centrality in this world of change where he can have his place only when he is dead. The "most painful sight" of that corpse (Teucer's words at 992) may have been represented on the eccyclema at the back of the scene.[7] It certainly compels the attention and focuses the conflict of all the characters in the last third of the work. Near that corpse, Teucer stations the child Eurysaces as a suppliant (1171ff.), a gesture that some have thought to refer to Ajax's status as a cult-hero at Athens.[8] Teucer's penultimate statement in the play leaves the audience with a vivid depiction of that painful sight: "Still the warm channels blow upward the black strength" (1411–13). The chorus' closing gnomic utterance too is about "seeing" (*idousi, idein,* 1418f.).

Such scenic imagery not only focuses the main theme but also helps depict nuances of human interaction and relationship. Such effects are characteristic of Sophoclean ethos. In the scene immediately after Ajax's death on the sword, Tecmessa discovers the body, utters a cry of lamentation, and then covers it with her cloak. No one who loved Ajax, she explains, could bear to look on his grim wound, the blood

7. Ajax' body must be visible from at the latest line 1000 and possibly earlier: see Jebb (note 4) 915; Taplin, *Greek Tragedy* (note 5) 189 n.5.

8. See Jebb (note 4) xxx–xxxii; Peter Burian, "Supplication and Hero Cult in Sophocles' *Ajax*," *GRBS* 13 (1972) 151–56; and Martin Sicherl, "The Tragic Issue in Sophocles' *Ajax*," *YCS* 25 (1977) 97f.

Sophocles

gushing out of the nose, and the cut (915–19). Her language renders the visual horror of the corpse's appearance as strongly as possible. But the scene does something else. It acts out in visual terms the contrast between the rigid upright sword of Ajax, imbedded deep in the body exposed on the lonely beach, and the enveloping cloak of Tecmessa.[9] As usual, the language reinforces the effect, for the verbal description of "concealing" in the "enfolding cloak" closely echoes the description of the body itself, some fifteen lines earlier, "enfolded in the concealed sword," in the sword's "enfolding embrace":

κρυφαίῳ φασγάνῳ περιπτυχής. (898)
ἀλλά νιν περιπτυχεῖ/φάρει καλύψω τῷδε παμπήδην. . . . (915f.)

The embrace of the sword in the body (898) and the cloak's embracing of the corpse imply very different relationships to the mortality of the human form: utter rejection in the name of the absolutes of timelessness on the one hand, acceptance of the time-bound ties of kinship and love on the other.

Ten lines later on, the chorus calls Ajax "hard of spirit," *stereophrôn* (926), and we are reminded of his famous and ambiguous simile of dipping iron (650–52), as he describes how he is "made woman-like" by Tecmessa's plea. The scene of the cloak visually concretizes the tragic distance between this rigid warrior and the woman who loves him. He has perished, as he wished, on his firmly fixed sword; all she can do is cover him in her softly enveloping cloak. Both the distance and the closeness between them are infinite, and the stage action catches them both in one of those large, paradigmatic gestures characteristic of Greek poetry at its best. The two modes of life, the warrior's and the woman's, are juxtaposed there, frozen for eternity, each in its characteristic pose.

The *Trachiniae,* for all the vividness of its narrative of past events and its offstage action of the present, is not a play of powerful visual symbolism, except in one respect: the robe of Deianeira. Taken from the interior space of the house, where Deianeira has also locked away

9. The visual power of this tableau is brought out by the scene on a red figure cup by Brygos, ca. 470 B.C. (Bareiss Collection, Metropolitan Museum, New York, L.69. 11.35), illustrated in Taplin, *Greek Tragedy* (note 5) plate 11. Taplin's own discussion of the sword, however, though excellent, omits the effect of the cloak (85–87).

the poisonous blood of the Centaur Nessus (587ff., 685ff.), and brought forth for Heracles to wear at his fatal victory sacrifice at Cape Cenaeum, the robe symbolizes the destructive bond between the two protagonists, Deianeira and Heracles.[10] It is the physical link between their two worlds, the enclosed realm of the house and the wild places where Heracles battles monsters and sacks cities. Deianeira herself carries out the robe and gives it to Lichas to bear to Heracles (660ff.). This occurs in the third episode, just after the choral ode on the power of Aphrodite and the violent physical struggle between Heracles and Achelous for her bed (497–530). In this scene she also relates for the first time the rape attempted by Nessus and tells of the supposed love charm that she has kept hidden all these years in the depths of the house (555–81). Anointed with the Centaur's poison, the robe connects the interior darkness of the house and the destructive beast world of Heracles' adventures, each in its destructive power. Sending it forth from house to the light of day, from Trachis to Cenaeum, Deianeira releases those deadly poisons of the primitive past from their enclosure in the house and transmits their destructive force to the present scene.

The robe and its poisons are kept firmly in the spectator's mind in the next scene. Deianeira again enters from the house to describe the disturbing effects of sunlight upon the tuft of wool with which she had anointed the robe. Some visual indication of her action probably accompanied the speech: she may have carried the implement with which she applied the poison or possibly some piece of fabric, garment, or container to indicate the kind of association with robes and the domestic spaces connected so often in Greek literature with women's work of weaving and storing clothing. In any case, Hyllus at once announces the calamitous sacrifice at Cenaeum (734–812). The robe plays a major role in his narrative (758ff.). Deianeira, whose two previous entrances were marked by long and elaborate speeches, now exits in silence (813–20), never to be seen again.

The following choral ode evokes again the dangerous beast world of the past and its poisons (cf. 831–40), after which the Nurse enters

---

10. For the robe and its connections with the poisons, the monstrous elements in the background, and the spatial contrasts of the play, see C. Segal, "Sophocles' *Trachiniae:* Myth, Poetry, and Heroic Values," *YCS* 25 (1977) 109–13, 126f., with the further literature there cited.

(again from the house) to describe in detail what we have feared and anticipated, the suicide of Deianeira (896–946). Here too the loosening of a robe has a major role (*peplos*, 924ff.).

The next entrance is Heracles', not from the house but from the parodos, representing the sea from which he has arrived as he crossed from Cenaeum to Trachis. Coming from a wider realm, he wears the robe that links him in a fatal bond to the house. Because of a garment drawn from its proper static interior spaces, this hero of vast travels (who, like Cleopatra's Antony, "bestrid the ocean" and spanned continents), is totally immobilized on a narrow bed in front of the palace.[11] At the end he will have to make his final journey carried by others.

Heracles' first long speech opens with a vivid description of the robe, stuck fast to his brawny shoulders because of the venom in which it was dipped (1054). Calling it "a woven net of Erinyes by which I am destroyed" (1051f.), he gives it an almost supernatural status. How different is this robe (which enfolds the male in an embrace of death) from Tecmessa's sheltering garment in the *Ajax*. The different functions of the two cloaks might be interpreted as emblems for the different views of woman in the two plays.

Heracles goes on to describe the robe as a living being, a ravening monster or beast that "feeds on my deepest flesh, lives with me and sucks the breath of my lungs and drinks up my pale blood" (1053–55). Later he applies the same imagery of devouring to the disease inflicted by the robe (1088f.), so that through the visual symbol of the robe, there before us on Heracles' body, the dark invisible power of lust, passion, bestial desire embodied in the monsters in the background of the play—the Hydra and the Centaur—comes alive and assumes a corporeal reality on the stage. Visually as well as metaphorically, Heracles is imbued with the poisons of this robe, which are also the poisons of his past and of the unconquered monstrosity within himself. Sophocles in the middle scenes of the play has carefully built up these associations of robe, poisons, sexual desire, and

---

11. For Heracles' immobility see C. E. Sorum, "Monsters and the Family: The Exodos of Sophocles' *Trachiniae*," *GRBS* 19 (1978) 65. For Heracles as a gigantic figure striding continents in *Trach.* 101f. see H. Lloyd-Jones, "Sophoclea," *CQ* 4 (1954) 91ff.; J. C. Kamerbeek, *The Plays of Sophocles, Commentaries*, Part 2, "The Trachiniae" (Leiden 1959) *ad* 101f.; Thomas F. Hoey, "Sun Symbolism in the Parados of the *Trachiniae*," *Arethusa* 5 (1972) 137, 144–46.

bestial monsters of a primeval past. Now they are embodied in the mighty figure wrapped in that envenomed robe. He wears on his very body the tragic bond between himself and his neglected house, between his present and his past, between his great civilizing victories and his defeat by the lust within himself,[12] symbolized by the fire from the monster's poisonous blood.[13]

The visual symbolism reaches its climax when Sophocles, here as in the *Philoctetes,* pushes at the limits of our repugnance for physical pain. As Heracles tries to tear off the robe that eats into his flesh, we actually *see* the poison's effect on the massive frame (1076–80):

> Now come up here and stand near your father, my son, and observe by what kind of misery I have come to these sufferings. For I shall *show* you these things outside of the coverings that conceal them [*deixô gar tad' ek kalummatôn,* 1078]. *Look,* all of you, *behold* this wretched body. *See* this ruined man, my piteous state [*idou theasthe . . . horate*].

As in the *Oedipus Tyrannus* and the *Ajax,* so here Sophocles finds a single visual symbol in which to condense the tragic paradoxes of his central themes: the man of invincible strength made weak by a woman's robe; the tamer of beasts overcome by the beasts; the conjunction of wife and husband, internal and external spatial fields, through an agent that can only destroy them both; Heracles' mighty physical force helpless before a power that is as much inside as outside him, the power of eros before which he, for all his vast physical strength, is impotent (cf. 354ff., 441ff., 488f.).

No visual symbol in Sophocles has a more powerful and far-reaching ethical and psychological meaning than the bow of the *Philoctetes,*

---

12. Although Sophocles adumbrates the myth of Heracles' apotheosis, as I believe, he still leaves the tragic suffering by keeping the final resolution of Heracles' fate ambiguous. Heracles' defeat by lust, which seems total, is then made good, in part, by his recognition of the oracles and by the purifying fire at Cenaeum but without any softening in the kind of heroism that Heracles embodies. For the interpretation of the play in this light see my "Sophocles' *Trachiniae*" (note 10) 97–158, especially 130–58, and with further bibliography, pp. 139f., n.95–97; also the sensitive study of Thomas F. Hoey, "Ambiguity in the Exodos of Sophocles' *Trachiniae,*" *Arethusa* 10 (1977) 269–74.

13. For the association of the literal fire of the poison and altars and the metaphorical fire of lust cf. 145 and 368 with 697, 765ff., 1036, 1082. See Segal, "Sophocles' *Trachiniae*" (note 10) 110f.; Dorothea Wender, "The Will of the Beast: Sexual Imagery in the *Trachiniae,*" *Ramus* 3 (1974) 12.

Sophocles

and no symbol of this type is more deeply expressive of the central issues of its play.[14] The opening scene defines the bow as a dangerous weapon (105) and as the object of the antagonist's quest: to Odysseus the bow is only the means of winning the victory at Troy (112ff.). Paradoxically, the very power of the bow, its "fearful boldness of might" in "arrows that can't be escaped, but bring sure death" (104f.) requires the use of unheroic guile and deceit against its owner, himself so far from any such strength in his own body (cf. 945–48). First object of remote discussion and calculation in a stratagem of trickery in the prologue, the bow then appears, with its wretched owner, on the stage. Suddenly, unexpectedly, it assumes a wholly different significance.

Just when the plot to carry off Philoctetes by guile seems complete, Neoptolemus turns to the bow. "Is that the glorious bow that you now hold?" he asks (654). "May I have sight of it close at hand and lift it, revere it like a god?" (656f.). Handing him the bow, Philoctetes replies with similarly sacral language (*hosia, themis*, 663) and for the first time intimates the heroic aura of *aretê* and generous action (*euergetein*) which surrounds the bow and emanates from its heroic past.

Although the young aspirant to the bow and its enfeebled possessor now stand at the furthest remove from its past glory, a spirit of heroic generosity still radiates from the bow. As Neoptolemus prepares to complete his treacherous design and to embark Philoctetes for Troy, the old warrior is overcome by an attack of his recurrent disease, hands Neoptolemus the bow for safekeeping, and after horrendous cries of agony falls unconscious. At that moment Neoptolemus might easily depart with the bow or the helpless man, or both, as the chorus in fact urges him to do (835–38). But having experienced something of the meaning of both the heroic weapon and the disease, both the wound and the bow, Neoptolemus cannot carry through his manipulative plan against the sleeping Philoctetes.

This scene contains one of the most powerful visual tableaux in Sophocles: Philoctetes unconscious and helpless on the ground, Neo-

14. The meaning of the bow has been well discussed by Cedric H. Whitman, *Sophocles, A Study of Heroic Humanism* (Cambridge, Mass. 1951) 182ff.; B. M. W. Knox, *The Heroic Temper,* Sather Classical Lectures 35 (Berkeley and Los Angeles 1964) 126ff.; P. W. Harsh, "The Role of the Bow in the *Philoctetes* of Sophocles," *AJP* 81 (1960) 408–14; Peter Rose, "Sophocles' *Philoctetes* and Teachings of the Sophists," *HSCP* 80 (1976) 69f. with n.48, and also p. 100.

ptolemus standing over him, now in full possession of the coveted bow. And yet Neoptolemus declares, in dactylic hexameters (the meter of epic and of oracle), that the "crown" belongs to the broken, feeble cripple stretched at his feet (841): *toude gar ho stephanos,* "His is the crown; him the god told us to bring." Nowhere, perhaps, does the visual impression more truthfully and concisely render the paradox of the situation, the inversions of strength and weakness, the discrepancy between appearance and reality, inner and outer areté, the distance between the hidden purposes of the gods and the carefully planned schemes of men. The sleeping invalid who lies collapsed before the strong, erect Neoptolemus looks like anything but the bearer of the crown of valor at Troy. Yet Neoptolemus begins to have a glimpse of the true strength and valor beneath the devastated exterior of the older man.[15]

In the previous scene Neoptolemus held the bow for a moment as a sign of trust between him and Philoctetes (654–75). That contact with the symbol of Philoctetes' heroic past and capacity for heroic companionship changes the meaning of the bow for him. It is no longer a prize to be captured under military orders but the mark of trust between men under the paradigm of the heroic friendship that once united Heracles and Philoctetes. Neoptolemus standing over Philoctetes with the bow in his hands is a visual replay of the young Philoctetes standing by the dying Heracles on his Oetean pyre. Neoptolemus now takes his place with earlier heroes as one of the bearers of the bow. Initially the bond of deception between him and Philoctetes (54–134), the bow now begins to function as a bond of personal trust, innate nobility of nature, and epic heroism.

The closing scene of the play harks back to the same visual image of the sleeping Philoctetes and of Neoptolemus standing beside him with the bow. In the earlier scene Heracles was present in the background when Philoctetes briefly recounted the bow's history (667–70). The chorus, soon after, celebrated Heracles' apotheosis on Mount Oeta (727–29), just before Philoctetes collapsed writhing with the attack of his disease. Now at the end Heracles appears on the stage. The pleonastic form of his announcement stresses the visual

---

15. On 839–41 see Whitman (note 14) 183; Knox (note 14) 131f.; Taplin, *Greek Tragedy* (note 5) 112; Segal, "Philoctetes" (note 2) 145f., with the further literature there cited.

authority of his epiphany (1411f.): "Know that you both *hear* the voice of Heracles, and *behold* his *visual* appearance" (*akoêi te kluein leussein t' opsin*). He gives instructions about the bow which refer back to the locale of its acquisition, the pyre on Oeta (1430–33). More important for our present purpose, he links Philoctetes and Neoptolemus together in an interweaving of personal pronouns and a simile evocative of Homeric epic (1434–37):

οὔτε γὰρ σὺ τοῦδ' ἄτερ σθένεις
ἑλεῖν τὸ Τροίας πεδίον οὔθ' οὗτος σέθεν.
ἀλλ' ὡς λέοντε συννόμω φυλάσσετον
οὗτος σὲ καὶ σὺ τόνδ'.

Neither do you without him have the strength to take Troy's plain, nor he without you. But as twin-pasturing lions do you guard him and he you.[16]

The visual image reinforces what syntax and imagery express on the purely verbal level: the men are bound together under the sign of the bow. In the quasi-ritual of the transmission of the bow, Heracles was present only verbally and symbolically (654–75, 727–29): here, at the end, after the bow has been exchanged and returned in a deeper and truer bonding of the two protagonists, Heracles is no longer a remote and invisible figure but a visible presence on the stage. This paradigm of heroic excellence, companionship, and endurance is not just in the mythic background but actually present, standing above the two mortals.

The three actors, all united under the sign of the bow—Heracles, Philoctetes, Neoptolemus—form a triangular configuration whose apex is the mythic embodiment of heroic values in the play, the god from whom the heroic meaning of the bow emanates. The triangle crystallizes the ideal of heroic friendship into one of those strong visual emblems which we have already seen in the *Ajax:* Tecmessa enveloping in her cloak the impaled body of the hero. What was instinctive but invisible in the complexity of Odysseus' plot and

16. On the effect of the pronouns and the possible visual gesture accompanying them see Wolf Steidle, *Studien zum antiken Drama* (Munich 1968) 187 with n.71; P. E. Easterling, "Philoctetes and Modern Criticism," *ICS* 3 (1978) 35.

Neoptolemus' conflict now gains the clarity and simplicity of visual action as the absent divinity returns to the human world.

The urn in the *Electra* deserves a place beside the sword in the *Ajax,* the robe in the *Trachiniae,* and the bow in the *Philoctetes* as one of Sophocles' richest visual symbols. The urn is the appropriate token of recognition between the surviving members of this doomed house.[17] It is the symbol of inverted life and death in Electra's world: Orestes' ashes are supposedly in the urn while the living Orestes stands before her. It is also the symbol of the living death which has been Electra's life in that house. On finding the disguised Orestes bearing the alleged remains of her brother, she addresses him as if the living brother and the ashes in the metal vessel were one (1165–67): "Receive me into this vessel of yours, nothing into nothing, so that for the rest of time I may dwell with you below." Even on giving up the urn, however, Electra is still involved in the experience of death which awaits her and Orestes. The joy of her cry of births (1232f.) is cut short first tentatively by Orestes (1288ff.) and then definitively by the Paedagogus' grim reminders of their task (1326ff.).

The urn is also the focus and symbol of other inversions: truth and falsehood, appearance and reality, strength and weakness, infinity and limitation, love and death. It is the final test of Electra's heroism, the "clear token" (*emphanê tekmêria,* 1108) of the isolation with which she must now reckon, in contrast to her sister Chrysothemis' false and premature "token" (*tekmêrion,* 904) of Orestes' return. It is an element in a progression of symbols through which men recognize who they are and where they stand in their world.

As in the *Philoctetes,* a young male protagonist radically changes his relation to a would-be victim of deception when he confronts the victim. Encountering the physical and emotional reality of the wound, Neoptolemus must come to grips with the pity that it arouses in him. The experience acted out on the stage affects him at a level below the rational control of language by which he expected to win his clearly defined success. Seeing Philoctetes recovered but still weak before him, the young hero cries out, "My speech has lost its

---

17. The most extensive discussion of the recognition scene is F. Solmsen, "Electra and Orestes: Three Recognitions in Greek Tragedy," *Mededelingen der Koninklijke Nederlandse Akademie van Wetenschappen,* Afd. Letterkunde, n.r. 30, no. 2 (Amsterdam 1967) 46–62, especially 53, 57, 59f. on the urn.

Sophocles

path [*aporon*]; where to direct it I no longer know" (897). So Orestes, overcome by the sight of Electra's wasted form (1177), can no longer keep his efficient stratagem of deceptive *logoi*. In terms very similar to those of Neoptolemus in *Philoctetes* (895–97) he says, "Alas, alas, what shall I say? At a loss for words, where [in words] shall I go? [*poi logôn amêchanôn elthô*]. For I no longer have the strength [*sthenô*] to rule my tongue" (1174f.).[18] In the *Philoctetes* the surrender to genuine emotion totally undoes the initial enterprise; in the *Electra* it only interrupts it but momentarily jeopardizes its success and endangers its perpetrators, as the Paedagogus points out soon afterward (1326ff.).

The emotional affect surrounding the urn, however, still cannot create the full recognition. That takes place only when Orestes, with difficulty, persuades Electra to put away the urn (1205–9) and to confront the living person before her. Then Orestes brings about the recognition through their father's signet ring (1222f.), an appropriate token for one whose concern has been the reattainment of power and patrimony through action. The urn, with its false ashes of a living son, however, continues its association with death when it is carried inside the house. Here it performs its intended function. It deceives Clytaemnestra, who is adorning it for burial at the moment of Orestes' attack (1400f.). Clytaemnestra understands only the death-bearing significance of the urn, its function as a token of murderous plotting, not of mourning and recognition between loved ones. But we do not see the urn at this point. Orestes has carried it into the house, at 1383, where it joins with the death-bound atmosphere of that dark interior into which Orestes later leads Aegisthus (cf. 1493–98).

In the deception of Aegisthus, however, Orestes and Electra no longer use the urn but the dead body of Clytaemnestra herself. This substitution, again a powerfully enacted scenic image, suggests a progression from falsehood to truth, from the logos of deceit embodied in the urn and the tale of Orestes' death which prepares the way for it to the *ergon* (deed), half of which has now been accomplished in Clytaemnestra's death. In apparently hopeless defeat, Electra prefers the supposed ashes in the metallic urn to the warm, living Orestes before her. At the end, now the deceiver instead of the deceived, she uses a real corpse to complete her victory. From the urn to the signet ring and then to the body wheeled out on the eccyclema, from fictive

18. On 1174 and the staging see David Bain, *Actors and Audience* (Oxford 1977) 79.

object to person, we gradually advance out of appearance toward truth. It is characteristic of the ambiguous justice of this play, however, that the shift from false ashes to real body is a movement closer to the horror of killing blood kin and of killing in general (cf. 1487–89, 1493–98).[19]

The urn was the token that brought together the separated brother and sister, a token of their love colored by the death and falsehood surrounding them in Mycenae. At the moment it appears onstage, Orestes is the active manipulator of the urn and the guile it serves, Electra the victim. Now, with Clytaemnestra dead, brother and sister have an equal share in the active execution of the plot. The partnership has already been established when Electra, answering Clytaemnestra's offstage death-cry, "Ah, I am struck," shouts exultantly, "Strike, if you have strength, a second blow" (1415). Now she too uses guile and logos, and she is the one to lead Aegisthus into the trap by clever acting and ambiguous speech (1442–57). The urn, token of love-in-death between true *philoi,* would be an inappropriate token for Aegisthus' recognition of Orestes. For him the dead body of his consort will be the instrument of his doom. Yet that body of a slain mother has now become the bond between brother and sister, joining them in their partnership of vengeance.

Electra had treated the urn with the religious respect associated with the treatment of the dead. Even Clytaemnestra had approached the urn in that spirit (1400f.). But not only do Orestes and Electra use the urn and the ashes it supposedly contains, they add to it in the second stage of their ruse the actual body of a murdered mother, hidden only by the light covering of a cloth, raised with horror on the one side but triumph and joy on the other (1468–71).

In its close associations with speech and actions, falsehood and truth, the urn also functions as a symbol of the deception of the theatrical situation per se. In this respect it is, like the severed head/ mask of Pentheus in the *Bacchae,* metatragic, a symbol of tragedy calling attention to its own medium as a literary fiction and as a set of conventions of language, action, music, and dance.[20] The urn embodies the paradoxical status of truth in a dramatic fiction. It is a

19. On the ambiguous justice of the play see C. Segal, "The *Electra* of Sophocles," *TAPA* 97 (1966) 536–39.

20. For Pentheus' mask see Taplin, *Greek Tragedy* (note 5) 98f.; C. Segal, *Dionysiac Poetics and Euripides' Bacchae* (Princeton 1982) 223ff., and also Segal, "The *Bacchae* as

work of art and elaborate artifice (cf. *typôma chalkopleuron*, 54) which gathers around itself the power of language to deceive or to establish truth. It functions, then, as a symbol of the play itself, a work whose falsehood (fiction) embodies truth.

As a vessel (*stegos*) filled with nothing (1165f.), it is, in one sense, the totally arbitrary signifier, an archetypal device for the deception—both by Orestes and by the playwright—which may be empty or full, contain nothing beyond itself or hold profound meaning. It is pure shell, "nothingness" to *mêden* (1166). But through its false contents of Orestes' alleged ashes, with which it is filled by a fiction of words, its nothingness is drawn into kinship with that paradoxical greatness-in-nothingness which lies at the heart of every Sophoclean hero's tragedy (*tên mêden es to mêden*, 1166). The exterior form of the urn holds false contents, but that very falsehood proves the means of winning back the truth. Electra's miserable outward form (cf. *eidos*, 1177), so different from the ideal image and so much at variance with inward nobility (cf. 354ff., 452), proves, by its very wretchedness, the means of breaking through the deception and cutting beyond appearances to the reality beneath. In this sense the urn is a mirror-image of Electra herself as well as an emblem for that paradoxical interplay of truth and illusion, honesty and deceit, inner substance and external husk, which lies at the center of the entire work.

Like Electra holding the urn, the audience must invest the fictive artifact (in this case, the play itself) with an enormous intensity of emotion in order for that truth to be established. It is, in fact, her very intensity of response to the object of falsehood, her desire to enter totally into the vessel containing the fictive center of her emotional life (cf. 1156f.), which so stirs Orestes that she overcomes the falsehood of the symbol, breaks through its shell of falsehood to the truth that it is about to reveal. Like Electra, too, the audience must be able to put aside the fictive envelope, the false and deceptive vessel, and turn back to the true forms of the living world when the fiction has done its work.

The urn scene gives full theatrical expression to one of the fundamental paradoxes of literary fictions. Only by accepting the fiction or, as Gorgias would say, deception (*apatê*), of the work can we find,

---

Metatragedy" in Peter Burian, ed., *Directions in Euripidean Criticism* (Durham, N.C. 1985) 159f., 166f.

experience, and benefit from the truth which that fictive shape contains and conceals.[21] The meaning of such a work consists in a never-resolved and never fully exhausted tension between the surface of its falsehood or fiction and the truth that lies beneath, at its core.

The seeing blindness of Oedipus, in both his plays, explores similar paradoxes of the theatrical fiction. Like Oedipus himself in the *Tyrannus,* who willingly submits to a self-blinding that makes him a second Teiresias, endowed with inner vision in compensation for the loss of physical sight, the audience submits to the blinders imposed by the poet's fiction. In its involvement with Oedipus and his drama it comes to experience, like him, the familiar identity of self and world as strange and problematical, whereas the alien now becomes the familiar. In the paradoxical light-in-darkness of this new truth, they find, as do the fictional spectators of Oedipus' last moments in the *Coloneus* (where blindness turns to mysterious sight before our very eyes), that the most fearful of the accursed heroes and the most terrible of the ancient myths also have the power to confer blessings—if one knows how to represent them and receive them correctly or, as Sophocles might say, reverently (cf. *Phil.* 1441–44).

III

Can any traits peculiar to Sophocles be discerned in the visual elements of his plays? I think that they can, although I must here venture somewhat beyond the realm of symbolism in the strictest sense and discuss visual effects a little more generally.

Though Sophoclean tragedy unquestionably has its share of violence and bloodshed, it differs from both Aeschylean and Euripidean drama in having a preponderance of ethical over emotional and pathetic effect. Though hardly serene, Sophocles is often restrained. He not only treats visual effects with the kind of intellectual and psychological thoughtfulness that we have seen in the plays studied above but also at times tones down—deliberately, it would seem—the raw energy of *ekplexis* (striking dramatic effect) in favor of other, quieter aims. The miracle of the blind Oedipus' transformation from a man

21. Gorgias 82 B 23 (D-K) see Giuliana Lanata, *Poetica Pre-Platonica* (Florence 1963) 204–7.

led to a leader in the *Coloneus,* to take one example, though prepared for by awesome signs from the gods, is held within the limits of a fifteen-line exit speech and a single strophic system (1539–78). The action thus sinks back from supernatural miracle to the reflective seriousness of human relationships: Theseus and the imminent doom of the house of Oedipus in Thebes to which the despairing Antigone will doggedly return (1670–1779).

The matricide of the *Electra* has the same subdued quality, though of horror rather than awe. The probable lacuna at 1427 makes certainty impossible, but it is arguable that Orestes reenters after the matricide without any visible evidence of the deed (*El.* 1424–36). At least the ensuing dialogue (1424–36) does not call attention to Orestes' appearance, unless those details were lost in the lacuna.[22] The chorus' remark about the "bloody hand" (*phoinia cheir*) dripping from "Ares' altar" (1422f.) could refer to actual scenic representation; but the combination with Ares' altar can equally suggest that the entire sentence is to be understood figuratively.

Comparison with the other tragedians' versions is instructive. In Aeschylus' *Choephoroe,* Orestes displays and expatiates upon the net that he brings out from within that bloodstained interior (*Cho.* 980ff.). Euripides' *Electra* too had a more vivid scenic indication of the crime, for the chorus cues in the murderous pair with the lines, "Now they set forth their foot from the house, befouled in the new-slaughtered blood of a mother [*mêtros neophonois en haimasi/ pephurmenoi*], trophy signs [*deigmata*] of victory over her wretched cries" (1172–74). With the murder of Aegisthus still before them, Sophocles' pair cannot yet openly reveal what they have done. This muting of the visual effect is nevertheless in keeping with the quiet, tense tone of the entire play, a play of inner struggle and long silent suffering rather than bold external acts.[23]

---

22. The chorus' *stazei* at 1423 need not mean that Orestes actually appeared with a sword dripping blood, as is suggested by J. H. Kells, *Sophocles, Electra* (Cambridge 1972) *ad* 1422–41. The text actually says "bloody hand" (1422).

23. The horror of the matricide, however, remains a major issue in the play, even if its presentation and character differ markedly from those of the Aeschylean and Euripidean versions. For recent views of its importance see H.-J. Newiger, "Hofmannsthals *Elektra* und die griechische Tragödie," *Arcadia* 4 (1969) 146f., with references to earlier literature; Kells (note 22) 4ff.; J. C. Kamerbeek, *The Plays of Sophocles, Commentaries,* Part 5, *The Electra* (Leiden 1974) 17f. The most recent discussion, P. T. Stevens, "Sophocles' *Electra:* Doom or Triumph," *G & R* 25 (1978) 111–20, tries to

In like manner the *Oedipus Tyrannus* has almost no action carried out on the stage. The action is really verbal, the unraveling of the hidden meanings of the ambiguous oracles, prophecies, and decrees.[24] But the visual images that Sophocles does show us on the stage cut to the very heart of the play's meaning: the inversions of vision and blindness, strength and weakness. Presumably Oedipus at the end bears the *skêptron* that he carried as king at the beginning. Now, however, as Teiresias had prophesied, the skêptron is the blind beggar's staff (456) as well as the reminder of that interweaving of passion, chance, and ignorance in Oedipus' killing of Laius (*skêptrô tupeis*, 811). We can only conjecture the presence of the skêptron at the end. It would be a powerful effect of opsis and *êthos* of Oedipus were weakly leaning upon it for the last exchange with Creon, where the subject is rule and power (*kratein*, 1522f.; cf. *kratunôn*, 14).[25]

It is particularly instructive to compare Sophocles' use of the third actor as silent onlooker with that of Aeschylus, from whom he may possibly (but not certainly) have inherited the device. Such scenes of

assert the older view, against Kells, that the matricide is simply approved and taken for granted. His interpretation, however, takes only superficial account of the arguments accumulated against this position since the studies of R. P. Winnington-Ingram, "The 'Electra' of Sophocles: Prolegomenon to an Interpretation," *PCPS* 183 (1954/55) 20–26, and Holger Friis Johansen, "Die Elektra des Sophokles—Versuch einer neuen Deutung," *C & M* 25 (1964) 8–32. For a balanced view, clearly showing the moral issues of the matricide, see G. H. Gellie, *Sophocles, A Reading* (Melbourne 1972) 106–30: "But the play remains a play about matricide, and Sophocles is always using our unfocused but constant uneasiness to keep us aware of his primary concerns" (106).

24. See, e.g., Florence Dupont, "Comment parlait le roi Oedipe," *Revue des Sciences Humaines* 36 (1971) 23–32: "La seule action qui ait lieu à l'intérieur du temps de la tragédie, se passe derrière les portes du palais" (23). For a somewhat different view, with an important definition of what constitutes action here, see Taplin, *Greek Tragedy* (note 5) 160f.

25. For the multiple meanings in the skêptron see Seth Benardete, "Sophocles' *Oedipus Tyrannus*," in Thomas Woodard, ed., *Sophocles; A Collection of Critical Essays* (Englewood Cliffs, N.J. 1966) 106, who would like to imagine a "crippled Oedipus . . . before the Thebans leaning on a staff, a staff which indicates as much his present authority as the use he once made of it to kill his father. . . ." Taplin, *Greek Tragedy* (note 5) 110, however, would realize this scene quite differently: Oedipus "looms above the suppliants, fatherly, dominant, wise—the nearest thing among men to a god (see 31ff.). . . ." In the paradoxes of this play the two possibilities are not mutually exclusive and may in fact be mutually necessary. For the skêptron see also Hay (note 5) 31–33, who would have Oedipus "gesticulating joyfully" with that same ambiguous skêptron at the news of the Messenger from Corinth (968ff.).

tense, significant silence heighten the symbolic potential inherent in the visual confrontation of the figures onstage: Cassandra in the *Agamemnon* witnessing in silence the meeting between her lord and his wife he left behind at Mycenae; Electra in Sophocles hearing the detailed account of the death of the one person who she thought could save her. The main protagonists, gathered before us on the stage, are all knit together and gripped by the crisis. Through the silence of a major protagonist, the dramatist creates a verbal vacuum more powerful than any speech could be. One could say of such scenes what Shakespeare's First Gentleman says in the finale of the *Winter's Tale* quoted in the epigraph to this essay: "There was speech in their dumbness, language in their very gesture."

Aristophanes' amusing parody in the *Frogs* (911–26) attests to the theatrical effectiveness of these Aeschylean silences. The spectator sits expectantly, Euripides complains, waiting in suspense for the veiled Niobe or Achilles to say something (*Frogs* 911–13). When the play is half over, the protagonist utters a few syllables, "big oxen words, bettle-browed, high-crested, terrible and ghastly-visaged, a mystery to the audience" (920–26). We can gauge the tremendous power of the device of the silent onlooker ourselves from the Cassandra scene of the *Agamemnon*.[26] Aeschylus' third actor here effects an over-powering dramatic revelation of an inevitable act; Sophocles' stresses the final, deliberate unfolding and confirmation of tragic character. With his greater attention to the inward development of character, to êthos, Sophocles uses a silent third actor to focus on self-understanding, resolution of an inner conflict, personal knowledge and acceptance of a tragic situation, rather than to expand or highlight the meaning of action per se. Cassandra's silent presence serves more to clarify the ritual and theological background of the doom in the house of Atreus and to concretize the sexual conflict in the *Agamemnon* than to explore her internal emotional life as a character. The difference between the two dramatists is telling: the silence of Sophocles' Electra or Neoptolemus is the silence of a character whom the audience already knows quite well; the silence of Cassandra is that of a new character who has not spoken at all and is not necessarily expected to

---

26. See B. M. W. Knox, "Aeschylus and the Third Actor," *AJP* 93 (1972) 104–24, especially 110ff.; Taplin, *Stagecraft* (note 1) 318f.

speak (cf. Aristophanes' parody). In Aeschylus, therefore, the effect lies in the surprise of speaking rather than in the silence.

In such situations in Sophocles we know that the events unfolding before us are of vital importance to the silent figure. The visual configuration leads us to fill that silence with the imagined reaction of that character, the actuality of which the poet withholds until a later event or a later point in the scene. Jocasta listens in silence to Oedipus' cross-examination of the Corinthian messenger, and then Oedipus, in silence, hears that messenger's cross-examination of Laius' old herdsman (*OT* 989–1056, 1132–46); Deianeira, silent, hears from her son of the dreadful effects of the anointed robe on Heracles at Cenaeum and then exits in silence (*Trach.* 749–820); Electra attends silently to the disguised Paedagogus' long account of Orestes' supposed death in a horse race at Delphi (*El.* 681–787). Silent for a hundred lines, Neoptolemus watches the tense verbal struggle between the two bitter enemies, Odysseus and Philoctetes, paralyzed by his conflict between military duty and instinctive nobility and compassion (*Phil.* 974–1074).[27] In both the *Tyrannus* and the *Trachiniae* the silences are approximately the same length, sixty to seventy lines. In both cases the character, a wife and mother, exits to suicide. In the *Electra* and the *Philoctetes* the silences are just over a hundred lines. If the *Electra* is a late play, close in date to the *Philoctetes,* as many scholars believe, then it would seem that Sophocles, as he became older, experimented with stretching these silences to longer, more suspenseful periods.

The Polyneices scene of the *Oedipus Coloneus* lends support to this hypothesis. Oedipus stands by in terrible silence during the ninety lines of Polyneices' entrance and speech (1254–1345). The latter's anxious question outside the meter "Why are you silent," *ti sigais* (1271), adds to the tension.[28] Antigone's short gnomic utterance on

27. "One of the great dramatic silences," says S. M. Adams of 974ff., in *Sophocles the Playwright, Phoenix* supplement 3 (Toronto 1957) 153. See also A. J. Podlecki, "The Power of the Word in Sophocles' *Philoctetes,*" *GRBS* 7 (1966) 233–50, especially 241; Knox, *Heroic Temper* (note 14) 131 on the auditory effects in general; also Karl Reinhardt, *Sophokles,* 3d ed. (Frankfurt a.M. 1947) 191 n.1.

28. "An anxious pause while Oedipus remains strangely silent," R. C. Jebb, *Sophocles, The Plays and Fragments,* Part 2, *The Oedipus Coloneus* (Cambridge 1885) *ad* 1271. Max Imhof, "Euripides' Ion und Sophokles' Oedipus auf Kolonos," *MH* 27 (1970) 83f., points out the contrast between the long set speeches in which father and son

the value of speaking (1280–83), though it divides Polyneices' continuous speech into two halves, only calls further attention to the theme
of silence. When Oedipus finally does reply, he addresses not his son
but the elders of Colonus who form the chorus (*andres*, 1348), and he
refers to his son in the third person (1351–53). Only in the eighth line
of his speech does he address Polyneices, turning on him the full,
crushing force of "O you basest of men," *ô kakiste*, in mid-sentence
(1354). Oedipus' ninety-line silence preceding makes this sudden direct address a powerful climax. As in the *Electra* and the *Philoctetes*,
the visual configuration of actors onstage shows that this silence has a
three-way effect, for Antigone too has been a silent, deeply feeling
auditor. The emotional impact on her is clear from her desperate,
futile plea to her brother not to attack Thebes (1414–46). The force of
these emotions remains strong to the end: the last thing Antigone has
to say in the play is to express her determination to return to Thebes
and prevent the fratricidal slaughter presaged not only in the actual
curse of Oedipus (1383–96) but in the long silence that preceded it.

Related to these effects of êthos and the intensification of the visual
configuration by dramatic silence is Sophocles' almost sculptural aus-
terity in the composition of scenic tableaux. Tecmessa placing her
cloak over Ajax is a good example. Another is the exodos of the
Antigone: Creon holding in his arms the body of his son—the last
remnant of his shattered house—which has been carried from the
dark cave of Antigone's union with death. There, before the house,
with the grim burden in his arms, Creon receives the final blow
"from within the house" (1279), the news of his wife Eurydice's
death. The spatial configuration, so obvious and simple, is part of the
suggestive economy by which Sophocles produces the sense of tragic
inevitability. Having denied the nonrational, noncontrollable, mysterious dimension of life, especially the ties of blood and mystery of
death, Creon is forced to descend into the dark cavernous spaces of
the earth, "the house of Hades" which sees love and death united
(1240f.); he then brings forth from the cave the sad burden that he
must bear to his own house. The figure of the father carrying his
son's corpse before his own house condenses into a powerful visual

communicate and the vivid *antilabai* of the discourse between brother and sister
immediately after (1399–1446).

image of this king's ruin when he tries to assert the autonomy of civic order over the ties of blood.

It is interesting to compare this scene of father and son with that at the end of Euripides' *Hippolytus*. There pathos predominates as the two men continue their dialogue to the end, until Hippolytus' absolution of his father proves his own nobility (*gennaiotês*, 1453ff.) and leaves us with a heightened sense of tragic waste and loss. In Sophocles the end, no less disastrous and wasteful, is more static; it is a sculptural tableau of the mourning king, the sinister recesses of the house behind him (cf. 1294), and the corpse he carries, simultaneously result and symbol of his own blindness in that very area which destroys him.

The *Electra* may have concluded with a similar effect if the last scene were staged with the heroine standing alone before the accursed house of her murdered parents.[29] Orestes and Aegisthus have reentered for the final deed of bloody vengeance. Justice is done, but a brooding, ominous mood remains, and Electra bears its full burden (cf. 1483–90), alone with that "much-destroying house of the Pelopids" (10) as she was at the beginning. The symbolic role of the house is comparable to that of vision in the *Tyrannus,* a symbol so pervasive that it cannot be separated from the basic constituent elements of the play: plot, character, setting. At the end Orestes and Aegisthus exchange foreboding words about that house as the site of "the evils of the Pelopids in present and in future" (1497f.; cf. 1495f.). But it is Electra who has been consistently in closest contact with that house and its evils, their victim and avenger (92ff., 190ff., 257–90, 308f., 812–19, etc.). If the chorus' closing address to the "seed of Atreus" refers to her (1508), we should perhaps recall her first appearance in the play as she stands alone before the sinister house (cf. 86ff., 818f.). The circularity of such a visual image would be appropriate for the static mood of this play, where pulling free from the past is so difficult, so uncertain.

Sophocles' visual symbolism and visual effects reveal the basic traits of his drama as a whole. His visual symbols are characterized by economy, clarity, and directness of focus on the issues of greatest human concern, the ability to condense the full range of tragic suffer-

29. See W. M. Calder, III, "The End of Sophocles' *Electra*," *GRBS* 4 (1963) 213–16; Segal, "*Electra*" (note 19) 529f.

ing into configurations of sculptural grandeur and simplicity, and (*pace* Tycho von Wilamowitz-Moellendorff) a refusal to sacrifice the deep ethical and philosophical issues to merely pathetic or narrowly theatrical effects. These qualitites play no small role in forming that impression of unity, proportion, and severity, the hallmarks of the Sophoclean "classic" style admired by critics from Aristotle to the present day.[30]

30. E.g., Paul Shorey, "Sophocles," *Martin Classical Lectures* 1, ed. L. E. Lord (Cambridge, Mass. 1931) 57–95, especially 88ff.

CHAPTER 5 /

Sophocles' Praise of Man and
the Conflicts of the *Antigone*

It is no coincidence that the most influential interpretation of the *Antigone*—and one of the most influential interpretations of any Greek tragedy—comes from a philosopher of idealism and dialectics.[1] The *Antigone* is certainly a play of antitheses and conflicts, and this state of conflict is embodied in the presence on stage of two protagonists, each diametrically opposed to the other. Yet as a result of Hegel's famous analysis, much discussion of the play has focused on the question of which of the two protagonists has more of the right on his side. This approach runs the risk of conceptualizing the protagonists too simply into antithetical principles that somehow are, and dialectically must be, ultimately reconciled.

This is not to say that no conceptual issues are involved in the characters of Creon and Antigone. But the issues are too complex to be satisfactorily reduced to a single antithetical formulation. We must avoid seeing the protagonists as one-dimensional representatives of simple oppositions: right and wrong, reason and emotion, state and individual, or the like. Such oppositions have some validity, but it is a validity purchased at the price of oversimplification and ultimately a misunderstanding of Sophocles' sense of the tragic. The characters,

---

1. For Hegel's treatment of the play see A. C. Bradley, "Hegel's Theory of Tragedy," in *Oxford Lectures on Poetry* (London 1909) 69–95, with the references there cited. Hegel's views, along with Bradley's essay, are now most easily accessible in *Hegel, On Tragedy*, ed. and trans. A. and H. Paolucci (New York 1962): see esp. 73–74. On the limitations of Hegel's treatment of the play see Victor Ehrenberg, *Sophocles and Pericles* (Oxford 1954) 33 with n.1; F. J. H. Letters, *Life and Work of Sophocles* (London 1953) 159ff.

137

like the play itself, have many levels that fuse organically, sometimes indistinguishably, into a complex unity; and here the confrontations of the two protagonists create an ever-ramifying interplay between interlocking and expanding issues.

It is the essence and the marvel of works of the classical period that concrete and generic so perfectly meet and unite. In this quality Sophocles is preeminent. In the *Antigone* the characters *are* the issues, and the issues the characters. But the characters are not only issues. They are individuals moving as all men do in a complex entanglement of will and circumstance, passion and altruism, guilt and innocence. Their searching, suffering, growth to understanding, and death give to the philosophical issues substance and the breath of life. Hence they can move us with a statement that does not falsify the intertwining of idea with particular, concept with action, loss with attainment, which forms the structure of our reality.

Recent critics, abandoning the simple thesis-antithesis opposition and looking at the play in terms of the action itself, have made it clear that it is hard to find much pure right on Creon's side, though this is not to say that his fate entirely lacks a tragic dimension or that the conflict is settled merely by a kind of moral default.[2] Antigone, on the other hand, is vindicated by the end of the play but only at the cost of tremendous suffering, her own and that of those closest to her. Indeed, since she disappears a little after the half-way point of the drama, one may wonder whether it is not the gods, Teiresias, and the rights of the corpse that are vindicated rather than Antigone herself.

Antigone and Creon are clearly the central focus of the play, yet together they give the play a double focus. The "double center of gravity" in the work, as one critic has called it,[3] creates a tension and richness that makes it possible for the action to reflect back upon itself

2. The problem of Creon's "tragedy" has been much discussed. C. H. Whitman surely goes too far in asserting that "there is nothing tragic or even morally interesting about him": *Sophocles, A Study of Heroic Heroism* (Cambridge, Mass. 1951) 90. He is not simply a bad man who gets his desserts, for as Ehrenberg (note 1) 59, points out, he does not alienate all sympathy, and he does, toward the end of the play, become increasingly human. For a discussion of Creon's role and character see also A. J. A. Waldock, *Sophocles the Dramatist* (Cambridge 1951) 123ff., who shares Whitman's view. At the other extreme is Letters (note 1) 168ff., who sees Creon as "technically" the hero.

3. R. F. Goheen, *The Imagery of Sophocles' Antigone* (Princeton 1951) 97.

in complex ways. And, as another critic has aptly pointed out, the decisive quality of the moral judgment expressed at the end of the tragedy requires a movement in which there can be complexity sufficient to make the play an adequate artistic expression of the complexity that exists in life.[4]

The complexity lies in part in the fact that the two protagonists, though totally opposed in their views, are nevertheless each bound to the other, "demonically bound" as Karl Reinhardt has put it.[5] Each is necessary to define the other. On the one hand, as C. H. Whitman has well remarked, "Antigone is the balance in which Creon is weighed, and found wanting";[6] on the other, Antigone's harshness would make no sense without Creon's authoritarian willfulness. It is the essence of the tragedy that the one figure seems to generate the other, that the two coexist as complementary parts of a whole. This whole is not necessarily a Hegelian synthesis of two opposing "spiritual substances" but something both infinitely simpler and infinitely more complex, something that is antecedent to and more basic than the conceptual formulations about spirit and absolutes. It is nothing less than the nature of man, his place in the world, and the possibilities and limitations of his actions. Around these issues and derivative from them revolve the antinomies that have been conceptualized in so many different ways: divine versus human law, individual versus state, religious versus secular, private versus public morality.

The conflict between Creon and Antigone has its starting point in the problems of law and justice. At any rate, the difference is most explicitly formulated in these terms in Antigone's great speech on the divine laws (450ff.), a speech that is both confession and defense, both plea of guilt and self-vindication, almost encomium. Against the limited and relative "decrees" of men she sets the eternal laws of Zeus, the "unwritten laws of the gods." She couples her assertion of these absolute laws with her own resolute acceptance of death (460). Thus she begins to extend the conflict outward to issues of wider scope. She chooses the divine command over the human compulsion and rejects life with its compromises for the absolutes of death. In-

4. See C. M. Bowra, *Sophoclean Tragedy* (Oxford 1944) 66–67.
5. Karl Reinhardt, *Sophokles*, 3d ed. (Frankfurt a.M. 1947) 74.
6. Whitman (note 2) 86.

deed, in her terms these absolutes are, paradoxically, just the things that "live always" (456–57).

This speech is also the focal point for themes that reverberate throughout the play. Antigone opposes the "decrees" (*kerygmata*, 454) of Creon to the "laws" (*nomima*) of the gods and thus sharpens the issue of what constitutes law (*nomos*). By implication she introduces the distinction between the man-made and the natural, the artificial and the eternally existent. The two words "decree" and "law" have been used confusedly and indiscriminately by Creon (*kerygma*, 162; *nomoi*, 177; *nomoi*, 191; *ekkekeryktai*, 203, etc.); and they now are seen to diverge.

The same divergence occurs with justice (*dike*). Antigone here appeals to the "Justice that dwells with the gods below" (451), whereas Creon is later to define the justice of a man solely in relation to the polis, the state, and to identify justice in private life with that in public life; "For he who is a good man in his domestic affairs will be shown just in the city too" (662–63). The certainty of this identification is severely shaken in the following scene, where the question of justice comes up in the most intimate of Creon's domestic relations and drives a wedge between public and private justice. Creon taunts his son with "going to law" (in Greek, "being at a case of justice," *dia dikes*) with his father (742) and is told in reply that he is mistaken in the matter of what is just (*ta dikaia*, 743). The chorus is to accuse Antigone of having "fallen against the lofty seat of Justice" (854–55) but will exclaim, at the end, to Creon, "Alas, you have seen justice late, as it seems" (1270).

Antigone's unqualified declaration for absolute values thus precipitates a redefinition of some basic moral and ethical categories. They do not fit her and have consequently to be remade. She is "a law to herself," *autonomos* (821); and as she is well aware (46off.), she must pay the price for standing outside the conventional definitions of law and justice. She challenges human law with an absolute that she backs up with the resolve of her own death, for this is the fullest assertion she can make of the intensity of her moral convictions. She can assert what she is only by staking her entire being, her life. It is by this extreme defense of her beliefs that she rises to heroic and deeply tragic stature; and simultaneously, by the same gesture she makes herself incomprehensible to the other actors, Creon, Ismene, the chorus. Only Haemon, who at a lower level makes and fulfils a similar resolve to die, comes close to understanding her; and in his final act, affirming himself truly her betrothed, he is indeed married to her in death. Death is the only possible union of such natures (1240–41):

> A corpse upon a corpse he lies, the unfortunate, having got his marriage portion in Hades' house.

In Antigone's speech on the unwritten laws, emphasis naturally falls upon law and justice, for the setting is a juridical one and Antigone is, as it were, on trial. But in the close-knit fifth-century city-state, "law" and "legality" have a far wider range of application than they would in the more compartmentalized ethics of modern civilization. For Sophocles and his contemporaries they involve the entire public and private life of the citizen, his relations with the gods and with his fellow men, and all the responsibilities, moral, political, and social, implied in those relations.

A sense of this wider realm of conflict is given in Antigone's repeated use of the word *kerdos,* "profit," "gain," in her great speech (461–64). She counts it "profit" to die before her time (461–62), "For whoever lives amid many woes, as I do, how does not such a one win *profit* in dying" (463–64). "Profit," however, is one of the words used throughout the play to characterize Creon's narrowly rationalistic and materialistic view of human motivation.[7] But in Antigone's mouth it carries exactly the opposite significance: emotion, nonrational (though equally firm) determination that willingly accepts or even seeks self-destruction, not self-advancement.

In the face of Antigone's resistance all of Creon's rationalism breaks down and is helpless. "Who is so foolish as to love to die" the chorus said at the announcement of Creon's decree (220). Yet Antigone exults in her foolishness and turns the word back upon her judge: "But if I now seem to you to be engaged in foolish deeds, perhaps I am accused of foolishness by one who is foolish himself" (469–70). In the very first scene of the play Antigone has asked to be left to suffer the consequences of her folly (95–96), and her attitude continues to the end. Hers is the woman's emotional resistance to the ordered male reason of the state. And she reinforces her action by the least rationally com-

---

7. For the theme of gain and Creon's character, see Goheen (note 3) 15ff. and passim.

Sophocles

prehensible of human acts, the sacrifice of her life. It is not that she acts
on unreason but rather that Creon's kind of reason is inadequate to
grasp her motives and her nature. This challenge to Creon's supposed
rationalism is to make itself felt even after her disappearance from the
stage, for the theme of reason and intelligence (*phronein*) dominates the
last three hundred fifty lines of the play. Creon is to see too late the
mistakes of his ill-founded intelligence (*phrenôn dysphronôn hamar-
têmata*, 1261), and the chorus' admonition about proud words teaching
intelligence in old age ends the play (1350ff.).[8]

Given the close interconnections in Greek civilization among all the
major aspects of life—intellect, morality, religion—it is natural that
this theme of intelligence should be firmly linked to the problem of
man's relation to the gods. In Sophoclean tragedy, as in much of Greek
thought before and after Sophocles, it is primarily the realm of the
gods which defines the boundaries of what man can know. Where the
one realm ends, the other begins, and to overstep the boundary line is a
dangerous violation of the things that are. It is a matter of "know
thyself" generalized to the human condition as a whole. In this play, as
in the later *Oedipus Rex,* knowledge, or the presumption of knowledge, reflects the limits of human power and man's responsibilities to
the areas of the unknown, the uncontrollable, the sacred.

To return to Antigone's crucial speech, it is thus significant that in
discussing the divine laws, she makes a point of man's not knowing
their origin ("and no one *knows* when they appeared," 457). Later in
her rapid exchange with Creon she opposes a similar statement of
ignorance to his positive assertions about law, right, and piety: "Who
knows if these things are held pure and holy below?" (521).

Creon understands nothing of the limits on human power and
control. For him, to know the ways of men is also to know the ways of
the gods; he sees the human realm as exactly coextensive with the
divine. He expresses this presumption, with characteristic blindness,
in his repeated invocations to Zeus; and these slowly build up in a
crescendo of arrogance and disaster.[9]

8. The conflict of Creon and Antigone in terms of rational versus emotional or
intuitive modes of apprehension is well discussed by Goheen (note 3) 75ff. And on the
phronein-aphrosynē motif see also 83–84.
9. On the religious significance of Antigone's Zeus in 450 B.C. see R. C. Jebb's
note *ad loc.* in his edition of the play: *Sophocles, The Plays and Fragments: Part III, The
Antigone* (Cambridge 1891) 89.

His first references to Zeus seem pious enough, though danger signs are tensely present. He first calls upon Zeus (184) after describing the guilt-stained death of the two brothers (170ff.) and asks that the god bear witness to his own principle that the state comes before everything (182ff.). This oath is followed, significantly, by the decree itself, the announcement of a deed that all Greeks would recognize as an unusually cruel and severe punishment, if not an actual violation of accepted religious usage.[10] He next calls upon Zeus (304ff.), also in an oath and when discussing piety and impiety. Yet here he is not even the calm, assured statesman of the earlier passage; hot with anger and perhaps fearing for his own position, he threatens the guard with death and worse if he fails to capture the violator of the decree. What gives this passage special point is the flash of impatience and the intolerant jibe at the chorus' foolishness and old age when they suggest, shortly before (278ff.), that the burial might be the result of divine intervention. Anger and irreverence both mount in Creon when, shortly after Antigone's great speech, he swears her and Ismene's punishment, "even if she is a sister's child, even if she is closer in blood than any who worships Zeus at the altar of our house" (486–87):

ἀλλ' εἴτ' ἀδελφῆς εἴθ' ὁμαιμονεστέρα
τοῦ παντὸς ἡμῖν Ζηνὸς ἑρκείου κυρεῖ. . . .

Literally, the second line goes "closer in blood than the whole altar of Zeus Herkeios" (Zeus who stands in the forecourt as the household god). This statement is outmatched only by his reply to Teiresias, shortly before the tragic reversal (1038–41):

You will not cover him in burial, not even if the eagles of Zeus wish to snatch him up and carry him off as food to Zeus' throne.

This from the man who first entered with "the gods" on his lips (162). And, a line and a half later, he adds, in a characteristic fusion of the

10. On the Greek view about burying the dead, even enemies, see Bowra (note 4) 64–65, 68. He notes, for instance (92), that the Greeks buried the Persians killed at Marathon and argues persuasively (69–70) that not even Polyneices' treason would justify this violation of the religious code. See also Ehrenberg (note 1) 28ff. and I. M. Linforth, "Antigone and Creon," *University of California Publications in Classical Philology* 15, no. 5 (1961) 191–93 and 248. Instructively parallel are Eurip. *Suppliants* 306–13 and 524ff.

intellectual and the religious themes, "For I *well know* that no man can pollute the gods" (1043–44).

It is, then, not by accident that Antigone begins her great speech with Zeus (449ff.):

> *Creon.* Dared you then to transgress these laws?
> *Antigone.* It was not *Zeus* who made these decrees of yours, nor are such the laws that Justice who dwells with the gods below established among men. . . .

Zeus is relevant, of course, because he is the supreme god and, as sky-god, is especially affected by the pollutions involved in the corpse. But as a focal reminder of Creon's *hybris* and, more important, as the fullest single embodiment of the realities of the universe, he is the measure of Antigone's dissent and of her heroism.

The gulf between Creon and Antigone thus becomes immense. It is among the ironies of the play that he who talks constantly of "pollution" and "reverence" (*sebas*) understands them only in the narrowest and least reverent way. He who has risked total pollution of the city in exposing Polyneices' corpse will seek to avoid pollution by the limited expedient of burying Antigone alive (773ff.). (The decree originally demanded death by stoning, 35–36.) It is Antigone, condemned for "impiety" (*dyssebes,* 514, 516), who is far closer to understanding what piety and the gods mean: "In acting piously I have gained [the charge of] impiety" (*dyssebeian eusebousa,* 924). Her very last words in the play reiterate her claim: "See what I suffer, and from whom, reverencing piety" (942–43). Her piety, as her paradox (924) makes clear, is not easy nor easily grasped by others, least of all the chorus (872), who assert that "self-willed passion" destroyed her (875). Yet it is almost an essential part of Antigone's action that it be not understood, that she stand alone against Creon's socially convenient claims of piety, the easy and popular inconsistencies that all agree upon and follow. It is only the tragic character who sees things through to their logical conclusions and so dies. Antigone, like Ajax, rejects life as compromise, gives up existence when it ceases to come up to the measure of the heroic self-image. "For you," she tells Ismene shortly after her great speech to Creon, "chose to live, but I to die" (555). Here both Ismene's gentleness and Creon's self-willed rationality are left furthest behind.

It is again among the tragic paradoxes of Antigone's position that she who accepts the absolutes of death has a far fuller sense of the complexities of life. Creon, who lacks a true reverence for the gods, the powers beyond human life, also lacks a deep awareness of the complexities within the human realm. Hence he tends to see the world in terms of harshly opposed categories, right and wrong, reason and folly, youth and age, male and female. He scornfully joins old age with foolishness in speaking to the chorus (281) and refuses to listen to his son's advice because he is younger (719ff., esp. 726–29). Yet his opposition of old and young is later to be turned against him by Teiresias (1088ff.), and he is, in the end, to be taught by the young son (725–26) who dies, Creon laments, "young with a young fate" (1266).

All these categories imply the relation of superior and inferior, stronger and weaker. This highly structured and aggressive view of the world Creon expresses perhaps most strikingly in repeatedly formulating the conflicts between Antigone and himself in terms of the woman trying to conquer the man (484, 525, 678, 746, 756). He sees in Antigone a challenge to his whole way of living and his basic attitudes toward the world. And of course he is right, for Antigone's full acceptance of her womanly nature, her absolute valuation of the bonds of blood and affection, is a total denial of Creon's obsessively masculine rationality.

Antigone's acceptance of this womanly obligation stands out the more by contrast with Ismene's rejection of it: "We must consider," Ismene says, "that we were born as women with women's nature, and are not such as to fight with men" (61–62). Ismene feels her womanhood as something negative, as a weakness. Antigone finds in it a source of strength. Ismene capitulates to Creon's view; Antigone resists and finds in her nature a potent heroism that cuts across Creon's dichotomizing of things and has its echoes even after her death in the equally womanly, though less significant, death of Eurydice.

It is Antigone's very nature, even more than her actions, which stands in such challenging opposition to Creon. Thus she concludes her first, and most important, clash with Creon with the pointed line: "It is my nature not to share in hating [*synechthein*], but to share in loving [*symphilein*]" (523). Her words not only answer Creon's charge that Polyneices is an enemy and hence deserving of hate not love (522) but also expose more of the fundamental differences between the two protagonists. In the conflict over such basic terms as "law," "piety," and "profit" lies much of the movement of the play.[11] The words for "love" and "hate" used by Creon and Antigone (522–23 and passim) have a certain ambiguity. *Echthros,* "enemy," means also personally "hated"; *philos,* "friend," means also an intimately "loved one." Creon simply identifies the two meanings; that is, he identifies personal and emotional love (*philein*) with political agreement (e.g., 187) and hate with political enmity. But Antigone's being and her action place into dramatic conflict the question of who deserves love and who hate. Hence at the end of their first encounter Creon answers Antigone's "It is my nature not to share in hating but to share in loving" with one of his characteristic dichotomies of man-woman, superior-inferior: "Go below then and love them, if love them you must; but no woman will rule me while I live" (524–25).

Creon's definition of man by his civic or political relations alone extends to areas other than love. He can conceive of honor only for benefactors of the state (207–10) and angrily rejects any idea that the gods could honor a traitor (see 284ff.). He again presumes that human and divine—or political and religious—values exactly coincide. Antigone, on the other hand, looks at honor in terms of what is due to the gods (77); and Haemon can find Antigone, a woman and a violator of the ruler's edict, "worthy to gain golden honor" (699).[12]

Not merely human relations are involved in the conflict between Creon and Antigone, but basic attitudes toward the whole of existence. It is the first stasimon, the famous ode on man (332ff.), which marks the first significant expansion of the meaning of the action to this broader level. The ode is not without its ambiguities and ironies, for its praise of man's intellectual achievement is severely qualified in the course of the play. It is preceded, moreover, by several blasts from Creon of very nonintellectual anger; and immediately before, the guard, a simple and conventionally pious man, dilates on the element of chance in human life (328) and exits with a statement of gratitude to "the gods" (331).

11. Goheen (note 3) 17 observes the importance throughout the play of such a "recurrent split of the two protagonists over certain common words" and traces this split at length through diction and imagery.

12. In the phrase "golden honor" (699) is implicit also the money image that especially characterizes Creon's materialistic reasoning. On this image in the play see Goheen (note 3) 14ff. and passim. In this connection too it should be noted that *timē,* "honor," has another meaning in Greek: "price," "value," in a strictly material, calculable sense.

The ode itself is also perhaps not so confident as might at first appear. The adjective that describes man, *deinos,* means not only "wonderful" but also "terrible," "fearful," as several commentators have pointed out.[13] But the greatest ambiguity lies in man himself. Man claims control and domination, yet he cannot control himself, has difficulty in controlling other men, and perhaps cannot even control the natural world. The irony of self-control is pointed up by the word used to describe man's civic and legal "temper" (*orgas,* 356) in the ode, for this word means also "anger" and is so used shortly before in the scene with the guard (*orge,* 280). Similarly the word for "thought" in the ode (*phronema,* 354) signifies also "pride" and has that sense in the ensuing scene with Antigone (459) as well as at other crucial points in the play.

There is little question that the ode reflects much of the optimistic rationalism of Sophocles' time: the Sophistic view of man's ability to work creatively upon his environment and the probably Protagorean concept that the state, the polis, along with law and justice, is a human creation and perhaps the most important stage in man's assertion of himself over against a hostile or indifferent world. The enumeration of man's cultural advances may itself derive from Sophistic culture-histories, or at least from the new rationalistic, anthropological view of man which treats of human civilization as the result of a gradual, slow advance. Similar ideas are already present in Aeschylus' *Prometheus Bound,* written perhaps some twenty years before the *Antigone.*

Though Sophocles draws heavily on these rationalistic views, he does not necessarily fully approve them. Through this ode he throws them into the dramatic action of the play and allows them to be weighed in the balance of the tragic outcome. It is not that he denies their validity, for he too is obviously much impressed with the range of human achievement. But he can no longer regard progress and a Promethean conquest of nature as having the heroic possibilities that Aeschylus—and perhaps Protagoras—saw in them. Sophocles sees in reason and technical control not simply a source of human freedom, as Aeschylus did, but also a potential source of human bondage and

13. On the multiplicity of meanings involved in deinos see J. T. Sheppard, *The Wisdom of Sophocles* (London 1947) 46–48. Also Goheen (note 3) 53 and 141 n.1 with the references there cited. Scholars have suggested, plausibly, a reminiscence of the far more sinister *deina* of Aeschylus' *Choephoroe,* 585ff.: see Jebb (note 9) *ad loc.,* Ehrenberg (note 1) 61ff., and Linforth (note 10) 196ff.

limitation. And his reflections on this subject are to mature in the *Oedipus Rex* where, it will be recalled, knowledge and intelligence are by no means unambiguous goods, though they are nonetheless inseparable parts of man's endowment.

Thus, to come back to the ode on man, when the chorus takes up the creation of law and justice after the praise of man's other achievements, they say that men may come "now to good, now to ill" (367). He may be "high in his city" (*hypsipolis*) but also "without city" (*apolis*) should he be led to an act of rashness (*tolma*).[14] His nature then, as this rashness or daring suggests even here, contains an irrational or violent and destructive potential. Perhaps in this shift of emphasis Sophocles means to suggest that success in law and justice, the areas that concern relations with other human beings, is more difficult and less certain than control over the lower orders of nature. Though the Sophist Protagoras is probably more optimistic, it is interesting that Sophocles' suggestion of the greater difficulty of law and justice would correspond roughly with Protagoras' emphasis on the difficulty and importance of justice and reverence, the qualities that make it possible for men to unite in cities or societies, in the myth that Plato puts in his mouth (*Protagoras* 320c–323a).

This complex connection between control and human relations has a further significance for Antigone. Her womanly nature, centered on sharing in love, opposes Creon's attitude of domination which stands apart from the otherness both of men and of nature and looks upon them as a potential enemy to be subjugated. Thus it is Antigone the woman—or perhaps, at another level, the woman in him—that Creon must subdue or, in one of his favorite metaphors, must yoke.[15] It is interesting in the light of this opposition that when Antigone seeks a heroic exemplar for herself, she invokes the figure of Niobe, a loving mother but also a human being who is at the same time organically fused with the natural world: she whom "the growth of rock, like intensely winding ivy, subdued" (826–27). Antigone's Niobe belongs both to humanity, with its feelings and sorrows, and to inanimate nature; and she symbolically unites the two realms. Thus the snow and rain are not hostile missiles to be warded off, as in the first stasimon

---

14. For this interpretation of hypsipolis see Ehrenberg (note 1) p. 64 n.1.
15. See Goheen (note 3) chap. 2, passim.

(356ff.), but are as her own tears, which she feels running down the rocky ridges of what is now her face (828–32):

> Still, as she wastes, the rain
> and snow companion her.
> Pouring down from her mourning eyes comes the water that soaks the
>   stone. (Wyckoff's translation)

Niobe, like Antigone, suffered from excessive love and pride; yet in her, as in Antigone, loneliness and sorrow are transmuted to a higher plane.

It is significant that the limitations in Creon's attitudes are borne in upon him not only in the area of his personal relations but also in language that makes another connection between human relations and the natural world and points toward a view resembling the Niobe image (though less profound), a view in which man does not dominate nature but learns from it sympathetically. Hence in urging his father to yield, Haemon chooses, as examples of yielding, trees that bend in the winter flood rather than straining stiffly against it (712ff.), and he prefaces his advice with a statement about human wisdom (*sophos*, 710) which echoes the praise of wisdom in the ode (365).

To yield is exactly what Creon finds most difficult, and there is perhaps a further irony in his statement after the encounter with Teiresias, "To yield is terrible [*deinon*], but to resist and strike my proud spirit with disaster stands also in [the realm of] the terrible [*deinon*]" (1096–97). Thus when forced by confrontation with the uncontrollable to yield, he echoes the lead-word in the earlier praise of man's power of control: "Many are the wonders [terrors, *deina*], and nothing more wonderful [terrible, *deinon*] than man."

Antigone, who in her own way also refuses to yield, images more fully the greatness of man. But this greatness is measured also against Creon's limitations. The contrast between the two kinds of not yielding is well exemplified in the single, concentrated line with which Antigone cuts through Creon's long rant (473–96): "Do you want anything more than my capture and death?" (497).

The scene with Haemon which follows and first explicitly introduces the yielding motif brings out more fully the limitations of Creon's strength. Though Creon spoke for his son's feelings in the previous scene (569ff.), he nevertheless fears to encounter in Haemon

Sophocles

the same emotional temper and spirit of resistance which he found in his betrothed. He indicates his fears in opening the interview with the question, Are you here *raging* at your father . . . ?", thus applying to Haemon the same verb that he used of the two women earlier (*lyssainōn*, 633; *lyssōsan*, 492; the word itself is not common and occurs only in these two places in the play and, indeed, only twice more in the extant plays). The verb is expressive not only of the way in which Creon regards those who oppose him but also of the areas where he feels himself most exposed and most uncertain. He is obviously reassured at Haemon's "Father, I am yours," the first words that his son, wisely, chooses to utter (635); and he expresses his relief in the expansive speech that follows (639–80), full of his favorite commonplaces about rule and authority.

In another way too the scene suggests that Creon's position is perhaps not so unshakeably firm as might appear. It reveals that Creon in fact relies heavily on the support of others, whether his son or the chorus. He cannot brook disagreement. He cannot, like Antigone, stand alone, and those who disagree he will coerce into agreement. At the same time he lacks the calm definiteness of Antigone and is actually far less reasonable than the raging womanly natures he insults. Indeed, nothing perhaps better illustrates the instability of his supposedly rational and consistent views than his treatment of Haemon here. Reconciliation and praise in the first part of the scene are followed not only by sharp insults in the second but even by the cruel threat to have Antigone put to death in her "bridegroom's" very presence (760–61). In these sudden shifts of mood Creon undermines the rational bases of his action on which rests, in part, his authority. But also he, the ruler, the man of consistent policy, indicates an increasing qualification of the image of man in the first stasimon as the reasoning being, the artificer whose intelligence is shown in the cities he creates and rules.

Another qualification of this ode comes to center on Antigone. The ode included the catching of birds as one of man's triumphs. From the beginning of the play, however, birds battening on the exposed corpse are sinister reminders of Creon's authority (e.g., 29ff.) and hence also of his subordination of religious usage to political decree. Yet it is these birds which carry to Teiresias the warnings about Creon's violation of that to which human control does not pertain. The birds too are the subject of an art (*techne*, 998), prophecy, which in its sympathetic listening to the voices of nature stands apart from the more systematic arts of control and device (*to machanoen technas*, 365–66) which man has "taught himself."

It is significant, then, that the guard, in describing Antigone's capture, compares her to a bird lamenting its young: "She raises the sharp cry of lament of a mother-bird in bitter grief, as when, in the empty nest, it sees the bed stripped of its nestlings" (423–25). And a little later the guard speaks of "hunting" Antigone (433). Yet though he thus connects his action with the imagery of domination in the preceding ode, he has also shown himself capable of a different attitude in the bird simile, one marked by pity for the hunted creature. At the same time, however, Antigone is the victim and is the one identified with a part of the subjugated natural world (and, as noted earlier, she is herself to deepen this identification in her Niobe simile, 823ff.). The guard, though aware and sympathetic, still allows himself to be forced into the position of the hunter, the controller. Like Ismene, he has good instincts but lacks the force to carry them through (esp. 439–40, "But it is my nature to count all other things as less important than my safety"). He fails where Antigone, his prisoner, succeeds; and her success, in death, has effects that create a drastic change in the attitude of the master-hunter, Creon.

The guard's simile not only underlines the sex of Antigone but also prepares for Creon's far cruder use of the imagery of animal conquest after Antigone's speech (473ff.); there too Creon connects conquests of nature with domination of male over female (484–85, 525). The parallels sharpen the difference between the guard's pity and the master's unfeeling severity.

Thus it is exactly the womanly element in Antigone which Creon cannot grasp. He must reduce her act to terms analogous to his own in order to understand it, and this he does most clearly in the language in which he voices his suspicions about Ismene (though he means his words to apply to Antigone as well):

φιλεῖ δ' ὁ θυμὸς πρόσθεν ᾑρῆσθαι κλοπεὺς
τῶν μηδὲν ὀρθῶς ἐν σκότῳ τεχνωμένων.

The mind of those artfully devising [*technōmenōn*] nothing honest in the dark is wont to be caught beforehand in its thievishness [literally "as a thief," *klopeus*]. (493–94)

Sophocles

The word "thief" used of Antigone's deed immediately classifies it in Creon's mind with the calculating desire for "gain" (*kerdos*), one of his favorite concepts. The verb "artfully devising" contains the root *techne*, "device," "craft," which, as already noted, figures prominently in the ode on man. But as the techne of the ode on man is answered (in part) by Teiresias' god-directed techne of prophecy, so the reduction of Antigone's motives to a narrowly conceived thieflike calculation is answered, also by the gods, in Creon's cry when he hears his son's voice close to the end: "Am I deceived, thief-like, by the gods" (*theoisi kleptomai*, 1218).

The themes of the birds, techne, and male domination over female are all linked as parts of a single complex, the multiple aspects of control and authority; and in this complex, which involves Antigone's death and the prophetic birds of Teiresias, it is perhaps suggested that the world of nature, to say nothing of the world of man, is neither so helpless nor so easily controllable as the first stasimon might lead one to suppose.

Antigone, as a woman and hunted victim, and Teiresias as interpreter of the signs from the gods and as a helpless, blind old man, are closely related to each other in their attitude of sympathetic relation with this natural world (and the comparison of Antigone to a screaming bird helps reinforce this association). Both have a special reverence for the divine which deeply antagonizes Creon. Both belong to an order of being or a stage of life of which Creon is contemptuous; and yet both in the end are vindicated at Creon's expense.

In putting Antigone to death, Creon has indeed gained his object, solidified his authority, crushed the refractory element that opposed—and this was the only element, so far, that did oppose. He expected men (248, "Who of men [*andrōn*] dared to do this deed") and gain-seeking calculation and finds instead a girl who seeks her only gain in death (461ff.) and looks to the gods, not to men. Rebellion there is, as he feared, but rebellion against a profounder and more deep-seated aspect of himself and his rule than he yet suspects. It is with the vindication of these rebellious areas, the womanly, the divine, the nonrational, that the latter half of the play is largely concerned; and it is perhaps this reason which in part accounts for the increasing prominence of Eros and Dionysus; the mythical embodiments of the least rational or controllable elements in human experience, in the odes of the second half of the play.

The answer to Creon, then, is twofold. In the person of Antigone is revealed Creon's reduction not only of womanly nature but of human nature in general. In his reply to Antigone's speech on the divine laws, Creon uses not only the language of technical control (fire and metallurgy, 474–76) and animal subjugation (the taming of horses, 477–78) but also implicitly compares Antigone to a slave (*doulos,* 479). The progression of the thought is highly significant, for it reveals the link between man's proud conquest of nature and Creon's debasement of man. Antigone's ability to resist the weight of argument and civic authority brought against her is itself a reply, a vindication of the unconquerable dignity and worth of the individual. She replies to the insult of slavery quite specifically, and her answer is the love and devotion of one individual to another under the sanctity of ties that are independent of the artificial aspects of the social order. It is the irreducible humanity of her bond, her refusal to let Polyneices become less than what she has felt him to be, that forms the kernel of her terse reply: "It was no slave [*doulos*] but a brother who died" (517).

The other part of the reply to Creon comes from the subdued realm of nature, wherein the gods are most manifest. This answer too is necessary for the wholeness of the play, for Creon has violated not only personal relations but something in the relation of man to the world, a sense of the sanctity in things, in nature as in man. These realms, the divine and the human, the natural and the divine worlds, fuse in the rapid movement of events which precipitates Creon's disaster: first, Teiresias' birds, then the terrible encounter between Creon and his son. The language used in this latter scene creates an even more decisive and more bitter inversion of the man–nature, human–animal theme. There is here an ironic alternation of tameness and wildness, but fearfully presented at the height of the peripety in Creon's own son. Haemon's voice, Creon cries out, "fawns on me" (σαίνει, 1214); and the verb recalls the terms for animal-like servility both in the ode on man (340, 350–52) and in the exchanges between Creon and Antigone (477–78, 509). Immediately after, however, Haemon is like a wild, untamed animal, with "wild [*agriois*] eyes," spitting, and finally turning on himself in his savagery (1231–36). Like an animal too, he has lost man's proud achievement of speech (354) and seems not to understand his father's words (1230).

Creon's brutalization of his human relationships has thus rebounded upon him and with it the tameness and obedience he demands from his own environment. Creon pays through his son for a reduction of man which he has previously inflicted on him. He had totally rejected, or refused to see, any possible love between Haemon and Antigone and thus rejected too the human individuality of his son. In the words "There are other fields for him to plow" (569), he brings the most intimate of human relations, with its traditional sanctities, down to the level of a brutish act and makes a connection too with the attitude in the ode on man (note the emphasis on plowing at the end of the first strophe, 337ff.). This degradation of the marriage tie continues in Creon's cruel taunt to Haemon that Antigone will die "in the presence of her 'bridegroom'" (760–61) and in Antigone's long, ensuing lament that she is "wedding" Acheron (816) and that her tomb is her "bridal chamber" (891). The pattern is fulfilled in Haemon's marriage, in death, to Antigone (1240ff.) with the consequent destruction of Creon's marriage and the son it produced.

Creon thus comes to learn the consequences of his attitudes and actions on two levels, which might be labeled internal and external, the personal realm and the outside world. Internally, through his sufferings in his own most essential relations, those which both define and express what a man is, he learns that one does not devalue the human realm without doing harm to one's own humanity. Antigone, with her absolute valuation of human ties, would then express the fullest development of this humanity and in her Niobe-image rises to almost godlike stature. Creon, having demeaned the sanctity of these ties, is left without any and hence scarcely human, a nonentity, as he says at the end, "existing no more than a nobody," or, as Wyckoff translates, "I who am nothing more than nothing now" (1325).

Externally, through the intervention of the divine powers in the person of Teiresias, Creon learns by coercion that there are areas of existence which cannot or should not be subjected to control and authority. But this compulsion from the realm of the gods and the natural world is at once brought home to him in terms of his own fate, and he is touched by the broader reversals connected with the birds through the animal imagery of his son's attempted parricide and death. Thus the two realms, internal and external, human world and natural world, are inseparably linked, and the play, in its greatness and complexity, is an expression of this unity.

The confounding of tameness and wildness in Haemon's death is connected with an even more fundamental reversal in the play and with another qualification of Creon's views of civilization. This appears in the theme of shelter. In the second scene with the guard, which follows the ode on man and is an obvious pendant to the first scene in this symmetrically structured play, the guard dwells on his and his companions' exposure to the elements as they watch the body: the force of the winds, the heat, the open air, the barren hills (410ff.). The fact that these details come so soon after the ode is significant, for there shelter from storm and the open air was prominently enumerated among civilized man's achievements (356–59):

> . . . δυσαύλων
> πάγων ἐναίθρεια καὶ δύσομβρα φεύγειν βέλη. . . .

(Statecraft is his,)
And his the skill that deflects the arrows of snow,
the spears of winter rain. (Fitts and Fitzgerald's translation)

A literal translation makes the connection a little more explicit:

He has taught himself to flee the missiles of frosts of the open air [*enaithreia*] that make hard lodging and the arrows of storm.

The storm described by the guard fills "the open air" (*aither*, 415, 421), and the image of arrows or missiles was used in Creon's previous angry interview with the guard (241, keeping the reading of the mss. with Jebb) and is to be used again by him, also in anger, against Teiresias (1033–34). Creon himself is responsible for a storm of sorts, for the guard begins his second scene with Creon by describing his first interview in terms of "the storm of your threats to which I was subject" (391) before going on to the real storm (417ff.). Combine this with the animal and hunting images (423ff. and 433), and the contrast with the ode is impressive.

That these themes of shelter and exposure have also the broader implications of communal life in general appears from Haemon's cross-examination of Creon (739–40).

> *Creon.* Is not the polis considered as belonging to the ruler?
> *Haemon.* You would exercise a good rule alone, over a deserted [*eremos*] land.

Sophocles

And something of this suggestion is acted out when, subsequently, Creon makes Antigone "deserted," "isolated" (*eremos,* 887, 919), and her cave is in a wild and "deserted" (*eremos,* 773) place. Thus Creon, for all his praise of law, has failed to grasp some of the essential qualities of civilization taken in its broader, more humane sense; and he appears as reversing, as it were, the process of civilization itself in exposing man to the desolation and violence of the world he has supposedly conquered.

This regressive tendency is present in the fundamental situation of the plot itself, the exposure of a man's body to dogs and birds. In the corpse, as in the storm and in Antigone's cave, we are reminded of the reality of the still untamed wildness that lies outside human civilization. Like the plague in the *Oedipus Rex,* the moldering corpse, quickly but effectively described (e.g., 29–30, 205f., 410) makes us uncomfortably aware of something disturbing, offensive, nauseating.

In the Greek view, however, these physically offensive elements have a profounder religious significance. They constitute, as Teiresias brings home, a *miasma,* a "pollution," an infectious taint that is the concrete manifestation of a violation of some religious sanction.[16] The exposed corpse is both an outrage of moral sanctions and a source of real pollution, a possible cause of plague, blight, barrenness, of the outbreak against man of all the uncontrollable and mysterious forces on which his survival depends. When the right relation with these forces is broken, man's very existence is threatened, on the level both of political coherence (1080ff.) and personal happiness (as Creon is to learn).

As leader of the polis, Creon must be concerned with such pollutions; yet it is only superficially that he grasps the significance of a pollution coming from a violation of the divinely established order of things. In his limited concern for the way in which the city will "escape pollution" (776), in the case of Antigone's death and, more markedly, in his hybristic statement about man's not being able to "pollute the gods" (1043f.), he shows his lack of a sense of the larger sphere of which the polis, and every human creation, may be a part.

16. For the significance of the miasma and related ideas in Greek religious thought see E. R. Dodds, *The Greeks and the Irrational* (Berkeley and Los Angeles 1951) 35ff. Also C. Segal, "Nature and the World of Man in Greek Literature," *Arion* 2, no. 1 (1963) 25ff. and 36ff.

Near the very end, in a final utterance about pollution, he conveys his newly gained sense of the limitations of human action: "O harbor of Hades, *hard to purify,* why, why do you destroy me" (1284f.; see also 1142).

Thus the corpse, in its connections with the themes both of shelter and of pollution, serves as an active link between the two aspects of Creon's irreligious attitude, his degradation of man and his disregard of the divine sanctions. The two themes are linked, of course, in Antigone too, for her burial of Polyneices is both a vindication of the divine sanctions and a more authentic statement of the dignity of man than the assertion of human independence and control affirmed by Creon. As the presence of the exposed and animal-torn body makes clear, the purely man-centered magnification of human achievement may involve, paradoxically, a debasement of man.

It is not that the confidence of the first stasimon is utterly negated. The image of man's greatness persists throughout the play, but it persists in the figure of Antigone rather than Creon.[17] The qualification of the view of man implied in the ode only works toward a clearer definition of the wholeness of man, the feminine with the masculine, the weakness and uncertainty that are always there, even in his most splendid achievements, the nothingness in the face of which his greatness is asserted. This greatness, as Sophocles sees it, has not reached its full measure unless is has confronted its own negation in death. This Antigone alone does. Death is merely brushed aside in the ode on man (361–62) and used as a threat of punishment, another instrument of control, by Creon.

Yet here the fates of the two protagonists, Antigone unshakeably firm and accepting death heroically, Creon crushed to "nothingness" (1325), are at extreme polarities. Though the original positions of strong and weak are reversed, the two are still separated each from the other as by an infinite gulf. In the *Oedipus Rex* of perhaps a decade later, Sophocles' statement about the complex interplay of human greatness and human weakness will be more fully unified in a single protagonist. And at the end of his life he will again use the figure of

---

17. It is interesting in this connection that Whitman (note 2) 91 takes the first part of the ode on man as referring to Antigone, "under the heroic type of humanity, limited by mortality and moral law, but unlimited in the scope and daring of her soul."

Oedipus as his prototype of a still more profound restatement of this complex relation.

The forceful presence of death, whether in the exposed dead body or in Antigone's acceptance of a living death, sharpens the problem of the nature and dignity of man. Death can be a degradation or an affirmation of human value in the face of inflexible necessities. Antigone's death affirms this value not only for herself but also for the dishonored corpse. For her it is still a human figure, still inseparable from a human personality. Creon, in maltreating the corpse, devalues also the image of living man. It is interesting to consider Creon's act in the light of the heightened emphasis on the human form in the mid-fifth century. Sophocles presents a play that centers about the desecration of a human body at the very time that his contemporaries working on the Parthenon were discovering and expressing the beauty and nobility of man's body as it had never been expressed before.

Again, therefore, Creon's act has implications that he himself does not realize. In regarding death as another instrument of control, not as a necessary condition of existence to be approached with compassion and understanding, Creon disvalues his subjects and ultimately himself. He denies that the state has a place for death in this latter, generic sense. Yet at the end he who had imperiously ordered the maltreatment of a body enters, himself carrying a corpse, and one that is "not another's" but his own (1257–60). As a king, he has dismissed or used death only to discover and experience it as a man, mortal and tied to mortal beings. Hence Creon's state-centered view of man reveals its inadequacies in widening areas as the play proceeds and is shown to involve the loss of the full humanity not only of the subject citizen but of the ruler as well.

A political or historical interpretation of a work of the magnitude of the *Antigone* is, of course, inadequate; yet the historical side has some wider ranges of significance. The play, at one level, is almost certainly a statement about the nature and ideals of Athenian democracy. It rejects the autocratic materialism and narrow rationalism implied in Creon's outlook, which restricts man's nature to a functional capacity, reduces him to a member of a political unit only. What Antigone demands, on the other hand, is that the state take into itself the sanctity of blood relations, the value of affection and emotional ties, the uniqueness of the individual. The conception seems not unlike that put forth in Pericles' Funeral Speech:

It is true that we are called a democracy, for the administration is in the hands of the many and not of the few. But while the law secures equal justice to all alike in their private disputes, the claim of excellence is also recognized; and when a citizen is in any way distinguished, he is preferred to the public service, not as a matter of privilege, but as the reward of merit. (Thucyd. 2.37.1, Jowett's translation)

In such a state an Antigone could exist—perhaps in a fuller way than Pericles intends—demanding her rights and thereby shaping the state after the best elements in herself, making it an expression of her own full humanity.

It has often been suggested, as noted earlier, that Sophocles intended the play, at least in part, as a qualification of the rational optimism of the fifth-century enlightenment as expressed in the speculations of Protagoras, Anaxagoras, Democritus, Hippocrates, and Hippodamus of Miletus.[18] It may be too, as Victor Ehrenberg has maintained, that behind the picture of Creon lies some reference to the "proud and austere" Pericles himself, "who with all his belief in humanity was so much less 'human' than, for instance, Sophocles."[19]

But the issues go far beyond the reference to specific men or classes of men. They are concerned with defining that in which man's humanity consists. Man would like to believe, the play seems to say, that he has developed wonderful resources for understanding and commanding his world. Yet man the artificer or deviser is not enough. Thus in the course of the play all the apparent conquests enumerated in the first stasimon prove to have a double edge. The sea, controlled proudly in the ode (335ff.) and for Creon, from his first appearance, boastfully associated with political control (the ship of state: 162ff., 189–90, etc.), returns in subsequent odes in connection with the helplessness of irrational suffering (see 584ff., 953ff., 966ff.), until Creon himself speaks of his disaster, ironically, as a "harbor" (1284). The animals and birds described in the antistrophe (343ff.) become the messengers of the violated divine order of things

---

18. For the connection of the ode on man with Sophistic and other philosophical speculation in the fifth century, see Ehrenberg (note 1) 61ff.; Goheen (note 3) 91ff., with the references cited in 152 n.28. See also B. M. W. Knox, *Oedipus at Thebes* (New Haven 1957) 107ff. and E. A. Havelock, *The Liberal Temper in Greek Politics* (New Haven 1957) chap. 3, passim, esp. 66ff.

19. Ehrenberg (note 1) 157.

Sophocles

and, in the imagery connected with Haemon's death, almost the immediate instruments of Creon's doom. Speech and communication (354) degenerate into ranting and insult or the utter, animal-like silence of Haemon at the end. Shelter and the fruits of man's city-creating temper (355–56) are denied the corpse and even the guards who watch it, and are negated also in Antigone's desolate place of burial. Even the conquest of disease (363–64) rebounds on man in the "divine disease" of the storm (425) and, more seriously, in the pollution with which the city "is diseased" as a result of Creon's "thought" or "intelligence" (1015).

It is only death, that alone which man cannot control or "flee," as the ode says (361), which proves the fullest touchstone of man's greatness and the truest means to his assertion of his humanity. The *Antigone* is still bleak and dark by comparison to the sublime finale of the *Oedipus Coloneus* where the hero discovers his greatest powers in his self-guided movements at his call to death. Yet in the *Antigone* too a self-accepted death is the source of what is beautiful and heroic in the play. But if Antigone, with her heroic acceptance of the unknown, of death, most fully vindicates the dignity of man,[20] Creon comes to act out the equally tragic process of becoming fully human. With Antigone's death there comes, through the blindness and helplessness of the seer, the rebirth of Creon's humanity, until he too is plunged amid loss and suffering into his own experience of the unwritten laws that all men must face as mortal beings who sometime encounter the unknown and unknowable. And in his encounter he passes from his communal position as head of state to a loneliness and isolation perhaps more terrible than Antigone's.

Antigone's view, then, for all its idealism, is more realistic, in the full tragic sense, than Creon's. To live humanly, in Sophocles' terms, is to know fully the conditions of man's existence; and this means to accept the gods who, in their limitless, ageless power (604ff.) *are* those conditions, the unbending, realities of the universe.

Sophocles never says that to accept the conditions is easy. Yet he seems also to assert that man not only must accept the conditions but

20. See Whitman (note 2) 82–83: "Antigone, with her precise and unshakeable perception of divine law, is the embodiment of the heroic individual in a world whose institutions cannot change but have usurped a right to existence apart from the justifiable interest of the citizens. For such an individual every moment of life is tragic. . . ."

has, or finds, the strength to do so. Even Creon, though far from the broken but still imperious Oedipus at the end of the *Tyrannus,* does not kill himself, crushed as he is. He suffers and endures.

It is in his appreciation of human greatness that Sophocles is the true contemporary of the statesman who sponsored the new Acropolis and Parthenon and of the thinker who said that "Man is the measure of all things." But he is a universal tragic poet in his deeply felt knowledge that man's human qualities, in all their greatness, involve recognition of the unyielding factuality of "the things that are," the gods. The first stasimon is justly described as a praise of man; but exactly what in man Sophocles is praising can be seen only in terms of the entire play. In another chorus the elders sing, "Nothing of magnitude comes into the life of mortals without suffering and disaster" (613–14).

III /

EURIPIDES

CHAPTER 6 /

The Tragedy of the *Hippolytus:*
The Waters of Ocean and
the Untouched Meadow

IN MEMORIAM ARTHUR DARBY NOCK (1902–1963)

The clash of human will and divine power is basic to the tragic sense of Greek drama. Not only may the gods serve to set the tragic action into motion, but they may themselves embody its meaning. As this meaning usually involves some of the most complex and difficult issues of human life, so the nature of the gods and their mode of acting upon the human world are. often puzzling, full of real or apparent contradictions or hard, painful truths.

The *Hippolytus* has its full share of these difficulties.[1] The human motivation in the play is totally comprehensible and satisfying in itself;[2] yet the gods, Aphrodite in the prologue, Artemis in the epi-

---

1. The text used is that of Gilbert Murray (1902; Oxford 1951). Fragments are cited after Nauck. For a bibliography of the *Hippolytus* see Albin Lesky, *Die tragische Dichtung der Hellenen* (Göttingen 1956) 165–66 (3d ed., 1972, 313–14); more recently, Froma I. Zeitlin, "The Power of Aphrodite," in Peter Burian, ed., *Directions in Euripidean Criticism* (Durham 1985), 189ff. I have touched upon some aspects of the imagery in a more general context in C. Segal, "Nature and the World of Man in Greek Literature," *Arion* 2, no. 1 (1963) 41–42.

2. The adequacy of the human motivation is stressed by L. H. G. Greenwood, *Aspects of Euripidean Tragedy* (Cambridge 1953) 44ff.; Gilbert Norwood, *Essays on Euripidean Drama* (Berkeley and Los Angeles 1954) 106ff.; R. P. Winnington-Ingram, "*Hippolytus:* A Study in Causation," in *Euripide: Entretiens sur l'antiquité classique*, vol. 6 (Geneva 1960) 183; Max Pohlenz, *Die griechische Tragödie*, 2d ed. (Göttingen 1954) 1:272, and many others. For the relation of human and divine in the play see in general the principle stated by Lesky (note 1) 168: "Hier nicht vom Menschlichen aus die Götter gesucht werden, sondern die göttlichen Gestalten den Menschen verständlich

165

logue, have significant dramatic, as well as thematic, roles. Their function in the play has often been explained by the claim that Euripides uses them to attack the anthropomorphic religion.[3] While certainly true to some extent, this explanation does not account for the meaning of the play as a whole or for the substantial independence of the human action, which is yet interwoven with the opposed natures and wills of the two goddesses.

It is, as will appear, largely through imagery that these gods are bound into the poetic fabric of the play. Through certain recurrent images of the natural world, notably that of the sea, their power is presented as an effective reality acting upon the human world. The imagery thus leads back to the gods and to the broader issues that their natures and actions raise. Thus, however critically Euripides may have regarded the gods of the traditional religion, he can use them poetically and dramatically to enlarge the scope of the tragedy[4] and to extend its meaning beyond the inward struggles of the protagonists to the question of man's relation to the order (or disorder) of the universe.[5]

The powers of the universe, the objective demands of man's world upon him, the forces of nature to which he is subject: these are central issues in the play. From their origins the Greek gods stand in close connection with these natural powers, and hence through them Euripides can state these broad themes and conflicts without losing dramatic or poetic vividness.[6] He exploits these connections most

---

machen sollen, auf den es dem Dichter ganz vorwiegend ankommt." See 3d ed., 323. Similarly, Winnington-Ingram, 188–89: "It is by the tragedy that we understand the gods, not by the gods that we understand the tragedy."

3. The view that Euripides' purpose in the *Hippolytus* is primarily to satirize the gods has been most fully restated in recent years by Greenwood (note 2) chap. 2, passim.

4. So Louis Méridier, *Euripide*, vol. 2, Budé ed. (Paris 1927) 23: "Par elles [the two goddesses] la tragédie acquiert une ampleur singulière."

5. See Norwood (note 2) 109. This view is perhaps most fully elaborated by B. M. W. Knox, "The *Hippolytus* of Euripides," *YCS* 13 (1952) 1–31.

6. There is a full and interesting statement of the advantages enjoyed by the ancient poet in this regard in Wilamowitz' introduction to his translation, U. von Wilamowitz-Moellendorff, *Griechische Tragödien übersetzt*, I (Berlin 1899) 110–11: "Aber er [the Greek poet] bedient sich des ungeheuren Vorteils, dass er die höchst realen ewigen Mächte, die in dem sittlichen Leben der Menschen walten, nicht als körperlose Abstraktionen belassen muss, wie sie sich dem Denken darstellen, noch zu symbolischen Schatten aus eigner Phantasie gestalten muss: die Phantasie seines Volk-

fully in linking the power of Aphrodite, as it acts throughout the play, with the force of the sea. As an image of the unfolding violence of Aphrodite's power, the sea becomes also a symbol for the demanding realities of the world—which are the gods.

Aphrodite, born from the sea, has all its irrational elementality. She is, as Seneca describes her in his *Phaedra* (274), the goddess *non miti generata ponto*. The imagistic significance of the sea, with its focal position for other images and themes in the play, is a natural outgrowth of the goddess' own nature and the forces with which the Greek mind, in its mythical formulations, had always associated her.

Euripides' imagery, therefore, does not become arbitrary or artificial, a forced or self-conscious literary device, but remains intimately related to a deeply rooted, age-old perception, already stated in poetic or proto-poetic form, about the nature of the love goddess and the love force. Here, as often in classical Greek poetry, the poet finds himself aided in his individual creation by the crystallization of traditional experience and perception in the myth. The myth may thus not only give the poet the general content of plot, characters, setting, and so on, but also, as it seems to do here, may suggest his basic images, his underlying poetic structure.

The relevance of Aphrodite's connection with the sea has, of course, been noted before, and it is well stated by Gilbert Norwood: "In her might and relentless cruelty there dwells 'something of the sea' that gave her birth and across which Phaedra, dogged by her unseen curse, voyaged from Crete." And again: "Aphrodite, the Sea-Queen, wonderful and ruthless like the ocean, bringing joy or grief with indifferent hands."[7] My purpose, however, is to show how the imagery of the sea and related images operate structurally throughout the tragedy, formed as it is under the shadow of the sea-born, sea-

es beut sie ihm dar als leibhaftige Götter, zu Personen, man möchte sagen von Fleisch und Blut, ausgestaltet in der ununterbrochenen dichterischen Arbeit von Jahrhunderten. . . . Lebenserfahrung und Gewissen lehren uns gewiss die tiefe Wahrheit, dass die Negation des Geschlechtstriebes nicht gut ist. . . . Aber wie grau und blass sind diese Gedanken gegenüber der Erscheinung Aphrodites. Die Göttin spricht das alles gar nicht aus. Ihren Willen spricht sie aus, ganz konkret, als mitthätige Person des Dramas," etc. See also Pohlenz (note 2) 1:273–74: "Für den Dramatiker war es ein einzigarter Vorteil, wenn er statt der schwer darstellbaren göttlichen Liebesmacht die Aphrodite des Volksglaubens einführen konnte, die sofort in jedem Zuschauer bestimmte Vorstellungen wachrief."

7. Norwood (note 2) 104 and 105.

wild goddess, and how this imagery underlies the unity of the play and deepens the dimensions and intensity of the tragic action.[8]

It would be mistaken to regard Aphrodite, that jealous, all too human female, as a symbolical figure and nothing else. Yet she obviously signified to Euripides and his audience a great natural force, the instinctive sexual drive in all its relentless power. In this aspect she is Kypris, and is so referred to in the play almost to the exclusion of the more general name, Aphrodite, which occurs, in fact, only three times (532, 539, 765). She had been so treated explicitly in Aeschylus' *Danaids,* and so she recurs, in an unknown play of Euripides, as the authoress of the love and commingling of earth and sky, on which all life depends (frag. 898 Nauck).[9]

Her terrible ambiguity lies in the fact that she is not only a power of the natural world but in a sense also within man: she is that part of him which responds instinctively to the elemental forces in nature and obeys, spontaneously, the same impulses as the animals, as earth and sky. Here through Aphrodite, as through Dionysus in the *Bacchae,* the external and internal aspects of human reality interpenetrate. It is this double aspect of Aphrodite, fused symbolically in the sea, which creates the fullness of the tragedy in the *Hippolytus:* on the one hand, a psychological tragedy, the result of man's futile attempt to suppress a basic part of his nature, and on the other hand, a tragedy of human helplessness before divine power. In other terms, the tragedy juxtaposes man as a part of nature, a creature among creatures, and man as a sentient being with a will and an inner life. Aphrodite,

8. Critics of the symbolist approach, such as Greenwood (note 2), often distort the possible symbolic roles of figures like Aphrodite or elements like the sea by viewing them apart from the poetic fabric of the whole work and only in terms of plot, as if this were the only significant part of the work. They then detach the element in question and ask, What does it represent? See, for instance, Greenwood's discussion of Poseidon (42): "Poseidon could of course represent the sea and all that is therein. . . . But how could the sea and its inhabitants be subject to the will of Theseus so as to become the instruments of his vengeance?" To try to give a single, final meaning to something like the sea in the *Hippolytus* is to misunderstand the nature of poetry. The sea does not represent Aphrodite any more than Poseidon represents the sea.

9. For the connection of Aeschylus' *Danaids* and Euripides frag. 898 with the Aphrodite of the *Hippolytus,* see L. E. Matthaei, *Studies in Greek Tragedy* (Cambridge 1918) 80; also H. D. F. Kitto, *Greek Tragedy* (London 1939) 202; Pohlenz (note 2) 1:274. For this elemental aspect of Aphrodite, see also R. Y. Hathorn, "Rationalism and Irrationalism in Euripides' *Hippolytus,*" *CJ* 52 (1957) 215ff.

whose reality is both biological and psychological, enforces the tragic linking of these two basic parts of the human condition. Her power is exercised both internally and externally; and in both aspects she is, like the sea, irresistible.[10]

These two aspects of Aphrodite correspond to the twofold nature of her dramatic role. She appears in the prologue as part of the external reality, an actor in the tragedy, and so she is spoken of in the exodos. In between, however, she is half real, half metaphorical, a force rather than a person. Thus as the action moves to the purely human sphere, her reality becomes internal rather than external. The same ambiguity is present in her status as a god. As part of external reality, she is indeed a god, an actor who affects the environment in tangible, concrete ways. Yet as an internal force, an instinctive drive pervading all of nature, she is "something greater than a god" (360). It is interesting that in introducing herself she does not say "I *am* a god," but "I am called a god," θεὰ κέκλημαι (2) not θεά εἰμί. Even her role as a dramatis persona is not free from this ambiguity, for as Norwood has well noted, she is more removed from the immediate action than Artemis, though paradoxically the cause of it all;[11] and unlike Artemis, she does not address directly any of her victims, or indeed any human character.

Thus the sea, in its vastness, power, and inscrutability, helps expand her significance beyond the anthropomorphic figure so objectionable to modern critics[12] into an invincible, eternal force. And, as imaged in the sea, this force appears as a surd, preexisting human nature and human questioning and impenetrable to human reason. Aphrodite, like the sea, *is*.

The ambiguity of the sea too makes it an apt symbol for the complexity of Aphrodite's position and her action upon the human characters, for as Euripides and other Greek poets present it, the sea

10. Thus Kitto's limitation of Aphrodite to an internal power seems to lose one of the dimensions of the tragedy: "It is of course because Aphrodite is this, an internal not an external tyrant, that the *Hippolytus* is a tragedy. She is not a "goddess" who torments us for his sport" (note 9, 201 n. 1). Yet in a sense, she *does* so torment us, for her jealousy if not "for her sport."

11. See Norwood (note 2) 102ff. He goes on to distinguish two aspects of Aphrodite in Euripides' mind: for the poet she is a "world-goddess" (104), for the philosopher "a spurious deity" (105). See also Matthei (note 9) 46–47.

12. See, for example, Greenwood (note 2) 45 and Wilamowitz (note 6) 112.

possesses the extremes of beauty when calm and of destructive power when disturbed.13

The symbolic dimensions thus conferred upon the gods are especially important for Euripides. Because of the problematical position in which he places his gods, he needs such active symbols perhaps more than a poet who simply accepts the traditional religion. In an age of growing skepticism and rationalism, these symbolic counterparts of the gods are, at one level, perhaps more real and true to him than the actual anthropomorphic figures.

Within the *Hippolytus* itself, the sea has several levels of significance, not always easily separable. In purely literal terms the sea is a simple physical element, neutral in itself but, like all aspects of the physical world, potentially destructive. The sea in this aspect has also a historical reality: associations with the past, as the sea that Phaedra crossed from Crete. On the mythical level the sea is connected with powerful divinities, Aphrodite and Poseidon; it is the sphere ruled over by gods whose power is active in human affairs. At this level the inert matter of the physical world becomes potent with divine, often sinister force. Finally, the sea, detached by one step from its gods, becomes symbolic of the unfathomable forces that course through the universe and human life. Its effectiveness as a symbol lies partly in the fact that its scope is without precisely definable limits. It can be viewed, for example, psychologically or metaphysically. Its range is as wide as the scope of the tragedy itself.

The range of the play's significance is established in the opening lines (1–6):

Powerful and not without name, I am called the goddess Kypris, both among mortals and in the heavens; and all who look on the light of the sun and dwell within the ocean Pontos and the limits of Atlas—those who revere my power I put first in honor and those who think big toward me I trip up.

13. For the beauty of the calm sea, cf. *Hel.* 1451ff., *IT* 421ff. For its association with violent passion, cf. *HF* 861 and frag. 1089, where an angry woman is compared to the sea. For the significance of the sea in Attic tragedy generally, see Albin Lesky, *Thalatta* (Vienna 1947) 215ff. For its connection with violent forces, see esp. 227–29, and for the sea in Euripides in general, 246ff. with the bibliographical references in notes 261 and 294.

It includes mortals and heaven (1–2), the sea and the sun (3–4). Aphrodite, the sea-born goddess, defines in terms of the sea the boundaries of the mortal realm over which she has power: "Those who dwell within the ocean Pontos and the limits of Atlas" (Πόντον τερμόνων τ' Ἀτλαντικῶν, 3). The human world is placed between two seas, and in the following action the sea will well up and destroy a representative portion of the human world it surrounds. What here only marks the geographical limits of human life will soon play an active part in its substance. The course of the action can be followed in terms of the advance of the sea; and because the outcome is known beforehand, the power of the destroying element is the more terrible and its release the more inevitable.

Aphrodite's prologue, in stating the situation, states also the basic opposition between herself and Hippolytus in terms of the sea. The "pale-green woods" (χλωρὰν δ' ἀν' ὕλην, 17) wherein the youth associates with his virgin goddess (παρθένῳ)[14] are a foil for the darkness of the surging sea. The instrument of his destruction will be the woman whom Theseus transported across the sea (ναυστολεῖ, 36); and the vengeance will be completed in the destructive aspect of the sea that belongs to Poseidon "the sea lord" (ὁ πόντιος ἄναξ, 44–45; see Πόντου, 3). The sea is thus associated at once with the female passion of Aphrodite (and Phaedra) and the male anger and violence of Poseidon (and Theseus). In both these aspects it will overwhelm the devotee of the virgin woodland goddess.

In the first lines, Aphrodite speaks of her power in the heavens (οὐρανοῦ τ' ἔσω, 2) as well as on earth; but Hippolytus enters, in a dramatic contrast, immediately after the prologue, singing of "the heavenly [οὐρανίαν] daughter of Zeus, Artemis" (59–60). The contrast is sharpened by the hunters' chorus (61ff.), which takes up his prayer and, though praising Artemis, blithely echoes parts of Aphrodite's sinister speech (64–69):[15]

14. The theme of the *parthenos* is a recurrent motif in the play. Hippolytus maintains his "virgin soul" in the face of his father's accusations (1006) and is to be immortalized finally in the songs of maidens (*parthenoi*, 1428). Artemis speaks also of her "maidenly joy" in opposition to Aphrodite (1302). On the other hand, Phaedra, when struggling to maintain her honor and virtue, speaks of time's revealing the evil men "as if holding up a mirror before a young maiden" (429).

15. The chorus' invocation to Artemis as *semnotatē* (61) perhaps also helps establish the association between the goddess and her follower, described shortly after as *semnos* (see 93ff.) though in a far more negative sense (see also 957, 1064, 1364).

Euripides

> . . . ὦ κόρα
> Λατοῦς Ἄρτεμι καὶ Διός, [cf. Ἄρτεμιν, Διὸς κόρην, 15]
> καλλίστα πολὺ παρθένων [cf. παρθένῳ, 17],
> ἃ μέγαν κατ' οὐρανὸν [cf. οὐρανοῦ τ' ἔσω, 2]
> ναίεις [cf. ναίουσιν, 4] εὐπατέρειαν αὐ- / λάν . . .

As Aphrodite is here juxtaposed with Artemis, so sea is opposed to sky, and the latter, as will be seen, appears throughout the play as a place of futile escape until it too is finally touched by the sea that destroys Hippolytus (κῦμ' οὐρανῷ στηρίζον, 1207).

Hippolytus' first significant speech (73–87) develops the theme of his purity and devotion to his pure goddess. The untouched garden from which he offers her the wreath is an ambiguous symbol of chastity (see *Song of Songs* 4:12: "A garden inclosed is my sister, my spouse"; also Catullus 11.22ff.: *velut prati ultimi flos . . .*). The gift of the crown "from an untouched meadow" is a symbolic offering of his sexuality to the virgin goddess, a concrete embodiment of the offer that he makes every day of his life. This scene thus presents a symbolical enactment of Hippolytus' whole way of life, and it does so in terms of the pure woodland to which Aphrodite had referred bitterly in her prologue (17). This sheltered woodland, however, will soon encounter the violent sea. The bee of spring which goes around it (77) will recur as the sign of the ever-present Kypris (563).[16] The modesty (*aidos*) that waters this "untouched meadow" with the moisture of its rivers (ποταμίαισι κηπεύει δρόσοις, 78) will reappear shortly as a motive force in the mind of the passion-filled, Kypris-swayed Phaedra (see 385ff.).[17] Even the adjective "untouched" (ἀκήρατος, 73, 76) will be flung bitterly back at Hippolytus, accused of unchastity, by the angry Theseus (σὺ σώφρων καὶ κακῶν ἀκήρατος, 949) and will reflect the chorus' hope for something to be found only in the realm of prayer, "a mind untouched by sufferings" (1114), when Hippolytus' banishment is a reality.

It is in the parodos, directly after the old servant's attempt to

16. For the parallel between 77 and 563 see Knox (note 5) 28.

17. For the role of aidos in the tragedy, see E. R. Dodds, "The *Aidos* of Phaedra and the Meaning of the *Hippolytus*," *CR* 39 (1925) 102–4. For the religious nature of Hippolytus' aidos and its connections with his "untouched meadow" and his sophrosyne, see A.-J. Festugière, *Personal Religion among the Greeks,* Sather Classical Lectures 26 (Berkeley and Los Angeles 1954) 12–13.

reproach Hippolytus for his neglect of Kypris (88–118), that the sea makes its first extended appearance in the play. The intricate first strophe begins with "Ocean," and develops a quiet and lovely scene: the spring and the sun-warmed rocks where the women of Troezen wash their clothes. Thus is an immediate contrast created between this women's world, with its pleasant domestic tasks, and Hippolytus' troop of hunters. Here sea contrasts with woodland, ocean with pure river, the languid flowing of water over the rocks with the strenuous activities of the austere young men. The contrast is sharpened by the echo of Hippolytus' "river dews," ποταμίαισι . . . δρόσοις (78), in the chorus' ποταμία δρόσῳ (127). The sea is here calm, beautiful, the gathering place for the good matrons of Troezen. Yet sea is the element of Aphrodite, and it is toward the end of the first strophe that we hear first of Phaedra, unnamed as yet, only "my mistress" (δέσποινα, 130). The antistrophe develops the full picture of Phaedra's passion-caused "sickness" (131ff.); and it is a fine stroke of Euripides' poetic imagination that the passion-sick queen should be introduced in this setting, by the sea. At the mention of Phaedra, the gentle sea of the first strophe becomes sinister and dangerous. The death to which her self-starvation is leading her is described, in one of the recurrent metaphors of the play, as a shipwreck: θανάτου θέλου- / σαν κέλσαι ποτὶ τέρμα δύστανον ("wishing to reach shore at death's grim end," 139–40). The first strophic system thus begins to create a juxtaposition between the peaceful, domestic life of woman and woman as passionate, unstable, self-destructive. The calm sea, with its happy associations, is what Phaedra is leaving behind. It is a reference point back to her life before Kypris entered it. Henceforth she—and we—will know the sea in its disturbed and destructive aspect.

With this first description of Phaedra's sickness in the antistrophe, there appears also a fuller intimation of the wildness of the natural world. The chorus asks if Phaedra is afflicted by Pan or Hecate, or the Corybantes or the Mountain Mother (141–44), all ambiguous divinities associated with the elemental powers of nature. Then they ask about Dictynna, whose connection with the wild is emphasized by the epithet πολύθηρον ("of much hunting," 145). Dictynna is, paradoxically, an aspect of Artemis (see e.g., *IT* 127) and, as πολύθηρος, would be, one might expect, connected somehow with Hippolytus. Yet here she is associated with Phaedra's passion and the sea: "For she [Dictynna] travels also through the marsh and over the dry land by the sea in the brine's sea-whirls" (149–51). There is perhaps a certain suspense and irony built up by the chorus' failure to name the goddess who is really responsible; they increase the irony by dwelling instead upon her enemy, Dictynna-Artemis, in terms of the element that symbolizes Aphrodite's own power. Yet the invocation of Dictynna is perhaps more to the mark than the chorus knows. She belongs to the Cretan past, to the dangerous, passion-filled ancestry of Phaedra, for in legend she was pursued nine months by Minos, Phaedra's father, before plunging into the sea to escape (see Callimachus, *Hymn* 3.189–203), and her worship was especially prominent in Crete.[18] The aspect of the sea associated with her too is different from the peace of the first strophe: there the warm rocks, dripping with pure water; here the giddy whirl of sand by the shore, something of the passion and desperation surrounding Dictynna's leap. The Marsh (*Limna*) referred to here is probably also the sanctuary of Artemis at which Hippolytus exercises his horses,[19] and as such is soon to be called upon with longing by the Aphrodite-possessed Phaedra (228; see 1131ff.). The reference to Dictynna, especially in conjunction with the sea, thus leads deeper into Phaedra's passion and begins to adumbrate the involvement in it of Hippolytus and his world.

In the antistrophe the chorus continues questioning and asks if anyone sailing from Crete has brought bad news (155ff.). The sea is again the conveyer of misfortune, and the crossing of it a token of disaster. The chorus has already spoken of Phaedra's coming death as a shipwreck (140); and Aphrodite referred briefly to Theseus' carrying Phaedra over the sea (ναυστολεῖ, 36). In a later ode the ship that brought Phaedra will be pronounced ill-omened (752ff.). In the present ode, however, though the reference is not to Phaedra's own crossing, the chorus establishes her connection, through the sea, with Crete, the land of sinister passions to which Dictynna already points.

The chorus ends, in the epode (162ff.), with a woman's prayer to Artemis, goddess of childbirth—"the heavenly Artemis who gives

18. For Dictynna, see "Britomartis" in W. H. Roscher, ed., *Ausführliches Lexikon der griechischen und römischen Mythologie* (Leipzig 1884–86) I.1, 822ff. Also Jessen, "Diktynna," *RE* 9 (1903) 584ff.

19. See Wilamowitz (note 6) 178 (*ad vs.* 150): "Die Beziehung auf das auch 228 und 1132 gennante Lokal Limne konnte nur Verstocktheit noch leugnen."

good births" (εὔλοχον οὐρανίαν). Thus as the women of the chorus turn back from the dangerous passions of their Cretan mistress to the burdens of normal wifehood and motherhood and the goddess who helps them therein, they also turn back from the turbulent sea to the sky (as they are to do later in the "escape" ode, 732ff.). A sinister connection with the wild remains, however, in the other epithet they give Artemis. They call her "mistress of arrows" (167), the weapons that connect her and her hunter-follower, Hippolytus, with the wild, weapons that she will use to destroy Aphrodite's favorite in the future (1422, 1451).[20]

With Phaedra's appearance and the first episode (170–524), the tension is deepened between woodland and sea, fresh waters and troubled sea, Artemis and Aphrodite. Phaedra's longing for a draught of "pure waters" (209) and for a "grassy meadow" (210) recall the pure waters of Hippolytus' aidos (78) and the "untouched meadow" from which he brings his offering (73–74). She longs too for the woodland (ὕλαν, 215) and the hunting of wild beasts, and desires "to hurl the Thessalian javelin holding the barbed missile in my hand" (220–22). The Nurse echoes her plaint in words that underline (unknown to her) the connection with Hippolytus' haunts (cf. κρηναίων ναομῶν, "streams from springs," 225; δροσερά, "dewy," 226). Then Phaedra calls upon "Mistress Artemis of Limne by the sea" (228) and expresses her desire to train horses in her sanctuary, so that the Nurse again wonders at her "love for horses by the waveless sands" (234–35). The language here draws both upon the earlier description of Hippolytus' surroundings (74ff.) and upon the sea imagery of the preceding choral ode.

With Phaedra's entrance, then, the innocence of woodland and mountains (233), of hunting and horse riding, becomes touched by a more complex element, her hidden erotic desires. She gives the "meadow" in which she would recline the sensuously suggestive epithet κομήτῃ ("with tresses of grass," 210). Indeed, for Phaedra the meadow has associations exactly opposite to those it had for Hippolytus.[21] She, or the Nurse, uses repeatedly the verb ἔραμαι ("love," 219, 225, 236, and note πόθον, "desire," 234). The ambiguity is, of

---

20. For Artemis' arrows in her revenge, see Knox (note 5) 30–31.

21. For the erotic implications of the meadow here see Knox (note 5) 6 n.8, citing Eur. *Cycl.* 171. Compare Shakespeare's *Venus and Adonis* 229ff. Ovid puts a similar metaphor, with deliberate erotic implications, into the mouth of his Phaedra: *Heroides*

course, inherent in her situation, that she cannot reveal the truth of her longing though it is of itself seeking release and expression in these cryptic desires. This very ambiguity, therefore, tinges the natural world, as here presented, with a complexity that it lacked in the statements of either Hippolytus or the chorus. For Phaedra, too, these elements of wild nature are dangerously near. The chorus spoke of them as something remote and terrible (see 141ff.), but Phaedra actually wants to enter the wild. Hence, too, her appeal to Artemis has a new ambiguity. It is to give utterance to her passion that she calls upon the pure, maidenly goddess, invoked before by Hippolytus and the chorus: δέσποιν' ἁλίας Ἄρτεμι Λίμνας ("Mistress Artemis of Limne by the sea," 228) are her words. The adjective "of the sea"[22] thus recalls not only the chorus' disturbed invocation to Dictynna but also the goddess under whose power she really lies. In the name of Artemis she is in fact calling upon Aphrodite; and through the ambiguity of her situation the calm world of Hippolytus and the chorus, the wilds and the gentle sea, begin to be invaded by her restless passion and become transformed into the images of her desire.

The ambiguity of her situation is increased by the emphasis on horses (with an obvious erotic allusion in 231).[23] The horse will, in fact, recur in the play as an erotic metaphor (546, 1425). At the end of this exchange, however, the Nurse speaks of Phaedra as being "reined out of her path" (ἀνασειράζει, 237) by one of the gods. The horse, in Phaedra's transformation, refers no longer to Hippolytus' chaste pursuits but to Phaedra's ardent desire, no longer to Artemis (with whom Phaedra ostensibly associates it) but to Aphrodite who has, in truth, reined back Phaedra like a horse. Possessed by the sea-wild goddess, she dwells on the free-running violence of the horse. The connection is complex, for the horses, though associated with Artemis, are connected explicitly with the sea through Limne and the "waveless shore" (235–36). Here *eros* (see ἔρασαι, 236), sea-sand,

---

4.29–30. So too the *belos* that Phaedra wishes to hold and hurl (220–22) may have erotic connotations. Note its explicit connection later with Eros in 530.

22. The reading δέσποινα δίας . . . Λίμνας found in some manuscripts is surely only a scribal error for the much more appropriate δέσποιν' ἁλίας . . . Λίμνας, Λ and Δ lending themselves easily to such a confusion, compounded by a misdivision of the words.

23. For the erotic association of the horse here see Knox (note 5) 6 with note 8, citing Anacreon frag. 75 D. See also Horace *Odes* 3.11.9ff.

and horses are united—albeit in a still indefinite way—in Phaedra's desire; and so they will be finally, in Hippolytus' end.

The tension relaxes somewhat in the ensuing dialogue between the Nurse and the chorus (267ff.);[24] but, as it builds up again toward the terrible revelation, the power of the sea returns. The Nurse complains that Phaedra is not "softened" or "moistened" (ἐτέγγετο) by her words (303), using the verb that occurred in the parodos of the women's innocent washing by the sea (127)—the calm sea that Phaedra is leaving behind. Then, turning to Phaedra abruptly in the next line, she urges her to be "bolder than the sea" (304–5). The change of address from the chorus to Phaedra and from the third back to the second person in these lines (300–305), an effect of which the ancients were well aware,[25] marks a heightening of the tension. As Phaedra's passion was introduced earlier by the sea, so the sea here accompanies the revelation of the fearfulness of that passion. The horse, too, is present at this new critical point, in the Nurse's oath by "the Amazon, mistress of the horse" (ἄνασσαν ἱππίαν, 307), echoed immediately after in Ἱππόλυτον (310), the name that wrings from Phaedra her first cry of weakness—οἴμοι—and sets in motion the final revelation. A few lines later she speaks of her subjection to her passion in terms of a storm (χειμάζομαι, 315), an image of helplessness before a raging sea, recalling the image of shipwreck which the chorus used of her approaching death by starvation in the parodos (140). The violence of the sea, now full upon her, is about to burst upon the Nurse and the chorus. Under the Nurse's cross-examination she calls upon her sinister Cretan heredity (337ff.) and finally can bring out ὁ τῆς ᾽Αμαζόνος, which the Nurse quickly completes with Ἱππόλυτον (351–52), repeating the telling words from 307–10. The Nurse then ends with the famous statement of Kypris' power: "Kypris, then, is found to be no god, but something greater than a god, whatever it is, who destroys her and me and the house" (359–61). The sea, virginity (the Amazon), Kypris, and finally Crete at the end of choral song (362–72) thus combine to introduce Phaedra's first coherent statement of her position (373ff.).

---

24. The pattern of the alternating relaxation and heightening of tension is well noted by Matthaei (note 9) 86, 89–90, and passim.

25. See for example, ps.-Longinus, *De Sublim.* 26–27, on τῶν προσώπων ἀντιμετάθεσις.

The interplay between emotion and logic, lyric and dialogue, is especially intense here. Phaedra's confession and the Nurse's statement of Aphrodite's power (359–61) seem of themselves to release the disturbed and passionate dochmiacs at 362; and these significantly end with another statement about the τύχα Κύπριδος ("ill fortune from Kypris," 371–72) and with the chorus' pitiful cry, ὦ τάλαινα παῖ Κρησία ("O unhappy Cretan child," 372).

It is with these last words ringing in her ears that Phaedra begins her famous speech to the women of Troezen (373ff.) in which she sets forth her attempt, and failure, to "conquer Kypris" (401) and her resolution to die. The sea plays a small though significant part in this scene and the following chorus; but the sense of the approaching violence is carried by other lines of imagery. The elemental force of eros manifests itself in phrases like μ' ἔρως ἔτρωσεν ("love wounded me," 392), νικῶσα ("conquering," 399), Κύπριν κρατῆσαι ("to overcome Kypris," 401); and these contrast tragically with the quieter words of will and intention (ἐσκόπουν, 392; προυνοησάμην, 399; βουλευμάτων, 402). This imagery of conquest and violence will emerge even more fully later in the language of the chorus.

In the midst of her ensuing denunciation of adulterous women (407ff.), however, Phaedra calls upon "Lady Kypris of the sea" (δέσποινα ποντία Κύπρι, 415). Thus at the moment when she is most fully resolved to preserve her marital purity, she calls upon the goddess who is causing her ruin and addresses her in the name of the malignant element through which her power will be made manifest. This epithet, ποντία, evokes again the vastness of Aphrodite's power and the ruthless will behind it which the goddess announced in the opening lines (Πόντου, 3). Phaedra's invocation of "Aphrodite of the sea" perhaps recalls too her earlier appeal to "Lady Artemis of Limne by the sea" (228). Then she was still concealing her passion and, one might say, invoking Artemis with Aphrodite in her heart and mind. Now, however, the truth of her domination by Aphrodite is revealed, and the revelation is coupled with the sea.

The Nurse, in her counter-speech (432ff.), completes the revelation with a fuller statement of Aphrodite's power; yet she lacks the full knowledge of what it is that she is releasing. Thus she tells Phaedra, "the goddess' wrath has fallen upon you" (438), but has no sense of how implacable and destructive is this wrath. Actually, of course, the Nurse is mistaken, for the object of the goddess' wrath is Hippolytus, not Phaedra; and it is only the indifference of the goddess which is to involve Phaedra's death with his: ἣ δ᾽ εὐκλεὴς μέν, ἀλλ᾽ ὅμως ἀπόλλυται, / Φαίδρα ("Phaedra is of good fame, but even so she shall be destroyed," 47f.). Her ruthless power is then presented in terms of the sea: "Kypris is not to be endured if she flows full on" (ἢν πολλὴ ῥυῆι, 443). She is like an onrushing wave, and the image is developed a few lines later: "Kypris travels in the air, she's in the sea-surge [ἐν θαλασσίῳ / κλύδωνι]; everything is born from her" (447–48). The juxtaposition of sky and sea again suggests Aphrodite's words in the opening lines, here restated by one of the mortals who is to prove subject to them (cf. also πολλή, 1 and 443). No part of nature is free of Aphrodite. Earlier the chorus rather innocently saw the cause of Phaedra's condition in Dictynna (Artemis) who frequents the sea (149ff.), but the power and essence of the sea as the force behind Phaedra's tragedy are to be found instead with Dictynna's opposite, Aphrodite.[26] The Nurse here gives instances of her power in the sky (Zeus, Eos),[27] and when the tragedy is complete, the truth of her omnipresence will receive its full and final formulation (see 1268ff.).

The Nurse continues the imagery of the destructive sea in asking Phaedra how she will "swim out" (ἐκνεῦσαι, 469) of the misfortune into which she has fallen. Phaedra, in the power of Aphrodite, is like a swimmer, helpless, in a wild sea, thanks to the will of the goddess (θεὸς ἐβουλήθη τάδε, 476). It is part of the tragic helplessness of both Phaedra and the Nurse that the latter uses these images of the raging sea and the feeble swimmer when she hopes to save. The imagery thus reflects the tragic pattern that marks the whole course of the Nurse's interference in Phaedra's passion.

At the end of her speech the Nurse, having failed by rational means (her verbal arguments), resorts to irrational: the hope of enchantment, spells, or charms, ἐπῳδαὶ καὶ λόγοι θελκτήριοι, as a possible drug or cure (φάρμακον) for Phaedra's "disease" (478–79). Here again the Nurse's short-term expediency involves her in a limited grasp of the situation and even in self-contradiction. She who admit-

26. Compare φοιτᾶι γὰρ καὶ διὰ λίμνας of Dictynna in 149 with φοιτᾶι δ᾽ ἀν᾽ αἰθέρα, κ.τ.λ. of Aphrodite in 447. The parallel is noted also by G. M. A. Grube, *The Drama of Euripides* (London 1941; rpt New York 1961) 182 n.2.

27. This passage on the power of eros among gods and men may be modeled on the earlier *Hippolytos Kalyptomenos:* see frag. 431, where men and gods, gods and sea, are juxtaposed as victims and subjects of Eros, and Zeus is also mentioned.

ted the power of Aphrodite as a pervasive force in nature (447–50) hopes to escape this force by means outside nature, by spells and magic. Phaedra, however, still resists, and does so in language that recalls the Nurse's initial despair on hearing of her mistress' passion. There, before she had time to make her "second thoughts" (436), the Nurse spoke of the more-than-divine Aphrodite as "destroying the house" (δόμους ἀπώλεσεν, 361). Here Phaedra uses the same phrase (δόμους τ' ἀπόλλυσι) of the "fine words" *of the Nurse* (487). Thus as Phaedra moves closer to her doom, her would-be savior comes to embody the very power she would evade. In seeking to circumvent Aphrodite's destructive power, the Nurse only becomes her agent. Mortals fulfill Aphrodite's will by their very means of escape.

Phaedra's brief statement of continued resistance is met by the Nurse's accusation of σεμνότης (σεμνομυθεῖς, 490), haughtiness toward the gods and the necessities they represent, the same reproach as was made, for a similar reason, to Hippolytus (93ff.). Thus the fates of the two victims begin to converge in terms of the goddess who is destroying them. And at this point Phaedra begins to weaken, first in 498–99, and more significantly in 503ff.: Speak no further, she says; my soul is "subdued" (ὑπείργασμαι) to eros; if you go on, I shall be taken by that which I flee. The verb ὑπείργασμαι continues the violent, warlike imagery noted above (392ff.), especially if, as one commentator has claimed, the metaphor refers to the undermining of a town (though no such usage is clearly attested). The verb is also used, however, of plowing a field and thus metaphorically does take Phaedra back "to that which I flee," to Aphrodite the "sower [ἡ σπείρουσα, 449] of eros," the giver of all generation on earth (448–50). It is not, of course, impossible that both metaphors, the violent and the sexual, are intended: the mixture of destructive and creative or procreative is essential to the ambiguity of Aphrodite's nature.

The Nurse, however, takes up her advantage and presses at the point where Phaedra is vulnerable, the charms, the magical and irrational, that which is beyond the strict logic by which Phaedra has held down her passion (see 391ff.). It is part of the tragedy of Phaedra's nature that she who maintained her strength of will and rational control for so long should yield so quickly to the irrational hopes held out by the Nurse. The surrender to the magical charms is the surrender of her reason, as the reversion to her childhood trust in the

Nurse is the surrender of her will.[28] She becomes a tragic exemplar of her own dictum (381–82):

τὰ χρήστ᾽ ἐπιστάμεσθα καὶ γιγνώσκομεν,
οὐκ ἐκπονοῦμεν δ᾽ . . .

We know what is right and understand it, but do not fulfil it.

Thus Phaedra seizes upon these "love charms" (φίλτρα . . . θελκτήρια ἔρωτος, 509–10) which she ignored shortly before (see 478–79); and asks, perhaps half-conscious of what her question implies, "Is the drug [φάρμακον] something to be used as ointment or to be drunk?" (516). At the beginning of her long speech previously, Phaedra had spoken confidently of her resolution and clear moral perceptions, affirming that no "drug" (φάρμακον) could make her change her mind (388–90). But now she has accepted, against her well-reasoned intention, a drug of a very different kind, one that vitiates her reason, indeed all rationality, and with it her life.[29] When her ruin is complete, the Nurse is to exclaim, "I searched and found

28. The point of Phaedra's surrender of her will to the Nurse is well made by Knox (note 5) 11: "She is now a child again, and the Nurse does for the grown woman what she had always done for the child—evades her questions, makes light of her fears, relieves her of responsibility, and decides for her." Phaedra, however, must still bear the guilt and the consequences of her acquiescence, passive though it may be, to the Nurse's scheme. Euripides leaves it ambiguous—intentionally, it would seem—as to what Phaedra thinks these pharmaka will do, dispel her passion or get her the man. The ambiguity is part of the complexity of her character and the delicate insight and handling of Euripides, which the harshness of textual surgery should not destroy. The subtlety of Euripides' handling of the *pharmaka* and Phaedra's submission to the Nurse is admirably pointed out by W. S. Barrett, *Euripides, Hippolytus* (Oxford 1964) on lines 507–24 (pp. 252–53); see also his comments on lines 509–12, 513–15, 516–21 (pp. 254–56). The complex entanglement of guilt and innocence in Phaedra are stressed at the end of the play too; see 1300–1301 and Barrett *ad loc.* (p. 399). On 1305 (οὐχ ἑκοῦσα) he remarks, "Those who believe that Phaedra consented in the end to the Nurse's scheme are doing so in the face of the poet's own denial: Artemis has no axe to grind for Phaedra, and her judgment here is certainly the poet's own."

29. These charms or drugs, like Phaedra's surrender of reason and life to Aphrodite's power, are to continue to work destructively upon Hippolytus, for he appears later in Theseus' eyes as a deceitful enchanter. Again, that which would save or cure only brings worse ills and deeper involvement in Aphrodite's design. The repetition of the theme of enchantment, moreover, perhaps suggests the same conquest of reason by passion working on Theseus as in Phaedra.

drugs [φάρμακα] for your disease—but not those I wished" (698–99).

And here, into this breach in Phaedra's will and reason, the destructive sea pours. The Nurse gives utterance to her hopes of saving her mistress with another invocation to Kypris of the sea: "Only may you, Lady Kypris of the sea, be a helper" (522–23). The phrase δέσποινα ποντία Κύπρι is identical (in verse-position also) with Phaedra's earlier invocation of the goddess in her tirade against adulterous wives (415) and makes clearer her tragic helplessness before the goddess and the ultimate weakness of resolve and reason: Phaedra is to become, through Kypris, one of those women whom she has cursed in the name of Kypris.

The repetition perhaps intimates also a certain ambiguity in this earlier resolve: even there, in the vehemence of her asseverations, Kypris and the sea were acting upon her will, although it is by them that she swears her purity. The sea here is thus in part a psychological symbol, reflecting a complex subjective aspect of the protagonist. It reflects powerful drives operating inwardly but repressed.[30] In line 415 Phaedra attempts to transform into its opposite this element of sea-Kypris latent in her; but here in line 522 it begins to emerge for what it is. In this sense the goddess whom the Nurse invokes as a "helper in the deed" (συνεργός, 523) has already been helping her from within Phaedra. She is the unconscious part of Phaedra's psyche which wishes to yield. On the level of the literal narrative, too, the invocation to Kypris as a helper is deeply ironical: the Nurse has no idea how willing a helper the goddess already is and how destructive is the sea power by which she calls upon her.

It is with the sea, then, ποντία Κύπρις, that the first great crisis in the tragedy is reached. The following powerful chorus on Eros (525ff.) develops the theme of violence and human helplessness latent in the preceding scene (392, 399, 401, 470) and complements the destructive power of the sea with its opposite, *fire*. No missile of fire is more powerful than that of Eros (530–34). Eros gave Iole to Heracles amid blood and smoke (551). The union that joined Zeus and Semele for the birth of Dionysus was accompanied by the "fiery thunder" (βροντᾷ ἀμφιπύρῳ) which took Semele's life (559ff.). In Semele, who is consumed by the fire of her lover and yet brings forth

30. For the theme of repression see Dodds (note 17) 102–4.

the divine child, is imaged the fearful ambiguity of Kypris as a generative and destructive force. Aphrodite breathes fearfully (δεινά) upon everything, and yet she is a bee, the maker of sweetness, that flits through the air (563–64).[31] The fire, followed by the image of the bee flying, is perhaps to be associated with the presence of Aphrodite in the air. With the reference to the stars in line 530, these images continue to widen the scope of Aphrodite's power in accordance with her opening words in the prologue.

This power, fully revealed in its destructiveness, is now turned against the calm world of the past. The verb στάζεις ("drip," 526) recalls the "rock dripping [στάζουσα, 121] the waters of Ocean" and the pure, clear waters of an untroubled domestic happiness in the parodos. Here, however, it is "desire" that is dripping, and the verb is also suggestive of the dangerous *pharmakon* through which Phaedra has yielded to the Nurse and Kypris (516). The missile (βέλος, 530) is no longer the weapon of the pure hunter in the wild (222) but the fire-blazing dart hurled by Eros. The bee is here associated with the destructive, omnipresent Aphrodite, not the "untouched meadow" of virginity and Artemis (77). The horse, too, connected with Hippolytus' pure and austere life, is here an unambiguously erotic metaphor, joined with fire, blood, and (if the text is right) marriage-songs that bode disaster (545ff.). The elemental force of Kypris thus invades and disturbs the calm world of Hippolytus and Artemis, of Troezen before Phaedra.

In the second antistrophe the violence of Eros is presented in dangerous proximity to spring-waters. The imagery of calm water is familiar from Hippolytus' speech on aidos (78) and the parode. Here the "mouth of Dirce," the Theban fountain, is called upon as a witness to the fiery marriage and parturition of Semele. Yet it is not the clear water of Dirce alone that is called upon, but the "holy wall of Thebes" itself. The enclosed life of the town, with its traditions and sanctity, calm as the waters of its springs, is threatened, or at least awed, by Aphrodite's power. Nor is the introduction of Dirce and the Theban wall merely fortuitous, for Eros in the ode is truly a destroyer of civilizations, approaching like an army (see ἐπιστρατεύσῃ, 527) with dreadful weapons (530), a sacker of cities (πέρθοντα, 541) bringing

---

31. Cf. also what the Nurse says of love in line 348: ἥδιστον, ὦ παῖ, ταὐτὸν ἀλγεινόν θ᾽ ἅμα.

fire, smoke, blood (545ff.). Both the fire and the military imagery thus converge destructively upon human order as embodied in the city wall and the city springs.[32] The ode thus universalizes the power of Eros and carries the implications of his impact beyond the individual life to human civilization as a whole. Yet at the end it leaves us with the delicate picture of the flitting bee.

At the dramatic climax of the play, where Phaedra and Hippolytus' personalities clash most directly, sea again becomes a controlling image. In his angry denunciation of women, Hippolytus reverts to the pure streams of his first speech (78): he will wash out his ears with "swift-flowing streams" (ῥυτοῖς ναϲμοῖϲιν, 653), dashing the water into them (ἐς ὦτα κλύζων, 654). The purity of the streams belongs to his life as he has lived it hitherto, with its calm and serenity. Now, however, the flood has broken, and this past world is being transformed by the violence of Aphrodite. The word ῥυτοῖς "flowing," recalls the onrushing flood of Kypris (ῥυῆ "flow," 443); the κλύζων (properly of the dashing of waves, a violent word: see *Ag.* 1181–82) suggests the "sea-flood" of Kypris (θαλασσίῳ κλύδωνι, 447–48). Hippolytus is led by his vehemence into the same kind of violence as that which has come from the sea-surge of the love goddess to overwhelm Phaedra. And this vehemence, of course, brings about his doom. He follows up this assertion by a characteristic, and equally disastrous, affirmation of his self-righteousness: "How then would I be evil who think that I am not pure if I but hear such things?" (654–55). Yet the impact of Aphrodite's violence upon his untroubled purity is perhaps reflected in his wish, shortly before, that women be allowed no maids but only "voiceless wild beasts" (ἄφθογγα . . . δάκη θηρῶν, 646–47). These beasts no longer belong to the innocent wild of Artemis; instead, the dangerous, passion-filled violence of Aphrodite begins to affect Hippolytus' world. Again there is an ironic connection between his own violence, wherewith he plays into Kypris' hands, and his coming destruction: his passionate outcry that a woman should have only voiceless companions will confirm Phaedra's suicide and her plan to leave behind a tablet that will "shout" (βοᾷ βοᾷ δέλτος ἄλαστα, 877) and "have voice" (φθεγγόμενον,

---

32. For the association of springs with the order and traditions of civilization, see *Od.* 17.205–11. Compare also the association of the Trojan springs with peace and domesticity before the coming of war and the Greeks in *Il.* 22.147–56.

880). On another level, this violence is the force of Kypris latent in him; but because repressed, it emerges as its opposite, with overcompensation in the extravagance and virulence of his denunciations.

At this point, then, the peaceful woodland of Hippolytus becomes touched by the sea world of Aphrodite and begins itself to become ambiguous, to turn against the hero as will his own horses later. In Phaedra's eyes, Hippolytus begins to become one of the wild beasts he hunts, sharing their cruelty and recklessness, their instinctive, unreflecting action. Earlier, when she first heard his denunciations, she associated him, by a verbal play, with his horse-loving Amazon mother, a creature of the wild, lacking ordinary womanly feelings (581–82: ὁ τῆς φιλίππου παῖς ᾿Αμαζόνος βοᾷ / ῾Ιππόλυτος . . . ; also 307–10). Then after his outburst, immediately upon her new resolve to die, she speaks of him as having "his mind sharpened by anger" (ὀργῇ συντεθηγμένος φρένας, 689). The verb is commonly used of wild boars sharpening their tusks savagely.[33] It thus reveals what Phaedra here sees in Hippolytus: the negative, inhuman aspects of the wild he loves. It is again part of the ironical ambiguity in which Hippolytus' world—and his goddess—are placed that later, in a striking metaphor, the tablets that Phaedra has left, which Hippolytus' extreme reaction has forced her to write, are said to "fawn upon" Theseus (προσσαίνουσι, 863). The wild animal is led to his doom by his very wildness, and the destroyer is the tame animal, the fawner. Hence, too, when Phaedra has formed her design, she swears the chorus to silence by "revered Artemis, daughter of Zeus" (713), the goddess of Hippolytus and the goddess of the untouched wild.

This untouched wild, however, with what belongs to it, is so far only a secondary, though contributing, agent. It becomes active and dangerous only through its contact with and opposition to the surging sea. Sea is still the primary motive force, and Phaedra is to be its first victim. She who could barely "swim out" (470) of her troubles is now totally overwhelmed by the sea: her suffering is like a great flood "not to be passed" (δυσεκπέρατον) save at the cost of her life (677–78). The divine force behind the flood is hinted at in her desperate

---

33. See, e.g., *Il.* 11.416, 13.474–75; also Eur. *Phoen.* 1380: κάπροι δ᾿ ὅπως θήγοντες ἀγρίαν γένυν; see Aristoph. *Lys.* 1255–56 and *Frogs* 815 with the scholion *ad loc.* These last three passages indicate that the metaphor was still concrete and vivid in the late fifth century. Cf. also Aeschyl., *Sept.* 715.

question, just before: "Who of gods or mortals would appear as an accomplice or an associate or a helper [ξυνεργός] in evil deeds?" (675–77). The ξυνεργός harks back to the Nurse's appeal to Sea-Kypris (ξυνεργὸς εἴης, 522). Kypris has been a "helper" indeed, and the sign of her work is the rising sea.

In accordance with the pattern of alternating tension and relief in the play, this climax is followed by the so-called escape ode (732ff.), with its lyrical expression of flight over the sea and its expansive half-mythical geography that, temporarily, lifts us beyond the tragic locale with its concentrated action. The chorus would rise over the sea as a bird and come finally where the sea, or sailing, is not, "where the sea-ruler of the dark lake no longer permits a path to sailors" (744–45). Here, too, recur pure springs, the ambrosial springs of Zeus, recalling the pure, untroubled world presented early in the play. Sea and sky here meet in harmony (746–77), not the fearful clash that is to come (1207); and earth, too, joins in providing abundance and happiness (749–51). Yet this world, beyond passion and beyond violence, is a world for the gods alone; and with them the first strophic system significantly ends (εὐδαιμονίαν θεοῖς, 751).

Even this world of escape and divinity, however, knows suffering, but only because of a mortal's entrance into it. Hence the amberlike tears that "the unhappy sisters of Phaethon drip into the dark flood [οἶδμα] of their father in pity for him" (738ff.). The swelling sea (οἶδμα) as mortals know it means grief; but here, in this mythical, imaginary world, tears can be transformed into something precious and beautiful (ἠλεκτροφαεῖς, 741). The "dripping" (σταλάσσουσιν) of tears, however, recalls the previous two odes—the peaceful dripping rock by the sea of the parode, and the dripping of desire into the eyes by Eros in the first stasimon. It suggests, then, even here the persistence of mortal suffering and the continuing power of Aphrodite working to destroy the calm past.

Similarly, the sea and sky that unite in the paradisiacal vision of the first strophe have been established from the very beginning of the play as the realm of Aphrodite. Hence in the second strophic system with the shift from the divine to the human world, the two elements, sea and sky, are united again but now for destruction rather than peace. The first words, "O white-winged Cretan bark" (ὦ λευκό-πτερε Κρησία / πορθμίς) bring them together in a sinister association:[34] we are reminded of the previous unhappy associations of a ship from Crete (155ff.; see 36) and indeed of Crete itself (cf. especially παῖ Κρησία, 372).

This sea, moreover, significantly carries Phaedra *away* from happiness (ὀλβίων ἀπ᾽ οἴκων, 755), not toward it, as the sea of the first strophe. It is now stormy, violent: κῦμ᾽ ἁλίκτυπον ἅλμας ("seabeaten wave," 753); and the ship passes directly through, not over it. No wishful transport upon the air here. True, in the next lines (756ff.) the ship is said to have "flown" (ἔπτατο) like a bird, but it is a bird of ill omen (δύσορνις). It is, furthermore, moored to the harbor in Piraeus by "woven [πλεκτάς] cables" that foreshadow the woven noose (770) with which Phaedra is to hang herself (note the emphasis on knots, figurative and literal, in 671, 774, 781).[35]

In the antistrophe the destructive power of Aphrodite is made explicit (767), and with it the power of the sea; Phaedra becomes the boat swamped with water, overwhelmed by the sea: ὑπέραντλος (which occurs only here in Classical Greek) is the word used.[36] The "white neck" about which Phaedra will fit the noose not only suggests the tragic waste of Phaedra's youth and beauty but also cancels, finally, the hope to escape the sea like a "winged bird" uttered in the first strophe (esp. 733; cf. also the "white-winged" bark in 752). The "hung-up noose" (κρεμαστὸν . . . βρόχον, 770) evokes also the gruesome truth of Phaedra's "escape" into the air, the corpse swinging suspended above the ground (see also 779, κρεμαστοῖς ἐν βρόχοις ἠρτημένη, and 802). It is thus that she "flies away" (828–29); and the tablet that will continue her act of destruction is also "hanging" (ἠρτημένη, 857).

Thus—to come back to the escape ode—with the return to reality and to mortal men in the second strophe, the bird and the sea pass

34. The connection between the two parts of the ode through the adjective *leukopteros* as the epithet of Phaedra's ship and the interconnected themes of the sea and flying are well noted by H. F. Graham, "The 'Escape' Ode in *Hippolytus* 732–75," *CJ* 42 (1947) 275–76.

35. The metaphor of the knot has been noted, in a different connection, by Wesley D. Smith, "Staging in the Central Scene of the *Hippolytus*," *TAPA* 91 (1960) 170.

36. Stephanus, *Thes. Ling. Graec.* defines it as follows: Ναῦς ὑπέραντλος, *Cuius sentina, vel aqua per fatiscentes rimas illabente, vel tumidis fluctibus desuper infusis, tanta copia exundat ut intra limites contineri amplius, neque exhauriri possit, atque ideo periculum instet, ne mersa navis intereat.*

from being sources of hope to being instruments of disaster. It is therefore with the reality of Phaedra's passion that the ode ends. The chorus' concluding words about her "painful love" (ἀλγεινὸν . . . ἔρωτα) recall what the Nurse said about the two forms of love "sweetest and painful" (347). This love is to prove painful to Theseus too (ἀλγυνοῦσι, 798; ἄλγιστα, 800). Phaedra has in a sense escaped this love, as the chorus says (ἀπαλάσσουσα, 774–75), but at the cost of her life. Thus there is no aspect of the universe that provides escape or refuge from Aphrodite. Phaedra, who would have escaped into the calm woodland (see 208ff.) is caught, ὑπέραντλος, by the sea, triumphant over its resisting victim; and the bird with which the chorus would escape the human reality becomes the omen of her death.

This presage of her death is at once fulfilled with the Nurse's cries (776ff.). Theseus enters at this point, and it is through him that the remainder of the tragedy will be executed. At the news he hurls to the ground his crown of leaves, woven together (πλεκτοῖσι, 807) like the cables of the ship that brought Phaedra across the sea to her doom (πλεκτάς, 761). The throwing down of this crown is also the symbolical counterpart to Hippolytus' presentation of the "woven crown" (πλεκτὸν στέφανον) to Artemis at his entrance, the scene from which the play's title, στεφανίας, derives. In both scenes, of course, the visual enactment would reinforce the verbal repetition; and the two events, as images of action, mark two cardinal points in the structure of the play. Theseus' act now shatters Hippolytus' peaceful life, symbolized in part by the crown gathered from the "untouched meadow" and offered to his goddess. The throwing down of the wreath by Theseus, standing as he does at the opposite pole of character and experience from his son, prefigures for Hippolytus the closing off and destruction of the world into which he has "escaped." The theme is thus analogous to the second strophe of the escape ode, with its forebodings of the realities to come; the weaving image (73, 761, 807) in fact connects all three passages. Significantly, then, when Hippolytus' death is imminent, the chorus sings that the resting-places of his goddess will henceforth be "without crowns" (ἀστέφανοι, 1137). In itself, of course, Theseus' flinging down of the sacred wreath of his θεωρία is ominous enough.[37] For him too it

37. For the crown motif and the *theoria* see Hans Herter, "Theseus und Hippolytos," *RhM* 89 (1940) 285–86.

marks the sudden and violent interruption of a peaceful life, the pleasant official and ritual duties that are a part of his kingly honor.

As the crown imagery looks back to Hippolytus and Artemis and the world that is being destroyed, so the following imagery points to the irrupting forces, Phaedra and Aphrodite—the victim who is also the agent, and the superhuman power underlying all the action and all the destruction. Theseus bewails his loss thus (822–24):

κακῶν δ' ὦ τάλας, πέλαγος εἰσορῶ
τοσοῦτον ὥστε μήποτ' ἐκνεῦσαι πάλιν,
μηδ' ἐκπερᾶσαι κῦμα τῆσδε συμφορᾶς.

Alas, I behold a sea of troubles such as I shall never swim out of again nor pass beyond the wave of this disaster.

The language echoes Phaedra's earlier utterance of her subjection to the power of the sea (cf. ἐκνεῦσαι, 470; δυσεκπέρατον, 678) and suggests the gradual spreading of the calamity as the force of the sea and Aphrodite break forth as what they are.

Theseus, continuing his lament, addresses the dead Phaedra thus: "For like some bird you have gone off out of my hand to disappear, bounding in a swift leap to Hades" (828–29). This bird imagery continues the theme of the escape ode and, in conjunction with 822–24, marks the universal power of Aphrodite, manifest in both sea and sky. It denotes here not the fancy of escape but the closing in of the reality of the mortal world, not freedom and potentiality but bondage to the elemental forces of nature. The possibility of escape is cut off by death, the death for which the bird here stands. This now negative significance of the bird touches the future as well as the present, for when Theseus is about to read the tablet, the chorus, like a prophet (*mantis*), senses a bird of ill omen (οἰωνόν, 873).

Whatever hopefulness was previously associated with bird and sky now gives way to the destructive reality of sea as through Theseus it touches its new victim. Directly upon the chorus' presentiment of disaster (873), Theseus reads the tablet and calls his woe "hard to pass beyond" (δυσεκπέρατον, 883), echoing Phaedra in 678 (this word occurs only in these two passages in Euripides' extant works). Then he utters the fatal words, "Hippolytus dared to touch my bed" (885), whereupon follows his curse, in terms of the sea: "Exiled from this country, a wanderer to a foreign land, shall he bilge out [ἀντλήσει] his bitter life" (898). This last metaphor, along with the preceding δυσεκπέρατον, again take us back to Phaedra (cf. ὑπέραντλος, 769). The repeated image thus extends her fate to Hippolytus and involves him, too, in subjection to the mounting power of the sea. There is more truth than Theseus knows in his first despairing words to his dead wife: "You destroyed rather than perished yourself" (ἀπώλεσας γὰρ μᾶλλον ἢ κατέφθισο, 839). But behind her it is Aphrodite who is the destroyer (δόμους ἀπώλεσεν, 361, 487).

With Theseus the force of the sea is continued in its wild, irrational power, but now under another aspect: the violent, male anger associated with Poseidon, who fulfills Theseus' angry curse (887ff.). Just before Hippolytus' cool and rational defense, Theseus reiterates his decree of banishment by calling to witness "Sinis of the Isthmus" (977) and "the Skironian rocks that neighbor the sea" (αἱ θαλάσσῃ σύννομοι Σκιρωνίδες . . . πέτραι, 979–80). The sea, in its connection with the Isthmian robber and the rock-dwelling tormenter of travelers, suggests the whole realm of cruelty and bitter experience that the wide-traveled Theseus has known, in contrast to the innocence of his woods- and mountain-loving son. These rocks too, unlike those by which the chorus of Troezenian women sang of their quiet, domestic tasks, belong in the world of violence and bloodshed which Theseus is calling down upon his son. Among these rocks, murder was violently done and violently punished. Here, then, the sea widens its symbolical range to include another manifestation of the instinctive life of man. With Theseus the two aspects of the sea converge and bear down together upon Hippolytus' peaceful world. The sea that Theseus calls upon thus creates a new contrast of innocence and experience, and in so doing it sharpens the tragedy of Hippolytus' undeserved punishment. He is at the opposite pole from "evil men," *kakoi,* like Sinis and Sciron; and the tragic irony of Theseus' introduction of his triumphs over these brigands is intensified by Hippolytus' repeated, if self-righteous, statements that he is not nor could be "evil" or "base" (kakos, 654, 1191).

The tragic irony deepens and foreshadows the peripety as Hippolytus shortly after, in averring that he is not kakos, calls upon the very sea that will destroy him: "Let neither sea [πόντος] nor earth receive my flesh if I have been an evil man" (κακὸς ἀνήρ, 1030–31). His oath only angers Theseus the more, who replies with a counter-wish involving the sea: "If I could [I would drive you] beyond the sea and the limits of Atlas" (πέραν γε πόντου τερμόνων τ' 'Ατλαντικῶν, 1053).[38] This line is almost identical with Aphrodite's statement of her power in the opening lines (3). It thus marks the continuation through Theseus of her relentless, irrational force in the face of all logical arguments, of even the ties of blood and filial affection. It recalls, too, the chorus' hope to escape beyond the sea and sail to "the holy limit of the sky which Atlas holds" (746–47) and marks the cancellation of this hope by the reality that is growing ever stronger and more threatening. The allusion to this ode, moreover, provides another link between the fate of Phaedra, to whose situation the ode refers, and Hippolytus, who is gradually engulfed by the same power. These references back and forth and the pervasive power of the sea which they reveal show how unified a structure the play in fact is, how closely intertwined the two parts are, and how strongly into the second part persists the presence of the two female figures, Phaedra, dead, and Aphrodite, absent.

This complex evocation of the power of the sea at the point of Hippolytus' exile, with the echoes both of the escape ode and Aphrodite's initial statement of her power, also helps to focus and clarify a central theme in the play: man's attempt to escape from the demanding, often savage, realities of his world by excluding a part of it from his existence. In the climaxing tragedy of Hippolytus, it is his past world, the removed and limited environment of woods and mountains, which is analogous to the chorus' longing for escape, and like it, is confronted and destroyed by the implacable reality of the sea. His hunting, for example, recurs in a sinister context in Theseus' long tirade against him: "For they [hypocrites like Hippolytus] go hunting [θηρεύουσι] with solemn words, while devising disgraceful deeds" (956–57).

As has been shown above, it is with Phaedra and her passion that this change in the significance of his past pursuits begins, first in her longing for his world (208ff.) and more dangerously in the wild-animal imagery she uses to describe his violent behavior (689).

38. Murray reads καὶ τόπων 'Ατλαντικῶν, whereas there is equally strong, if not stronger, manuscript authority for τερμόνων τ 'Ατλαντικῶν (accepted by Méridier) which would make the line practically identical with line 3. Καὶ τόπων is poetically extremely weak, aside from making rather dubious sense. Even with Murray's reading, however, the reference back to line 3, and to 746–47, is unmistakable.

Euripides

Through Phaedra, too, and the situation that she creates, his fondness for athletic contests (ἀγῶνες), which he sets above political power (1016ff.), takes on a sinister coloring. He is now involved in a much grimmer contest, one that is verbal, not physical, and in which it is his honor and his life that are at stake (ἠγωνιζόμην, 1024; cf. ἀμιλλῶμαι λόγοις, 971). This new contest, moreover, is the direct outcome of Phaedra's own contest, for she was engaged, said the Nurse, in a contest for her life (496), one that she lost by a "wrestling fall" of her own hand (σᾶς χερὸς / πάλαισμα μελέας, 814–15). Now this contest has spread to Hippolytus and transformed his free ἀγῶνες into something tense and dangerous. As Phaedra's language earlier reflected the inhumanity of Hippolytus as hunter, so the contest imagery, as developed in the ἄμιλλα λόγων with Theseus, reflects the human limitations of his athletic ideal: there are more serious contests in life which Hippolytus knows not of.

Still another image marks the collision of Hippolytus' world with Phaedra's (and Aphrodite's). The figure of disease, which is used exclusively of Phaedra in the first part of the play and is one of the most frequent metaphors there,[39] is here applied to Hippolytus. As he is forced to accept a contest as deadly as Phaedra's, so he becomes touched by the effects of her disease as they spread outward from her final act. Thus in the midst of his agon with Theseus, he exclaims, "We are afflicted [νοσοῦμεν], guiltless though we are" (933).

The disease image, transferred from the lovesick queen to the austere prince, has a further appropriateness, for his present calamity, viewed in terms of his previous life and his ideal of purity, is apparently as unrelated to justice and right as is a disease that spreads, irrationally and indifferently, from one victim to another. The Athenians knew well the irrationality and unpredictability of contagion from the plague of the preceding year (see esp. Thucyd. 2.51 and 2.53); and the extension of the *nosos* image from Phaedra to Hippolytus suggests a similarly uncontrollable irrationality in the multiplication of disaster.

The theme of wish versus reality, calm and limited past versus

39. For the nosos image see 40, 186, 205, 269, 279, 283, 293, 294, 394, 405, 463, 477, 479, 512, 597, 698, 730, 766 (a total of eighteen instances). It recurs in the second half of the play (aside from 933) only in 1306, significantly of Phaedra's passion, now revealed by Artemis. See also frag. 428 of the *Hippolytos Kalyptomenos*. For the image in general see Pohlenz (note 2) 1:273, with the note at 2:114–15.

expanding and dangerous present, is taken up again in the third stasimon (1102–50), sung at the moment of suspense between Hippolytus' departure for exile and the announcement of his death. Connected through this wish theme with the escape ode, this song, too, precedes a great disaster. The first strophic system creates a strong antithesis of hope and reality, the latter expressed, fittingly, by Hippolytus' austere companions (1102–10), the former by the gentler, more timid Troezenian women (1111–19).

Significantly, what immediately precedes the ode is another instance of man's inability to grasp the full, complex realities of his world and himself. Hippolytus leaves the stage in lines 1100–1101 shouting, "Never will you see another man more chaste [σωφρονέστερον], even if my father thinks not so." *Sophronesteron* is, of course, loaded with irony and ambiguity, for not only is this parting shot singularly devoid of *sophrosyne* but Phaedra, at the analogous point in her tragedy, had made her last spoken word a promise to teach Hippolytus sophrosyne (731)—for her not "chastity," as Hippolytus narrowly intends it, but "good sense," "soundness of mind," "moderation."

With Hippolytus' tragic and hybristic boast quivering in the air, the chorus of his companions turns sadly and finally from the hope in the divine realm voiced in their first song (61ff.) and reiterated in the escape ode to a more barren, but perhaps truer, view of reality (1102–10):

> ἦ μέγα μοι τὰ θεῶν μελεδήμαθ', ὅταν φρένας ἔλθῃ,
> λύπας παραιρεῖ· ξύνεσιν δέ τιν' ἐλπίδι κεύθων
> λείπομαι ἔν τε τύχαις θνατῶν καὶ ἐν ἔργμασι λεύσσων·
> ἄλλα γὰρ ἄλλοθεν ἀμείβεται, μετὰ δ' ἵσταται ἀνδράσιν αἰὼν
> πολυπλάνητος αἰεί.

Thoughts on the gods [or, the gods' thoughts for us] when they come to my mind greatly diminish my griefs; but, though I hold understanding concealed in hope [or, hope for some (divine) Intelligence], I am left in the lurch in men's fortunes and acts as I gaze upon them. Things change with one another from every side, and men's life shifts about, full of wandering always.

The chorus thus turns back from hope (note also τὰ παρ' ἐλπίδα λεύσσων, 1120) and from the infinite possibilities of the gods to the bare, unprotected realities of human finitude, "men's fortunes and acts."

The women's chorus in the antistrophe (1111–19) cannot yet accept such a vision. They remain attached somehow to hope in the gods (εὐξαμένα θεόθεν, κτλ, 1111); and with a woman's hold on life they can still regard change and flux as not profoundly threatening. Their world is still essentially the warm and gentle sea of the parode. Thus they pray for good luck, wealth, the adaptability of their behavior to the situation, and the easy, pleasant acceptance of the "fortune" (tychan) of each day.[40]

In wishing not to have a δόξα ἀτρεκής ("accurate opinion," 1115) they seem in fact to be rejecting the possibility of a clear, accurate view of the terrible reality with which they are being presented.[41] The Nurse too, it will be recalled, warned with disastrous results against excessive "accuracy" (akribeia, 469; cf. 261) in moral conduct. In reechoing her warnings the women thus attempt to separate themselves as far as possible from the fates of the two protagonists who lived—and died—because of their over-precise, uncompromising approach to life (βιότου δ' ἀτρεκεῖς ἐπιτηδεύσεις, 261).

40. The division of the strophes of this chorus between the Troezenian women and the hunters has been made by Murray, following Verrall's suggestion, on the basis of the alternation of masculine and feminine participles. See Murray's critical note to vv. 1102ff. of his Oxford text. His division of the choruses has been generally accepted: see Grube (note 26) 190 n.1. Barrett (note 28) 365–69 is reluctant to accept Verrall and Murray's division of the chorus at 1102ff. and inclines to suspect textual corruption. Yet his objection that Hippolytus' companions who appeared at 61–71 "are now away with his horses by the shore (cf. 1173ff.)" is not decisive. It would be natural for them to have come at the news of Hippolytus' accusation and then to exit after him. The time sequence is admittedly awkward, as Barrett points out, though it is highly dubious that the audience would be disturbed by such an inconsistency at this point. Even so, we need not assume that *all* of Hippolytus' companions follow him to the sea at once. Some could linger to commiserate his fate. The chorus of companions would also form a nice balance with Hippolytus' entrance. Their reappearance creates a bitterly ironical link between past innocence and present complexity, happiness and disaster. Through them Hippolytus' way of life seems to pass in review at the very moment when it is about to be destroyed in its totality. Note too the verbal parallels between the two scenes (with 1138–39 cf. 17, 64–65, 73–74).

41. The meaning of *doxa atrekês* is ambiguous, as Méridier (note 4) 72 n.4 points out: *"une opinion exacte* (par suite *dépourvue d'illusions*), *sur la réalité*, ou: *des principes de conduite trop rigoureux* (comme ceux d'Hippolyte?)." Wilamowitz (note 6) preferred the former view in his translation, "Nicht verlangt mich zu tief in das Wesen der Dinge zu blicken," which seems to suit παράσημος better (he continues, "aber auch nicht in das Dunkel des Aberglaubens zu sinken").

Such accuracy is perhaps closer to a simplistic rigidity than a just
appreciation of the total reality. It may be that *akribes* or *atrekes* in this
sense carries some connotations of an aristocratic way of seeing the
world, an undeviating devotion to a neatly circumscribed ideal. The
Old Oligarch saw akribeia as an aristocratic quality (ps.-Xenophon,
Ath. Pol. 1.5):

> In every country the aristocracy [*to beltiston*] is opposed to the democ-
> racy, for in the aristocrats [*tois beltistois*] there is least licentiousness and
> injustice, but most accuracy [*akribeia*] about the good things; but in the
> common people there is most ignorance, disorder, and malice.[42]

If this is so, then the chorus, following the path opened up by the
plebeian Nurse, rejects the aristocratic desire to master the world in
terms of well defined categories and absolutely valid aims, to see life
clearly, simply, as conquerable by human excellence or *arete*. It is
precisely because of the complexity of divinities like Aphrodite, Artemis, Poseidon, however, and the conflicting drives they instill in
men that this simple view is doomed. To try to see a world wherein
such powers are rampant through an ordered neatness or exactness of
mind or will is σεμνότης—an accusation, it will be remembered,
brought against both Phaedra and Hippolytus.

Yet the chorus' solution, though perhaps more feasible than that of
the two protagonists, serves only to evade the problem and hence to
sidestep involvement in a heroic attitude and a tragic fate. Though far
from the Nurse's attitude of practical expediency, the women of the
chorus are proven similarly inadequate to grasp and deal with the
reality. They prefer to live day by day without, as it were, looking
life in the face. Their wish for "a mind untouched [ἀκήρατον] by
pain" (1114), however, recalls, as noted earlier, the "untouched
meadow" (76–77) of Hippolytus' past life, the simple happiness now
about to be destroyed. In this context the word "untouched" adds an
ironical warning note that vitiates the optimism of their prayer and
their wish for escape.

Yet in their retreat into wish here and in the earlier ode, they are
portrayed, as in the parode also, with a sympathetic humanity. They

---

42. I am grateful to John Finley of Harvard University for calling my attention to
this passage.

failed to save Hippolytus—which, presùmably, they could have done—as they failed to respond decisively to the first news of Phaedra's death (776ff.). But in these failings they are shown simply with the natural weakness of the mass of men, accepting the pleasures of their daily existence and ever seeking an escape from the elemental realities of their world.

In the second strophic system, however, the clash between past and present, between Hippolytus' severe pursuits and his disgrace and approaching death, is made as sharp as possible. All the aspects of his previous world are recalled at the point of their destruction: the sands by the shore, the mountain groves, the hunts and Dictynna (1126–30), the horse racing by Limne (1131ff.), the crowns he gave to Artemis (1138), the deep green wood (βαθεῖαν ἀνὰ χλόαν, 1139; cf. χλωρὰν δ' ἀν' ὕλην, 17). All the parts of his life which have been sheltered from the turbulence of Kypris are destroyed by her; her power and that of the sea have destroyed his refuge. These haunts and pursuits recur now to mark the end of his innocence and his full exposure to the violence of Aphrodite's power. At the same time, their restatement here indicates the relentless progress of Aphrodite through the tragedy, for most of these aspects of Hippolytus' life were presented first either in connection with Phaedra's subjection to Aphrodite (so Dictynna, 145) or actually through her eyes at the height of her love sickness (the sands by the shore, 234; the hunt, 215ff.; the horse racing by Limne and Venetian colts, 228ff.). The verbal echoes thus mark the turning of Phaedra's love destructively upon Hippolytus and his world. The beginning of his disaster is thus brought full circle with its end as Phaedra's involvement of him in her love, now become hate, is complete.

Her passion, her lovesick dreams and longings, embraced the whole of Hippolytus' world, his surroundings, his activities (see 208ff.). But she can grasp them only in dream or in wish. When she seeks to possess them in their reality, her passion destroys them and the life they make up. The meeting of their two worlds is perhaps symbolized and dramatized by the joining of the two choruses here, one of Phaedra's women companions, the other of Hippolytus' fellow-hunters. Yet together they can sing only of the loss of the simpler past; and presumably it is this chorus of hunters which will bring in Hippolytus' mangled body. When the two worlds become intertwined, they destroy one another. The joining of the choruses perhaps marks the interlocking of the two fates, a symbolical sharing of the double tragedy. In a sense Phaedra is as much Hippolytus' victim as he is hers. Yet the destruction of his world is more complete, or at least more completely dramatized. It cannot bear the full weight of complex reality which Phaedra brings to bear upon it.

The chorus ends by echoing Hippolytus' previous affirmation of his innocence (οὐδὲν ἄτας αἴτιον, 1149; see οὐδὲν ὄντες αἴτιοι, 933); and almost in the same breath they announce the arrival of the Messenger. The climax that has been long awaited and has been seen gradually building up now bursts full upon us. Euripides uses this Messenger's speech not to introduce a crisis in the middle of the play but to state the finality of the outcome. The speech thus produces the sharpest possible juxtaposition of calm past and violent present, of woodland and sea, wish and reality, before the final catastrophe and the loss of all hope.

Before his long account of the disaster itself, the Messenger re-introduces the theme of prayer, or wish, in referring back, almost by way of prologue, to the curses Theseus called down upon his son, "the curses of your mouth which you prayed for to the lord of the sea concerning your son" (1167–68). Theseus replies with an invocation to the gods and Poseidon for hearing his "prayers" (κατευγμάτων, 1169–70); and the tale of Hippolytus' death follows at once (1173ff.). The connection of prayer and sea, however, recalls both Hippolytus' imprecation, "Let neither sea nor earth receive my flesh . . ." (1030) and Theseus' wish to drive Hippolytus "beyond the sea and the limits of Atlas" (1054). Wish, the sea, and Poseidon take us back also to the escape ode, where Poseidon as ruler of the sea was hopefully included (cf. ποντομέδων, 743–44; πόντου κρέοντι, 1168). Yet only the destructive prayers are fulfilled. The prayers that become reality are the deadly ones, and their fulfillment implies something about the reality in which men live or can hope to live.

The scope of the power of the sea and another level of contrast with what it destroys are suggested in the Messenger's opening words to Theseus: he calls him, naturally enough, ruler of the land (γῆς ἄνακτα, 1153) and declares that he has to relate a matter of importance "to you and the citizens who dwell in the city of the Athenians and the limits of the Troezenian land" (1158–59). Theseus is thus summoned in his political or social capacity, and the disaster is presented as one of political as well as merely personal significance. He, as ruler of the

Euripides

land, and the ordered society he represents are confronted by Poseidon "lord of the sea." We are reminded of the similar opposition in the first stasimon on Eros, "sacker of cities" (541), bringer of fire and smoke, his power attested even by "the holy wall of Thebes" and the spring of Dirce (555–61). Both Poseidon and Eros embody forces outside civilization which civilization is forced, with pain, to recognize.

The Messenger's speech then sets forth in detail this elemental power. It begins at once with the sea not as something remote from our land-based existence but in its closest contact to human life, "the sea-receiving shore" (ἀκτῆς κυμοδέγμονος, 1173), the place where its force ever dashes unspent (note κυμοδέγμων: it is waves that the shore receives here, not just swirling sand as in 151). The shore by which the women washed, where Hippolytus trained his horses, here becomes a dangerous place of contact with elemental powers, a border country between land and sea, order and violence. The opposition is sharpened through the fact that the shore of Hippolytus' horse racing in the previous chorus was described as πολιῆτις (1126) and hence was associated with man's civilized life, the life of the polis. The shore by which he is killed, however, is fully exposed to the savage, open sea: it lies "beyond this land, already toward the Saronic sea" (τοὐπέκεινα τῆσδε γῆς / πρὸς πόντον ἤδη κειμένη Σαρωνικόν, 1199–1200). This shore, therefore, now reveals the destructive potentialities that lie just beyond it. At the moment of the terrible apparition, when Hippolytus' companions looked "toward the sea-roaring shores," land is concealed by the sea: "The Skironian shores" and the Isthmus and "Asclepius' rock" are all "hidden" by the swelling sea and the foam rushing toward the shores (1210ff.).

As land is overwhelmed by sea and as the border-ground between them becomes a place of violence and destruction, so human control and reason are overborne by the same power. Hippolytus' futile attempts to control the maddened horses are described in the metaphor of a sailor pulling on the oar (1221) or a steersman directing his course by the rudder (1224, 1227). The imagery here suggests the total engulfment by the sea: he is, literally as well as metaphorically, no longer upon the familiar, sheltered land he knows. All has become sea. He is thus made to share the fate of the (figuratively) shipwrecked and drowning woman who has destroyed him. Metaphor and reality are interchanged with a terrible oscillation, for while the imagery here completes all the previous images of shipwreck and sailing, it is, at the same time, literal reality. The chorus' earlier hope to escape sea and sailing (743ff.) is thus totally frustrated, for the "sailor" is destroyed not only by the sea but by his own "ship." And their wish to escape to a peaceful shore (ἀκτή, 737, 742), the fabled "apple-bearing coast of the Hesperides" (742), is ended on the shore of their own land.

With the sea, other elements of nature are released in their violence. The fire associated with the destructive force of Eros in the first stasimon (525ff.) is present in the horses' "fire-born" (πυριγενῆ, 1223) bits, which no longer serve as a check or control but only add to the breaking forth of elemental violence.[43] Sky, like fire an opposite of sea but forming with it the stated realm of Aphrodite's power (2ff.), joins violently in the wave's dash against the heavens (κῦμ' οὐρανῷ στηρίζον, 1207). And finally the rocks by the sea, once the calm place of untroubled womanly tasks, reveal their sinister potential in mangling the horse-drawn body (πέτρῳ, 1233; σποδούμενος μὲν πρὸς πέτραις, 1238; also λεπαίας . . . χθονός, 1248). These rocks then, like the shore itself, lose their association with the gentleness and order of civilized life and become connected instead with the cruel, pain-filled rocks in the name of which Theseus banished Hippolytus and sent him to his death (see 977ff.; Pind, *Pyth.* 2. 41ft).

Here, then, all the aspects of the natural world, even elemental opposites, draw closer together and destroy the peaceful, innocent life that man, though in their midst, hopes to live among them. Through them Euripides suggests the contiguity of this elemental violence, whether within man or without, with the ordered structure of human life, and the fineness of the barrier that keeps the two realms apart.

The irruption of Aphrodite's power into the human world breaks down this barrier and transforms the once familiar environment—the shore, the rocks, the horses—into something savage and destructive.

---

43. Norwood (note 2) 93, notes the unusual elaboration of this description of the sea (esp. 1205ff.) and suggests that in adjectives like πυριγενῆ Euripides is imitating Sophoclean diction. Euripides, of course, doubtless wished to make his presentation of the sea here, at the high point of the tragedy, as splendid and powerful as possible. Yet in the light of the previous imagery, πυριγενῆ may be more than a mere *epitheton ornans*.

The horses, once the restraint of rational control is broken (see 1218ff.), become wild animals, no longer recognizing the human master who has fed and cared for them (1240); and they, like the Bull (ἄγριον τέρας, 1214), disappear afterward (1247–48). They thus revert to their original wild state and share the destructive wildness of the Bull. Ironically, Hippolytus' scorn of Aphrodite was first shown through his care of his horses (see 110ff., where he turns away from the old servant's appeal on her behalf with a command to his followers to care for the horses). He would use for his own chaste purposes these mettlesome, unstable creatures. Yet as instruments of her vengeance they recall the stringency of her demands and the persistence of her destructive will. Since the horses, as noted earlier, are an erotic symbol in the play, they can also fittingly serve as conduits of Aphrodite's power. They are, in fact, elsewhere associated with the goddess (see Sappho, frag. 2, v. 9 [Lobel-Page] and Schol. on *Il.* 2.820). Her part in the rising up of the sea, however, is suggested not only in the horses but also in the tossing up of foam (ἀφρόν, 1210), popularly connected with the goddess' name (*aphros*—Aphro-dite). Her presence here in sea and foam becomes explicit in the following ode (1268ff.).

The horse, however, is associated also with Poseidon who, as Hippios, god of horses, is a god of male sexuality and fertility (note the legends of his coupling with Demeter in the form of a horse, Paus. 8.25.5ff., 8.42.1).[44] In addition to these legends of the stallionlike virility of Poseidon there are other connections of the horse with wild and exuberant male sexuality: the horse-tailed satyrs, often ithyphallic, on the vases of the sixth and fifth centuries and the lecherous, violent Centaurs on the west pediment at Olympia and on the Parthenon metopes (the hybristic licentiousness of the latter is also a theme of tragedy: cf. the role of Nessus in Soph., *Trach.* esp. 1095–96; also Eur., *HF* 181; Pind. *Pyth.* 2. 41ff.).

The Bull, of course, is an obvious sexual symbol and, like the horse, is also associated with Poseidon (both bulls and horses are regularly sacrificed to him). Yet its significance in the play may be

---

44. For Poseidon Hippios and Demeter see also Pausan. 8.37.9–10. For Poseidon's connection with sexuality, fertility, and vegetation (as *Phytalmios*) see in general the recent study by Bernard Dietrich, "Demeter, Erinys, Artemis," *Hermes* 90 (1962) 129ff., 134–36. Dietrich notes also the connection of the horse, through its association with fountains and water, with vegetation and fertility.

more complex. Though the Bull is a direct result of Poseidon's inter-vention, its appearance is also a continued manifestation of Aphro-dite's power, for it recalls the bull of Pasiphae, Phaedra's mother. Phaedra herself referred to the legend earlier, for her sex-ridden, guilt-laden ancestry comes out when she confesses her love for Hip-polytus (337–38)

> *Phaed.*   Alas, mother, what a love you loved.
> *Nurse.*   The love she had for the Bull, my child? Or what is this you mean?[45]

Here, then, the force of her love and the violence it has released are again called up in the Bull. Yet in Pasiphae's bull, too, are fused, in sinister fashion, the angered powers of both Poseidon and Aphrodite. Pasiphae's love for the bull was attributed to both divinities. In one version Aphrodite sent it to punish her; in the other (followed by Euripides in the *Cretans*) Poseidon sent it to punish Minos.[46]

In the Bull are summed up not merely the powers of Aphrodite and Poseidon but all the violent instincts within human life and the natu-ral world: the passion of Phaedra, the anger of Theseus, the tenuous basis of control over such domesticated animals as the horse. The Bull serves as the symbolic extension of the bestial element in man, his insatiable lusts and unreasoning anger. It recalls too the Minoan passion, pride, and savagery in Phaedra's heredity which Aphrodite could work upon. There is indeed something Minoan—and some-thing animal-like—in the way Phaedra has died: her passionate deter-mination to protect her name and her children, and her wild, ruthless desire to be avenged. Her action came from the springs of her in-stincts, with its roots in her ancestry (myth makes both Pasiphae and Minos headstrong, passionate, and ruthless; and the *paternal* part of

45. For the connection of the Bull of the Messenger's speech with Pasiphae's bull, see Winnington-Ingram (note 2) 175 with note 2 and 196: "Pasiphae's bull is, sym-bolically speaking, the same bull that came out of the sea to destroy Hippolytus (and the same bull with which Pentheus wrestled in the *Bacchae*)."

46. Aphrodite's connection with Pasiphae's bull is asserted in Hyginus, *Fab.* 40, with Poseidon's in Apollodorus, 3.1.3–4. See also J. G. Frazer on the latter passage in the Loeb Classical Library ed. (London 1921) 1:305 n.3. Also "Pasiphae" in Roscher (note 18) 3.2 (1902–9) 1668. For Euripides' treatment of the legend in the *Cretans*, see D. L. Page, *Select Papyri*, 3: *Literary Papryi, Poetry*, Loeb Classical Library (London 1950) 71ff.

Phaedra's heritage should not be forgotten: Minos also had certain irregularities in his sexual life, *iungitur semper nefas*). The Bull serves to connect Hippolytus' doom with the deepest roots of Phaedra's passion, and, through her, with Aphrodite's anger.

At the same time, the Bull is the objectification of Theseus' anger, wild, charging blindly, yet an anger also rooted in Aphrodite, in the most primitive and instinctive form of sexual rivalry and jealousy— that between father and son. Theseus is himself strongly subject to Aphrodite: he is a man of passion and a strong sexual temperament, whose numerous amours are well known (Hippolytus is himself the fruit of one of them!). He is, as would be expected, keenly sensitive to the power of sexual desire in men (τὸ δ' ἄρσεν αὐτοὺς ὠφελεῖ προσκείμενον, 970, and, in general, 966ff.). It is partly his own temperament, lustful and passionate, which makes him incapable of believing Hippolytus innocent. Thus, as L. E. Matthaei long ago remarked, "Theseus, in a sense, replaces Phaedra and exhibits the malignant aspect of Aphrodite's power in another form."[47] The Bull is the symbol of this new form: as a psychological symbol it is the product of his sexual jealousy and violent anger. Like Aphrodite, it is born from the churning foam and springs from the symbolical reservoir of elemental forces in the play, the sea.

It is, however, the horses that are the immediate instruments of Hippolytus' death, and the interplay between horses and Bull, on the symbolic level, is complex. Both, through their association with Poseidon, are connected with male sexuality; yet the horses throughout the play are ambiguously connected both with Hippolytus' virgin pursuits and with sexual desire. They are associated with virginity in the metaphor of the virgin as the untamed or unyoked colt or filly (πῶλον ἄζυγα, 546; κόραι γὰρ ἄζυγες γάμων, 1425, of the girls who will sing of Hippolytus' fate). Hence the patron of this horse racing is Artemis, or Dictynna, the virgin goddess (228ff., 1126ff.). So, too, Hippolytus' mother, the Amazon devoted to a rigorous and chaste life, is scornfully called "horse-loving" by the sexually preoccupied Phaedra (581). Yet in the first two instances of the metaphor the maidens are about to give up their virginity (and in the former, through the violence of Eros himself), and in the third, the Amazon's chastity has been violated. In their connection with maidens who are

47. Matthaei (note 9) 105.

about to know Eros, therefore, the significance of the horses is ambiguous. Hippolytus keeps them in the service of the maiden Artemis, but the impact of the full sexual passion and anger of Phaedra
and then of Theseus disturbs the delicate balance in Hippolytus' control over them. It forces him to drive too close to the dangerous
border between the two realms, the sand and the sea, Artemis (see
234ff., 1126) and Aphrodite or Poseidon.

It would be perhaps too extreme an application of the symbolism
to see in the affrighted horses fleeing before the Bull the inability of
Hippolytus' limited way of life to withstand the reality of the sexual
forces he has always denied. Through the horses, nevertheless, he is
destroyed by a part of his own life, by something he has reared
himself and always believed he could control yet perhaps did not fully
understand. When confronted by the power of the sea and the monster it produces, he is unable to maintain control and is killed. In the
destruction the horses show their other side and in their newly released wildness become the actual instruments of the disaster. Thus
Hippolytus' destruction comes both from something that is within
his world and from something outside of it, something that is basically akin to himself (his very name adumbrates the connection and the
tragedy—*furiis direptus equorum*)[48] and something that is antithetical
to himself, which he has rejected as foreign to his nature.

It is the interplay between the opposites, however, which gives his
fate, and the whole tragedy, its richness. The Bull triggers the latent
wildness in the horses, as Theseus had triggered the mounting savagery of the sea. Yet Phaedra, with whom the whole is set into motion,
had found in and elicited from Hippolytus a wildness and animal-like
cruelty (see above) for which he is to pay manyfold. Thus in a sense
the Bull, the ἄγριον τέρας, is of his own creation. From another
point of view, it could be seen as the projection of his own sexuality,
suppressed but returning back upon him with redoubled, irresistible
force, before which flight and dismemberment—both physical and
psychological, like Pentheus'—are the only results. But Hippolytus is
not a Pentheus. His character has still a wholeness, nobility, and

---

48. Ovid, *Fasti*, 3.265, *Met.* 15.542–44. See also Verg. *Aen.* 7.767, *turbatis distractus*
equis. On the connections made in antiquity between his name and his fate see "Hippolytos" in Roscher (note 18) 1.2 (1886–90) 2683; also Wilamowitz (note 6) 95–96;
Herter (note 37) 275.

Euripides

humanity through which he can retain a hold upon life long enough
to redeem his previous inhumanity by a deepened understanding and
a broader generosity.

There is, however, an ironical justice, worthy of the spiteful Aphrodite, in the destruction of the virgin protagonist by this creature of
proverbial virility and sexual appetite. The justice—or injustice—
involved is reflected in another of the images associated with the Bull
and the sea: the terrible sound. Hippolytus earlier cried out that
"voiceless [ἄφθογγα] wild animals" should associate with women
(645–46), but it was the voiceless tablet that "shouted" and "gave
voice" (877ff.). When accused, however, he calls upon the house—
δώματα, the house Aphrodite has destroyed (361, 487)—to give
voice (φθέγμα) to his innocence (1074–75). To this Theseus replies
with irony that he is taking flight to "voiceless" (ἀφώνους) witnesses
(1076) and that "the deed, without speaking, lays information" that
he is base (1077). The final answer, however, comes from the re-
sounding sea (ἠχώ, βαρὺν βρόμον, 1201–2) and the terrible voice
(*phthongos*, 1205; *phthegma*, 1215) with which the whole earth re-
sounds (ἀντεφθέγγετο, 1216). Again, the savagery of his earlier statement about voiceless beasts (645f.) returns upon him redoubled. It is
fear of the impassioned shouting of his voice which leads Phaedra to
her deed (see 581–82 and 692: πλήσει τε πᾶσαν γαῖαν αἰσχίστων
λόγων). And Hippolytus' own shouting in his interview with the
Nurse is perhaps not unlike Theseus' roar of anger when he reads the
tablet (877ff.). Thus again the roar of the Bull is, at least in part, his
own creation. It is the composite of all the anger and passion—
Phaedra's, Theseus', Hippolytus'—which men can release in their
moments of unreason, when the primitive animal roar of pain or
wrath breaks forth before the articulate human voice can find form
for utterance. Hence the voice Hippolytus calls for (1074–75) comes
back not as a human voice, speaking truth and justice, but as a bestial
roar that drowns out justice, reason, intelligible human speech.[49]

Euripides' use of the Bull in close connection with the sea thus
involves a complex range of associations. Theseus had prayed to

49. It is interesting in this connection that Strabo (10.2.19, 458C) gives the roaring
as one of the reasons why rivers (esp. the Achelous) were likened to bulls. See also R.
C. Jebb, *Sophocles: The Plays and Fragments*, Part 5, *Trachiniae* (Cambridge 1894), on
line 11.

Poseidon only to kill his son, not specifying the form; and presumably Hippolytus might have been killed by the sea alone, as was the case in a Troezenian version of the legend.[50] The Bull, however, springs from the sea almost as the spontaneous product of the desires and passions generated among the chief characters. At the same time the Bull's sexual symbolism expands and deepens the psychological complexities of Hippolytus' character and his tragedy. It belongs to a level of man's instinctive life which Hippolytus would deny or repress. It is the embodiment of everything that is not human, yet it is man who calls it up out of the sea.

With the destruction of Hippolytus, Aphrodite's power is restated in its most triumphant and inclusive form. The ode of 1268–81 recognizes her "queenly honor" and power over all the elements of the world:

You, O Kypris, lead the unbending mind of gods and of mortals, and with you flies Eros with wing of many hues, casting about [them] his swiftest wing. He flies over the earth and the deep-sounding salt sea. And upon whose maddened heart he rushes winged with light of gold, him he charms, even the young wild beasts of the mountains and of the sea and all that the earth nourishes and the blazing sun [reading αἰθόμενος] looks upon, and men: over all these, Kypris, in your queenly honor you alone rule.

Again sea is fused with sky, for here, after the manifestation of her power in the sea, in the Messenger's speech, her companion Eros is likened to a bird, ποικιλόπτερος, flying with "swiftest wing" (1270–71). The passage evokes the previous bird imagery, especially its association with flight and escape (see esp. 731ff.), now proved futile by the power of winged Eros (1272–73). The Nurse's words about Aphrodite in the sea-surge (447–48) are proved more completely and terribly true than she could know. Her subsequent words, πάντα δ' ἐκ ταύτης ἔφυ, κτλ ("Everything has its birth from her," 448–50), are also here recalled, on a much deeper and more inclusive level

50. For the Troezenian version of Hippolytus' death see Pausanias 2.32.10 and in general Carl Robert, *Die griechische Heldensage* II (in L. Preller, *Griechische Mythologie* 2.2) 4th ed. (Berlin 1921) 740 with n.2. The Bull, however, would seem to have been an integral part of the legend in Athens by Euripides' time, and Plutarch (*Thes.* 28) attests that the version of the story in the various tragedians was substantially the same. See also Preller-Robert, 743 with n.3.

(1276–80). Aphrodite's realm thus includes not only the basic elements of sea and sky but all aspects of the natural world. The "mountain creatures" point back once more to Hippolytus' quiet mountain retreats and the animals he hunted, now too overwhelmed by and subjected to Aphrodite, as the horses and the land in the preceding scene were overwhelmed by the sea.

This chorus echoes not only the Nurse's words (447ff.) but Aphrodite's own speech that opens the play. Here, as there, her power is said to extend over both gods and mortals (cf. 1–2 and 1268), sea and sky; and the end of the ode reminds us that the power and honor (κράτη, 5; τιμώμενοι, 8) which she demanded of men are now acknowledged to the full (βασιληίδα τιμάν, 1280; μόνα κρατύνεις, 1282).

In the play, of course, it is the recognition of her power by men that is the central theme, and hence they are given special emphasis in the enumeration of the spheres of her dominion. They come, emphatically, last in the series at the beginning of a verse (1280). The position of the phrase itself, however, leaves somewhat ambiguous the reference of the words that come immediately after: ἄνδρας τε· συμπάντων βασιληίδα τιμάν / Κύπρι, τῶνδε μόνα κρατύνεις ("and men; over all these, Kypris you alone rule in queenly power," 1280–81). The more obvious and immediate reference of "all those whom you, Kypris . . . rule" is probably all the aspects of the physical world here enumerated. It is also possible (though admittedly less likely with συμπάντων) to take the reference to be to "all *men*," both those who openly admit her power and those who deny it.

The ode occurring at this crucial point presents also a dramatic and essential duality in Aphrodite's nature. This ambiguity is deepened in the stress upon birds and flying, for previously, too, the bird imagery had an ambiguous significance, expressing both man's hope for escape to a world of untroubled beauty (731ff.) and the reality of death (see 828ff. and cf. λευκόπτερος, 752, of Phaedra's ship, with ποικιλόπτερος here, 1270). The epithet χρυσοφαής (1275) recalls also the amber tears shed for Phaethon in the beautiful West (ἠλεκτροφαεῖς, 741). Yet those gentle tears there still belonged to a human world full of sorrow and compassion, whereas the brightness of Eros here has no relation to human feelings. It simply marks his power over all of creation, including men. The beauty of Eros—and Aphrodite—thus stands out only the more sharply against the destruction they have caused; and it is significant for the meaning of the tragedy that Euripides has placed this rich ode on their beauty and their creative agency in all of life at the point where their destructive potentialities have been most in evidence.

Artemis' entrance here, immediately after the hymn to Aphrodite, is something of a *coup de théâtre*. It also reemphasizes the basic conflict of the play, the opposition of the two goddesses, at the point when that opposition has completed its destruction of human life. Yet even Artemis continues to bear witness to the power of the sea, blaming Theseus' use of his gift from his "sea father" (πατὴρ . . . πόντιος, 1318) and exclaiming to him, at the end of her speech, "these evils have broken upon you" (σοὶ τάδ' ἔρρωγεν κακά, 1338). This verb from Homer on is used of the breaking of waves. Aeschylus' *Persians* (433) provides a close parallel: κακῶν πέλαγος ἔρρωγεν.

In recalling the sea, moreover, the goddess who has come ostensibly to soothe the pain of the human tragedy also takes up the familiar theme of the closing off of escape. She addresses Theseus aggressively thus (1290–93):

How will you not hide your form in shame beneath the earth or taking wing upward [πτηνὸς ἄνω] not change your life and hold your foot outside of this grief.

The familiar image of flight here reflects the total impossibility of the once longed-for escape now that disaster and grief have closed about the human protagonists. The sky that Hippolytus invoked with his goddess at the beginning (οὐρανίαν Ἄρτεμιν, 59–60), connected perhaps with his own form of escape from the complex reality of human life, is now possessed, like the sea, by the opposite and rejected power.

The final opposition between this broader, more violent reality and the unreality of the previous wishes is again stated, in the exodos, through the theme of prayer. What both Theseus and Hippolytus pray for now is death. When Theseus hears Artemis' words he can only utter δέσποιν', ὀλοίμην (1325), echoing perhaps the ὀλοίμην of Hippolytus' oath that Theseus would not believe (1028). Hippolytus himself now prays for death to come as healer, Παιάν (1373), and for Hades to bring him to his final rest (1386ff.), while Theseus wishes again to die, to be a corpse instead of his son (1410).

Euripides

Hippolytus' last wish, however, is both the most impossible and the most terrible. Hippolytus wishes men could curse the gods, εἴθ' ἦν ἀραῖον δαίμοσιν βροτῶν γένος (1415). This wish, coming from the "pious" (1419) Hippolytus, takes even Artemis aback, and she cautions, ἔασον (1416). Yet while the most fanciful of all the wishes, it is, in a sense, the most real and tragic statement in the play. It completes now his companions' earlier hesitation about a divine Providence or Intelligence (1102ff.) and reflects the total futility and helplessness of human effort and aspiration, all of man's bitterness and despair toward a universe in which he can see nothing but capriciously destructive, jealous, and pitiless powers.

Prayer, then, becomes, at the last, curse, and as such recalls the curses (ἀραί, 888, etc.; cf. ἀραῖον here) which Theseus called down upon his son. It sums up the futility of wish and prayer, perhaps of hope itself. All the wishes turn out to be totally impossible of fulfillment (as in the escape ode); or else they are fulfilled only if they are destructive (Theseus' curse, Hippolytus' oath in 1028ff.); or, if positive, they are fulfilled in a negative way. Thus Hippolytus' prayer to Artemis at the beginning (85–87),

With you I associate and converse with words, hearing your voice but seeing your face not. And as I began, so may I round the end of my life [τέλος δὲ κάμψαιμ' ὥσπερ ἠρξάμην βίου],

is fulfilled with a bitter reversal at the end. Hippolytus does, in a sense, end his life as he began, conversing with Artemis and "seeing her face not" (see 1391ff., where the dying youth infers his goddess' presence from the perfume—ὦ θεῖον ὀδμῆς πνεῦμα—but presumably cannot see her: cf. also Soph., Ajax 14ff.). Yet his τέλος βίου is far different from what he has prayed for, and fulfillment has come not through the goddess to whom he prayed but through her opposite, to whom he refused prayer. All hope to escape reality is thus confronted with a more basic and bitter reality. The only thing men can pray for in the end is death or the power to curse the gods, which is tantamount to cursing life.

It is, of course, in Aphrodite that the complex nature of this inescapable reality is reflected, though Artemis will play Aphrodite's role in some future tragedy (1420ff.). Hence this last part of the play also adumbrates the ambiguity of the love goddess. Love and death fuse in

Hippolytus' appeal for death in language that recalls the erotic roots of his disaster. He speaks of his "love [ἔραμαι] for the double-edged spear [λόγχας]" to put to sleep (εὐνᾶσαι) his life (1375ff.; cf. also κοιμάσειε, 1386). The longing for the spear recalls Phaedra's desire for it at the beginning of the play (ἐπίλογχον, 221; ἔραμαι, 219, etc.). Artemis speaks of his being yoked (συνεζύγης, 1389) to his disaster, an image with familiar erotic associations (ἄζυγα, 546; ἄζυγες, 1425). Finally, when Hippolytus is about to die, his request, "raise my body" (κατόρθωσον δέμας, 1445), echoes the languor of the lovesick Phaedra earlier (cf. ἄρατέ μου δέμας, ὀρθοῦτε κάρα, 198) and recalls the carrying out of her lifeless body (ὀρθώσατ' ἐκτεί-νοντες ἄθλιον νέκυν, 786).[51] Indeed, Hippolytus' pitiful state at the end, his entrance among companions who bear his almost lifeless body, is vaguely parallel to Phaedra's entrance, in a state of collapse and near to death, at the beginning (e.g., λέλυμαι μελέων σύνδεσμα φίλων, 199). These connections suggest again the tragic interweaving of the deaths of the protagonists, the ambiguity of who is agent and who is victim, and the power of love to destroy both the lover and the beloved. The circle is thus closed, and Hippolytus in his death reenacts horribly the languid condition—the weakness and help-lessness—of the woman whose love, scorned, has killed him and herself.[52] Yet against the goddess whose will comprises the indif-ferent interplay of elemental opposites, love and death, procreation and destruction, the human characters come to assert their own hu-manity. As Bernard Knox has well said, the forgiveness that passes between them is "an affirmation of human values in an inhuman universe."[53] In this mutual forgiveness both father and son discover a lost basis of understanding and love. And in finding one another, each loses something of his previous intransigence and limitation of feeling. This change is already working within Theseus even before

51. ὀρθόω is used metaphorically of Phaedra's conflict and moral struggle: see 247, 680. The parallel between Hippolytus' condition here and Phaedra's love-sick state earlier has been noted briefly also by Grube (note 26) 193.

52. There is perhaps a further adumbration of the circular movement, the fulfill-ment of Aphrodite's will, in Hippolytus' statement that he sees the gates of Hades (ὄλωλα καὶ δὴ νερτέρων ὁρῶ πύλας, 1447), which recalls Aphrodite's concluding words in the prologue (56–57): οὐ γὰρ οἶδ' ἀνεωιγμένας πύλας / Ἅιδου, φάος δὲ λοίσθιον βλέπων τόδε.

53. Knox (note 5) 31. For the gradual growth of the compassion and reconciliation at the end of the play see also Matthaei (note 9) 104ff.

Hippolytus confirms it and adds to it his own. Theseus' first reaction to the news of Hippolytus' death was triumph, almost joy, at the fulfillment of his prayer (1169ff.); and he met the first announcement of the Messenger with the cruel remark, "At whose hand? Did he fall into the hatred of someone whose wife he violated, like his father's?" (1164–65). After the full account of his death, however, he softens, admits the tie of blood (οὕνεκ' ἐστὶν ἐξ ἐμοῦ), and states that he no longer either rejoices or is grieved (1259–60). He still wishes, however, to "examine him with words" (λόγοις τ' ἐλέγξω, 1267) and refute his previous denial of the deed. Artemis, however, taking up this phrase, reveals Theseus' own culpability in not having "examined" (οὐκ ἤλεγξας) the matter more fully through divine and human means (1321ff.). She cannot absolve or forgive his guilt, only set forth, objectively, the way through which absolution, or at least mitigation of guilt, might come: "First your ignorance of your error looses you from baseness; and, second, your wife in dying took away examinations of words" (λόγων ἐλέγχους, 1335–37). The repeated expression "examine" (or "examine with words") points up the hastiness and irrationality of Theseus' previous action and traces his share in the disaster to the unchecked and unexamined release of his anger. He who, in his wrath, would not believe his son's repeated oaths that he was not kakos (1031, 1075, 1191)[54] is proved himself kakos in the eyes of both the goddess and the son: σὺ δ' ἔν τ' ἐκείνῳ κἀν ἐμοὶ φαίνῃ κακός (1320). He comes, however, to repent fully; but only Hippolytus, the victim, can forgive him for his anger (τί δ'; ἔκτανές τἄν μ', ὡς τότ' ἦσθ' ὠργισμένος, 1413) and absolve him (1449 and 1335). The anger (ὀργαί, 1418) of Aphrodite, however, is unforgivable, and Hippolytus wishes to curse her as his father cursed him (1415). Men can forgive one another, but they cannot forgive the gods any more than the gods can forgive them. To quote Knox once more, "These gods are, in both the literal and metaphorical senses of the word, inhuman."[55] Their inhumanity, however, is the resisting matter of the universe against which man's humanity comes to life.

Thus Hippolytus, who showed himself Theseus' son negatively in his impulsive and pitiless dismissal of Phaedra and total lack of at-

54. The thrice-repeated εἰ κακὸς πέφυκ' ἀνήρ stands also in ironic contrast with Hippolytus' earlier self-righteousness about not being kakos, 654.
55. Knox (note 5) 29.

tempt to understand her suffering, recognizes his kinship to his father at a deeper and more meaningful level. To reach this recognition, however, he must suffer from his father the same cruelty and anger that he showed to Phaedra. The impulsiveness and vehemence of the two men make the reconciliation all the more significant, as well as psychologically possible. This reconciliation in turn helps redeem their previous callousness and is the more moving and tragic coming after they have suffered the full consequences of their rash natures. Theseus' blind wrath made him incapable of pity for his son. As he threatened to drive Hippolytus from the palace with his own hand, his final words were, "For no pity [οἶκτος] for your exile comes upon me" (1089).[56] Now, however, it is the father who is an object of pity to his son; and the son gives the pity he was himself formerly denied (1405, 1407, 1409):

> I lament too then my father's disasters . . . Alas, most wretched for this misfortune, father . . . I lament your error for you more than for me. . . .[57]

And as Hippolytus rediscovers Theseus as father, Theseus recognizes him, finally, as son (1452, 1455):

> Θη. ὦ φίλταθ', ὡς γενναῖος ἐκφαίνῃ πατρί.
> Ἱπ. τοιῶνδε παίδων γνησίων εὔχου τυχεῖν.
> (with Wilamowitz's transposition)

> *Thes.* O dearest one, how noble you show yourself toward your father.
> *Hipp.* Pray to find your legitimate children thus.

In this recognition, each finds a new level of humanity in both himself and the other.

56. It is perhaps interesting that previously "pity" was found only in the mythical world into which the chorus longs to escape: *oiktos* is used but one other time in the play, of Phaethon, lamented by his sisters, in the escape ode (740).

57. Euripides' emphasis upon Hippolytus' forgiveness of his father and his delicate and beautiful treatment of this theme are interesting in the light of another legend of Hippolytus, that involving his rebirth and transfer to Aricia, in which special emphasis is given to his *refusal* to forgive his father: see Herter (note 37) 292 and Pausan. 2.27.4: ὁ δὲ ὡς αὖθις ἐβίω, οὐκ ἠξίου νέμειν τῷ πατρὶ συγγνώμην, ἀλλὰ ὑπεριδὼν τὰς δεήσεις εἰς Ἰταλίαν ἔρχεται, κ.τ.λ.

The reconciliation, spreading from father to son, touches even Phaedra who, though not actually forgiven, is at least explicitly included among the victims (1404) and given a part in the future cult-song about Hippolytus (1430).[58] Indeed, the language with which Theseus pardons his father recalls and cancels some of the inhumanity in his violent rejection of Phaedra. His nobility in not leaving his father's hand "impure" (ἄναγνον, 1448) stands at the opposite extreme from the self-righteous and narrow priggishness in his denunciation of Phaedra: "How then would I be base who think I am impure [οὐδ' . . . ἁγνεύειν δοκῶ] if I but hear such things" (654–55).

Whatever positive element the tragedy contains, however, appears in the contrast between Phaedra's death and Hippolytus'. She died "betrayed" (590, 591, 595) by the Nurse and, in a sense, by Hippolytus. Hippolytus at the end holds firm in his father's entreaty not to be "betrayed" (μή νυν προδῷς με, τέκνον, ἀλλὰ καρτέρει, 1456). Her death came amid hatred and anger, as her love turned to the lust for vengeance; and in its train it brought only more hatred, anger, and death—all the violence that the sea and the Bull symbolize. Although this violence, and the tragic waste and loss it entails, cannot be wiped out, they are at least in part mitigated by the love, the understanding, and the deeper avowal of kinship at Hippolytus' death.

But the gods do not forgive, nor do they wish to be touched by human suffering (1437–39). Artemis may provide the objective material out of which the humanity and forgiveness may grow, but in herself she is indifferent and remote, even cruel so far as Theseus is concerned. She can state coldly that Theseus' ignorance excuses him (1334–35); but only Hippolytus can speak the personal, emotionally effective, and truly comforting absolution: "I free you from this death of mine" (σε τοῦδ' ἐλευθερῶ φόνου, 1449). Contrast the way in which Artemis speaks her "absolution." She uses the third-person, abstract form of statement τὸ μὴ εἰδέναι . . . ἐκλύει κάκης (1335), which is itself given as part of a logical enumeration, πρῶτον μέν . . . ἔπειτα δέ, in the remote, cool language of a judge (1334–37). Scholars of recent years have thus rightly criticized older interpretations that saw in her appearance all sweetness and light, serenity and divine

58. For the position of Phaedra at the end, see Matthaei (note 9) 110.

pity.[59] She does, it is true, ask Hippolytus to forgive Theseus[60]; yet it is after her departure, when the two men are left alone with their suffering, that they turn to one another, father and son, and make the most significant, and for Hippolytus the final, discovery of their lives.

Artemis thus remains true to her nature, as Aphrodite to hers: she is still the goddess of the wild, of the nonhuman world. Her only words of comfort are that the gods do not rejoice at the death of pious mortals (1339–40), and she can but assure Hippolytus that he dies dear to her (1397–98):

Ιπ. οὐκ ἔστι σοι κυναγὸς οὐδ᾽ ὑπηρέτης,
Αρ. οὐ δῆτ᾽ ἀτάρ μοι προσφιλής γ᾽ ἀπόλλυσαι.

Hipp. No longer have you hunter or servant.
Art. No; but you die dear to me.

It is part of Hippolytus' tragedy that he, whose death resulted from his very devotion to Artemis and from something of her wildness in his treatment of Phaedra, should find his goddess true to her nature at the end: "Easily you leave a long association [ὁμιλίαν]," he chides (1441), and his words recall Aphrodite's spiteful warning in the prologue about his "falling in with more than mortal association" (μείζω

59. The positive view of Artemis here has been restated as late as 1935: see S. M. Adams, "Two Plays of Euripides," *CR* 49 (1935) 118–19. He sees Artemis as speaking in 1326–41 "with a gentle statement of the gods' invariable law" and offering Theseus "such comfort as she can" (119). Similarly Méridier (note 4) 23–24. See *contra* Knox (note 5) 29–31; Kitto (note 9) 206; Norwood (note 2) 96ff. Their views were anticipated, however, as early as Matthaei (note 9) 112, who finds, with her usual sensitivity and honesty, "Something . . . of the unsolved in the cruel relations between gods and men" and "the biting, cruel, truly Euripidean atmosphere of sarcasm against the so-called 'divine.'"

60. Hippolytus' reply to Artemis' request in 1443, καὶ γὰρ πάροιθε σοῖς ἐπειθόμην λόγοις, might also mean in the context that he has already forgiven his father even before Artemis' injunction: "For even before [your request] I was obeying your words [i.e. what you are now enjoining]." Euripides does use *paroithe* of the recent as well as of the more remote past (see, e.g., *Phoen.* 853). The generally received interpretation, however, "For in the past too I was wont to obey your commands," is perhaps more suited to the ironical and bitter tone of Hippolytus here and is probably to be preferred, but the other should be kept in mind. It is not impossible that there is an intentional ambiguity in Hippolytus' words.

βροτείας . . . ὁμιλίας, 19). But Artemis by her nature can do nothing else, and it is only at her departure and the unsolaced approach of
his own death that Hippolytus discovers his own humanity. Her
departure thus marks symbolically his relinquishment of the wild that
he has loved and in which he has lived.[61] His death is thus also the
rebirth of his humanity.

The conclusion of the play, then, does contain positive elements,
but it is far from optimistic. The tragic mixture of grief and compassion, of humanity gained at the price of suffering and death, is suggested in the image with which the play ends, significantly an image
of the sea (1462–67):

> A common grief to all the citizens this came unexpectedly. There will
> be a rhythmic plashing of many tears [πολλῶν δακρύων ἔσται
> πίτυλος]; for the stories of the great that are worthy of grief are more
> wont to endure.

The word πίτυλος introduces a common but complex metaphor that
is practically untranslatable. It is used figuratively of the rhythmic
beating of breasts or falling of tears in lamentation but literally denotes the regular sound of the oars produced by the coordinated
efforts of the rowers as on a trireme.[62] Hence it is well used here to
mark the human social world (cf. κοινὸν . . . πᾶσι πολίταις, 1462),
which thus expresses its common participation in grief and loss. It
was in terms of the whole society that Hippolytus' death was first
announced (see πολίταις, 1168–69), and the tale of his disaster will be
preserved in a social context (1423ff.). His fellow-citizens are capable
of feeling and lamenting his suffering as a god cannot. The goddess
who cannot weep (ὁρῶ· κατ' ὄσσων δ' οὐ θέμις βαλεῖν δάκρυ, 1396)
can give only the "greatest grievings" of *others'* tears for his sufferings

---

61. On Artemis' departure see Kitto (note 9) 207: "We breathe a little more freely
when this sub-human goddess has taken herself off, leaving the stage to the reconciliation between father and son."

62. For pitylos in its literal sense see Aeschyl. *Pers.* 976; Eur. *Tro.* 1123; *IT* 1050,
1346, etc. Euripides uses it frequently of lamentation (see *Tro.* 1236) or even of other
strong emotions like fear (*HF* 816) or madness (*HF* 1189, *IT* 307). The best and fullest
elaboration of the connection between the rhythmic beating of oars and lamentation
occurs in Aeschylus (*Sept.* 854–60) for whom the metaphor, as with his sea metaphors
generally, is extremely vivid. For a full discussion of the meanings of pitylos, with
abundant parallels, see Barrett (note 28) 418–19.

(πένθη μέγιστα δακρύων καρπουμένῳ, 1427). The rhythmical lament and falling tears of the chorus, therefore (see δακρύων, ἀξιοπενθεῖς, 1464–65), are the human equivalent for the goddess' gift. At the same time these are bitter tears, unmitigated by the gentle unreality of the wished-for world of the escape ode and hence not transformed into the beautiful brightness of amber, like those shed by Phaethon's sisters "into the swelling sea of their father" (738–41). In the pitylos image, grief and tears are again associated with the sea, but without any suggestion that the sea provides comfort or consolation.

This image, on the contrary, sharpens the juxtaposition between the human world and the elemental forces that have crashed destructively into it. It evokes all the power of the sea and the whole sequence of the previous imagery, the shipwreck or storm in terms of which the coming disaster of Phaedra was presented (36, 140, 155ff., 315, 752ff., etc.) and the wreck of Theseus too upon a "sea of troubles" (822ff.). Most poignantly, it recalls the description of the doomed Hippolytus as a steersman who has lost control of his ship (1221, 1224, 1227). As the image for the measured sound of man's control over one of the elements of this world, the pitylos points up, finally, man's helplessness against the measureless and the uncontrollable.[63]

It is this lament, then, which answers the previous attempts to control or escape the sea. Like the hunters' song earlier (1102–10), it marks a sadder but more realistic acceptance of all that the sea implies. Hippolytus' attempt to resist its elemental force is only reflected tragically back upon him in the oarlike beat of the lamentation at his death. Yet this lament combines in itself the images both of human weakness and of the possibility of human compassion. In its sealike rhythm it acknowledges the uncontrollable and the nonhuman yet transmutes its violence into pity. Thus the pitylos reasserts another side of man's capacity for measure. It resolidifies man's social bond against the unknown and gives final and enduring expression to the human—and humanizing—side of grief and loss, the compassionate understanding to which men, through suffering, can rise.

The god-sent violence of the sea thus overwhelms human life and when calm returns leaves behind a wreckage in which the only sound is the slow, steady lament, like the strokes of the oar. He who re-

63. For this aspect of the pitylos image, see Segal (note 1) 42.

jected what the sea meant is destroyed by it yet is himself mourned in terms of it. It remains as the symbol for the realities, more bitter than consoling, surrounding human life, the realities that, like the gods, endure eternally while the individual life comes and passes away.

Through the sea, then, we come back to the question of the nature of the gods raised at the beginning of this essay. Aphrodite is not only in the sea but of the sea. The sea is the necessary correlative of her power and nature, the demanding nature of the reality of our world. Hence its imagistic function in the play is indispensable for establishing the scope of the action. Through the imagery of the sea the problematical role of the gods is raised above the question of Euripides' religion to become a mirror for the broader questions of the nature of human existence, human action, and the "total reality" amid which human life is lived.[64]

Commentators have, of course, objected ceaselessly to this dehumanization of the gods.[65] Yet it is essential to the tragic action that the powers against which the protagonists struggle and to which, ultimately, they yield be inhuman, pitiless, totally regardless of man's constructs and his ideals. These powers and their poetic embodiment in the wild sea serve as the foil for the humanity that is finally affirmed and as the measure of the effort involved in the affirmation.

In the sharpness and bitterness of this polarity lies one of the basic differences between Sophoclean and Euripidean drama. In Sophocles we may feel that the gods are somehow responsible for human suffering, as in the *Oedipus Rex* or in the statement that ends the *Trachiniae*, "There is nothing of this that is not Zeus" (1278). But their responsibility in Sophocles is vaguer and less pointed. His gods are less intelligible in terms of human passions and more remote from human life. They look upon man's suffering across the cold, vast distances of space, like the constellations moving for eternity along their "circling

64. Winnington-Ingram (note 2) 190: "Of this total reality from which there is no escape the gods are symbols." Norwood (note 2) 105, also speaks of Euripides' gods as symbolizing "the permanent facts of the Universe and of human life."

65. See, among others, Greenwood (note 2) 41, 45 (rather one-sided); Wilamowitz (note 6) 112–13, who speaks of Euripides' gods has having "des Menschlichen zu viel" while lacking "das Beste des Menschen"; yet he sees the "disharmony" between human nobility and divine baseness as part of his intention and dramatic technique. For the conflict of humanity and the inhuman see Lester Crocker, "On Interpreting *Hippolytus*," *Philologus* 101 (1957) 245: "It is man *against* the universe—insofar as he wants to be human." See also the references cited above, note 59.

paths" (see *Trach.* 130–31). For him, then, the definition of humanity comes exclusively through man, his greatness and his blindness and the uncertainty of his life, and not, as in Euripides, through the opposition between man and a divine inhumanity.

The prologue of the *Ajax* perhaps comes closest to the *Hippolytus* in depicting a pitiless divinity (note especially the contrast between Athena and Odysseus, 118ff.); but even Sophocles' Athena is far from the wanton spite of Euripides' Aphrodite. Athena's role in the play is much less significant, and her wrath is not unjust (see 760ff.) and, perhaps, not inexorable (see 756–57). In Euripides, on the other hand, divine inhumanity makes the affirmation of humanity necessarily more tenuous, hesitant, and uncertain. It is perhaps doubtful whether the human compassion asserted in the last scene of the *Hippolytus* is an adequate or fully satisfying counterforce to the divine indifference. The dirge is nevertheless *something*. It is the final term in the progression from the wild shouting of Hippolytus (581ff.) and the rancorous letter of Phaedra which "shouts" though silent (877ff.) to the ritual songs of the disaster to be sung by the Troezenian girls (1423ff.) and the pain-wrung forgiveness of the son-victim toward the agent-father. But it marks perhaps the ultimate helplessness of man in such a world. To be human means to die at the hands of the gods, but it also means to be able to lament.

The divinities of the *Hippolytus,* then, possess both the indifference and the power of the elements with which they are associated (in fact the *combination* of indifference and power defines in large part their divinity); and these elements, sea and woodland, come to play as large a symbolic role in the action as the gods themselves. Together they comprise a whole, no part of which can man neglect or seek to escape without incurring the risk of its striking back. It is this wholeness of the world which makes it dangerous to men. The Greeks generally did not separate the positive and negative aspects of divinity. Apollo is the god who cures diseases as well as he who sends them; and Dionysus is a god "most terrible" as well as "most mild" (*Ba.* 861).[66] The gods thus themselves contain something of the duality of the natural world, both life-giving and destructive.

These antinomies in the gods, which are therefore the antinomies faced by human life, run throughout the play. Love is "sweetest and

66. See A. R. Bellinger, "The *Bacchae* and *Hippolytus,*" *YCS* 6 (1939) 25f.

painful at the same time" (348), and so its goddess brings both eros and thanatos. Destructive and spiteful in the prologue, she is hymned as a beautiful and life-giving power just after she has done her worst.[67] And Phaedra, who enters determined to die, surrenders to Aphrodite with the return of her desire to live (see 441ff.: "Will you then because of love destroy your life . . ."). Yet, through Aphrodite, she generates death on a wider and more violent scale. Similarly, as Aphrodite's sea can be warm and soothing in the parodos, and violent and destructive as the action develops, so too the peace and removal of the woodland has its negative aspect in some of the imagery associated with Hippolytus (646–47, 689).

Conversely, there is the suggestion of a similar duality in Artemis. As Aphrodite is associated both with the joyous, creative release of sexual energy and with its thoughtless, blind violence, so Artemis, the cold, chaste goddess, can be called upon as the gentle helper of women in childbirth (161–69).[68] The play presents us with the paradoxical associations of Aphrodite and death, Artemis and birth. Artemis too is associated with the sea (148ff., 229), the element of her enemy and opposite. Indeed, in the exodos she seems to share Aphrodite's sea qualities, with her indifference to the "third" victim (1404) and her willingness to involve, on her own initiative, a fourth (1420ff.). She seems, furthermore, to have been worshiped at Troezen as a goddess who saves from the sea, and it is perhaps to this aspect of her that Phaedra refers in 229, "Lady Artemis of Limne by the sea."[69] She is thus Hippolytus' goddess in her association with both woodland and Limne by the sea. Another Troezenian legend, however, involves her in the death, by the sea, of one of her followers, also a hunter: Saron, for whom was named the sea from which death comes to Hippolytus (1200).[70] Thus despite the basic

67. See ibid. 26: "But compare her [Aphrodite's] unlovely appearance in the prologue with the exquisite song in her honor strangely put just before the entrance of Artemis, her foe." Equally significant, however, is what comes *before* this song. So too Eros, in the same sentence, can be a sacker of cities (541ff.) and the "keeper of keys to Aphrodite's dearest chambers" (539–40).

68. For Artemis as a birth goddess see Plato, *Theaet.* 149b, and, in general, M. P. Nilsson, *Geschichte der griechischen Religion,* 2d ed. (Munich 1955) 1:492ff.

69. For Artemis' connection with the sea at Troezen see Wilamowitz (note 6) 95; also Jebb (note 49) on Soph. *Trach.* 636; Apollon. Rhod. 1.571: Ἄρτεμιν, ἥ κείνας σκοπιὰς ἁλὸς ἀμφιέπεσκεν.

70. See "Saron" in Roscher (note 18) 4 (1909–15) 388. Wilamowitz (note 6) 95 n.2,

opposition between the two goddesses there is, as several scholars have noted, a terrible likeness between them,[71] which on the psychological level perhaps signifies something of the ambivalence of the human mind toward the elemental passions and desires it must both live with and repress. Phaedra, possessed by Aphrodite, longs for the purity of her opposite; and Hippolytus, serving the chaste Artemis and desiring the calm woodlands and removal from human affairs (1013ff.),[72] denounces sex with a vehemence that itself violates the severe sophrosyne he supposes himself to possess.

On another level this likeness between the two goddesses expresses the ineluctable wholeness, the unity in complementaries, of the elemental world. Men may try to divide up this wholeness against itself, to transform it mentally by claiming to worship one of its aspects, though, as in Phaedra's case, they may be using the opposite only to conceal the power to which they are really subject. Yet whatever divided forms this reality takes in the human mind, its wholeness is still inescapable. That which is longed for becomes that which destroys. Phaedra's love for Hippolytus causes her death, just as his devotion to Artemis causes his. She seals her death with an oath in the name of the goddess opposite to the one to whom she is in fact bound (σεμνὴν Ἄρτεμιν, 713–14) and with words that repeat the prayer of her beloved's chaste followers (see 61ff.). His death comes from the forces he has most resisted, the wildness of the sea, the sexuality of the Bull, and from the creatures he has reared and loved. Thus the ambiguities in both Aphrodite and Artemis and the interplay between them reveal how easily and mysteriously eros leads to thanatos, how one instinct leads to its opposite, and how dangerous and complex generally are the basic instincts, even the life instincts, that rule our existence.

It is this complexity, this dangerous wholeness, which Hippolytus seeks to ignore or escape. Perhaps there is even an aspect of the goddess he worships, and worships exclusively, which he does not

---

regards Saron as "ein Doppelgänger des Hippolytos nach der einen Seite seines Wesens, der wohl aus ihm differenziert ist."

71. See Knox (note 5) 28–29, who notes other parallels. On Phaedra's concealing of "Aphrodite" by "Artemis" see the "Discussion" of Winnington-Ingram's paper (note 2) 197; also Dodds (note 30) 103–4.

72. For this *topos* of the peaceful private life see in general G. Heintzeler, "Das Bild des Tyrannen bei Platon," *Tüb. Beitr.* 3 (1927) 26ff.

Euripides

know, just as he does not know an aspect of the horses he trains in her service. She is invoked, as we have seen, as the goddess of childbirth; and it is significant that Hippolytus specifically denounces childbirth, like everything connected with sex, in the most violent and extravagant terms (618–24). In this he denies the most immediate of the realities of life, the act wherein men are most bound to the necessities of their animal nature, where the boundary between the controlled human world and the wild, pain-filled world of the beasts is narrowest. Thus he refuses to know a basic aspect of his goddess, one wherein she too is perhaps touched by the wildness of the sea, the inevitable risks of man's participation in the process of creating life. To these risks the women of the chorus are closer, as women have always been. (Euripides also appears, atypically for his society, highly sensitive to the supposed ἀκίνδυνον βίον of women: *Med.* 248–51.) Hence they can find the sea gentle and peaceful in the parode, while Hippolytus, abominating women, is to know only its violence. In seeking to banish the creative powers of life, he renders inevitable his full exposure to its destructive powers. Indeed, his chief occupation, the hunt, is destructive, and again serves only a partial aspect of his goddess, the πότνια θηρῶν, the goddess connected with wild animal life. The Artemis whom the women know and invoke, however, is the complement, not the enemy, of Aphrodite. She wields the bow (167) but also gives good births (εὔλοχον, 166). Thus it is the gentle, pitying, life-giving aspect of his goddess, as she manifests herself to women, which Hippolytus ignores; and hence he is destroyed by her complement, also a goddess of life, in her most cruel and inhuman form.

Hippolytus' rejection or ignorance of this other aspect of Artemis is, of course, deliberate. His life is a pure expression of the masculine desire to re-form his world, to make himself as free as possible of the physical and animal exigencies of his existence, to which women must yield (or at least from which they can less easily escape). Hence, to assert his freedom he must reject them and their bondage to the creation of life. His freedom is ultimately the spiritual freedom men have always sought, and the search cannot but be tragic.[73] There is an

73. See Crocker (note 65) 242: "His [Hippolytus'] total rejection of sex is the rejection of enslavement to a disorderly, non-rational, non-moral force, which women, the arousers and objects of our desires, embody. It is a tragic assertion of will—the

element of true idealism in his aims and in his uncompromising rigidity (his akribeia) which contrasts favorably with the Nurse's amoral expediency or the chorus' wish for easy adaptability, wealth, and principles that are not too firm (see 1111ff.).[74]

Yet in his idealism he is opposed by one of the strongest and most relentless realities of physical existence, symbolically associated with the equally forceful and resistless power of the sea. In trying to resist, Hippolytus almost destroys his own humanity, only to rediscover it at his death and with it his own tie, rooted in physical generation, to his father. With his humanity and compassion he triumphs, as a man, over the wildness of the sea. But as his body is borne away, it is the rhythm of the sea that echoes behind him as a dirge.

---

will to surpass the animal in us, to live on purely human terms of idealism, mind, and spirit." See also Méridier (note 4) 24. To see these possibilities in Hippolytus' tragedy is not, of course, to maintain that Euripides intended us to regard him as an Orphic. See D. W. Lucas, "Hippolytus," *CQ* 40 (1946) 65–69; Winnington-Ingram (note 2) 186–87; Knox (note 5) 21 with note 22; Méridier (note 4) 20 n.1. The religious character of Hippolytus' worship of Artemis is well discussed by Festugière (note 17) 14ff. with note 19, pp. 145–46. The mystical element that Festugière emphasizes in this worship, however, seems to me only to deepen and embitter his tragedy rather than mitigate it, as Festugière seems to imply in his discussion of the final scene (pp. 16–17). It must be remembered too that Hippolytus shows no belief in an afterlife. In such a situation Artemis' "No; but you die dear to me" (1398) is cold comfort; and his curse in 1415 and his final address to the goddess in 1441 indicate that he is not in fact comforted. Here, as in the *Bacchae*, it is very difficult to determine what actually are Euripides' religious attitudes or how favourably he regards the kind of worship which Hippolytus practices. On the religious implications, positive and negative, of Hippolytus' *sophrosyne* see Barrett (note 28) 172–73; and on Hippolytus and Orphism, 342–43.

74. There is perhaps an interesting affinity between Hippolytus' outburst against sex and women with a more famous and more influential idealistic proposal for gaining a measure of freedom for the human spirit: Plato's construction of his ideal state. Compare Hippolytus' suggestion for "buying the seed of children" from temples with a certain weight of gold or bronze or iron each according to his value (620–23) with *Repub.* 3.415aff. and 8.547aff. The resemblance is, of course, superficial (Plato is using Hesiod, *Op.* 109–201 without any reference to Euripides), and Hippolytus is simply here overemotional and negative rather than serious and constructive, but it is essentially the same universal limitation of human freedom which is in question. Euripides' attitude about the possibility of this freedom is, as the course of the play makes clear, quite different from Plato's.

CHAPTER 7

The Two Worlds of
Euripides' *Helen*

I

Euripides' *Helen* has justly been called a comedy of ideas.[1] That is only half the story. The *Helen* is also a romance. In addition to its setting in the Egyptian never-never land, the play also includes the reunion of long-separated lovers, the loss and recovery of identity, the supernatural knowledge of a magicianlike princess, and (like Shakespeare's *Much Ado About Nothing* or *Cymbeline*) a calumniated heroine whose virtue will carry her and her beloved through the perils of delusion and restore them to their own kingdom to live happily ever after.[2]

Euripides has intertwined these hoary and popular themes of the romantic plot with the Sophistic intellectualism of his own day. The combination is extraordinary. The closest parallels are perhaps Sophocles' *Philoctetes* and Aristophanes' *Frogs,* but Euripides has pushed the two sides, romance and intellectualism, to their furthest extremes. He has thus created a Chimaera-like tour de force in which amusement and puzzlement follow close upon one another.

The analogies with *A Midsummer Night's Dream* or the *Tempest* cited by Schlegel, Verrall, and others were largely pejorative, supportive of their dismissal of the *Helen* because it is not "tragic" and

---

1. See Anne Pippin (Burnett), "Euripides' *Helen:* A Comedy of Ideas," *CP* 55 (1960) 151–63.

2. On this female figure in romance see Northrop Frye, *A Natural Perspective: The Development of Shakespearean Comedy and Romance* (New York 1965) 63–65.

therefore not "serious."[3] The idols of high seriousness and dramatic realism have tended, until recently, to usurp the whole of the domain of criticism, banishing the more conventional and unrealistic forms, like romance, to the remote corners.[4] Northrop Frye's distinction between Iliadic and Odyssean critics is helpful here. Classicists, like Aristotle and "Longinus," tend to be Iliadic.[5] Romance, on the other hand, requires a suspension of critical judgment and an acceptance of noncommonsense situations and conventions. Thus an approach to the *Helen* based on psychological realism can elucidate individual scenes but misses the heart of the play because psychological realism, however helpful for the parts, is not an appropriate response to the whole. The play has suffered from a peculiar kind of reductio ad absurdum from which it is only slowly beginning to recover. What has long been observed of Shakespeare is equally true here: it is easy to make a Shakespearean play look ridiculous by refusing to accept its convention.[6]

One of the recurrent devices of romance is the division between two worlds, a real world of pain and trouble and an ideal world of peace, serenity, simplicity, and rustic ease.[7] The plot often centers on the passage between these two worlds and especially on the hero's return from the ideal to the real world. By the very fact of envisaging a second world superior to the humdrum everyday world in which most of us live, romance operates within a framework of antitheses. Not every romance need develop this potentially antithetical structure, but the possibility is inherent in the convention. The *Helen* exploits it very fully.

With this contrast between real and ideal worlds the *Helen* combines the theme of recognition. The romance and the recognition play are distinct forms, but they have affinities that allow happy marriages to occur.[8] Recognition easily fits into the movement in

3. See, for example, A. W. Verrall, "Euripides' Apology (*Helen*)," in *Essays on Four Plays of Euripides* (Cambridge 1905) 46; August Wilhelm von Schlegel, *Vorlesungen über dramatische Kunst und Literatur*, Krit. Ausgabe von G. A. Amoretti (Bonn and Leipzig 1923) 1.123.

4. See Frye (note 2) 9; also his *Anatomy of Criticism* (Princeton 1957) 51–52.

5. Frye (note 2) 12.

6. Loc. cit.

7. See the discussion of the three realms of late Shakespearean romance in Frye (note 2) chap. 4, especially 136–59.

8. See Richmond Lattimore, *Story Patterns in Greek Tragedy* (Ann Arbor 1964) 53:

romance between different worlds or different levels of truth. Since the passage between worlds and the recovery of a lost loved one and/or a lost truth also correspond to the awakening from a deluded state and to the reacquisition of a lost vitality, romance makes frequent use of the archetypes of death and rebirth. The pattern is already established in the *Odyssey* and ingeniously varied in the late Shakespearean romances.[9] But the *Helen* provides the first extant example in Western literature of the full-blown fusion of romance and recognition.

The passage between real and ideal worlds, when compounded with the mistaken identities and delusions of the recognition play, invites paradox and irony to a high degree. In the *Helen* the irony and paradox have a bitter tone,[10] especially, as we shall argue, toward the end of the play. Like comedy, the *Helen* plays upon a contrast between normality and abnormality, the expected and the fantastic. Yet the normal world in the background (especially in the lyrics) is not the everyday life of a Dicaeopolis or a Peithetaerus but the hellish world of Troy, with the grim associations carried by Troy from the *Iliad* and *Agamemnon* to the *Ajax* and *Troades*.

The central irony of the *Helen* lies in its antithesis of appearance and reality.[11] What is the real nature of the world? What is "word"

"The theme of the *Helen*, beyond all other extant Greek plays, is illusion. All dramas which are truth-plays: the founding stories; the stories of lost persons recovered, of mistaken identity; the stories of character defamed and vindicated; all have this in common. A lie has been perpetrated on the dramatic world. However lively the activity, it is all shaped toward the revelation of the truth: which comes, indeed, after the darkest moment."

9. See Northrop Frye's remarks on the different groups of characters in the *Tempest:* "Each goes through a pursuit of illusions, an ordeal, and a symbolic vision." Frye, Introduction, *William Shakespeare, The Tempest* (Baltimore 1959) 15.

10. For a good appreciation of the bitterness of the *Helen's* irony see Paul Friedländer, "Die griechische Tragödie und das Tragische," *Die Antike* 2 (1926) 105: "So bitter, dass von dorther das Komische überall einen bösen und schneidenden Ton empfängt."

11. See Burnett (note 1) 152: "The language, the plot, and the very form of the *Helen* all have been made to express this tension between what is and what only seems to be." See also Günther Zuntz, "On Euripides' *Helena:* Theology and Irony," in *Euripide: Entretiens sur l'antiquité classique* 6 (Vandoevres-Geneva 1960) 223ff.; D. J. Conacher, *Euripidean Drama: Myth, Theme and Structure* (Toronto 1967) 290–93; Richard Kannicht, ed., *Euripides, Helena* (Heidelberg 1969) 1.57ff., especially 62–68; also Hans Strohm, "Trug und Täuschung in der euripideischen Dramatik," in E. R. Schwinge, ed., *Euripides*, Wege der Forschung 89 (Darmstadt 1968) 367–68; Rich-

(*onoma*) and what "fact" or "deed" (*pragma*)? Helen is herself the symbol of this mysteriousness of reality, a quality that she retains from the *Odyssey* to the adaptation of the Euripidean drama in Hofmannsthal's *Ägyptische Helena* and Seferis' Ἑλένη.[12]

Helen has a double existence: she lives in the world of both appearance and reality. Men have treated an empty cloud image as the real Helen and have fought a long and bloody war to possess it—a real war in the real world, with as the price the ultimate reality, death. The real, or at least the corporeal, Helen, however, dwells in remote Egypt, which, despite its geographical factuality, is closer to the island of an Alcinous or a Prospero than to an actual place. Even this Egyptian fairyland has its divided aspect. It has its fairy princess, but also its ogrelike, dangerous ruler. Together this royal pair present opposed images of virginal purity and lustful (if vulnerable) desire.

The ultimate irony in Euripides' treatment of these basic antitheses lies in the fact that the play never completely resolves the question of which aspect of reality is the true one. We cannot be certain that the potential order and purity conveyed by the figure of Theonoe may not be an illusion, a pleasant, hopeful, even necessary illusion, but an illusion nonetheless.[13]

These questions about the nature of reality cut deep into the concerns of the late fifth century. Is there a stable reality? If there is, can we know it? If so, can we communicate it: is its nature reducible to language? These are the questions that Gorgias and his contemporaries were raising (D-K/82B3). They are also, at least in part, the questions that the *Helen* raises, for this play, with its recurrent antitheses between appearance and reality, onoma and pragma, is simultaneously about the nature of reality and the nature of language and art.[14]

---

mond Lattimore, *The Complete Greek Tragedies, 3, Euripides* (Chicago 1959) 485: "The dominant theme is paradox, illusion, surprise, all summed up in the relation of Helen to that other self, the idol who is not, but in some way is, Helen herself."

12. See for example the conclusion of Hugo von Hofmannsthal's "Ägyptische Helena," *Gesammelte Werke, 4, Dramen* (Frankfurt a.M. 1958) 301–2, or the end of Act 3 of Goethe's *Faust*, part 2, e.g., the words of Phorkyas, "Die Göttin ist nicht mehr, die du vorlorst, / Doch göttlich ist's."

13. For further discussion see below, section VII.

14. See Friedrich Solmsen, "*Onoma* and *Pragma* in Euripides' *Helen*," *CR* 48 (1934) passim; John G. Griffith, "Some Thoughts on the 'Helena' of Euripides," *JHS* 73 (1953) 36–37.

Behind these issues lies a deeply felt rift in the late fifth century between man and his world, between the constructs (broadly speaking, *nomos*) with which man orders and organizes the phenomena around him and the alien substance of that realm (*physis*) which he seeks thus to order.[15] One result of this familiar cleavage between nomos and physis is a loss of confidence in the belief that the traditional forms of thought and action are adequate to grasp and to deal with what is now felt to be the truth or the reality. For men like Protagoras, Gorgias, Antiphon the Sophist, successors to the still (relatively) innocent logic of the Eleatics, truth and reality (*alêtheia, ta onta, einai*) are now problematical terms.

In the *Hippolytus* and the *Medea*, Euripides had explored this rift in its psychological dimensions: the split between inner and outer worlds.[16] In the *Bacchae* he was to explore radically its social as well as its psychological implications: the division between the order of society and the potential disorder within man, within the very man who, as king, embodies that order.

In the *Helen* the psychological and social implications of these conflicts are marginal. Yet its antitheses between appearance and reality, onoma and pragma, are deeply akin to these critical rifts between nomos and physis. If works like the *Medea*, the *Hippolytus,* and the *Bacchae* ask whether the ultimate reality is reconcilable with human order and human society, the *Helen* asks the anterior question: Is reality perhaps so problematical, so divided against itself, that we cannot even say what reality is at all, or cannot even be sure that anything is real?[17]

The *Helen* thus has a more epistemological and ontological focus

15. See William Arrowsmith, "A Greek Theater of Ideas," *Arion* 2, no. 3 (1963) 38: "What Euripides reported, with great clarity and honesty, was the widening gulf between reality and tradition; between the operative and the professed values of his culture; between fact and myth; between *nomos* and *physis;* between life and art." For these matters with other reference to fifth-century literature and thought see Kannicht (note 11) 1.57–60; Felix Heinimann, *Nomos und Physis* (Basel 1945) 46–58; W. K. C. Guthrie, *A History of Greek Philosophy,* 3, *The Fifth Century Enlightenment* (Cambridge 1969) 55–134.

16. For the correlations between inner and outer worlds and appearance and reality see C. Segal, "Shame and Purity in Euripides' *Hippolytus,*" *Hermes* 98 (1970) 278–99.

17. Compare also the way in which the divided nature of the gods (who embody, in part, the nature of our reality) is related to divisions within the psychological and moral realms in plays like the *Electra, HF,* and *Ion.* See also Arrowsmith (note 15) 47ff.

than the above-mentioned plays, with their extreme crises in the realms of action and society. This fact accounts in part for the playfulness and questionable seriousness of the drama. The theory of relativity can be taken more lightly than immediate issues of good and evil. But the *Helen's* antitheses between truth and appearance embrace the ethical side of the questions about the nature of reality as well as the epistemological questions about the role of language, myth, and art in communicating that reality. One cannot fully separate the meaning of the play as a criticism of life from its meaning as a criticism of art.

II

Helen's beauty mediates between the epistemological and the ethical themes, illusion and war. It signifies, as it did for Goethe and Hofmannsthal, a promise of happiness in a strange and violent world. Yet this beauty is also an object to be coveted and possessed. Hence, as Helen says again and again, it is also a curse (27, 235–36, 261–63, 304–5, 383–84). It carries with it the hint of the eidolon's vacuity (262)[18] and memories of irremediable loss and fearful suffering. This ambiguous status of Helen's beauty—and of beauty, *kallos,* generally in the play—is another aspect of the question of the nature of reality. Is even the supreme beauty of a Helen, object of long and hard wars, not only illusory but even destructive?

It is natural that the real Helen, whose "image" has destroyed Troy, should feel more keenly than any other character the horror of its fall and pity for its victims (39, 109, 196–202, 229–40, etc.). Yet as the embodiment of a purer kind of beauty, Helen also appears against the background of a quasi-pastoral "green world" of Pans, echoing flutes, Nymphs, and Naiads (179–90, 349–50). Even here, however, the peacefulness of these settings is tinged by suggestions of violence and specifically the violence of the rape of Persephone to which Helen's rape is closely parallel. When Hermes carried Helen away (ἀναρπάσας δι' αἰθέρος, 246), she was plucking flowers by the Eurotas, as

---

18. The wish in 262 that she could wash her beauty away like a painting (or like a painted statue) uses the same word (*agalma*) as that used for the empty phantom in 705 and 1219 (νεφέλης ἄγαλμα).

Persephone, in the Homeric Hymn, was plucking flowers in "that fair field of Enna."[19] In a later lyrical passage, shortly after another reference to her homeland (349–50), Helen again speaks of a myth of rape and addresses the "maiden Callisto" (375).[20] Though rape is probably not involved in the story of Kos to which she next alludes (381–83), Kos too has suffered violence "because of beauty" (καλ-λοσύνας ἕνεκεν, 383).[21]

Hermes' "snatching up" of Helen in 246ff. is the obverse of the eidolon theme and involves the same antitheses of appearance and reality, name and body. Hermes, says Helen, carried her off "through the aether" (δι' αἰθέρος, 246), and we recall the aether theme of the prologue (cf. 36 and 44–45). Immediately after these words Helen explains that her name (onoma) was a subject of "empty talk" at Troy (μαψίδιον ἔχει φάτιν, 251).[22]

The rape theme also raises the related questions of the nature of the gods and their connection with human morality. Hermes' snatching up (ἀναρπάσας, 246) replaces the actual rape of Helen by Paris (cf. ἀναρπαγάς, 50).[23] In the prologue Helen described her removal to Egypt as part of the plans of Zeus (46–50). There it reflected the larger order of a directing divine power. In the parode, however, the chief agent is Hera, representative of the chaos of anthropomorphic gods. It is she, says Helen in 241–43, who has sent Hermes. Thus the removal of Helen to Egypt appears under two different aspects. In the prologue it appears as a benign protection; in the parode it appears as the disruptive act of a jealous goddess with accompanying images of rape in the background. One recalls also Apollo's seduction of Creusa— also as she was plucking flowers (*Ion* 888–96)—an act equally ambiguous in its implications about the gods' relation to morality.

The two aspects under which Hermes' snatching up of Helen appears restate the prologue's antithesis between Zeus and Hera in a

19. See Homer, *h. Cer.* 6–18; Ovid, *Met.* 5.390–401; in general C. Segal, *Landscape in Ovid's Metamorphoses,* Hermes Einzelschriften 23 (Wiesbaden 1969) 34 with n.65.

20. Verrall (note 3) 122 strongly objected to this passage as "Alexandrian poetry, not Attic, learned, frigid, and hollow at the heart"—a judgment that the interpretation here offered should mitigate.

21. For the myth of Kos see A. M. Dale, ed., *Euripides, Helen* (Oxford 1967) and Kannicht (note 11) *ad loc.*

22. For the problem of the interpretation of this passage see Kannicht (note 11) *ad. loc.* (2.85).

23. The noun is a *hapax legomenon,* as Dale (note 21) *ad loc.* observes.

new form and carry to another level the divisions within the fabric of reality. This division corresponds also to the two sides of the Persephone myth that lies in the background: death versus rebirth, joy versus sorrow, the beauty of Helen's song (183–91) or the flowers she plucks (243–45) versus the horror of Troy. Yet in raising the question of these divisions within the divine order, the parode also places the sufferings of Helen against the background of a universal archetype of rape and restoration, loss and recovery, and hints at a large rhythmic pattern to be reenacted in her sufferings. At the same time the violence of Paris' act (see 50) looms even larger against the mythical background of the rape of Persephone.

The play's very first word, "Nile," creates, as Günther Zuntz remarked, the setting of "a far away, fabulous land."[24] The paradox of the "white melting snows" that feed the "maiden-lovely streams of Egypt's warm fertile fields" in the third line evokes the atmosphere of wonder and fascination with which the Greeks were wont to regard the sources of the Nile.[25] The marine setting of lines 5–15, the suggestive names of Psamathe and Nereus, the mysterious power of Theonoe with her double name (reminiscent perhaps of the double names of Homeric epic)—all conduce to the same effect.

Verrall, giving, as often, the wrong answers to the right questions, asks why Proteus should be the king of Egypt.[26] The answer may be simply Euripides' desire to recreate something of the fairy tale mood of *Odyssey* 4 and of the *Odyssey* generally. Like the Odyssean Phaeacia, Egypt is a mysterious point of transition between worlds, a point where the past can be relived and in some sense transformed. Helen and Theonoe, like the mysterious and helpful goddesses and knowing women of the *Odyssey*—Leucothea, Circe, Calypso, Nausicaa, Arete, even the Helen of *Od.* 4.219–64 and 15.125–30—hold the keys to life and death, loss or recovery of the past from which the hero is separated.

The removed beauty of Egypt where Helen laments like a Nymph

24. Zuntz (note 11) 202.
25. Cf. Hdt. 2.20–28; Eur., *Archelaus,* frag. 228 Nauck. See also Helen H. Bacon, *Barbarians in Greek Tragedy* (New Haven 1961) 159; Dale (note 21) *ad vs.* 3.
26. Verrall (note 3) 73. Hugo Steiger, "Wie Entstand die Helena des Euripides," *Philologus* 67 (1908) 202–8 has fully illustrated Euripides' indebtedness to the *Odyssey,* but his interpretation of the data (Euripides' parody of the epic) is not necessarily to be accepted.

or Naiad among echoing mountains (184–90) bears a strong similarity to the gentle, serene setting of Helen's Sparta in 243–45 and 349–50. There are other verbal associations between Egypt and Sparta. The "streams of the Eurotas" (Εὐρώτα ῥοάς, 124 and 162) recall the "streams of Nile" (1). The echo of that first line is even stronger in the expression ῥοαὶ / τοῦ καλλιδόνακος . . . Εὐρώτα, ("streams of Eurotas of the lovely reeds," 492–93), especially as Νείλου παρ' ὄχθας ("beside the banks of the Nile") immediately precedes (491). Egypt's tranquility, like the Spartan home of Helen before Paris' intrusion, has associations of a happiness and an innocence either outside or anterior to the complexities of passion and war. Both places have traits of an Edenlike world of youth and sheltered maidenhood. They exemplify a *locus amoenus,* like Ibycus' "grove of the Maidens" or Hippolytus' meadow, where a fragile and virginal beauty takes refuge from a harsher world.[27] Here too the associations of the Persephone myth behind 243–45 are again relevant.

That aspect of the figure of Helen which is innocent and faithful has a natural kinship with the serenity of this Egyptian-Spartan setting. Egypt's recent king was "the most chaste of mortals" (πάντων . . . σωφρονέστατον βροτῶν, 47). His *sôphrosynê* stands at the opposite pole from the evil reputation of the Trojan Helen which torments the real Helen. Here, in his kingdom, she can "preserve her bed pure [ἀκέραιον] for Menelaus" (48); and one is again reminded of those virginal *loci amoeni* cited above.

There is, however, a difference between the Eurotas and the Nile. The former has a concreteness and a local familiarity that set it apart from the make-believe atmosphere of distant Egypt. Egypt, therefore, is the ideal symbol for the exploration of the tensions between reality and appearance. It lies between Troy and Sparta, between mortals and gods, between a fabulous and an actual geography. Herodotus had impressed the stamp of his incomparable charm upon the remote and fanciful qualities, the πλεῖστα θωμάσια, which so delighted him in Egypt (2.35.1); and Euripides has exploited the imaginative and symbolical possibilities.

The contrast between Egypt and Troy is also the contrast between *Odyssey* and *Iliad.* Indeed, Egypt's "lovely-maidened streams" (1)

27. Ibycus, frag. 5 Page or 6 Diehl; *Hipp.* 73ff. For other parallels see my *Landscape* (note 19) 24, 46, 68–70.

contrast sharply with the death-filled "streams of the Scamander" (52–53):

ψυχαὶ δὲ πολλαὶ δι' ἔμ' ἐπὶ Σκαμανδρίοις
ῥοαῖσιν ἔθανον . . .

On account of me many souls died at the streams of the Scamander.

The contrast is even more pointed for line 53, with its opening *psychai pollai* is surely meant to recall the proem of the *Iliad* and the "many strong souls of heroes" (*pollas . . . psychas*) sent down to Hades by the war (*Il.* 1.3–4).[28]

This contrast becomes a matter of visual and scenic effect when Teucer steps upon the stage. The worn, ravaged warrior from Troy is astounded by the lushness of Egypt and the richness of the palace (69). Helen's allusion to "the fields of Nile" (Νείλου . . . γύας, 89) both echoes the description of the prologue (3) and contrasts with Teucer's description of the deaths at Troy (94ff.).

It is now clear that the play's central antithesis between appearance and reality has a number of different ramifications. The meaning of the *Helen* reveals itself in terms of this basic structure or core of antithesis, to which more and more elements are seen to cohere as analysis probes deeper. Those which have so far emerged can be presented in the following diagram:

Reality	*Appearance*
Real Helen	Eidolon
Zeus	Hera
Beauty as positive good	Beauty as a curse and source of strife (the three goddesses)
Helen's removal to Egypt as protection	Helen's removal to Egypt as rape
phrenes	*soma* (160–61)
Innocence	Guilt
Egypt	Troy
Odyssey	*Iliad*
Life ← Persephone Myth → (173ff., 243–45)	Death

28. Unhomeric, however, is the notion of these *psychai* "dying," as Kannicht (note 11) notes *ad. loc.* (2.32).

Euripides

This simplification should not suggest that the themes here presented in sequence are subordinate one to another. They are not so much logical deductions from a single antithesis as simultaneous aspects and expressions of that antithesis at other levels and in other areas.

III

Generally speaking, the male characters of the play stand on the negative side of these antitheses, the female on the positive. The division is reminiscent of the *Odyssey*, with the prominence which that poem gives to clever and mysterious women. But they are also related to the exotic flavor of the Egyptian setting. In this strange world the male, heroic values of mainland Greece, perpetually kept before us in the theme of the Trojan War, prove ineffectual and even encumbering. Hence Menelaus' discomfiture by the Portress is not just a bit of humorous stage play but dramatizes the alienness and inappropriateness of those martial, Trojan values which Menelaus embodies. The incongruity of the king in rags reflects not only a loss of personal identity but a questioning of cultural identity.

The opposition to war which this rejection of heroic values implies is part of a larger issue important in late fifth-century thought, an increasing movement away from the public toward the private realm.[29] Within the public world of the polis, action is the exclusive prerogative of men. Women have no place. In Euripides' fictional Egypt—as in Herodotus' "real" Egypt—the situation is just the reverse.[30] The men may bluster and threaten, but the real power lies with the women. In the *Lysistrata* of the following year, Aristophanes exploits a similar inversion and makes some of the same criticisms of traditional Greek values. In both these plays masculine aggressiveness has to yield place to the life-fostering, private, mysterious ways of women. In Euripides' play the hero whose pride lies in the open challenge and the man-to-man conflict on the field of battle or (in

29. For this subject in relation to Euripides see the useful remarks of Friedrich Solmsen, "Euripides Ion im Vergleich mit anderen Tragödien," *Hermes* 69 (1934) 453–56.

30. Hdt. 2.35; Soph. *OC* 337–41.

fifth-century terms) in the straightforward shock and clash of matched lines of hoplites can be saved only by one woman's guile and another's complicity. Thus at the point when Menelaus is dissuaded from his initial impulse to violence, he hands the job of persuasion over to Helen as "woman's work" (σὸν ἔργον, ὡς γυναικὶ πρόσφορον γυνή, 830).

Menelaus' monologue (483–514) after the fiasco with the Portress proves this blunt and simple warrior no match for the problems of name and act raised in the Egyptian world (see onoma at 487, 490, 498).[31] He falls back on the "simple name" of the heroic past (ἁπλοῦν δὲ Τυνδάρειον ὄνομα κλήζεται, 494) and the renown of his name (502) as the one who "lit the glorious flames of Troy" (503–4):

κλεινὸν τὸ Τροίας πῦρ ἐγώ θ' ὃς ἧψά νιν,
Μενέλαος, οὐκ ἄγνωστος ἐν πάσῃ χθονί.

Glorious is the fire of Troy, and glorious am I who kindled it, Menelaus, not unknown in every land.

In a setting where war and Troy are called into question, an identity defined by Troy's fall is highly problematical. "Glorious armies" (453), brilliant cloaks (423–24), and the pomp of generalships (392–96, 503–4) have all been lost on the seas that separate Troy from Egypt (400, 423–24).[32]

Helen is not, to be sure, entirely free of the theatrical heroics of Menelaus. She too wants to die "nobly" and gain *doxa* (298, 841).[33] But this concern with her fame in the public world plays a much smaller role in her characterization than in her husband's. Behind it stands always an intense consciousness of shame. Euripides has built upon the self-consciousness and guilt of the Iliadic Helen,[34] even though, in a typically Euripidean paradox, he is following the anti-Homeric version of her story.

31. See Karin Alt, "Zur Anagnorisis in der Helena," *Hermes* 90 (1962) 20; Burnett (note 1) 153; Griffith (note 14) 38.
32. Verrall (note 3) characteristically considers Menelaus' loss of his garment merely as a "joke" (97). For a different view see Burnett (note 1) 152.
33. On the passages see Steiger (note 26) 211–12. Compare the parody in Aristoph., *Thesm.* 868. Lines 299–302 may be interpolated, but 298 is probably genuine: see Kannicht (note 11) *ad. loc.;* but *contra* Dale (note 21) *ad. vs.* 297.
34. See Alt (note 31) 10–11.

These contrasts cut below the surface of the two characters' situations to larger, representative attitudes behind them. Menelaus' orientation is all toward the outer world of action. The contests he mentions in his opening lines (386–87) are emblematic of his whole vision of the world. Helen's world view has an inward dimension. This contrast is, in turn, an aspect of that between appearance and reality, body and spirit (160–61).

The central section of the play defines the differences in a context of new urgency. Confronted with the problem of escaping from Egypt, Menelaus resorts to the rhetoric of Troy (ἄνανδρά γ' εἶπας Ἰλίου τ' οὐκ ἄξια, 808). He rejects any "shaming" of his reputation, his *kleos* (845), or any "blame" (ψόγος, 846) he might incur (also 948–49, 993). Helen, however, feels "shame" in a more deeply moral and inward sense (922), and speaks of the moral bases of her *kleos*, her reputation as an adulteress (926–28). A little later she even defines the "noblest fame" (*kleos . . . kalliston*) as lying in ethical character (*tropoi*, 941–43).

The couple's response to Theonoe follows the same pattern. Menelaus threatens to stain Proteus' tomb "with streams of blood" (αἵματος ῥοαί, 984). The phrase suggests the violation of the sheltered serenity of Egypt's *kalliparthenoi rhoai* (1). Helen, on the other hand, appeals to the memory and the goodness of Proteus (909–16, 940–43) and invokes justice and morality throughout her speech (cf. 894–943, esp. 919–23). Menelaus also calls on Proteus before he utters his threat (961–68); but, characteristically, he stresses Proteus' *kleos* rather than his moral character (εὐκλεέστατον, 967; κακῶς ἀκοῦσαι, 968).

Menelaus' solution to the problem of escape is violent and, as Helen calmly points out, wildly unrealistic.[35] He will act (cf. δρῶντας, 814) even if it means his death.

To this death-bent desperation Helen opposes the resiliency of Odyssean guile and adaptability. She plays Odysseus to Menelaus'

35. It is mistaken to regard this scene merely as "quite delightful comedy," as does E. M. Blaiklock, *The Male Characters of Euripides* (Wellington, New Zealand 1952) 90; so also G. M. A. Grube, *The Drama of Euripides* (1941; London 1961) 344–45. The high pathos of the scene was enthusiastically appreciated by Wieland, who in 1808 considered its "Ausdruck stiller Grösse, Gefühl und Energie" moving "wie vielleicht keine andere Stelle in irgend einer Tragödie, die ich kenne": cited by Steiger (note 26) 211, who has a good discussion of the interplay of life and death in the passage (210–11).

Achilles. "Hope" (*elpis,* 815, 826), "device" (*mêchanê,* 813), and "persuasion" (*peithein,* 825, 828) are the key words. The contrast of her hope and persuasion to Menelaus' death is especially marked in the stichomythies of 814–15 and 824–26. Though Helen agrees readily enough to the death pact of 835–54, it is Menelaus who pronounces the decisive word θανεῖσθαι (836) and expounds the idea at length and with enthusiasm (842–54). Later, in a striking passage, Menelaus invokes Hades as an ally, so many men has he sent there with his sword (969–71).[36] In the deliberations that follow upon Theonoe's conversion to their cause, Menelaus again proposes violent and murderous expedients (1039–46). He finally acquiesces in Helen's *sophia* (1049–52), though his heart again warms to thoughts of an eventual combat (1072). In both of these scenes of plotting Helen appears as the saving female figure of superior guile which Euripides had exploited in the *Iphigeneia in Tauris.*[37] Ironically, Euripides' innocent Helen has a model in her mythic opposite, the chaste Penelope.

We can hardly expect that Menelaus, having sacked Troy for Helen's sake, will give her up easily (cf. 806). Even so, his possessiveness has a distinctly negative significance. His determination to keep the real Helen reenacts his earlier possessiveness toward the false: he clings to the real Helen with the same desperation and delusion with which he clings to the eidolon in the early part of the play. In the first case his possessiveness affirms a choice of appearance over reality. In the second it accompanies a choice of death over life. When Helen urges, "It is better to leave me than have my marriage bed kill you" (807), Menelaus adduces the honor of his Trojan success (808).[38] His relation to both the real and the false Helens brings together illusion,

36. The striking quality of Menelaus' rhetoric was warmly admired by Verrall (note 3) 104: "Here is a grand bold handling of big ideas! Here is something to humble Aeschylus' Clytaemnestra and her cry to the fiends of Hell . . . ," citing *Eum.* 106.

37. See *IT* 1017ff., especially 1032 on the *technai* of women. Theoclymenus at 1621 complains that he has been "caught by women's *technai.*" See also *Danae,* frag. 321 Nauck, and in general Friedrich Solmsen, "Zur Gestaltung des Intrigenmotivs in den Tragödien des Sophokles und Euripides," *Philologus* 87 (1932) 1–17, reprinted in Schwinge (note 11) 332–33; Walter Zürcher *Die Darstellung des Menschen im Drama des Euripides* (Basel 1947) 158–59.

38. On the life-giving of Helen's reaction to the situation in 805ff. See Steiger (note 26) 210: "In ihrer sorgenden Liebe will sie ihn lieber wieder verlieren, als ihn der Gefahr des Todes ansetzen."

death, war, Troy, and male aggressive values on the same side of the play's basic dichotomies. The Menelauses of this world in a sense always cling to phantoms: life is full of prizes to be possessed, enemies to be killed, glory to be won. Yet after all their slaughter what they have in their hands may turn out to be an empty "cloud's image" (705)—unless a saving figure like Helen recalls them through her sophia to hope and the gentler remedies of persuasion and device.

This division between husband and wife who so passionately desire reunion is another of the paradoxes created by the two worlds of the play. It is latent in the couple's very first scene together. In the other recognition plays of about this time, the *Ion* and the *Iphigeneia in Tauris,* the lost pair feels an instinctive affinity, a spontaneous communication, before they actually know who they are.[39] This is a common feature of romance and is exploited, for example, by Shakespeare frequently in the late romances. In the *Helen* this feature of the recognition theme is lacking. Helen's first response is to flee in fear (541ff.). Menelaus in turn indignantly rejects her advances when she realizes who he is (564ff., esp. 567). To some extent Euripides is simply varying the formula of anagnorisis. But the lack of the instinctive, subconscious recognition may also indicate a gulf separating the two characters. Despite their emotional ties, conceptually they belong on different sides of the play's antithetical camps.

Menelaus' recognition of Helen is, in fact, a double anagnorisis.[40] The joyful discovery of his real wife is balanced by the grim, mocking discovery of the emptiness of the prize of war. All in vain, all for a phantom (704–10).

Winning Helen back from the dangers of Egypt has a similar double aspect. The recognition of Helen and the challenge posed by her rescue revive the hero's lost identity. But this Trojan identity is in itself one of the problems framed by the play's antithetical structure. Menelaus holds to a potentially destructive as well as to a saving

---

39. See Alt (note 31) 25 and in general 17–20 on the recognition scene. On the parallels and differences between the techniques of recognition in the *Helen* and the other plays of anagnôrisis see also Solmsen, *"Ion"* (note 29) 428ff.: Wolfgang Schadewaldt, *Monolog und Selbstgespräch*, "Neue philologische Untersuchungen" 2 (Berlin 1926) 23–24; and most recently Peter Rau, *Paratragodia: Untersuchung einer komischen Form des Aristophanes*, Zetemata 45 (Munich 1967) 53–56, with the literature there cited.

40. See Kannicht (note 11) 1.54–55; L. A. Post, "Menander and the *Helen* of Euripides," *HSCP* 68 (1964) 104.

aspect of his lost heroism. To regain Sparta, the heroic martial self that possessed the false Helen dies, to be reborn in a battle for the real Helen. The first stage of the process is the loss of the false Helen and with this the loss of the accoutrements of his Trojan identity. The eidolon of the false Helen leaves of its own accord. The real Helen, in the second stage of the process, becomes the active figure. She will lead through a symbolical ordeal of death and rebirth (1049–52) the warrior who brings death and fire to cities and calls upon Hades (969ff.).

In the parode Helen is likened to the divinities of nature, Nymphs and Naiads who sing of Pan's marriage (186–90). She offers tears of grief to Persephone (173–78), but she herself is like the maiden carried to the underworld (243–51) who, as a later ode assures us, returns to the upper world amid the rejoicing of all nature (130ff.). The figure of Helen is itself a survival of a Mycenaean (or earlier) vegetation goddess and was so worshiped at Sparta.[41] On one level her Egyptian confinement preserves her purity (48), but on another it is a kind of living death for her, as she in fact says (τοῖς πϱάγμασιν τέθνηϰα, τοῖς δ' ἔϱγοισιν οὔ, 286). Euripides, with his repeated references to Persephone here and his interest in primitive cults in the later years of his life (especially in the *Iphigeneia in Tauris* and *Bacchae*), may have known of this aspect of Helen and incorporated it into the structure of his play.

Helen appears both as the grieving, bereft mother who mourns her dead consort and as the daughter or Maiden whose restoration revivifies in its train the sources of life hidden under the earth. Menelaus, she laments, was "among the corpses under the ground" (344). When he finally casts off the spell of the phantom Helen, his life is renewed, as the Messenger's joyful words imply (722–25):

νῦν ἀνανεοῦμαι τὸν σὸν ὑμέναιον πάλιν
ϰαὶ λαμπάδων μεμνήμεθ' ἃς τετϱαόϱοις
ἵπποις τϱοχάζων παϱέφεϱον· σὺ δ' ἐν δίφϱοις
ξὺν τῷδε νύμφῃ δῶμ' ἔλειπες ὄλβιον.

41. See M. P. Nilsson, *The Mycenaean Origin of Greek Mythology*, Sather Classical Lectures 8 (Berkeley 1932) 73–76, 170–71 and his *Geschichte der griechischen Religion* 1.2 (Munich 1955) 211; also Cecil Page Golann, "The Third Stasimon of Euripides' *Helena*," *TAPA* 76 (1945) 37–38, with the literature there cited. For the significance of the Persephone archetype in the play see Burnett (note 1) 156; Furio Iesi, "L'Egitto infero nell' *Elena* di Euripide," *Aegyptus* 45 (1965) 57ff.; Lattimore (note 8) 52–53.

Now I renew once more your marriage-rite, and I remember the torches that I carried running beside your four-horsed chariot; and you in the car, the bride with this man here, left your happy home.

The lines suggest not only the rebirth and renewal (ἀνανεοῦμαι) of a *hieros gamos* but also the movement from Hades to the light of the marriage torches. When the messenger again addresses Menelaus, it is with a new respect for his authority: he calls him for the first time by the Homeric title "lord," *anax* (744), having previously addressed him only as "Menelaus" (599, 700).

Helen is not herself entirely free from delusion. Despite her confident defense of herself against Teucer's inversion of appearance and reality (118–22), she becomes—like Teucer and Menelaus—a victim of this confusion too (576–90). She herself suffers the pain of "seeming to have, not having" (592; cf. 35–36, 611, 705–6). But this state is short-lived for her. It is her power to manipulate illusion and reality, *logos* and *ergon,* which secures true life for herself and her husband (1049–52). It is she, for example, who administers to Menelaus the bath and the change of garment (1382–84). Here too the ritually enacted restoration of life is combined with the ancient theme of the renewal of the maimed, weakened, or otherwise impotent king.

Like some of Shakespeare's heroines (one thinks of Portia in the *Merchant of Venice* or Helena in *All's Well That Ends Well*), she is the leader in the game of interchanging appearance and reality. She is herself the principal force in the rhythm that carries the action from sterility to union, sorrow to joy. Her powers are natural and feminine rather than magical, but she stands on the lower rung of a ladder that leads to Shakespeare's Prospero. And behind her, mysteriously enlarging her stature and significance, stands the great archetype of Persephone, whose "doublet" Helen's Mycenaean original was.

With these contrasts between Menelaus and Helen, we may extend the diagram of antitheses as follows:

Helen	Menelaus
Reality	Illusion
Feminine values	Masculine values
Odyssey	*Iliad*
Peace	War
Egypt	Troy

Shame over Troy	Glory in Troy
Private realm	Public realm
Inward life (cf. 160–61)	Outward action
Unselfishness (cf. 805–7)	Possessiveness
Persuasion, hope, device	Force
Rebirth (Persephone)	Death

IV

Theoclymenus stands on the same side of these antitheses as Menelaus. His dominant traits are violence and delusion. The first time that he is mentioned Helen describes him as "hunting" for her marriage (θηρᾷ γαμεῖν με, 63). On his next appearance, that hunting is literal rather than metaphorical, and it is bloody as well: "He's away," says Helen, "in beast-killing slaughter," (ἐν φοναῖς θηρο- κτόνοις, 154). The bloodthirstiness continues in the next line, which extends the killing (=*ktonos*) to bigger game: "For he kills [*kteinei*] whatever stranger from Greece he lays hands upon" (155).

These passages prepare our expectations for Theoclymenus' actual appearance on stage. After a brief address to his father's tomb he speaks of "nooses for wild beasts" (1169) and shortly thereafter of punishing wrongdoers with death (1172). The hunting image returns at 981 (θηρᾷ), 1169, and 1175 (θηρώμενον), with "death" following in the next line (1176).[42] Thinking that Helen has escaped, he calls loudly for horses and chariots (1180–83), only to check himself a moment later: "Hold, for I see those we are pursuing here in the halls and not in flight" (1184–85). There is humor here, of course, but there is a serious thematic relevance too. Like Menelaus (808–54 and 1039–52), Theoclymenus rushes precipitately to violent deeds and then, rather sheepishly, has to retreat. Like Menelaus too, he exemplifies the inadequacy of heroic values even in the kingdom over which he rules.

His opening obeisance to his father's tomb, comic as it may

---

42. Theoclymenus has affinities with the figure of the "black hunter" discussed by P. Vidal-Naquet, "Le chasseur noir et l'origine de l'éphébie athénienne," *Annales: Economies, Sociétés, Civilisations* (1968) 947–64; English version in *PCPS* 194 (1968) 49–64.

seem,[43] also has a function in the structure of the play. It exhibits that same material possessiveness which Menelaus expressed toward Helen (806–54). Theoclymenus needs the tangible remains of Proteus at his very doors for his daily salute. The idea is grotesque, and Euripides is doubtless having fun with the figure of the exotic king on the tragic stage. Theoclymenus completely fulfils the possibilities of a bizarre, *outré* idiosyncrasy that one might expect of an Egyptian monarch.[44]

Not only does Theoclymenus' material piety contrast markedly with the piety of his sister (see below), but it also plays directly into Helen's hands. Lacking the inward spirit of piety, he is taken in by its external trappings. The burial of Menelaus, with its ritual overtones of purification and rebirth, holds no mystery for him. Rather, it provides him with an opportunity to show off his wealth and to bind Helen to him (as he thinks) a little more securely. He sees in her pious act only the personal advantage of having a docile and obedient wife. "It's to our interest to bring up a pious wife," he says (1278). To underline the contrast between his conception of piety and the other dimensions of religion in the play, the *fabula sacra* of the Mountain Mother of the Gods follows almost immediately (1301ff.).

In one important respect Theoclymenus differs from Menelaus. He is to lose Helen. Losing Helen, he is never quite to emerge from the cloud of delusion, or at least not until the deus ex machina intervenes. When the Messenger reports Helen's flight, he asks, "Did she go off lifted on wings or with earth-treading foot" (1516). The phrase πτεροῖσιν ἀρθεῖσα recalls the disappearance of the false Helen who "disappeared lifted off [ἀρθεῖσα] into the aether's folds" (605–6). The echo suggests that Theoclymenus regresses into the unreality of the eidolon theme in the first half of the play. He reenacts Menelaus' earlier confusion between appearance and reality. Though the Dioscuri enlighten him at the end, the last picture we have of him before

43. R. P. Winnington-Ingram, "Euripides, *Poiêtês Sophos*," *Arethusa* 2 (1969) 131, ingeniously suggests that Euripides here intends "a hit at the conventional treatment of locality in the *Choephoroe* . . . ." For the lighter view of Theoclymenus in general see Verrall (note 3) 52ff., and Steiger (note 26) 212–16: to the latter the last third of the play is all comic parody, an *Überlistungskomödie*. Kannicht (note 11) 1.69–71 sees the deception of Theoclymenus as the tragicomic inversion of the tragic split between truth and appearance in the first half of the play.

44. Bacon (note 25) overlooks this possibility, I think, in her discussion of the tomb and the religious customs of the Egyptians in the *Helen*: 137–38, 148–49, 153–54.

he rushes off with murderous thoughts is of a man deceived. The chorus, loyal to Helen's request for silence (1387–89), glibly lies, "I never would have thought that Menelaus could have escaped our notice . . ." (1619–20).

The foil to Theoclymenus is, of course, Theonoe. She is associated, as Zuntz and Anne Burnett have shown, with a suprahuman cosmic wisdom and with a pure, spiritual conception of the gods which contrasts with the delusions of the other characters and with the petty jealousies of the anthropomorphism presented in the prologue and elsewhere.[45] She stands clearly on the side of reality and far from the appearances in which her brother is enmeshed. Her piety, though "not seeming" so (οὐ δοκοῦσ' ὅμως, 1020), is vindicated as truth at the end. The Dioscuri's praise of her just and righteous action (1647–49, 1656–67) cancels Theoclymenus' vilification (*kakistê*, 1632).[46]

Theonoe contrasts not only with Theoclymenus but also with Menelaus. Her entrance in a blaze of light which signifies both rebirth and purity (865–72) follows closely upon Menelaus' violent resolution of the death pact (836–54).[47] Her serenity and the vast scope of her mind, reaching out to the aether and "the pure breath of heaven's recesses" (866–67), stand out in sharp relief against the death-bent, Hades-invoking anxieties of the Trojan hero (cf. 863–64). The kleos sought by her defender, the servant, at the end of the play (1640–41) is very different from the martial, Troy-based kleos on which Menelaus stakes his identity. Her celebrated meditation of a "deathless *gnome* that dwells in the "immortal aether" (1013–16), is as A. W. Verrall put it, a gentle reproof to "the soulless philosophy of Menelaus."[48]

Whereas Theoclymenus needs to have his father's tomb at the very entrance to his palace, Theonoe's piety soars into the highest reaches

45. See Burnett (note 1) 157–59; Conacher (note 11) 294–97 and 301–2; Kannicht (note 11) 1.71–77; Max Pohlenz, *Die griechische Tragödie*, 2d ed. (Göttingen 1954) 1.386–89; Post (note 40) 101–2; Verrall (note 3) 59; Zuntz (note 11) 204, 213–16.

46. Note too Theoclymenus' denial of the servant's *eusebestatê* in 1632–33.

47. Grube (note 35) 344 n.1, suggests a parallel with the appearance of the Delphian priestess in the *Ion*.

48. Verrall (note 3) 106. Lines 1013–16 have, of course, given rise to a voluminous literature. See the "Discussion" in Zuntz (note 11) 234ff., Burnett (note 1) 159ff.; Henri Grégoire, ed., *Euripide*, Budé ed., vol. 5 (Paris 1923) 41ff. and his long note *ad loc.* (91–94); Iesi (note 41) 64ff.; and Kjeld Matthiessen, "Zur Theonoeszene der Euripideischen 'Helena,'" *Hermes* 96 (1968) 693ff.

of the cosmos (866–67). She, in fact, proves a far more effective protector of this tomb against the threats of Menelaus' desperate violence (980–90).

In her affinity with the highest and purest reality and her distance from the narrow, possessive localism of the two male characters (or three, if Teucer is included), Theonoe deepens the antithesis between male and female, martial prowess and life-giving, feminine gentleness, with a further contrast between materialism and vast philosophical perspective. Her presence embodies an opposition between intellect, abstract thought, mysticism, the eternal creations of the spirit on the one hand and force, bloodshed, war on the other.

Her philosophical nature, as well as her femininity, separate her from the active, competitive, exclusively male functions of the *polis* with which Theoclymenus and Menelaus are associated. Theoclymenus' conception of justice, for example, is to exact physical and indeed capital punishment like a judge in a real polis (cf. *dikazein*, 1637). Theonoe, however, conceives of punishment (*tisis*) in the broad philosophical terms that extend to an afterlife and to a consciousness that cannot die (1013–16).

This antinomy between the two sets of characters foreshadows some aspects of Plato's struggles between the *bios politikos* and the *bios theorêtikos*.[49] In the period of the *Helen* these tensions are nascent in various criticisms of the narrow, destructive exclusiveness of the polis. In Aristophanes' *Birds* the polis and the human nomoi are full of corruption, informers, and the joyless complexities of *polypragmosynê*, while the imaginary Cloud-city exists in a gentle and benign realm of physis where the mythical violence of Tereus becomes the songful reasonableness of the Hoopoe. Similar criticisms of the limited horizons of the polis appear around the same time in Aristophanes' *Lysistrata*, in Hippias, in Democritus, and in the *Truth* of Antiphon the Sophist.[50] In Euripides' own work of this period there is also Ion's famous speech on the evils and dangers of the public life of the polis (*Ion* 585–606, 621–47), and reinforcing it the warning exam-

---

49. See, for example, Werner Jaeger, "Über Ursprung und Kreislauf des philosophischen Lebensideals," *SB Berlin* (1928) 390–421. Zuntz (note 11) 215–16 well observes the contrast between the commonsense intelligence of the "man in the street" at 744–57 and the cosmic, mystical wisdom of Theonoe.

50. See in general H. C. Baldry, *The Unity of Mankind in Greek Thought* (Cambridge 1965) 32–51; Guthrie (note 15) 152–63, esp. 161–63.

ple of Creusa's patrician exclusiveness and possessiveness with their nearly disastrous consequences (*Ion* 1291–1305; cf. also 589–93).

As the embodiment of the highest reality ("pure uplift," remarked L. A. Post),[51] Theonoe is also the high point of the contrast between Egypt and Troy. If Theoclymenus leaves the suspended otherworldliness of Egypt somewhat tarnished, Theonoe portrays whatever is best in it. His buffoonish figure suggests the scorn that a decadent kingdom could arouse in the Greek mind, as in the story of Busiris, whereas her Egypt is the repository of the ancient mystical wisdom of the East.[52] The Egypt that surrounds her is a kind of ideal state harking back to the benign monarchy of Proteus, a Prospero's island in which she is Ariel to Theoclymenus' Caliban. Her maidenhood is the badge of her purity. Even before we hear her name, she is called *parthenos* (10), as she is throughout the play.[53] As the "maiden" par excellence, she thus embodies the essence of Egypt's "maiden-lovely streams" that introduce the play.

The purity and brilliance that flash forth at her entrance (865–72) unite the two main aspects of the reality-appearance antithesis, the ethical and the epistemological. This brightness signifies a lucid truth in contrast with the murky cloudedness of Troy, but it also signifies the hope of life and rebirth. The recognition scene in which occur the first movements out of delusion begins with Helen's appeal to Theonoe's knowledge ("she who knows everything truly," 530); and Helen's next words show us this knowledge in the service of light, life, and rebirth (530–31):

> φησὶ δ' ἐν φάει
> πόσιν τὸν ἁμὸν ζῶντα φέγγος εἰσορᾶν . . .

She [Theonoe] says that my husband is in the light of life and looks upon its gleam.

Correspondingly, Theonoe's "purity" (865–67) is both moral and intellectual. It combines both freedom from delusion and freedom

51. Post (note 40) 101.

52. See Pierre Gilbert, "Souvenirs de l'Égypte dans l'*Hélène* d'Euripide," *AC* 18 (1949) 79; Iesi (note 41) 63ff.

53. See, e.g., 894, 939, 977, 1032, and note the verb μιαίνω in 1000. Post (note 40) 103 suggests an identification between Theonoe and Athena (with dubious relevance

from passion. It is inward as well as outward, for it involves her body (*parthenos*) as well as her soul. We may contrast Theoclymenus' concern with the "outward" purity of his house when he reflects that Menelaus has not died in Egypt (καθαρὰ γὰρ ἡμῖν δώματα, 1430). In her the wisdom of the *physiologos* and the justice of the *agathos* are one and the same.

The tension between Theonoe and Theoclymenus, and hence between reality and appearance, also involves the question of which of them truly embodies the spirit of Egypt and which is truly the representative of the pious and good dead king, Proteus. The higher reality of Egypt, as Euripides makes clear, belongs to Theonoe. Not only does her maidenhood have a kinship with Egypt's "maiden-lovely streams" in the first line, but she too is associated with the distant, mysterious atmosphere of the sea and its mythical denizens in the opening lines (4–8). It is she who "has honor from her ancestor Nereus" (15) and is called "the maiden descended from the Nereid of the sea" (318; cf. 1647).

Theoclymenus, of course, has an equal title to this marine ancestry (e.g., 8), but he is never described in these mythological terms. He prides himself on being the devoted son of Proteus, as his opening words show (1167–68):

ἀεὶ δέ σ' ἐξιών τε κἀσιὼν δόμους
Θεοκλύμενος παῖς ὅδε προσεννέπει, πάτερ.

This son of yours—that is, myself, Theoclymenus—salutes you, father, always, both leaving and entering the halls.

But, as we have seen, it is Theonoe who proves to have the more legitimate claims to filial piety and to the spirit of Proteus (1028–29). She is, as Verrall remarked, "essentially his representative."[54] Her inward "shrine of justice" (1003–4) is a more authentic memorial to Proteus than the ostentatious tomb that Theoclymenus has erected for his daily salute (1165–68).[55] In the speech of the Dioscuri at the

---

to the play, in my judgment); Kannicht (note 11) 1.74, is more convincing in connecting Theonoe's physical purity with the pure aether and the nous of 1013–16.

54. Verrall (note 3) 79.

55. See also 1648–49. For a cautious approach to Theonoe's "shrine of justice" see Matthiessen (note 48) 702–3. Cf. also lines 1648–49.

end, Theonoe shares with Helen the virtue of *sophrosynê* (1657, 1684); and it was for sophrosynê that Zeus had singled out Proteus beyond all mortals (47).

Although Theonoe's virginity stands at the opposite pole from Helen's experience,[56] the two women are not in all respect opposites. Dramatically, Helen is the more complex. Theonoe will remain in her removed and mystical sea-realm. Helen has to return to the complexities of the human world where Menelaus is king.

Yet Helen can also speak Theonoe's language as can no other character in the play. In striking contrast to Menelaus, she appeals to Theonoe's purer conception of justice (920–21, 940–43), the divine (903, 914–23), and piety (900–901, 914–21). She can also rise to a generosity and universalism of thought that match Theonoe's. In 906–7 Helen speaks of the "heavens and earth common to all mortals," where we are reminded of Theonoe's opening statement (866–67) and her philosophical dictum of 1013–16. To Theoclymenus' casual dismissal of care for the dead as nothing but trouble, Helen answers with a riddling line on the existence of the dead "there as well as here" (1421–22).

Helen can also understand God in a mysterious, almost allegorical way. "God," she says, "is to know those dear to you" (θεὸς γὰρ καὶ τὸ γιγνώσκειν φίλους, 560). As Theonoe possesses an inward world of spirituality and piety and has a "shrine of justice" in her nature (1002–3),[57] so Helen too has vindicated her inward being, her *phrenes*, against the crimes attaching to the external image, the εἰκὼ φόνιον (73) of her supposed body (160–61). Both women, finally, are united in the last pronouncement of Theoclymenus in the finale (1680–87). In a sense Theonoe is Helen's purer self, the ultimate reality with which Helen is in touch, albeit not as steadily as Theonoe.

If Theonoe points to that higher reality in the realm of morality, theology, and philosophical and religious thought, Helen touches it

56. Griffith (note 14) 39 observes that Helen begins and ends with an address to Theonoe as "virgin," and comments that it is "not perhaps overtactful of her to stress poor Theonoe's spinsterhood." Theonoe, however, would probably not have been displeased, and Griffith's comment is somewhat in the direction of the "documentary fallacy."

57. Theonoe's πέφυκα at 998 indicates, I believe, that the physis of 1002–3 means "her nature" and not "nature," "human nature," in general.

in the realm of grace, beauty, and art. The two figures are complementary images of man's striving for spiritual strength and unity.
Helen's position is naturally the more complex, for she mediates
between reality and appearance as Theonoe does not and has to suffer
the complication of her identity through the existence of a licentious
other self.

The motif of the aether forms another link between the two wom-
en. Like Helen herself, the aether occupies a middle position between
reality and appearance. The eidolon—destructive, deceptive, lustful
(cf. εἰκὼ φόνιον, 73)—goes off finally into its kindred aether, leaving
Helen free and innocent (see 584, 605, 1219).[58] In this aspect the
aether is connected with the emptiness and delusiveness of clouds and
wind (cf. Hera's ἐξηνέμωσε, 32, and also 44, 705–6, 1219–20) or with
the passion of the gods (216). The aether of which Theonoe speaks,
however, is "solemn" or a "subject of reverence" (*semnos*, 866) and
immortal (1013–16). Helen's eidolon is composed of "sky"
(οὐρανοῦ ξυνθεῖσ' ἄπο, 34) and is a creation of Hera's jealousy and
spite (31–36). Theonoe's sky is associated with the "pure breath"
(*pneuma*, 768) of heaven and thus has affinities with bold philosophical concepts like the nous of Anaxagoras or Diogenes.[59] The one
stands in the mythical tradition of the poets' cloud images of lust and
deception, like that of Pindar in the Second *Pythian,* so brilliantly
exploited by Aristophanes in the decade before the *Helen.*[60] The other
belongs in a speculative tradition reaching back to the philosophers of
Ionia.

The antitheses focused by the contrasts between Theonoe and the
male characters expand the range of the central antithesis even further, and they may be diagrammed as follows:

Theonoe	Theoclymenus (and Menelaus)
Philosophical concept of God (*ta theia*)	Anthropomorphic gods (cf. 708)

58. Cf. also 613, where the eidolon goes off πατέρ' ἐς οὐρανόν; and compare the
eidolon's ἄστρων . . . βεβηκυῖαν μυχούς (617) with Theonoe's αἰθέρος μυχούς
(866), following the text of Kannicht who accepts (surely correctly) the emendations
of Hermann and Wecklein.

59. For the relevant fragments and discussion see Matthiessen (note 48) 699–702;
also Burnett (note 1) 160–61; Post (note 40) 103; Griffith (note 14) 40.

60. For the deceptive cloud image in early mythology see the useful discussion in
Kannicht (note 11) 1.33–38.

Purity and virginity	Lust
Inward morality (cf. 1003)	External morality (cf. 1626–41)
True respect for Proteus	Seeming respect for Proteus
Piety in spirit	Piety in outward forms
Cosmic and universalistic perspective	Narrow possessiveness and localism
Punishment after death and "immortal *gnomê*"	Corporeal punishment, physical death
Aether as a permanent and divine substance	Aether as transient and deceptive cloud image

V

The balance between Theonoe and Helen is a microcosm of the whole play's balance between the intellectualist antitheses of appearance and reality on the one hand and the archetypal themes of romance on the other. Helen has the major role in uniting these two sides of the play, for she is simultaneously the mysterious female ministrant to life and rebirth and the focus of the confusion between appearance and reality. But Theonoe and Proteus also contribute to uniting these two strands.

As the father of Theonoe, Proteus has a natural place on the philosophical or intellectualist side of the play. He is the remoter source of the real justice and piety that are finally vindicated in the person of Theonoe. But from the very beginning he also introduces the major archetypal motif, death and rebirth. He is himself an example of a maimed king whose authority has now become impotent with the ascension of his successor. Theonoe's decision to aid Helen and reject apparent for real respect for her father restores something of the old king's moral and spiritual vitality (cf. 1020–21 and Theonoe's address thereafter to her "dead father," 1028–29).

Menelaus' situation is, in part, that of Proteus: in both cases a dead king's authority has to be restored. In Proteus' case, of course, the restoration is possible only in a metaphorical and spiritual sense, as is appropriate for the father of Theonoe. His moral and figurative rebirth through Theonoe's inward struggle and decision is both a parallel and a foil to the more primitive ritual of rebirth through which Menelaus has, physically, to pass.

Proteus also stands behind the action as a symbol of the possibility of achieving a victory over death. His tomb is a visual reminder of the living power of the dead. It exercises a beneficent effect on the living. Helen observes that it has saved her "like the temples of the gods" (801).

The motif of death and rebirth not only governs the rhythm of the action but also helps clarify the ethical side of the play's antitheses. When Teucer early in the play says that Troy has been sacked "for seven fruitful circles of years" (ἑπτὰ σχεδόν τι καρπίμους ἐτῶν κύκλους, 112), he is not just indulging in a poetic periphrasis but setting the theme of Troy and war into the larger archetypal framework of the action (cf. references to the "green shoots" in the parode, 180 and 243, and, of course, the Persephone myth there).

The myth of Persephone and the renewal of the impotent king are the archetypal myths behind the situations of Helen and Menelaus respectively. The movement between life and death and upper and lower worlds runs through the early part of the play (61–62, 286, 344, 518–19, 529–30) and culminates in the "renewal" (ἀνανεοῦμαι) of Menelaus' marriage amid the torches of the wedding celebration (722–24).

As husband and wife soon realize, this rebirth is only partial. Menelaus' violent threats and especially the death pact, which comes exactly in the middle of the play (835–54 in a work of 1692 lines), turns the joy of reunion to their deepest immersion in death. The fact that they will execute this pact on the tomb (842, the first line of Menelaus' development of the idea) is a further negation of the hoped-for revivification of the powers of the dead king, Proteus. The speech in which the desperate Menelaus threatens to defile the tomb with "streams of blood" (984–85, a passage that, incidentally, echoes his initial exposition of the death pact: cf. τύμβου 'πὶ νώτῳ / νώτοις in 984 and 842) begins with the address to Hades as his ally. It is also at this point in the play that Menelaus is most deeply held by the glory of Troy and the forces of death which it signifies.

Here Menelaus does, in fact, stand in the realm of death, in a deeper and more real sense than Helen realizes when she speaks of his supposed literal death earlier (344, 518–19). Theonoe, with her light-bringing torches (865–72) and her talk of immortality (1013–16), swings the balance back to the side of life. She is seconded by Helen, who appeals to the living moral power of Proteus. If Menelaus were

dead, how, she asks, would Proteus' charge be fulfilled (910–12)?
"How would he give what is living to the dead" (913)?[61] And in her
next lines she couples "the god" with the "dead" father (τὰ τοῦ θεοῦ
καὶ τὰ τοῦ πατρός, 914–15). Theonoe's decision to help the couple is
also an affirmation of Proteus' life: "If he were alive, he would give
her back to you," she tells Menelaus (1011–12). It is immediately
after this statement that she makes her famous pronouncement on the
immortal consciousness of the dead in the deathless aether (1013–16).
Here not only is Proteus reborn as a life-giving force in the world,
but his life appears as part of a vast process of cosmic renewal far
transcending the individual and physical rebirth that Helen and Menelaus seek.

The spiritual and ritual or philosophical and archetypal forms of
rebirth reinforce one another in that same balance which Helen and
Theonoe hold between them. The two sides of the rebirth theme
exemplified in the two women are complementary aspects of Euripides' complex vision of human life, held in an eternal counterpoise
between ideality and actuality, abstract thought and primitive energy, mind and nature.

After this midpoint of life and death and this glimpse of rebirth in
the boldest, most imaginative terms (1013–16), Helen replaces Theonoe as the play's genius of new life.

The ritual death of Menelaus is also connected with the theme of
purification (note the carrying off of the λύματα, 1271). In finally
freeing himself of Troy, Menelaus moves a little closer to that pure
world which Theonoe inhabits, even though his purification follows
an archaic ritual quite remote from the developed spiritual and philosophical purity of Theonoe. As the eidolon freed Helen from the
burden of past guilt and shame, this purification frees Menelaus, at
least in part, from the suffering of his Trojan past. He too can now
take a part in the manipulation of appearance and reality, using the
terms "living" and "dead" in the riddling way that points toward the
escape from these inversions (see 1289–90).

The ode on the Mountain Mother of the Gods (1301–68) is the
culminating point of this theme of rebirth.[62] It comes just at the point

61. κεῖνος in 912 should be Hermes, but one wonders whether it may refer to
Proteus, as the dead king whose force is still felt in the world of the living.
62. Earlier critics tended to regard the ode as totally irrelevant. Gottfried Hermann,
Euripidis Tragoediae, vol. 2, part 1, *Helena* (Leipzig 1837) *ad* 1376 considered it an

Euripides

when the reality and the appearance of life and death have been reversed. Shortly before the ode, Theoclymenus, attempting in his rather heavy-handed way to console Helen, assures her that "the husband who is dead would not be able to come alive" (1285–87). Menelaus then takes up this play on his own supposed death and life (1288–89).

This ode is the mirror image of the parode.[63] It resumes and completes the motif of Persephone there stated and reflects the reversal that has occurred in the interim. In the parode Persephone is in the underworld (173–78). The indirect allusion to her rape (243–46) suggests that the long desolate period of her sojourn under the earth, corresponding to Helen's long, lonely sojourn in Egypt, is about to begin. The Mountain Mother ode also speaks of Persephone's rape (ἁρπαγὰς δολίους, 1322), using the same word that was used of Helen (50, 246). Its main point, however, is the return of Persephone and the renewed joy of nature.[64] Its movement is not from joy to grief, as is implicit in 243–46, but from grief to joy, from *lypê* (1344) to *terpsis* (1352).[65]

This movement from the parode to the second stasimon crystallizes what has been in effect the movement of the entire plot, which is in turn the cyclical movement from winter to summer characteristic of romance.[66] Yet here too the rhythm of romance blends with the intellectualist themes of the play. In the early part of the play the inversions of life and death are fused with those of appearance and

---

actor's interpolation. Verrall (note 3) 64 found it "absolutely irrelevant" and saw in it nothing but a "poet's compliment to the poetry and popular features of the legend and the celebration, that and nothing more" (108). Similarly Wilhelm Schmid, *Geschichte der griechischen Literatur,* 1.3 (Munich 1940) 506 and 513–14 (with useful bibliography); Grube (note 35) 349; and more recently Dale (note 21) xiii ("scarcely a pretence of relevance to the events of stage"). Golann (note 41) provides a useful survey of previous views, but his own interpretation is unsatisfactory. Recent interpretation has had better success: see Burnett (note 1) 155–56; Conacher (note 11) 300–301; Lattimore (note 8) 53; Zuntz (note 11) 226–27.

63. Note the echo of the parode's ἕλικα . . . χλόαν (180) and χλοερά (243) in ἄχλοα πεδία γᾶς (1327) and χλόα (1360).

64. Golann's view (note 41) 34ff. that the ode does not refer to Demeter and Persephone but rather to the cult of Helen is implausible. By the late fifth century the syncretism of Demeter and Cybele was well advanced: see Soph., *Phil.* 391ff. and in general Nilsson, *Geschichte* (note 41) 725–27.

65. Note also Zeus' help to "mother earth" in the prologue, 40ff.

66. See Frye, *Anatomy* (note 4) 182–83; *A Natural Perspective* (note 2) 57ff.

reality and have a negative significance for the protagonists. Now, however, as Helen and Menelaus themselves manipulate both of these inversions (1049–52, 1287–89), they have a positive significance. Appearance and death become the main instrument of their achievement of new life.

The life-death themes stated mythically in the ode continue in the action that immediately follows it. Helen explains how Theonoe has kept her promise, acceding to the lie that Menelaus is "dead in the earth and does not see the light" (1372–73).[67] Helen then describes how she changed his castaway's rags for a new cloak (1382), a change of garment signifying a renewal of identity (see also 1296–97), as Helen's own change from white to black (1087, 1186–87) accompanies her saving manipulation of life and death, reality and appearance. She washes Menelaus in pure river water (1384), thereby not only effecting the ritual transition from the death-dealing sea to life but also continuing the cosmic rebirth of the Mountain Mother ode.

In the exchange of garments, scenic effect and underlying mythic structure are again at one. Earlier, at the nadir of his fortunes, Menelaus stood in rags before the palace gate and felt a hero's shame (*aischynê, aidôs*) for his wretched garb (416–17). His attempt to conceal it (417) was a futile and premature movement out of his reduced state. He is, at this point, still preoccupied with appearances and still possesses the false Helen and all that she symbolizes. Giving up his rags, he also gives up something from the world of heroic vicissitudes (*tychê*, 417) in which he gained them. Ineffectual in this strange realm, somewhat like the shipwrecked sailors of the *Tempest*, he has to relinquish his regal and heroic scruples in matters of clothing (416–17) as of action (cf. 1050–52); and, like a mystic initiate, he must put himself into the hands of a mysterious power to be reborn.

Even here, however, there is still a distinction between Helen as dispenser of life and Menelaus as the violent soldier who has come from the death-filled atmosphere of Troy. While Menelaus "practises" (ἠσκήσατο, 1379) with arms, Helen "decks him out" (ἐξήσκησα, 1383) with the change of clothing. The two characteristic actions, one feminine and life-giving, the other masculine and mar-

---

67. The phrase ἐν χθονί suggests the chthonic themes connected with death and the underworld at the beginning of the play: see 168, 344, 518–19. Murray and Dale, however, are suspicious of the phrase, but it seems not to trouble Kannicht.

tial, are now brought together in the same verb. Though still indicative of opposing attitudes, the two gestures are both working toward the same end. Antithesis has become complementation. The union of contraries here holds out the promise of a fuller union in Sparta.

The third stasimon, sung as Helen and Menelaus exit for the last time, continues the themes of cosmic rebirth from the Mountain Mother ode but localizes them in a more directly personal situation. The movement from sorrow and death to the joy of a new life now takes place not on remote Olympus but in the local Laconian festival of the Hyacinthia (1465–75). The death of Hyacinthus becomes the occasion for the "nocturnal joy" of the festal dance (νύχιον ἐς εὐφροσύναν, 1468–70).

Hyacinthus, like Helen and Persephone, is connected with the death and rebirth of vegetation. The Hyacinthia was primarily a fertility festival.[68] Hence this allusion to his cult continues the rhythmic movement of renewal after sterility. There is perhaps the further intimation, as in the *Odyssey,* that the union of the king and queen in their own land, performing the rites that fall to their office, ushers in the fertility of which the land has been doubly deprived while both its king and its Persephone-like queen have been held in the realm of death or "under the earth."[69] Despite Proteus and Theonoe, Egypt also functions, in part, as a sort of Hades, a place of death; and Menelaus' return fulfils the folk tale or initiatory motif of a descent to the underworld.[70] In this respect Menelaus' experiences reflect those of Odysseus and are the male counterpart of the vegetation myth attaching to Helen.

In other ways too the cosmic myth of the return of Persephone echoes the private circumstances of Helen and Menelaus. The marriage of their daughter, previously thwarted by the shame of Helen (688–90), is anticipated in the blazing marriage torches of this third stasimon (1476–77). Yet the larger cosmic themes are not forgotten,

68. See Nilsson, *Mycenaean Origin* (note 41), and *Geschichte* (note 41) 316–17, 531; see also Golann (note 41) 39.
69. See *Od.* 19. 107–14 and C. Segal, "Transition and Ritual in Odysseus' Return," *PP* 22 (1967) 341.
70. See Iesi (note 41) 57–63. There may also be a play on the Hades-like quality of Egypt in 69, where Teucer compares the palace to "the house of Plutus," possibly alluding to the association Ploutos/Ploutôn: see Nilsson, *Geschichte* (note 41) 319 and Bacon (note 25) 137–38.

for the chorus refers to Hermione as the "heifer" (μόσχου, 1476), a word that suggests the connection of the human and natural worlds in a large, all-embracing rhythm.

The themes of life and rebirth here remain combined with those of reality and appearance. This real marriage of Hermione contrasts with Theoclymenus' delusion of marriage with Helen (1430–35). When he says shortly before that his house is "clean" (*kathara*) because Menelaus did not die there (1430–31) and that "all the earth should cry out with happy hymnals of Helen's and [his] marriage" (1433–35), he is ironically echoing the couple's real cleansing of the past and the reality of the cosmic rebirth that accompanies their union (1327–29, 1362–65).

The address to the swift Phoenician ship sailing across the seas (1451ff.) recalls the other Helen's journey to Troy (e.g., 229–38). The sea that has hitherto signified separation, wandering, and death[71] now becomes the literal means of recovering all that was lost and of passing from death to life. At the end of the ode the chorus calls upon the Dioscuri to cross the grey sea and the dark swell of its waves, sending the favoring breezes that will carry the united couple home (1501–5). They are then to "cast off from their sister the ill-fame [*dyskleia*] of a barbarian couch" (1506–7). The crossing of the sea thus cancels the shame and evil name that bulked so large in Helen's speeches early in the play. The sea performs the same restorative function for Menelaus. It receives his arms (1262) and washes off the stains (λύματα, 1271) of the polluted past. Having robbed Menelaus of his heroic identity, as he says at his first appearance in the play (424–25), it now renders that identity back to him.

In its restorative function the sea presents the appearance of "death" when in fact it confers new life. When Theoclymenus asks what kind of death Menelaus dies, Helen replies that he perished "most pitiably, in the sea's wet waves" (οἰκτρότατ', ὑγροῖσιν ἐν κλυδωνίοις ἁλός, 1209; see also 1271).

The two positive functions of the sea, restoring identity and purifying the past, not only repeat the contrasts between appearance and reality and death and life but also connect these contrasts with those between Troy and Egypt. Its healing and purificatory functions are the

---

71. See 202, 233ff., 400–401, 408ff., 423–24, 520ff., 531ff., 773ff., 1126ff.

Euripides

cosmic analogue to those of Theonoe (866–67) and stand at the opposite pole from Theoclymenus' narrow, limited purity (1430–31).

Even more important, the figure of Galaneia in the first strophe of
the ode (1456–64) recalls Theonoe's mythical sea ancestry: Proteus,
the Nereids, Psamathe (4–15). Galaneia is herself "the grey daughter
of Pontus" (1457) and like these other sea-deities is a beneficent figure. Theonoe's mythical marine ancestry, especially in its connection
with Proteus, has signified the possible existence of justice, piety, and
the higher reality of a purer moral order. This marine mythology and
Proteus, as symbols of that order, accompany the images of a joyful,
revivified nature, in contrast to the dying nature of the parode. This
kindly "Egyptian" mythology, more remote and less familiar than
the Olympian, also contrasts with the negative anthropomorphism of
Olympus in the early part of the play (e.g., the myths of Callisto and
Kos in 375–85). The reborn joy of nature, which is also the joy of
Persephone's return from the underworld, is then carried to Sparta in
the antistrophe that follows the address to Galaneia (1465–78). The
temple of Athena, previously the setting for the Persephone-like ab-
duction of Helen (243–48), now stands alongside the Spartan festival
of the Hyacinthia.

The marriage torches of Hermione which end the antistrophe
(1476–78) have an important role in defining these antitheses. We
spoke above of their role in signifying the private aspect of the protagonists' happy reunion. But Hermione too stands under the large
archetype of the maiden reclaimed. Her marriage torches mark a
return to life and light, analogous to the entrance of Theonoe (865–
72) and the renewed marriage of Helen and Menelaus (637–41, 722–
25). Like the Hyacinthia and the Spartan myths of the Leucippidae
(1465–1468), Hermione's torches resolve in local and intimate terms
the antithesis between life and death. They complete an antithesis
between the treacherous fire beacons of Nauplius at the remote
Cephiridean reefs (766–67, 1126–31)[72] and the flames that razed Troy
on the one hand and the purifying torches of Theonoe on the other
(865–72). Correspondingly, the destructive sea of the Nauplius story
in the Trojan realm contrasts with the kindly sea of Galaneia, linked
to Egypt's marine mythology in this ode.

72. Verrall (note 3) 110 notes how odd it is for the chorus to know of this detail at
767.

VI

Indispensable as Theonoe is, it is Helen who effects the decisive movement from death to life. She activates the life-giving possibilities that stand on one side of the play's polarities and form one side of the Egyptian locale. Her distinctive quality in effecting this movement is summed up in the word χάρις, which includes grace, charm, beauty, song, gratitude, love.[73] In its flexibility and range of meanings it is especially appropriate to the iridescent radiance of Helen herself.

Charis first occurs at the end of Teucer's speech on the oracle of the foundation of Salamis. Apollo has foretold that he will name his new land Salamis "for the sake of [as a sign of favor or gratitude toward] his homeland there" (τῆς ἐκεῖ χάριν πάτρας, 150). This *charis* in the new settlement suggests a benign movement from the Trojan world to peace, and thus it serves as a potential paradigm and encouragement for Helen and Menelaus: eventual escape from the grip of Troy, rest from wandering, and the acquisition of a stable home.

The life-giving significance of charis, however, is primarily associated with Helen. In the first strophe of the parode she asks Persephone to receive her songs of lamentation accompanied by her tears as a thank offering to the dead (173–78). We may compare the movement from lypê to terpsis in the ode on the Mountain Mother. Indeed, much of the meaning and beauty of the play lies in her phrase χάριτας . . . ἐπὶ δάκρυσι ("thank-offerings of grace accompanied by tears," or "upon tears," 176): the attainment of joy and beauty in the midst of the lamentations of death and war, a faith in life and creation which can envisage a higher reality of innocence and beauty through the deluded killings at Troy. Hence the related word χάρμα in 321 denotes the possibility that Menelaus is alive despite the "lamentations" (γόους, 321) of his death. That same antithesis is stamped on the reunion between Menelaus and the real Helen: his tears (*dakrya*, cf. 176) change to "joy" (χαρμονά, 654), and there is more joy (*charis*) than pain (*lypai*, 654–55).

The association of charis with a movement from pain to joy receives its most vivid formulation in the Mountain Mother ode. The

73. Conacher (note 11) 298–99 has well observed the importance of charis in the play, but not, I think, traced its significance far enough.

Charites sent by Zeus serve as the essential instruments of the rebirth and revivification of nature. These joyful and restorative songs, which provoke the Goddess' laughter (1349) and pleasure (*terpsis*, 1352), are in direct contrast with the parode. There Helen sang plaintive songs to the dead (176) and called upon the Sirens, "daughters of Earth," to come with their mournful music (168–73). These Sirens are not the spellbinding singers of the *Odyssey* but chthonic deities connected with funeral monuments and the grave.[74] Their music is appropriate to this underworld, death-bound half of the Persephone cycle. But the Charites of the second stasimon, like the Muses in the proem of Hesiod's *Theogony* but unlike Helen's tearful Charites of 176, are joyful and life-giving as they celebrate Persephone's return and, by analogy, Helen's release from her deathlike imprisonment at Proteus' tomb.

Charis as the joy of rebirth continues into the next scene when Helen, as part of her manipulation of death and life, tells Theoclymenus that she would die with Menelaus out of love for him (1401–2). But, she goes on, "What charis would there be in dying with the dead?" (1402–3). And she then reiterates her need for a ship "that I may receive full charis" (1411). In both of these lines, charis denotes her abandonment of death for life. Behind this apparent abandonment of the dead Menelaus for a living husband lies her real abandonment of a death-like state for the life and marriage signified by the return to Sparta. Hence the "full charis" of 1411 refers at one level to the "favor" conferred on her by Theoclymenus but at another level to the joy of life, rebirth, renewal contained in her escape with Menelaus.

Charis also means "charm," and especially sexual charm, a quality that Helen, if any woman, possesses in the highest degree. The play shows her, in contrast to her eidolon at Troy, using this aspect of charis in the service of life. In the scene with Theonoe she draws upon the multiple meanings of charis—gratitude, charm, grace—to persuade one who has renounced the sexual charis to aid the cause of love. Euripides must have savored this paradoxical understanding between the figure of Helen and the virginal Theonoe, but his Helen is careful to adapt her charis to Theonoe's moral purity.

---

74. For these chthonic Sirens and further literature see Kannicht (note 11) *ad loc.* (2.67).

It is with Theoclymenus that Helen most successfully deploys the full range of her charis. The credulous and loutish king is no match for this womanly grace, charm, and wit. Helen need only make a strategic reference to marriage (1231), proffer reconciliation (1233), and Theoclymenus is ensnared. "Let there be charis in return for charis," he promises (1234): "favor for favor" is what he means, but his words also suggest, ironically, the deeper "joy" of Helen's return for her present show of "charm." The disguised Menelaus adds that the ship would itself be a sign of "favor" (or "gratitude") for Menelaus (Μενέλεῳ τε πρὸς χάριν, 1273). Theoclymenus innocently pays tribute to Helen's "charm" when he promises to heap the ship with gifts, doing this, as he tells the disguised husband, "out of favor for her" (τῇδε πρὸς χάριν, 1281).

In Helen's last appearance on stage, charis occurs no fewer than seven times in some seventy lines. It describes her success in winning over Theonoe (1373), in deceiving Theoclymenus (1378, 1397, 1411), in abandoning death for the joy of life (1402). Her last use of the word brings together its fullest range of associations. Theoclymenus is concerned that Helen may weep too much for her "dead" husband. She reassures him with the words, "This is the day that will reveal to you my charis" (ἥδ' ἡμέρα σοι τὴν ἐμὴν δείξει χάριν, 1420). Theoclymenus is probably to understand *charis* to mean "gratitude" here. But to the audience it also signifies that "charm," "joy," "beauty" which are part of Helen's resilient hold on the vitality of existence and her capacity to bring forth life from death. "What charis is it to die with the dead," she has said a few lines before (1402–3). In his last lines on stage Menelaus prays to Zeus for "one favor" (μίαν χάριν, 1449). Helen's life-giving charis has already secured it in advance.

VII

The *Helen* not only points back to the Sophistic dichotomies of onoma and pragma but also looks ahead to the Platonic attempt to distinguish appearance from reality in a deeper sense. The young Plato, as a lad of sixteen, may well have been in the audience of the play's first performance.

Euripides, like Plato, suggests that the ultimate reality may consist in a purity and beauty that we reach through the violence and confusion of the eidola that deceive us with their false gods. Theonoe is, as Kannicht suggests, a poetic anticipation of Plato's concern with freeing the mind from the obscurities of the sense world in order to attain the purity and clarity of the noumenal realm.[75] Plato too used Stesichorus' myth of the phantom Helen as a parable of the evils we suffer when we are deceived by the "false" beauty and "false" pleasures of the sense world (*Rep.* 9.586BC). In Euripides' play not only Theonoe but also the true Helen—and perhaps, therefore, the true reality—are in touch with what is life-giving, innocent, and noble. So in Plato the ultimate reality is good, pure, and beautiful. It is our task not to mistake the mists of appearances for this reality, not to take the shadows in the cave for the true shapes of things in the light of the sun or confuse the murky depths in which most men live with the clear atmosphere that the philosopher breathes (*Rep.* 7.514Aff.; *Phaedo* 109A–11C). Menelaus, in more than a literal way, comes to see the world differently. The violence of his ten-year effort to regain the shadow of the real Helen contrasts ironically with the comparative ease with which the real Helen falls into his arms and devises the means for their reunion.

So much similarity there is, perhaps. Yet Euripides is not Plato. Menelaus returns with the real Helen, but he is no philosopher. Euripides remains more interested in the twists and turns of men's delusions than in the grasping of an eternal and ideal reality.

Hence, for all the antitheses between Helen's gentle arts and Menelaus' violence, between Egypt and Troy, feminine and masculine values, the action culminates in a swashbuckling scene of violence in which the veteran of Troy is totally in his element. Menelaus invokes Poseidon next to the "pure daughters of Nereus" (1584–86) and pours "streams of blood" (αἵματος ἀπορροαί) into the sea (1587–88). He thus pollutes with bloodshed those "maiden-lovely streams" of the play's first line, with its associations of Egypt's benign marine mythology. The action also recalls the "streams of blood" (αἵματος ῥοαί, 984) with which, in his desperation, he threatened to defile

75. Kannicht (note 11) 1.76, citing *Phaedo* 67A and *Theaet.* 176A–C. See also the interesting remarks of Grégoire (note 48) 43–46, who notes that aside from Aristophanes' parody in *Thesm.* the name Theonoe occurs only in Euripides and Plato (*Cratyl.* 407B).

Proteus' tomb (984–85). The destructive and divisive significance of the sea in the first half of the play now emerges as a possibility once more, even though life is winning out over death. When Menelaus creeps to the prow sword in hand "having no thought of any corpse" (νεκρῶν μὲν οὐδενὸς μνήμην ἔχων, 1583), the victory over death is assured; yet we are also reminded thereby of the ritual death through which he has had to pass.

The ensuing battle is itself one of those "contests of blood" (ἅμιλλα . . . αἵματος, 1155–56) which the chorus condemned in the famous antiwar passage in the first stasimon (1151–58). Menelaus calls upon his companions to "bloody" (καθαιματώσει) the heads of the Egyptians (1599). "Slaughter, massacre the barbarians," he shouts (σφάζειν, φονεύειν, 1594). Indeed, the battle virtually transforms the ship into a "stream of blood" like those of 984 or 1587–88: φόνῳ δὲ ναῦς ἐρρεῖτο (1602). Menelaus addresses his men here as "the sackers of Troy" (1560), and Helen calls upon the "Trojan glory" (1604). Throughout the play, however, Troy and the kleos of Troy's capture have had a primarily negative significance (especially 808–54).[76]

It may be, as some have argued, that we are not to take the death of the Egyptians too seriously.[77] The slaughter of the bull could even appear as a kind of ritual scapegoat for Helen's safe return. The burden of the dead past or the false, "destructive image" (73) must be sacrificed to reacquire innocence. Yet a real human sacrifice, barbarians though the victims are, follows the killing of the animal. Herodotus had included a grisly tale of human sacrifice in his account of Helen and Menelaus' escape from Egypt (2.119.2–3); and Euripides may have that passage, with its grim overtones, in mind here. Sacrifice in general is an ominous theme in the tale of Troy.[78] Euripides

76. With 1560 cf. 806; with 1603 cf. 845.

77. So Steiger (note 26) 217; Grube (note 35) 350. Verrall (note 3) remarks that the killing of the Egyptians "would be repulsive if it were not too silly" (54); see also 85: "Any audience fit for Euripides would feel this to be a hideous thing, a thing intolerable, unless, in some extreme circumstances, it might perhaps be presented as a stern necessity." "Coldblooded cruelty," he says on the next page (86).

78. Arrowsmith (note 15) 39 suggests that the Brauron cult in the *IT* serves "to lay bare the immense human 'blood-sacrifice' of the Peloponnesian war." See his further remarks on 44–45. The sacrificial animal is also handled in a way that makes for an ostentatious display of physical force (cf. 1561–64). The rather mysterious horse of 1567–68, which Dale finds "superfluous" and "an unwelcome anticlimax" (*ad* 1563–

does not dwell on it in this play as he had in the Taurian *Iphigeneia*. Yet Helen spoke of her suicide as a "sacrifice" to the goddesses' jealousy (354–57), and Menelaus had alluded to the preliminary shedding of blood with enigmatic relish (προσφάζεται μὲν αἷμα πρῶτα νερτέροις, 1255).

On the positive side, the concluding battle reenacts history in a way that wipes out the old guilt. The Trojan War is fought again, in miniature. But Helen is now on the right side, cheering on her husband. Her verb ἀνήρπασε at 1374 even recalls the rape that began the conflict (50), but now it is her husband (πόσις, 1374) who is doing the carrying off. In allowing Helen to relive as a virtuous wife her sinful Trojan past, Euripides is also availing himself of the imaginative possibilities of romance where the dead past may be relived and second chances are the rule.[79]

It is also possible to regard the battle scene in psychological terms: it is a cathartic, liberating reexperience of a traumatic, guilt-laden past. Dramatically, Helen's role in this scene is essential for the completion of her side of the story. As Menelaus recovers his identity as a heroic warrior, so Helen recovers hers as a virtuous wife. This dramatization of her recovery of identity is all the more important as the eidolon in the first part of the play has raised the question of that identity. Indeed, Helen feels the shame of the evils perpetrated in her name as a part of herself. As Richard Kannicht observes, "Without the beautiful Helen, then, no eidolon of the beautiful Helen either: just this fateful conjunction is the basis of the tragic paradox which alienates her from herself: to be ἀναίτιός θ' ἅμα παναίτιος."[80] The battle scene heals the split in her identity between onoma and pragma and is a final overcoming of her *Selbstentfremdung*.

---

68), may be there as a reminder of the martial character of Menelaus, the heroic identity being reborn: cf. the equine sacrifice in *Il.* 23.171 and also Hdt. 4.71–72, Tac. *Germ.* 27. On the rarity of horse sacrifices see L. Ziehen, *RE* 18.1 (1939) 591–92 s.v. "Opfer." At the same time the horse would be an appropriate sacrifice to Poseidon for one who seeks a safe return over the sea to his homeland: cf. J. G. Frazer, *Pausanias' Description of Greece* (London 1898) ad 8.7.2.

79. Hence the revival of the "dead" in the *Winter's Tale, Pericles, Cymbeline*. There is a good example of this imaginative cancellation of the burdensome past through reliving it in the section entitled "Alle Mädchen sind dein" in Hermann Hesse's *Steppenwolf* (*Gesammelte Dichtungen*, Suhrkamp ed. [1952] 4.373ff.). The descent to the underworld in *Od.* 11 and *Aen.* 6 also provides some analogies.

80. Kannicht (note 11) 1.61.

There are, of course, other positive features of the ending. The benign effect of Zeus' purposes stated in the prologue (36–37, 44–47) but obscured in the parode (241–43) are now confirmed: "Such is the will of Zeus" (Ζεὺς γὰρ ὧδε βούλεται, 1669).[81] The appearance of the Dioscuri also confirms the immortal (1659), and not the mortal, logos of their fate (21, 138–42, 284–85) and establishes Helen's virtue forever (1666–70, 1686–87). On the other hand their appearance is made absolutely necessary by the sanguinary fury of Theoclymenus. And, in any case, Euripidean *dexiotês* could have devised a less violent resolution to a play in which the Trojan War and war in general have carried nothing but the most negative associations. A work that has bitterly condemned violence requires violence, finally, for its resolution. The chorus' words at 1151–58 are an ironic, haunting echo as Menelaus, seconded by Helen, pours blood into the sea and invokes the sack of Troy and the "Trojan glory" (1560, 1603).

The point is not that we have to decide between a positive and a negative interpretation but rather that Euripides himself refuses to decide. There is ultimately no total reconciliation between the play's two worlds. The vision of the *Helen* is profoundly dualistic, and the dualism may cut too deeply to be bridged.

Parallel to this dualism in the dramatic structure stands the philosophical dualism connected with the aether and Theonoe, the contrast, broadly speaking, between spirit and matter. Anne Burnett's elucidation of this dualism is especially valuable, though the connection with Anaximander is perhaps not to be insisted on:[82]

The materialist, Anaximandrian theory of justice was altered by Euripides not only because of its alienation from the world and its morality, but also because it belonged at last to a monistic system. Anaximander's justice lay in the undifferentiated Boundless from which the Opposites came, just as Anaxagoras' *nous* stood single and sufficient behind the created world. By contrast, the justice which Theonoe serves is the phenomenon of a dualistic universe. In her own person Theonoe unites justice with *aither*, for she, who has an altar of *Dike*

81. Matthiessen (note 48) 695 notes the balancing of Helen's prayer to Aphrodite and Hera (1093–1106; cf. 1024–27) by Menelaus' to Zeus near the end of the action (1441–50). See also Conacher (note 11) 301–2 who notes the absence of "Zeus' plans" from Theonoe's explanation (302).
82. Burnett (note 1) 161.

within herself, is also the priestess of the divine *aither.* . . . But *aither,* the house of Zeus (Nauck², Frag. 491), or Zeus himself (Nauck², Frags. 836, 869, 903, 935, and many others), was not for Euripides the single first substance. Creation occurred only when *aither* was paired with earth (Nauck², Frags. 836, 1012). Reflecting this duality, the *Helen* recognizes a double system of causation and of morality, influenced perhaps by the Opposites of Anaximander, and looking forward to the coexistence of the Wandering Cause and the Mind, in the *Timaeus.*

Thus here at the end Helen's purity, innocence, resilience prove to be not enough. Violence is needed, and the male heroism of Menelaus supplies it. The "streams of blood" that he pours forth (1587) are not only a dark counterstatement to the virginal purity of Egypt's streams (1) but also a return to primitive ritual after philosophical mysticism and lofty spirituality. The antithesis between the primitive-archetypal and philosophical-speculative aspects of the play noted earlier is not resolved any more than that between the reality of war and the aspiration toward peace (1151–58). Egypt itself is dualistic: beside Theonoe there stands Theoclymenus, as beside Helen, Menelaus. The play contains bold speculations on spiritual immortality (1013–16); yet Helen and Menelaus' rebirth requires a deeply primitive sacrifice of blood.

The ending, therefore, gives an ironic turn to the antithesis of reality and appearance in the play and deepens the pervasive dualism with a profounder dualism that reflects basic cleavages in human life: philosophical principles and primitive rituals, abstract thought and vegetation myths, spiritual purity and fertility celebrations, immortal aether and the shedding of blood.[83] The antithetical structure of the play subsumes these final antitheses into those between Troy and Egypt, guilt and innocence, death and life. The mythic "language" of the plot and the intellectualist language of the philosophical problems enrich and expand one another with ever-widening horizons.

The fact that the dualism emerges at the end as a *necessary* part of our world structure, however, suddenly throws the clarity of those previous antitheses into confusion. The play's final irony in this supposedly happy ending is that the previous antitheses are shown to be simplistic. In the last analysis, human life cannot be reduced to clear-

83. See Burnett (note 1) 155.

cut dichotomies. Reality is elusive and ambiguous precisely because it is itself a perpetual dialectic between what seems and what is.

For this reason Helen, with her ambiguous status between corporeal and fictive being, is the central figure, and Theonoe and Menelaus remain simpler polarities at either end of the spectrum. We may emerge from the mists long enough to recognize the clarity and beauty of a Theonoe; but when we return to the realm of action, to real Sparta after fairyland Egypt, we find ourselves again in a dualistic world where the boundaries between reality and appearance are not sure, where a Helen needs a Menelaus and joins him in the war cry and the lust for blood. Once out of range of that suspended world of Theonoe's mysterious wisdom and Proteus' mild justice and sôphrosynê, we return to the strife, passions, possessiveness of men and the inevitable bloodshed to which they lead. The reenacted Trojan War at the end darkens the validity of a Theonoe's claims to superior truth and the reality of her philosophical realm after all.

Ending with battle and war enables Euripides to keep a certain bitterness of mood. In adapting Euripides' myth to his *Ägyptische Helena,* Hofmannsthal felt that the motif of the eidolon introduced the problem of dividing the work into two parts, a ghost story and an idyll.[84] One may demur at considering Euripides' *Helen* a ghost story (Hofmannsthal, like Goethe, exploited this facet of the legend), but it is clear that his ending is carefully planned to keep the idyll far in the background. As in the *Tempest,* the return to mainland reality brings a relinquishment of the infinite openness and hopefulness of romance. Euripides' ending, like Prospero's last action, figuratively buries the creator's book of spells and abjures the "rough magic" of his "so potent art."[85]

VIII

There is still another dimension of meaning in the two worlds of the *Helen.* Helen is a ministrant to life and renewal in both a physical and spiritual sense. Her charis is the joy of life and feminine charm. But it also includes the beauty of art. Her role as a manipulator of

84. The quotation from Hofmannsthal is given by Alt (note 31) 24 n.1.
85. *Tempest,* V.i.49–51.

technê and mêchanê, of deception and the double vision that confuses the more prosaic everyday mentalities of Menelaus and Theoclymenus, also signifies the restorative force of art itself. Like the poet, Helen rings the changes on illusion and reality and with falsehood achieves truth. Gorgias used the figure of Helen to reflect upon the nature of art,[86] and the Gorgianic elements in the antitheses of Euripides have long been recognized.[87]

Plutarch reports a remark of Gorgias, à propos of tragedy, as follows (82B23): "The one who deceives is more just than the one who does not deceive, and the one who is deceived is wiser than the one not deceived." Plutarch's context makes it clear that Gorgias is talking about the need for successful fiction ("deception") in representational art, which conveys its truth by exploiting the audience's acceptance of the appearances that it in fact knows to be a lie. Something of this idea, I suggest, underlies certain elements in Euripides' play, especially the fanciful Egyptian setting and the marine mythology of Psamathe, the Nereids, Proteus, Galaneia, and even Theonoe. Given the problematical character of reality itself, Euripides is saying, there may be a truth that goes deeper than our everyday vision of things, a truth that looks improbable and "deceptive," but yet is "wise" and "just" in Gorgias' sense. This is the visionary truth of art, imagination, and mysticism. By its light the apparent triumphs even of the physical prowess of a Menelaus may prove eidola. Theonoe's Egypt, akin to Gorgias' "wiser" deception, may harbor truths about our existence which are usually concealed from us, clouded by our passions and the impurities of our lives and our world.

As the kaleidoscope of the play's antitheses between appearance and reality turns before our eyes, we become aware that the play *qua* play is itself a term in those antitheses: the very fact that we watch with rapt attention a wildly improbable tale of fantastic characters indicates something of our own hesitation between illusion and reality. What Northrop Frye has said of the *Tempest* is in part applicable also to the *Helen:* "The play is an illusion like the dream, and yet a focus of reality more intense than life affords. . . . What seems at first illusory, the magic and music, becomes real, and the *Realpolitik* of

---

86. See C. Segal, "Gorgias and the Psychology of the *Logos*," HSCP 66 (1962) 99–155.

87. Solmsen, "*Onoma*" (note 14); see also Schmid (note 62) 504, with note 3.

Antonio and Sebastian becomes illusion."[88] That Euripides was conscious of such possibilities appears substantiated by at least one passage in which he deliberately breaks through the dramatic illusion and reminds us that we are, after all, watching a play, a fiction (1056).[89]

This tension between art and reality, like the more general tension between appearance and truth, also remains unresolved. Helen's mental *mêchanai* and "wise deceptions" yield place at the end to the hard truth of Menelaus' brawn. Unlike Plato, Euripides has no conviction of an ideal truth. He is content to reveal how problematical is the relation of all human life to what we suppose to be real or illusory. Unique as the *Helen* is, it also shares in what Zuntz has called "the tragic essence of Euripides' works, namely, the renunciation of a final truth [which] serves, in the *Helen,* to irradiate, ironically, the web of inescapable error and limited yet saving understanding which is life."[90]

Thus if the *Helen* explores art's magical power to transform reality and to present facets of it usually hidden to us, it is also willing to prick the bubble. Theonoe remains in the sealed-off realm of Egypt; and the threat of violence to her person, parallel with Helen's participation in the reenacted Trojan War, is a final compounding of the ambiguity of art and illusion. Euripides has taken us to magic realms and "faery lands forlorn," but he has also shown us their fragility. And that double vision of art's use of illusion to convey truth, its suspension between *onoma* and *pragma*, cloud image and solid body, belongs to the special quality of self-reflective romance which the *Helen* shares with the *Tempest:*

> These our actors,
> As I foretold you, were all spirits, and
> Are melted into air, into thin air;
> And, like the baseless fabric of this vision,
> The cloud-capp'd towers, the gorgeous palaces,
> The solemn temples, the great globe itself,

88. Frye, *Tempest* (note 9) 21.
89. See Dale *ad* 1050ff. (134). The chorus' rather stiff lines, τοὺς δὲ Μενέλεω πόθῳ / λόγους ἀκοῦσαι τίνας ἐρεῖ ψύχης πέρι (945–46), if not dismissed as careless and mechanical writing, also look like a self-conscious reflection, almost approaching parody, on the convention of the *hamilla logôn* in tragedy.
90. Zuntz (note 11) 221–22.

Euripides

> Yea, all which it inherit, shall dissolve,
> And, like this insubstantial pageant faded,
> Leave not a rack behind.

IX

The complexity of the two worlds of the *Helen* takes us back to the inevitable question of whether the play is a tragedy, a comedy, or something in between. Unquestionably there is much in the *Helen* that is comic, or at least amusing. Yet even the most comic scenes— Menelaus and the Portress or the appearance of Theoclymenus— have their serious side. While the motifs of *agnoia* and anagnôrisis point ahead to New Comedy, they have their fully tragic aspect too: the ignorance and blindness in which so much of human life is lived.[91] Indeed, the confusions and recognitions of New Comedy arose and were (and are) appreciated not just because of the titillation of the unexpected but because they too point to the uncertainty, ignorance, and instability of the human condition.[92]

The issue of whether the play is comedy or tragedy is, in the last analysis, irrelevant. Euripides, like many artists in the late stages of their work, has created a form that transcends the precise limits between genres. Shakespeare's late "tragic" romances—notably *Cymbeline* and *Pericles*—are a close analogy. The urge and the encouragement to go beyond the conventional form of tragedy must have come with the conception of the basic material of the plot: the complex interchanges of appearance and reality, the exotic setting, the philosophical mysticism, the ritual death and rebirth, the odes on Persephone and the Mountain Mother, the blend of Sophistic epistemology and ancient, Odyssean archetypes. The equally "romantic" and "comic" features of plays like the *Iphigeneia in Tauris* and the *Ion*—to say nothing of the heroless *Trojan Women* or the tripartite *Heracles Mad*—suffice to show that Euripides was in a period of intense artistic exploration and experimentation.

The *Helen's* very hesitation between tragedy and comedy is itself

91. See Solmsen, *"Ion"* (note 29) 434 and 452–53.
92. See Albin Lesky, *A History of Greek Literature,* 2d ed., trans. James Willis and Cornelis de Heer (London 1966) 386–87.

one term in the questions and antitheses that it poses: are truth and reality something akin to the gentleness, beauty, innocence of Helen or to the mystical purity of Theonoe, or are they rather akin to the "Trojan" violence of Menelaus (and Theoclymenus), for it is the action of these two male characters which stands out most vividly at the end of the play.

If a choice must be made, one can find legitimate grounds for considering the *Helen* a tragedy, albeit a tragedy of a very special form. It depicts, finally, not an escape into a transformed world, as Aristophanic comedy often does, or even the renewal of a disrupted social order, after the fashion of Menander and his successors, but raises disturbing and ironic questions about the place of violence and bloodshed in the reality in which men have to live. The necessity of reenacting the Trojan War, cathartic though that may be, and the brutal impulses of Theoclymenus toward the *miasma* of shedding kindred blood in the penultimate scene shatter the simplicity of a happy ending. The *Helen* is tragic if only because it recalls us to the horror of our immersion in a deluded world of passion, war, razed cities, empty goals. It makes us aware, on a multiplicity of levels, of the cost of choosing appearance over reality—a choice for which the play's purest and most idealistic character comes close to paying with her life.

Zuntz has beautifully described the play as "an ethereal dance above the abyss."[93] The play is a tragedy in so far as Euripides never lets us forget that the abyss is there, and is real.

93. Zuntz (note 11) 227.

CHAPTER 8 /

Pentheus and Hippolytus on the Couch and on the Grid: Psychoanalytic and Structuralist Readings of Greek Tragedy

I

Among the changes of perspective that the last two or three decades have seen in the study of classical culture has been a greater awareness of underlying social and personal tensions and of the various strategies, at all levels of the culture, to evade, mask, or sometimes reconcile these tensions. Structuralist and psychoanalytic criticism are valuable tools in laying bare these tensions and the mechanisms that serve to deny, understand, or overcome them. In many ways the two methodologies complement each other. Using patterns of binary oppositions in an attempt to grasp the underlying syntax of myth and focusing on the dichotomy between nature and culture, the "raw" and the "cooked," Claude Lévi-Strauss and his followers have paid particular attention to the relation between myth and society;[1]

For helpful suggestions and friendly criticism I thank Marylin Arthur, Kenneth Reckford, Peter Rose, Joseph Russo, Peter Smith, Philip Stadter, and Froma Zeitlin. I gratefully acknowledge a summer stipend from the National Endowment for the Humanities in 1977 which aided me in putting this essay into definitive form.

1. For classical applications, see Jean-Pierre Vernant, *Mythe et pensée chez les Grecs,* 3d.ed. (Paris 1974); Vernant, *Mythe et société en Grèce ancienne* (Paris 1974); Vernant and Pierre Vidal-Naquet, *Mythe et tragédie en Grèce ancienne* (Paris 1972); Marcel Detienne, *Les jardins d'Adonis* (Paris 1972). For further bibliography, see John Peradotto, *Classical Mythology: An Annotated Bibliographical Survey* (Urbana, Ill. 1973) 40–47; C. Segal, "The Raw and the Cooked in Greek Literature: Structure, Values, Metaphor," *CJ* 69 (1973/4) 289–308; *Tragedy and Civilization: An Interpretation of Sophocles,* Martin Classical Lectures 26 (Cambridge, Mass. 1981) chap. 2; also "Structuralism

yet their methods, both in their objectives and their modes of operation, tend to neglect the self, and especially the self as it unfolds and
develops in time.[2] Psychoanalysis, on the other hand, which aims at
grasping the hidden processes of the unconscious that speaks in the
symbolic language of dreams and unguarded Freudian slips, has been
accused of paying too little attention to cultural context and leveling
out cultural differences in its assumptions of universally valid subconscious processes.

Admittedly Freud and Lévi-Strauss make odd bedfellows. The former is concerned with the irrational impulses of the unconscious, the
latter with the rational structures with which the human mind tends
to organize reality. Yet the underlying similarity is perhaps as important as the obvious surface differences. Both deal primarily with the
mechanisms of thought and feeling through which puzzling, ambiguous, and contradictory aspects of reality are forced into bearable,
coherent forms for the inner life of man. Both insist that the hidden
mental processes yield up their secrets to the light of reason and can
be described in rational, scientific language. For both there is a systematic, logical, coherent pattern underlying the most random, minute, apparently trivial detail. Freud reads souls as Lévi-Strauss reads
myths and societies: nothing is without its significance; every item,
when properly understood, has its place in a pattern. For Freud the
language that unlocks the secrets of the unconscious is the language of
the physical sciences, with its notion of quanta of energy which are
displaced, transferred, repressed only to burst out in another direction and in another form. For Lévi-Strauss this language is that of
formal linguistics and mathematics. Symbols and diagrams abound.
"Every myth," Lévi-Strauss predicted in a moment of euphoric
confidence, "corresponds to a formula of the following type: $F_x(a)$

---

and Greek Tragedy," in this volume. For a concise introduction to and critique of
Lévi-Strauss see Edmund Leach, *Lévi-Strauss* (London 1970) and *Culture and Communication* (Cambridge 1976); Jonathan Culler, *Structuralist Poetics* (London 1975) 40–54;
G. S. Kirk, *Myth, Its Meaning and Function in Ancient and Other Cultures* (Berkeley and
Los Angeles 1970) 42–83 and 132–71; Richard S. Caldwell, "Psychoanalysis, Structuralism and Greek Mythology," in *Phenomenology, Structuralism, Semiology*, ed. Har-
ry R. Garvin, *Bucknell Review* (Lewisburg, Pa., April 1976) 209–30, which unfortu-
nately came to my attention after this essay was completed, provides a stimulating
theoretical comparison of structuralist, Freudian, and Lacanian approaches to myth.

2. See, e.g., Frederic Jameson, *The Prison House of Language* (Princeton 1972) 196.

$:F_y(b) \cong F_x(b) \ :F_{a-1}(y)$."[3] On the Freudian side, we have concepts like cathexis, abreaction, reaction-formation, projection, displacement, transference, countertransference, and so on.

Both the structuralist and the psychoanalytic reader are more concerned with the symbolic transformations by which the mental processes represent reality than with the objective reality per se. Indeed, reality for both is a mental configuration: the product of the structures and logic of the social organization in the structuralist view or of the alignment of forces in the ego's adjustments to the pressures of id and superego in the psychoanalytic view. The real mental life of the individual, for the Freudian, lies in the struggle to repress, integrate, sublimate, or otherwise accommodate the drives of the id. The creations of culture only express those conflicts in sublimated, symbolic form. For the structuralist too the real meaning of culture lies in the latent, not the surface, meaning because that contains the informing pattern, the deep structure of the myth, society, or ritual in question, the basic mental set that finds homologous expression in all the various codes of the society: dietary, botanical, sexual, architectural, familial.

Both a structuralist and a psychoanalytic criticism, then, will stress not the dominant ideal values openly proclaimed by the culture or the individual but rather the subsurface tensions that the culture or individual seeks to resist, smooth over, contain. Lévi-Strauss views myth as mediating logical contradictions (e.g., nature and culture, life and death) and thereby as enabling man to make his world intelligible. For Freud the emotional health of the individual depends upon his confronting and resolving conflicts between libidinal and aggressive drives which the conscious mind acknowledges only reluctantly and the realities enforced by his society and the external conditions of his life. Dreams represent these conflicts in symbolic form. Severe unacknowledged or unresolved conflict produces neurosis.

For both approaches, concerned as they are with the hidden meaning, the pattern observable only to the trained analytic eye, the *process* of transformations, adaptations, accommodations through which reality is made intelligible or endurable is more important than the absolute "meaning" of a given symbol; and such an absolute or

3. Claude Lévi-Strauss, "The Structural Study of Myth," in *Structural Anthropology,* trans. C. Jacobson and C. G. Schoepf (Garden City, N.Y. 1967) 225.

universal meaning becomes questionable anyway. In both cases the absolute signified per se takes second place to the complex relation between signified and signifier in a sign system, whether that system is part of the ego's web of neurotic defense-mechanisms and rationalizations or the society's attempt to deny logical contradictions through a system of mediations. Both approaches relate reality to a thinking subject rather than to an objective world "outside." To quote a French structuralist critic, "Ultimately one might say that the object of structuralism is not man endowed with meanings, but man fabricating meanings, as if it could not be the *content* of meanings which exhausted the semantic goals of humanity but only the act by which these meanings, historical and contingent variables, are produced. *Homo significans:* such would be the new man of structural inquiry."[4] Mutatis mutandis, something similar could be said of the rather older man of psychoanalytic inquiry.

Psychoanalytic and structural models also can help correct each other's deficiencies. Structuralism contributes a sense of the formal coherence of the work as a system of signs grounded in an underlying conceptual unity. It helps put into focus the relations between mental structures implicit in the society at large and the mythic structures used by the literary work. A psychoanalytic orientation brings a fuller awareness of the self and a greater sense of the dynamics of growth and change in time than is possible within the more static structuralist frame, with its emphasis on synchrony over diachrony, the paradigmatic over the syntagmatic plane.[5]

To turn briefly to the figure of Oedipus in Sophocles' *Tyrannus,* combining structuralist and psychoanalytic methods can help us toward a broader conception of character in Greek tragedy. The modern reader sometimes finds difficulty in understanding the complementarity of the generic and the individual in the Greek view of character. Oedipus is both an individual, with his conflicts and tensions, and a figure who performs the sacral and social functions of kingship. He occupies the symbolic center of the struggle to keep chaos at bay, to create a favorable and orderly relation between man

4. Roland Barthes, "The Structuralist Activity," in R. and F. DeGeorge, ed., *The Structuralists from Marx to Lévi-Strauss* (Garden City, N.Y. 1972) 153.

5. For these terms see Leach, *Culture and Communication* (note 1) 25–27; John Peradotto, "*Odyssey* 8.564–571: Verisimilitude, Narrative Analysis, and Bricolage," *Texas Studies in Literature and Language* 15 (1974) 818ff.

and the cosmos, to effect that mediation between the extremes of god and beast which constitutes one of the bases of human civilization. Paradoxically, the *Oedipus Tyrannus* gave Freud his name for the Oedipus complex; but the play itself pays very little overt attention to the psychological dimension of Oedipus' anomalous position.[6] Sophocles establishes a more even relationship than Euripides between the psychological and socioreligious meaning of the myth. Taken together, structuralist and psychoanalytic approaches allow us better to maintain this fine equilibrium and help us to appreciate the implications of Oedipus' ambiguous sacral kingship (he is both legitimate king and outsider, both the pollution and the source of purification, both the godlike savior and the scapegoat or pharmakos) without either insisting too emphatically on the Freudian levels of meaning or denying their presence in the configuration of plot elements given at the very surface of the narrative.

Whereas the structuralist study of myth seeks to discover the polarities that myth mediates and therefore makes acceptable as part of the basic structure of reality, the myths as used by tragedy destroy rather than affirm mediation. Clear differentiation gives way to fusion, ambiguity, paradox. Heracles in the *Trachiniae,* for example, is both the slayer of monsters and himself a monstrous, violent figure, both the celebrant at the victory sacrifice he offers and the beast consumed and devoured by a fire that points downward to the triumphant beast-man, Nessus, rather than upward to the Olympian realm where the flames ought to carry the sweet savor of the sacrifice.[7] Agamemnon and Cassandra in Aeschylus plunge from a godlike privileged status to bestial degradation, sacrificed like animals. Heracles (in both Sophocles and Euripides), Oedipus, Philoctetes, Pentheus are simultaneously at the lowest and the highest extremes on the scale of human values, both destroyers and saviors, accursed outcasts and noble heroes. The heroine of Euripides' *Iphigeneia in Tauris* is both the priestess of a savage cult involving pollution by human sacrifice and the central figure in the worship of the purest goddesses. Her brother, Orestes, is both a godlike youth of extraordinary beauty and a raging, bestial madman who has to be hunted.[8]

---

6. See Vernant, "'Oedipe' sans complexe" in *Mythe et tragédie* (note 1) 77–98.
7. See Detienne (note 1) 71–113; Segal, "Raw and Cooked" (note 1) 306f.
8. Cf. *IT* 269–74 and 275–80; cf. also 1163, 1324, 1426.

If tragedy, on a structuralist reading, dramatizes the collapse of polarities and the destruction of mediation, the tragic catastrophe, in a Freudian perspective, reflects the explosion of forces held in too precarious a balance in the psyche. The tragic justice, then, reflects the inexorable necessity of psychodynamic forces to reach an equilibrium. It is a law of the psyche that any blockage of the life forces has the most dangerous consequences. Fate, then, is the ineluctable power of our primal instincts, our oedipal and pre-oedipal drives. The grip of predestination in King Oedipus' tragedy, in Freud's view, is the grip of these forces upon us, at some level, during the whole of our lives: Oedipus' "fate"

> moves us only because it might have been our own, because the oracle laid upon us before our birth the very curse which rested upon him. It may be that we were all destined to direct our first sexual impulses toward our mothers and our first impulses of hatred and violence toward our fathers; our dreams convince us that we were.[9]

At the risk of some violence to both Freud and Lévi-Strauss, we may suggest that the internal stability of psychodynamics, that balance of opposing forces of the psyche which allows us to function according to a socially accepted standard of healthy, non-neurotic behavior, has some analogy, *grosso modo,* with the structuralist model of myth's mediation of polarities in the social order.

Combining structuralist and psychoanalytic perspectives has a particular usefulness and validity for the study of Greek literature and society, for here the distinctive quality of human civilization is defined in terms of the accommodation (ideally at least) rather than the repression of sexuality as the savagery of precivilized man adapts to the temperate forms required by city and family. To the raw and wild realm outside the city belong *both* the virginal hunter's rejection of sexuality (Artemis, Hippolytus, Daphne, Atalanta) and the unrestrained lust that characterizes the bestial Centaurs, the goatish Satyrs, the Nymphs who inhabit the forest's pools, and the seductive goddesses who inhabit remote, deserted islands: Calypso and above all Circe who entraps her would-be lovers in their own bestiality by

9. Sigmund Freud, *The Interpretation of Dreams,* trans. A. A. Brill, Modern Library ed. (New York 1950) 161.

changing them into swine, lions, or wolves. To achieve the proper emotional balance is also to claim humanity's intermediate position between the animal instincts of procreation and the gods' freedom from coming to be and passing away. Neither repression nor the untrammeled expression of sexual instincts is "civilized."

II

The two plays that we shall discuss in detail, the *Hippolytus* and the *Bacchae,* enact the two poles of deficient or excessive sexuality. In serving the virgin goddess Artemis and rejecting the love goddess Aphrodite, Hippolytus has his place truly in the wild, among the beasts that he hunts. In the *Bacchae,* on the other hand, the king, a rigid, authoritarian ruler, has a hidden animal self that will emerge not in the palace or the city which he supposedly controls but only in the wild forest and mountains where he is destroyed, dismembered, by those very instinctual forces that he has denied.

Overtly repressing his sexuality, Hippolytus begins and ends in the wild; latently repressing his sexuality, King Pentheus moves from the inner, civilized space of house and city to the wild realm where his concealed violence really belongs. At the other extreme from both these heroes stands the Heracles of the *Trachiniae.* His excessive sexuality has brought ruin to the house and city of his newest concubine, Iole, and soon brings that ruin to his own house as well. The play moves on an axis of inner and outer space, the inner, civilized world of Deianeira's house and the vast outside spaces of Heracles' journeys. Deianeira embodies the essence of the woman's inner space, Heracles the essence of the male hero's outward orientation.[10] One of the motive forces in the tragedy is the intensity of sexual desire that destroys both protagonists. The civilized space of the *oikos* is shattered by the intrusion of the wild spaces of the lustful beast-figures in the background. Heracles, behaving like the bestial monsters he has conquered, never enters the house that has been his goal; Deianeira,

10. See C. Segal, "Mariage et sacrifice dans les *Trachiniennes* de Sophocle," *AC* 44 (1975) 30–53, and *Tragedy and Civilization* (note 1) chap. 4, passim. For other aspects of the contrasts between inner and outer space see also Segal, "Sophocles' *Trachiniae:* Myth, Poetry, and Heroic Values," *YCS* 25 (1976) 123–30, 141–46, 148–51.

yielding to sexual jealousy, activates in the house the poisonous blood of the Centaur which has no place there. That Deianeira should use the blood of Nessus (and ultimately of the monstrous Hydra) to protect her house and marriage and that Heracles should woo Iole in the manner of the beast-men who carry off women by force state that collapse of the fundamental dichotomies in the sexual code which precipitates the tragic catastrophe. Viewing such events both psychologically (as the result of sexual repression or intemperance) and structurally (the collapsing of fundamental polarities and the resultant explosion of the structure of civilized life in the several codes) can only expand the dimensions in which we can understand these multi-layered works.

On both the psychoanalytic and the structuralist reading the hero of the *Hippolytus* stands outside the mode of life which makes normal functioning in society possible. His devotion to Artemis and exclusion of Aphrodite need no psychoanalytic comment. His worship of this goddess of the hunt and of wild places, however, also marks his ambiguous relation to the civilized world: as hunter he stands between city and wild, cooked and raw. Indeed, that position is even more precarious, for at the one extreme he resembles the Orphic mystic, a vegetarian who eats no meat at all (cf. 952–55), whereas at the other extreme he is a huntsman who devours the flesh of his prey (108–12).[11] On the structuralist model, that is, he is both god and beast, both above and below the human level, sharing a mystical union with the divine on the one hand but attributes of the carnivorous and hunting beasts on the other. In like manner, his refusal of Aphrodite separates him from the human reproductive cycle of birth, maturity, and death and thus places him *above* the human condition. That same refusal calls his very humanity into question in the beastlike violence (689; cf. 646) with which he reacts to the Nurse's proposition, thereby placing him *below* the human condition.

Hippolytus' extreme oscillation between unmediated extremes in the structuralist's dietary code is also the point of greatest ambivalence and conflict from the psychoanalytic point of view: the sublimation of physical instincts into a mode of life which has its creative, beautiful, and spiritual aspects but which, having its origins in

---

11. See C. Segal, "Euripides, Hippolytus, 108–12: Tragic Irony and Tragic Justice," *Hermes* 97 (1969) 297–306.

repression, also contains unresolved tensions, violence, and contradictions. The Hippolytus who rejects Aphrodite at his entrance (73ff.) has as his pendant the Hippolytus who appears as the savage hunter in 108–12:

> Come on, my followers, and enter the house and concern yourselves with food; joyful is a full table after the hunt. Then you must rub down the horses so that I may yoke them to the chariot and sated with food may practice the fitting exercises.

From a structuralist point of view the oscillation between a vegetarian Hippolytus who performs "mystic rites" (25, 952–55) and a Hippolytus who sates himself on the flesh of his hunted prey reflects an imbalance that needs but will not receive mediation. From a psychoanalytic point of view this same polarization is related to a central point in Hippolytus' neurosis. It is important to observe where the references to Orphic mysteries and vegetarianism occur. There are two places. In the more elaborate passage the Orphic theme comes from the father in his most dreaded manifestation. Here we see Theseus in his terrible wrath, threatening the son with exile or death. The other reference to these rites occurs in the mouth of Aphrodite in the prologue. Here Hippolytus is coming from the "solemn house" of his grandfather, the "pure Pittheus" who educated him (11), "to see the solemn rites and holy mysteries" in Athens (25). Hippolytus' own purity, then, which is religious as well as sexual (cf. 654–55, 1002–6) and plays a crucial role in the violence of his reaction to Phaedra's proposal (654–55), finds an echo in this other, benign side of the father figure, the grandfather, Pittheus, whose "purity" (11) matches and perhaps influences his own.[12] At the house of pure Pittheus he can escape the threatening father-figure in Athens, his biological father, Theseus, and find a pure foster father, just as in Artemis he can find a pure foster mother (we may recall her function as *kourotrophos*, "nurturer of children," and her loathing of the eagles' devouring of the pregnant hare in *Ag.* 135–38) to replace the Amazon mother he has lost.[13] But neither Pittheus' house nor Artemis' wild

---

12. See C. Segal, "Shame and Purity in Euripides' Hippolytus," *Hermes* 98 (1970) 278–99, especially 278f., 296ff.

13. On the processes of splitting and doubling of the maternal figure in the *Hippolytus* see Anne V. Rankin, "Euripides' Hippolytus: A Psychopathological Hero,"

forests and meadows constitute a realm where a young prince should expend all his energies, and hence they can provide no lasting solution to his conflicts.

In structuralist terms, neither the mystical activities of rites that bring him close to the gods nor his proximity to the beasts and the wild as a hunter can effect the mediations between god and beast embodied in the polis. As Aristotle remarks at the beginning of the *Politics,* the man who forms "no part of the polis" must be "either a beast or a god" (1.1253a28f.).

This splitting of the paternal figure into two, a gentle grandfather, a spiritual figure who enables the young man to bypass the conflicts with his biological father, and a threatening, violent father at that, has, as we shall see, a close parallel in the *Bacchae.* The *Bacchae,* however, reverses the terms and presents the same constellation of elements, but in their mirror image.

As a reflection of the "return of the repressed" or the revenge of forcibly denied life instincts, Hippolytus' death by the bull sent from Poseidon and the sea is a case of the double determination so common in Greek literature.[14] The remoter agent is the father in his anger and sexual jealousy who thus responds to a sexual threat from his son. His vengeance takes the form of that aggressive sexuality which Hippolytus had most feared and shunned. The symbolism represents what Hippolytus had most sought to avoid: it enacts his deepest anxieties, a confrontation with the male sexuality centered in Theseus, who is thus both the threatening, feared father and the embodiment of his own repressed sexuality. The play fulfills the child's deepest oedipal fears: despite his pleas of innocence, he is accused and convicted of sexually assaulting his father's wife (that is, punished for his repressed incestuous desire for the mother) and then mangled and killed by an emanation of his father's terrible wrath and his own repressed sexuality. The immediate cause, the instrument of Theseus' vengeance, is the god of the violent earth and sea, Poseidon, who is also the father of Theseus. The motif of the threatening father is thus reinforced by doubling, for Poseidon is also the father in his aggressive, threatening

---

Arethusa 7 (1974) 71–94, and Jean J. Smoot, "Hippolytus as Narcissus: An Amplification," *Arethusa* 9 (1976) 37–51.

14. See E. R. Dodds, *The Greeks and the Irrational* (Berkeley and Los Angeles 1951) 7f., 16, 30f.

aspect. He has given his son, Hippolytus' father, the power to destroy, the curses (*arai*, which are "curses" not wishes). On the other hand, the dying hero's farewell to his virgin goddess at the end, his forgiveness of his father and conferral of another kind of "purity" (1448–50), which is no longer his one-sided sexual purity, point toward a resolution of his neurotic conflict with his father and some relinquishment of the repressive mechanism that focuses on his virgin goddess. That this occurs only in his dying moments is, of course, essential to the tragic meaning of the play.[15]

In the psychoanalytic perspective the clash of mutually contradictory and therefore self-destructive projections (good father / bad father, pure mother / sexually threatening mother) is part of the hero's failure to confront the reality of adult sexuality and therefore leads to his dismemberment by the monstrous bull from the sea, a bull who is no doubt a not-too-distant relative of the bull with which Pentheus struggles in the dark dungeons of his palace in his resistance to Dionysus (*Ba.* 616ff.).[16] Defined in structuralist terms, these issues reflect a larger social and conceptual concern with the precarious position of man and of human civilization in general between bestiality and divinity.

Consorting with his goddess in the wild and thus outside the framework of civilized life, Hippolytus lives out the emotional consequences of having as mother an Amazon, a figure on the periphery of civilization, as Aeschylus stresses in the *Eumenides* (cf. 625–28, 685–90). The virginal female warrior shuns men and has no place in a normal oikos. Her status as Hippolytus' mother is due to Theseus' violent conquest and rape. Phaedra too, we may recall, also comes from the fringes of Greek civilization; and we may note the close association of Hippolytus and Amazon when she makes her first confession of her love to the nurse: "Are you in love, my child? With whom?—Whoever this man is, the Amazon's . . . —Hippolytus, you mean?" (350–52). A psychoanalytic critic might say that Hippolytus has dealt with his need for this remote and not very promising

---

15. Segal, "Shame and Purity" (note 12) 296–98.

16. For the bull in the *Bacchae* see R. P. Winnington-Ingram, *Euripides and Dionysus* (Cambridge 1948) 9 and 84, and William Sale, "The Psychoanalysis of Pentheus in the *Bacchae* of Euripides," *YCS* 22 (1972) 69f., 72f.; for the *Hippolytus* see C. Segal, "The Tragedy of the *Hippolytus:* The Waters of Ocean and the Untouched Meadow," 200–203 in this volume.

maternal figure by denying his own sexuality and finding a surrogate mother in the austere virgin goddess. But the solution is precarious, and the advances of Phaedra upset the balance and activate an image of the mother with which he cannot deal. This image of a mother as sexual being and sexual object awakens all his repressed instincts, now in their primal, incestuous form.[17]

From a structuralist point of view, the crisis that Phaedra provokes expresses the tensions already contained in Hippolytus' anomalous position between house and wild, between god and savage, between illegitimacy and kingship (as in the *Oedipus Rex*), between Orphic purity and the abomination of the exiled criminal. The crisis strains the polarity to the breaking point. The two sides fly apart. Hippolytus is driven from the city into the wild, loses any possibility of succeeding, Theseus as king of Athens (one of the points at issue in Phaedra's decision to commit suicide), and reverts entirely to his status as hunter and trainer of horses, moving not only outside the city but to an even more basically liminal point between sea and land.[18] In both the psychoanalytic and the structuralist reading the disaster occurs when the situation exceeds the limits that society has set up as the norms of basic human reality and identity. On the one hand civilization fails to effect the necessary mediation between divinity and bestiality; on the other hand the individual fails to integrate conflicting impulses as he relinquishes one of his primary defenses against his own sexual drives, the splitting off of the sexually pure from the sexually seductive mother.

Viewed structurally, the spatial symbolism expresses Hippolytus' anomalous position between god and beast, his failed mediation between Orphic vegetarian in close communion with a virgin goddess and savage, carnivorous hunter. Psychoanalytically, his extreme attachment to a sexually pure maternal figure, as a replacement for the Amazon mother he has lost, leads him to leave house and city for the wild forests. But those wild places where he hunts and consorts with his virgin goddess—the uncut meadow where no agriculture is practiced, the shore where he rides his horses and meets his death from the sea and the bull—are both symbols of unresolved sexual conflicts

---

17. See Rankin (note 13) and Smoot (note 13).
18. See Segal, "The Tragedy of the *Hippolytus*" (note 16) 198f.

and simultaneously places that negate the polis life which he has rejected.

The forests of his hunting, a typical place of male initiation (both martial and sexual) to adult status, are here a liminal place of savagery and danger which Hippolytus cannot fully leave behind, just as he, like Pentheus, cannot successfully negotiate the passage between youth and man, wild and civilized.[19] The uncut meadow has, of course, its specific sexual associations as a place of virginal purity (and especially female virginity) about to be lost;[20] but it also contrasts implicitly with the plowed fields of the fruitful earth on the Greek model by which agriculture is the civilized activity par excellence: unfruitful maiden is to married woman as forest or mountain is to arable land, as hunting is to farming, as untamed (raw) is to civilized (cooked).[21]

The uncut meadow, from a psychoanalytic perspective, also symbolizes Hippolytus' longing for a pre-oedipal union with his mother, a desire that must be relinquished or transformed if the youth is to become a mature man. Such a union, if consummated, can lead only to (symbolic) dismemberment and death.

The shore where the catastrophe occurs is a place of potential mediation between sea and land, wild and city, bull and tame horses. But as the transitional point of exile from the city it is the place where mediation breaks down in the overwhelming brute force of the terrifying and monstrous bull, embodiment of the threatening genital sexuality that Hippolytus has repressed.

All three locales, meadow, forest, and shore, have their different and specific functions in the symbolism of the play; but all, in different ways, embody a failure of accommodation to the demands of

19. For the significance of wild forest and hunting in initiatory and erotic symbolism see Marcel Detienne, *Dionysos mis à mort* (Paris 1977) 64–98, especially 74ff.; Pierre Vidal-Naquet, "The Black Hunter and the Origin of the Athenian Ephebia," *PCPS* n.s. 14 (1968) 49–64, and his essays on the *Oresteia* and the *Philoctetes* in Vernant and Vidal-Naquet, *Mythe et tragédie* (note 1) 135–58 and 161–84.

20. For the significance of the meadow see B. M. W. Knox, "The *Hippolytus* of Euripides," *YCS* 13 (1952) 6; Segal, "The Tragedy of the *Hippolytus*" (note 16) 172f.; K. J. Reckford, "Phaethon, Hippolytus, and Aphrodite," *TAPA* 103 (1972) 416 and passim.

21. For these equations see Detienne, *Jardins d'Adonis* (note 1) 187–226; Vernant, "Hestia-Hermès: Sur l'expression religieuse de l'espace et du mouvement chez les Grecs," *Mythe et pensée* (note 1) 140f., and his *Mythe et société* (note 1) 149ff. and 191ff.

mature, adult, civilized life. The unresolved sexual conflicts are both symbolically identified with and projected upon places outside the polis and its characteristic activities. Both Hippolytus' inward psychology and the external spatial dimensions of his life remove him from the normal course of self-fulfillment personally and socially open to the Greek male and thus define that constellation of qualities which marks him as a tragic figure.

As virgin and hunter both, Hippolytus is in a sense uncivilized. He meets his death in the wild realm, in a threatening borderland between earth and sea. Yet he gains a heroic status in the civilized world as a cult-figure to whom girls at marriage dedicate their offering of hair. That a youth who has rejected sex and marriage should receive this honor is an ironic inversion which corrects, too late, the emotional imbalances in Hippolytus' life. It does so, however, on the social and ritual, not the personal and psychological, plane, for others, not for himself, and at a point when his own repressed sexuality has brought him death and sterility, not marriage and procreation.

A structuralist approach reveals the appropriateness in the fact that this figure whose place has been on the margin of the city should be involved in the rite of passage which civilizes the "untamed" or "unyoked" maiden (*Hipp.* 1425) and marks her change from the implicit wildness of her virgin state to the civilized status of her place within the house (*Hipp.* 1423–27). The ambiguous status of the hero as both pure and impure, honored and degraded, is reflected in an ambiguity in the ritual code. In this case these "greatest honors" (*timai megistai,* 1424) which the virgin goddess gives her pure devotee in compensation for his death through the violence of the bestial and sexually potent bull and horses consist in a ritual of virgins who are moving into a realm where Artemis no longer applies, worshipers who are in fact taking leave of Artemis—as Artemis, within the action of the play, soon takes leave of Hippolytus (1437–41). The ritual act here faces both ways: it both resolves and crystallizes an ambiguity. Its mediation of opposites (honor / dishonor, purity / pollution, death / immortality, etc.) becomes as ambiguous as the tragic hero himself.

At another level of the cultic and mythic symbolism this irony and ambiguity correspond to the coalescence in the personage of Hippolytus of the hero who overcomes temptation (the familiar Potiphar's wife motif that recurs in the Greek myths of Bellerophon and Peleus) and the figure of the dying god / Hymenaios, beloved by the Great Mother as son and consort and mourned by her after his death.[22] Closer to the surface of the play's diction, the ambiguity operates in the doubling of the yoke of marriage with the yoke of destruction studied by Kenneth Reckford,[23] a true union of opposites raised to the second or third degree. Here the "yoked horses" and the "yoked maidens" embody pulls in opposite directions which cannot be reconciled; and the "co-yoked Graces," *syzygiai Charites,* potential mediators of death and immortality through art, can only lament the passing of unattainable innocence as virginal purity completes the crossing over to its violent and bloody opposite (1148–50).

III

The parental conflicts that a psychoanalytic reading clarifies in the *Bacchae* complement those of the *Hippolytus.*[24] In the *Hippolytus* the threatening father is the dominant presence, and the fostering, kindly father is only a remote, trace element (the pure Pittheus who gave the young hero his spiritual nurture or *paideia,* 11). In the *Bacchae* the biological father, the chthonic Echion, is absent, and the gentler father-figure, the actual grandfather, Cadmus, has the more prominent role. The son even bullies and maltreats this gentler father as the biological father of the *Hippolytus* maltreated the son. The situation of the *Bacchae* thus enacts, at one level, a child's oedipal fantasies, reversing the father-son relation of the *Hippolytus.* The maternal relationships, however, are more complex. The substitute mother of the *Hippolytus* gives way to the biological mother of the *Bacchae,* Agave, who proves the agent of the hero's doom. The mechanisms of repression and sublimation by which Hippolytus deals with his oedipal conflicts make both aspects of the mother-figure strong and vivid

22. See Reckford (note 20) 415–17.

23. Reckford (note 20) 419–22.

24. For some recent psychological readings of the *Bacchae,* see George Devereux, "The Psychotherapy Scene in Euripides' *Bacchae,*" *JHS* 90 (1970) 35–48; Patrick Roberts, "Euripides: The Dionysiac Experience," in *The Psychology of Tragic Drama* (London and Boston 1975) 33–53; Jeanne Roux, *Euripide, Les Bacchantes* (Paris 1970, 1972) 1.43ff.; Bernd Seidensticker, "Pentheus," *Poetica* 5 (1971) 35–63, especially 51f., 57–63; and Sale (note 16) 63–82. See also C. Segal, *Dionysiac Poetics and Euripides' Bacchae* (Princeton 1982) chap. 6, and in this volume chap. 9 on Euripides' *Bacchae.*

presences, both the virgin goddess of the hunt (and the remote Amazon behind her) and the sexually threatening, seductive and aggressive "mother," Phaedra, behind whom stands Hippolytus' enemy and destroyer, the goddess Aphrodite. The immediate occasion of Dionysus' assertion of power over Pentheus is the latter's acknowledgment of his erotic impulses toward the women in his mother's entourage, women who, led by Agave and her sisters, Pentheus' aunts, are surrogates for the desired mother. Indeed, some of the energy in Pentheus' animus against the Maenads comes from the ambivalence created by his repressed infantile desire to possess his mother (and, in this case, her collective substitute). Aspiring to adult masculinity, Pentheus wants to possess and master these women who directly threaten that male superiority; and the assertion of sexual, political, and military authority comes to the same thing. But another part of Pentheus, the repressed unconscious fantasies released by Dionysus, wants to retreat back to infancy and to enjoy the "softness" and "luxury" of being held in his mother's arms (968–70) and perhaps also the nurturing liquids that these women lavish so abundantly on the creatures of the wild (699–702; cf. 708–11, 142f.).

The *Hippolytus'* complex doubling and splitting of the maternal figure, however, do not occur in the *Bacchae*. The objects of Pentheus' repressed sexual impulses are more diffused (cf. 219ff.), and the maternal figure is more overtly destructive. The doubling that does take place only reinforces this aspect of the mother: the son, Dionysus, by his birth destroys the mother and is saved in the father's "male womb" (526f.), a denial of the procreative reality that so troubles Hippolytus (*Hipp.* 616–24). Yet the incinerated Semele is herself the victim of an ominous maternal figure, the threatening stepmother, Hera (9).

Read psychoanalytically, the *Bacchae* presents a son's fantasy-solution to his oedipal rivalry with his father. The threatening, vigorous, biological and sexual father is absent. The paternal figure who replaces him, the aged grandfather, Cadmus, is old and weak and has relinquished his (royal) power or *kratos* to his son. The mother is left to concern herself entirely with the son, who is offered infantile dependence on her, the "luxury" of being held once more, like a baby, in her arms (966ff.). The play, however, ends with the reassertion of the reality principle, but in a way very different from that in the *Hippolytus*. Whereas Hippolytus' death seems to contain some successful resolution of his oedipal conflicts, too late though it be, Pentheus' end represents the impossibility of the infantile fantasies that he is living out. He has only a moment of awakening when he recognizes himself in his filial relation to both Agave and the absent Echion (1115–21), just before the brutal murder. The mother's murder of her infantilized son acts out the impossibility of this fantasy solution to the oedipal situation. The son cannot have the mother on these terms. For him to return to infancy, to banish the virile father, and to be held once more in his mother's arms, after attempting to witness her secret activities of a supposedly sexual nature in a context suggesting delusions of phallic power, can lead only to his death by dismemberment, his psychic as well as physical disintegration.

Complementing a psychological by a structural approach reveals a larger significance in such figures as Echion and Dionysus. Echion, on the one hand, stands behind Pentheus' emotional instability. He is the "savage father," the aggressive and physical, biological father. His subordination to the gentler, somewhat ineffectual Cadmus enables Pentheus to inherit his father's power and kingdom (*kratos*, 213; cf. 43f.) without a direct confrontation with his father, without having to resolve the conflicts that succeeding his father might entail. On the other hand Echion is also one of the key elements that define Pentheus as a structural anomaly within the city: human but serpent-born, a champion of justice (*dike*) but a *theomachos*, an enemy of the Olympian gods like the monstrous giants who threaten the divine order with chaos (538ff.); autochthonous as a sign of the civic solidarity and continuity in Thebes but autochthonous as an aspect of the savagery that opposes the Olympian gods.

Likewise Dionysus is a threat not merely to the psychological coherence and integration necessary for Pentheus' successful passage from childhood to adulthood but also to that system of polarities on which Pentheus' rigid, authoritarian order rests. He is not only a symbol of all that Pentheus has repressed, the latent animality that turns back against himself in the god's tauriform epiphanies, but also a god who breaks down all the familiar mediations, dissolves differentiation on every level into sameness, and through his function as the god of tragedy and the tragic mask also challenges the capacity of myth and language to mediate contradictions. In his realm, fusion replaces boundary, and the mutually exclusive opposites of our everyday logic disturbingly coexist. In his rites the natural world joins with the human celebrants. In the lines so much admired by "Longinus," "The whole mountains and the beasts joined in the bacchic revel" (*symbaccheuein*, 726f.).

Dionysus is an outsider violently resisted by the king; but he is also a native of Thebes with a legitimate claim on the city's allegiance. He combines his Olympian birth with the bestial forms of bull, snake, or lion in which he appears to his worshipers. His personal appearance fuses male and female characteristics, and his geographical associations join both Greek and barbarian, both local and universal attributes. As a kind of eternal adolescent, he stands between child and adult. As a god of wine he embodies the life-giving forces of the earth, the moisture and sap of new vegetative growth; but he can also call the destructive power of the earth into his service when he shakes Pentheus' palace (*Ba.* 585). His presence on stage as an actor in the drama not only calls attention to the way in which tragedy and tragic myth open the secure structures of the society to the fluidity and changefulness inherent in the god, but also shows tragedy itself, as it were, demarcating before our eyes what Victor Turner calls the "liminal space," a space between order and disorder, a realm of disturbing but also potentially fruitful disintegration of familiar boundaries and identities.[25]

Entering Thebes as an outsider, a stranger from a barbarian land, Dionysus both repeats and reverses the work of the original culture hero, the aged Cadmus, who came from barbarian Sidon to Hellenic Thebes, killed the serpent, and sowed the teeth from which sprang the race of Thebans, the sown men from whom Pentheus is descended. He comes to Thebes bringing a new gift, but one with a much more complex and ambiguous relation to what men conceive of as civilization than Cadmus. Cadmus, the original founder, is then expelled, driven into the wild, transformed into the "savage form" (*physin . . . agrian*, 1358) of a snake, the creature he killed in his initial founding act. He who left barbarians for Greeks is condemned to lead barbarian hordes against Greek shrines and cities (1334–36, 1352–60).

In shattering the secure limits and well defined polarities of Pen-

---

25. Victor Turner, *The Ritual Process: Structure and Anti-Structure* (London 1969) chaps. 2 and 3, and more recently "Liminal to Liminoid in Play, Flow, and Ritual: An Essay in Comparative Symbology," *Rice University Studies* 60 (1974) 53–92.

theus' world, Dionysus reveals the hidden truth of the king's identity as both man and beast, both confident ruler and chaotic, bestial madman, both the celebrant and the sacrificial victim. Instead of reaching the "celestial glory" of the hoplite warrior (972), the king plummets to earth as hunted animal (1107–13) and meets his doom as a little child helpless before the gigantic figure of an overpowering mother (1114–28).

The gates that Pentheus defends so zealously (781; cf. 653) embody both the tightly drawn boundaries of his own repressed and rigidly circumscribed personality and also the carefully drawn limits between city and wild upon which Pentheus relies to keep Dionysiac religion and emotionality shut outside of Thebes. The collapse of the gates is thus significant in the dimensions of both culture and personality. Infiltrating Pentheus' defenses in a psychological sense, Dionysus reveals the king's repressed animality in his self through the appearance of the bull within Pentheus' very stronghold, the prison that was meant to contain the god, his Maenads, and all the emotionality that they signify. The structuralist reader, focusing on the nature-culture antinomy, directs attention to the havoc wrought or the joy afforded by the Dionysiac fusion of opposites. Violently resisted, the god as violently dissolves the clear distinctions between city and wild, man and beast, logic and emotion, in all the codes of the civilized order, sweeping away the symbols of psychological, familial, and political coherence and authority.

Psychologically, it is important that the king and lord (*despotēs*, 1046, 1095) now become a helpless child (1114–28), whereas the woman barks commands like a general (cf. 1106). In terms of the structuralist antitheses, the king who so vehemently defended civilized enclosure (463, 653, 781) is now trapped outside the city walls, hemmed in and cornered as a hunted beast by women, themselves far from the enclosed shelter of their oikos, who "surround him in a circle" (*peristasai kyklo(i)*, 1106; cf. Pentheus' image of the city enclosed "in a circle," *kyklo(i)*, in 463 and 653). The Dionysus who breaks down the king's defenses and walls against his own instinctual and animal impulses is also the Dionysus who leaps his carefully defended barriers between city and wild, man and nature. In terms of these latter, structural anthitheses, it is ironically significant that the king's city-defending tower (653) has now become a tree on the exposed mountainside (1095ff.). Here, in an exalted place, the ruler occupies simultaneously the lowest point in the polis as the scapegoat-victim; supposedly defended, he is the most threatened; a man, he is in woman's garb; a human being, he is about to become the sacrificial beast. Perched on this height he will defend not his whole city but only his own miserable life; and the enemies are not male warriors but Maenads whose crag opposite (if a mild mistranslation be allowed) is a kind of "antitower," *antipyrgon . . . petran* (1097).

We can conceptualize the peripety on two spatial planes, horizontal and vertical. On the horizontal plane Dionysus' penetration of Greek Thebes from barbarian Asia expresses the collapse of Pentheus' conception of the self and of the city. On the vertical plane Pentheus, shot up high into the fir tree as king, plunges abruptly down to earth as beast and victim (1110–14):

> They laid myriad hands upon the fir tree and pulled it up from the earth. And Pentheus, seated on high, from his high place falls in downward plunge to earth with myriad shrieks, for he came to know that he was near his doom.

The fall from high to low which is such a prominent feature of Pentheus' doom also lends itself both to psychoanalytic and structuralist interpretation. For the latter the king's fall from the topmost height of a tree to the ground below reflects that failure of mediation between Olympian and chthonic which runs through the whole play. The tree here functions in a manner similar to the "heavenly pillar" of Pindar's first *Pythian Ode* (17–20b): it symbolizes a cosmic unity that binds together sky, earth, and nether world. Closely associated with the sacral kingship, (pseudo-) divinity, and sacrificial status of Pentheus, the fir tree here resembles the Cosmic Tree or *axis mundi* so important in the religious imagery of many peoples.[26] The unsuccessful mediation between heaven and earth presented in the disastrous rise to and fall from the tree parallels the loss of a harmonious accord between man and nature and the disintegration of the social

---

26. See Mircea Eliade, *Patterns in Comparative Religion* (New York 1958) 265ff., and "Methodological Remarks on the Study of Religious Symbolism," in Eliade and J. M. Kitagawa, ed., *The History of Religions: Essays in Methodology* (Chicago and London 1959) 93ff.

order as symbolized in this violent death of the king and the ensuing bestial metamorphosis and exile of the founder of the kingship.[27]

Aspiring to delusions of godlike power (949–52) and to the "glory that reaches to the heavens" (972), Pentheus in fact plummets downward to the bestial condition of the beast-victim, from king to pharmakos. Both his own internal turbulence and the vengeful nature of an offended god combine to destroy that position of ordered human civilization where the opposites might be mediated rather than collapsed together. Hence when he is elevated and exalted in the "high-necked fir-tree" (1061), he is the "climber" (cf. *ambas*, 1061) who will soon be killed as the "climbing beast" (*ambatēn thēra*, 1107f.). The "miracle" (*thauma*, 1063) of this god who fuses male and female, chthonic and Olympian, human and bestial, consists in bending the "heaven-high topmost branch" to the "black earth" (1065). This initiates the terrible union of bestial and human in Pentheus and soon issues into the epiphany of the mysterious god as the bull who "leads" the king, now himself a calf or lion, to his death (cf. 1059, 1173ff., 1185ff.). At the same time this unleashing of bestiality contains the play's most detailed description of human technology, the bow and lathe of 1066–68. The simile of the bent tree as bow or lathe dramatizes the collocation of civilization and savagery in this god who oversteps and dissolves boundaries. Bow and lathe bring together the two discrete areas whose separation Dionysus destroys, hunting in the wild and practicing crafts that belong within the secure, enclosed space in the city, imaged perhaps in the enclosed circuit drawn by the lathe (cf. "drawn about the circumference," *graphomenos periphoran*, 1067). The king's attempt to reinforce these boundaries separating city and wild (cf. 463, 654, 781) ironically ends not only in the triumph of the god of the wild in his own element but also in this use of an image of enclosure for the destruction of enclosure.

If we move from the horizontal to the vertical axis, the mysterious pillar of light which unites earth and sky marks not the mediation of

27. For the sacral functions of kingship see *The Sacred Kingship, Numen,* Supplement 4 (Leiden 1959); M. Yamaguchi, "Kingship as a System of Myth: An Essay in Synthesis," *Diogenes* 77 (1972) 43–78; C. Segal, "Tragic Heroism and Sacral Kingship in Five Oedipus Plays and *Hamlet*," *Helios* 5 (1977) 1–10.

heaven and earth as an image of cosmic harmony but the collapse of polarities in the miraculous ephiphany of the god. The verb that expresses this idea of "joining," *stērizein (estērixe,* 1083), is also the verb that describes Pentheus' ill-starred reaching toward "heavenly glory" in 972. In fact, he is moving in just the opposite direction, downward to infamy, regressing from heroic fame to infantile help-lessness. Only a few lines before, stērizein described the shooting of the tree "straight up into the upright air" (1073), but this elevation is only the preliminary to his downward plunge in the spatial, ritual, and biological codes (cf. 1111ff.). In like manner the attack itself comes in language that fuses polarities in both the spatial and the technological codes: the Maenads, as they tear up the tree by the roots (1104), "shatter the branches with lightning," *synkeraunousai* (1103), a striking verb, associated earlier with the flashes of Zeus which attended Dionysus' fiery birth or the god's own ominous epiphanies (cf. 6, 244, 288, 594, 598). The Maenads use "levers not of iron," *asiderois mochlois* (1104), an oxymoron whose paradox condenses into a single phrase that anomalous fusion of savagery and civilized technology present in more expanded form in the simile of the lathe to describe Dionysus' power over wild nature (1066f.).

From a psychoanalytic perspective the episode of Pentheus' death suggests the hero's unresolved ambivalence between delusions of phallic potency on the one hand and rejection of his masculinity in submission to the mother (dressing as a Maenad) on the other. The phallic imagery of the elevation in the tree is obvious. It is fairly likely too that the uprooting of the tree and the wild women's consequent dismemberment of the youth who plunges violently to earth (1109ff.) reflect fears of castration by the mother. William Sale and Philip Slater have both analyzed this scene in these terms, focusing on the child's ambivalent attitude toward his own male sexuality and toward his mother.[28]

Sale's interpretation, which perhaps exaggerates the phallic elements,[29] can be refined in one important respect. Planning how he will spy on the Maenads in 953–54, Pentheus says to Dionysus,

28. Philip Slater, *The Glory of Hera* (Boston 1968) 298–301 and chaps. 9 and 10, passim; Sale (note 16) 73ff.

29. E.g., Sale (note 16) 67 and 74.

We must not conquer the women by force [*sthenei*]; but I shall conceal my body in the fir trees.

Dionysus' reply, "You will be concealed with that concealment with which you deserve to be concealed" (955), calls attention by its very linguistic form to the hidden meanings soon to be clarified: the inversion of active and passive, observer and participant, Maenad and victim of Maenads. From a psychoanalytic perspective, Pentheus' inability to confront and accept his full male sexuality takes the form not only of the regressive mode of voyeurism but also of refusing to confront the women directly by "force" (*sthenei*, 953, where a sexual meaning may also be latent). Pentheus here would use the phallic visibility of the fir tree for concealment. Unable still to accept his phallic sexuality, he regards the trees as a means of self-concealment, not self-revelation: they serve as an instrument in the substitute sexuality of looking rather than the overt sexual act of doing, which would require the full acceptance and exposure of erect phallus. Dionysus, however, will use the tree, as he uses the bull, for just the opposite purpose, namely to reveal the repressed libidinal energies of Pentheus, the animal in himself which he cannot face, the concealed tension between opposites which, when released, destroys his precarious psychic integrity and leads to the inevitable consequences, the *sparagmos,* as much a symbol of emotional events as the actual physical rending.

The death itself is the last stage in Pentheus' movement back from adult male heroism to infancy. He reverts to the position of the small child, lying on his back, having "fallen to the earth" (1112) and facing the "mother" (1118, 1120) who has "fallen upon him" (1115), a stranger who glowers at him with an enraged, terrifying face that gives no sign of recognition. She responds neither to his touch (1117f.) nor to the words in which he attempts to identify himself: "It is I, mother, your son, Pentheus, whom you bore in Echion's house" (1118f.). The lines convey a surrealistic image of the helpless infant confronting the Evil Mother who refuses her nurturing milk, withdraws her loving embrace, and does not heed his cries. The infantile situation, however, is nightmarishly replayed for a grown youth who is not in the safety of his "house" (1119) but on the wild mountainside. The mother is not physically but emotionally absent. Instead of the maternal look, there is the fearful glare of the maniac, with rolling

eyes and foaming mouth (1122f.), the Evil Mother in her most hor-
rific aspect.[30] Instead of the soft touch there is the furious attack that
tears the arm from the socket with more than human force (1125–27),
a "force" (*sthenos*) more potent than that which he, in his submissive
feminine disguise, could not bring himself to use against women
(953). Instead of life, finally, there is death as the once gentle mother
becomes the "priestess of death" (*hierea phonou*, 1114) in the rite of
the god of the wild.

From a more humanistic perspective one might argue that in the
extreme agony of this dismemberment Pentheus gains a certain degree of self-recognition. He throws off the mitra or cap that symbolizes his bondage to Dionysiac delusion (1115; cf. 833, 929). He
asks for "recognition" (*gnōrisasa*, 1116) from his mother and declares
his identity, giving both mother and father. Most important of all, he
admits his "errors" or *hamartiai* ("Do not kill your son because of my
errors," 1120f.). But the recognition only intensifies the pathos: it
comes too late for Pentheus and too soon for Agave. What Dionysus
has released in him, though it might have proved the means of an
ultimate integration of personality, can now lead only to the dismemberment or sparagmos. Agave's "recognition" too (*gnōrisasa*, 1285)
will come only when she has run the full length of the Dionysiac
madness that she, like the other Theban Maenads, opposed. There is
perhaps just the glimmer of growth in Pentheus' willingness to acknowledge "errors" or "faults" (the word used of his mother and
aunts' accusations of Semele in the prologue, 29). But this dropping
of his defense-mechanisms comes too late. He does not possess the
inward integrity and spiritual greatness that enable Hippolytus to
survive his sparagmos long enough to reach a new level of self-
understanding, forgiveness, heroic generosity, and endurance (*Hipp.*
1446–66).

Both from a structuralist and from a psychoanalytic point of view,
the hero's precarious position between sky and earth expresses the
basic tension of the situation: on the one hand a tension between
unmediated polarities that span the civilized and the savage potential
of man, on the other hand a tension between sexual repression (which
manifests itself in feminization, concealment, submission) and delu-

---

30. For the Dionysiac release of "the murderous impulses of the mother toward her
son" see Slater (note 28) 223ff.

sions of phallic potency which when acted out result in symbolical castration and dismemberment.

Here also the two approaches do not exclude each other. They offer complementary sets of coordinates which enable us to triangulate the areas of crisis and conflict from different directions. Structuralism concentrates upon the logical relations within society and in the cosmic order. In the *Bacchae* these are called into question by the paradoxical nature of Dionysus as a principle that dissolves boundaries; in the *Hippolytus* they are called into question by the structural anomaly of the hero's place in society, his restrictive pursuits, and his limited religious and sexual orientation. On a psychoanalytic reading, Dionysus symbolizes the uncompromising impulses of the id itself, which burst forth to shatter the uneasy balance of a neurotic personality with its outwardly aggressive masculinity, castration anxiety, latent ambivalence about (male) sexuality, and terror of an overpowering maternal figure. In Slater's interpretation of the psychodynamics of the Greek oikos, Dionysus releases both the mother's ambivalent attitude toward her male offspring whom she idolizes and resents and the male's anxieties toward the female, with her latent resentment and rage, hidden power, and the potentially destructive force of her emotional ambivalences. From this point of view the *Bacchae* offered its audience a powerful catharsis by revealing and acting out unconscious and repressed tensions, anxieties, and fears. On a structuralist view the play explores, makes visible, and holds up for inspection the tensions of opposites contained and kept apart in the logical structures of the civilized codes: ritual, sexual, biological, familial, political, and so forth.

The purpose of these remarks is not to add another detail to the psychoanalytic literature on Hippolytus or on Pentheus (where, however, the role of Echion has not received the attention that it deserves).[31] Rather, it is to stress the way in which approaches as di-

---

31. For Echion see C. Segal, "Euripides' *Bacchae*: Conflict and Mediation," *Ramus* 6 (1977) 103–20, esp. 108f., and *Dionysiac Poetics* (note 24) 131–33, 186–89; see also the brief remark of Slater (note 28) 299: "One also sees an echo of the weak marital bond, for Echion, Pentheus' father, is conspicuous by his absence." Sale's challenge (note 16) 77, "I defy any reader of the play to say a word about Echion except that he spawned Pentheus and then, so far as we know, vanished," neglects 537–44 and 995f. = 1015f. as well as the associations of Echion with the snake and the earth of early Thebes. For a corrective, with another approach to Echion and his role in the play, see Marylin Arthur, "The Choral Odes of the *Bacchae* of Euripides," *YCS* 22 (1972) 171–75.

verse as psychoanalytic and structuralist criticism can work together to illuminate from a number of different perspectives those points of tension and instability which constitute the matrix of the tragic character and hence of the tragic catastrophe.

Whereas some of these points could no doubt emerge from more traditional readings, the combination of structuralist and psychoanalytic approaches allows us not only to appreciate more fully the multifaceted and multivalent nature of Greek tragedy but also to grasp more clearly the parallelism between all the levels of meaning, the interlocking homologies of all the codes. If we take our stand in the psychoanalytic camp of *Bacchae* critics, for example, the emotional state of Pentheus is the primary reality, and the city of Thebes, the ambiguous meanings of autochthony, the imbalances between East and West, Greek and Barbarian, city and wild become metaphors for the psychological imbalances within Pentheus. If we take a structuralist point of view, Pentheus' emotional conflicts become a side issue, and his violence and instability become metaphors for and expressions of the failed mediations between beast and god which surround his kingship and are exposed by the arrival of a figure who serves both as a kind of anti-Pentheus and as a focal point for all that the organized authority of the polis finds most difficult to assimilate.

This reading, selective and incomplete as it must be, of two thematically related Euripidean plays may, I hope, illustrate that Freud and Lévi-Strauss do not necessarily form a binary opposition. Taking both approaches together gives us more than we might get from a single methodology. This is doubtless so because Greek (and other) myth and literature employ symbols that are not only polysemous but in their range of meaning also virtually inexhaustible. After the intellectual hybris of these powerful analytic systems, therefore, we should in humility remind ourselves that what Heraclitus said of the psyche is also true of tragedy and tragic myth: "You would not find its limits travelling every road: so deep a *logos* does it have" (DK 22 B45).

CHAPTER 9 /

Euripides' *Bacchae:* The Language of the Self and the Language of the Mysteries

IN MEMORIAM GEORGE DEVEREUX (1908–1985)

Overcoming classicists' traditional resistance to psychoanalytical interpretation, George Devereux's essay on the recognition scene of the *Bacchae* has been widely recognized as one of the most successful applications of a psychoanalytical approach to an ancient Greek tragedy.[1] Devereux has shown how Cadmus, using a "flawless psychotherapeutic strategy,"[2] brings Agave out of a psychotic episode by a question-and-answer technique that forces her to speak and thus to bring to consciousness material in her unconscious and preconscious.[3] The present essay seeks to develop some implications of Devereux's suggestive work both in a theoretical and in a linguistic-interpretive direction.

From a theoretical point of view, Devereux's study shows how closely consciousness is bound up with language. This connection is, of course, a cornerstone of Freudian theory and practice, wherein the analyst's task is to lead the patient to verbalize repressed desires and

---

I thank the John Simon Guggenheim Memorial Foundation for a fellowship in 1981–82, during which this essay was written. I note with sorrow the death of George Devereux, for whose Festschrift this essay was intended and with whom I discussed several of its issues, in Paris on May 29, 1985, at the age of 77.

1. George Devereux, "The Psychotherapy Scene in Euripides' *Bacchae*," *JHS* 90 (1970) 35–48. See, for example, Jeanne Roux, *Euripide, Les Bacchantes* (Paris 1972) 2.609, on *Ba.* 1264–67; citing Devereux's article, she remarks, "Cadmos recourt non à des exorcismes, mais à une thérapeutique méthodique telle que pourrait la pratiquer un psychiatre."

2. Devereux (note 1) 35.

3. Devereux (note 1) 43f.

fears and in the process bring to light the necessarily hidden sources of the neurosis. The exact relation between language and the unconscious, however, remains one of the most discussed questions of recent psychoanalytic speculation, particularly in the work of Jacques Lacan and his followers.[4] Does the unconscious in fact have the structure of language, as Lacan suggests? Or, with some Freudian critics, can one speak of the "non-communicating languages of the unconscious," for example, the symbolic language of dreams?[5] Is the oneiric discourse of this dream language of the unconscious akin to the transformative processes in figurative or poetic language, the displacements of familiar syntax in the rhetorical figures of metaphor, metonymy, synecdoche, and so on?[6]

From a different but complementary point of view, Devereux's essay also raises the question of the relation between the dramatic performance and the unconscious of the spectators.[7] In the case of the *Bacchae* in particular, Euripides seems to be using the stage itself as a kind of dream world where our most buried fears and fantasies—particularly of an oedipal nature—can be acted out. The space of the dramatic representation thus becomes a privileged place in which, thanks to the rhetorical transformations and symbolic displacements effected by the poet's language, we can evade the censor and view things that we do not normally allow ourselves to see, hear things that we do not normally allow to be spoken.[8] Greek tragedy exter-

---

4. See for example Jacques Lacan, "The Function of Language in Psychoanalysis," in *The Language of the Self,* trans. Anthony Wilden (Baltimore 1968; rpt. New York 1973) 3–27; Frederic Jameson, "Imaginary and Symbolic in Lacan: N rxism, Psychoanalytic Criticism, and the Problem of the Subject," *Yale French Studies* 55/56 (1977) 351ff, 365ff. Using a different approach but equally insistent on the role of language and the verbal transaction in the psychoanalytic exchange is the work of Roy Schafer, "Action and Narration in Psychoanalysis," *New Literary History* 12, no. 1 (1980) 61–85, and "Narration in the Psychoanalytic Dialogue," *Critical Inquiry* 7, no. 1 (1980) 28–53.

5. "Linguaggi non comunicanti dell' inconscio" is the terminology of Francesco Orlando, *Per una teoria freudiana della letteratura* (Turin 1977) chap. 1 (cf. p. 21); also 60ff.

6. See Lacan (note 4) 31 and 51; Orlando (note 5) 56ff.; Jameson (note 4) 367f.

7. See also Devereux's interesting remarks on staged versus narrated events in tragedy and their relation to dream and the unconscious in "The Structure of Tragedy and the Structure of the Psyche in Aristotle's *Poetics,*" in Charles Hanly and Morris Lazerowitz, eds., *Psychoanalysis and Philosophy* (New York 1970) 60ff.

8. It is important to distinguish, as Devereux carefully does (note 7) between what is visually shown onstage and what is only recited or narrated (63): "Greek tragedy

nalizes and concretizes, visually and verbally, what remains dim, suppressed, and unformed in the unconscious. The *Bacchae,* like Sophocles' *Oedipus Tyrannus* (which it resembles in a number of ways), has as its central theme the viewing and speaking of forbidden, secret things. As André Green asks, "Le théâtre, n' est-il pas la meilleure incarnation de cette *autre* scène qu' est l' inconscient?"⁹

The play as a whole, and particularly the "psychotherapy scene" studied by Devereux, is a mirror of the dramatic art itself in its power to reveal the hidden dimensions of the self and to effect a passage, perhaps an equilibrium, between unconscious and conscious knowledge. The illusionistic power of Dionysus, the god both of madness and the theater, is the power to create the involving fictions of the theatrical representation in the spellbinding magic of art. It is also the power of the poet to spin out the dream world of fantasy in which the terrors and desires repressed in the unconscious can be released. As an enactment of Dionysus' power and a reflection upon that power, the play reveals first the hypnotic power of the poet, as the mouthpiece of the god, to enfold us in his web of illusion and then the power of conscious knowledge to break the spell and return us to reality, but with a freshly experienced reintegration of conscious and unconscious.¹⁰ In the psychotherapy scene the latter process predominates. It both complements and answers the gradual release of the unconscious by Dionysus in the first part of the play.

The fact that Agave, after the revelation, flees the scene of her acts, never (as she hopes) to return (1381–87), is both a natural human revulsion and also the poet's recognition of how painful the surfacing of the unconscious is, how difficult and dangerous are the means that

---

simply takes place on two levels: the raw event occurs off stage; its psychological consequences are shown on stage." We may add that the presentation of psychological states offstage, in narration only, often has a more dreamlike quality and can depict more deeply repressed, threatening, and anxiety-provoking states. Thus Agave's carrying of Pentheus' head impaled on a thyrsus, with its implications of the castrating power of the phallic mother, appears only as a narrated, offstage event (1139–42), whereas when she appears onstage with Pentheus' head, she carries it "in her arms" or "in her hands" (1277, 1280). In an otherwise excellent study, Helene P. Foley, "The Masque of Dionysus," *TAPA* 110 (1980) 131, states that "the mask [of Pentheus] returns unchanged to the stage impaled on Agave's *thyrsus.*"

9. André Green, *Un oeil en trop* (Paris 1969) 11.

10. For these implications of the *Bacchae,* see Foley (note 8) and C. Segal, *Dionysiac Poetics and Euripides' Bacchae* (Princeton 1982) chap. 7, especially 234ff. and 259ff.

enable us to look into its depths, and perhaps also how gladly we would run away from what we have seen. This instinctive flight may be interpreted both as an individual reaction and as a cultural phenomenon. Euripides, writing in self-chosen exile in Macedonia, at the fringes of the Hellenic world, knows instinctively what his former compatriots most desire to see and to escape.

In the Cadmus-Agave scene the question-and-answer technique is employed by a father figure who embodies the reintegrative capacities of the ego. This scene is symmetrical with the previous scenes of question and answer between Pentheus and Dionysus (460–518, 648–59, 787–846, 912–70). These scenes are dominated not by a kindly authority figure speaking the voice of the ego but by Pentheus' ambiguous double, an alter ego of the same age, who speaks the voice of the id. The dialogue here effects not a progression to adulthood, consciousness, and ego integration but a regression to primary-process thinking.[11] The Agave-Cadmus scene shows a mortal coming out of the spell of madness cast over her by the god; the scenes between Pentheus and the Stranger show us a mortal gradually but inexorably falling under the god's mysterious power.

Corresponding to this basic difference of function between the two sets of scenes is a difference in the way in which the question and answer functions in each. Agave, confronting Cadmus with initial disappointment and annoyance (cf. 1251f.), asks her first question (not deliberately elicited by Cadmus) in a rather aggressive mood (1263): "What of these things is not well, or what is painful?"[12] Her mood changes to puzzlement as Cadmus bids her look at the sky and she asks why (1264–65). At this point Cadmus takes over the role of questioner for the crucial moments that bring Agave out of her madness (1266–79). His last question focuses on the most crucial detail of the passage between delusion and reality (1277): "Whose visage do you then hold in your embrace?" At this point the roles shift, and Agave becomes the questioner (1280): "Alas, what do I see? What is

---

11. I owe this technical term to George Devereux. I use it not to pretend to technical competence or to indulge in jargon for its own sake but to underline the extent to which Euripides' insights into the psyche anticipate the clinical observations of modern psychoanalysis.

12. Devereux (note 1) 41: "As late as 1263 Cadmus and Agave talk past each other." See also Roux (note 1) *ad* 1263: "Agavé interroge Cadmos avec un étonnement agacé, mais sa question marque le début de son retour à la conscience."

this that I am carrying in my hands?" Cadmus asks one last question (1283): "Does it then seem to you to resemble a lion?" The remaining questions (until the lacuna after 1300) belong to Agave, as she tries to find out what she has done (1286–98). This shift from the aggressive question of 1263 to the genuine requests for information as she takes over the role of questioner from Cadmus in 1280 marks the critical moments of her return to sanity and her genuine reclaiming of reality.

When we compare the analogous scenes of question and answer between Dionysus and Pentheus, we find almost the exact reverse of this relation. Here the question-and-answer technique of line-by-line exchange (stichomythy) has the function of bringing the questioner under the spell of the god's madness, of confusing subjective and objective vision, and thereby of blurring the division between reality and delusion. In the first face-to-face encounter between Pentheus and the Stranger, Pentheus occupies the position of apparent authority. He asks the questions, and the Stranger responds. The strict line-by-line query and response goes on for over fifty verses (460–518); but there is a crucial, if subtle, shift when for a brief moment Dionysus asks the question (492):

εἴφ' ὅ τι παθεῖν δεῖ · τί με τὸ δεινὸν ἐργάσῃ

Say what it is necessary to suffer. What is the terrible thing that you will do to me?

The question is a significant one, for it anticipates the massive reversal between doer and sufferer, active and passive, which Dionysus will soon effect as the victim and the captor change places.[13] Pentheus' only remaining question of this scene in fact reveals his helplessness and his ignorance rather than his power (501): "And where is he? Not visible to my eyes at least." From that point on, Pentheus never recovers his authority as questioner. He is on the defensive for the remainder of the scene (503–18). Dionysus attacks his ego at the places where Pentheus' defenses are most heavily concentrated and therefore most vulnerable: his identification of himself with the political power of the city (503), his implicit definition of that power as the

13. For the reversals of active and passive see Segal (note 9) 247–56; also C. Segal, "Etymologies and Double Meanings in Euripides' *Bacchae*," *Glotta* 60 (1982) 85ff.

ability to "bind" or constrain (505),[14] and his insecurity about his identity, about who or what he really is, as symbolized by the ambiguity of his name (503–8):

Pentheus. Seize him: he scorns both me and Thebes.
Dionysus. I tell you not to bind me, sane among you not sane.
Penth. I say to bind, having more authority than you.
Dion. You know not why you live nor what you do nor who you are.
Penth. Pentheus, Agave's child, my father Echion.
Dion. You are suited for misfortune in your name.

In the briefer scene of question and answer after the palace miracle, when illusion and reality are in fact thrown into confusion, Dionysus now answers Pentheus' questions with commands (647) or with other questions that reveal the hidden power of his own emerging authority:

Did I not say—or did you not hear—that some one will release me? (649).

What then? Do not the gods leap over even walls? (654).

Both of these interrogative sentences question the symbolical center of Pentheus' authority, the power to bind or constrain and the power to exclude by the civic and military force of the city all that Dionysus represents (cf. 504f., 653f.).[15]

At the turning point, as Pentheus' resistance changes to submission, the pattern of question and answer undergoes an interesting reversal. Pentheus' overcompensatory militaristic bluster slows down to a single brief question (803), which focuses on the ambiguity of active and passive (800–803):

Pentheus. We are at grips with this stranger who leaves us no path, who neither suffering nor doing will be silent.

14. On 506–8 and Pentheus' definition of his "authority" (*kyros*) by "binding" see Segal, *Dionysiac Poetics* (note 9) 93, and "Etymologies" (note 12) 83.
15. See Segal, *Dionysiac Poetics* (note 9) chap. 4. For the importance of walls and enclosures, see also William C. Scott, "Two Suns over Thebes: Imagery and Stage Effects in the *Bacchae*," *TAPA* 105 (1975) 333–46, especially 341: "It is Pentheus' misfortune to oppose a god who refuses to be bound by architectural structures."

Euripides

Dionysus. My friend, it is still possible to arrange these things well.
Penth. Doing what? Being a slave to my slaves?

Dionysus' line (802) leaves it deliberately ambiguous who is the active arranger. Pentheus' question implies that it is to be himself, but he has just admitted the confusion of active and passive (801). The god in fact tacitly assumes the role of power by taking over the questioning and trapping Pentheus through questions that reveal his (the god's) hidden knowledge of Pentheus' unconscious or repressed desires (806–19). The pivotal question leads Pentheus to avow openly his sexual curiosity and its voyeuristic form (811): "Do you wish to see [the Maenads] sitting all together on the mountains?" When Pentheus resumes the role of questioner in the latter half of the strichomythy, he is in nearly total subjection to the god who has now touched the hidden springs of his unconscious wishes (822–40). Pentheus' role as questioner here becomes exactly the reverse of what it was when he first encountered Dionysus (460–518). The question-and-answer dialogue is also exactly the reverse of that between Cadmus and Agave at the end.

The next scene completes Pentheus' submission to the power of Dionysus, and Pentheus' questions are again expressive of helplessness and complaisant acceptance rather than resistance and authority (cf. 922, 925–26, 941–42, 945–46, 949, 950). The scene ends with Pentheus finishing the sentences of Dionysus and Dionysus feeding him the lines that he will fill out with the ambiguous words of his doom (966–70):

Dionysus. From there another will lead you back.
　　Pentheus. My mother, surely.
　Dion. Conspicuous among all.
　　Penth. To this I go.
　Dion. Carried you will go.
　　Penth. To my soft luxury, you mean.
　Dion. In your mother's hands.
　　Penth. And you will compel me to be dissolved in comfort.
　Dion. Such dissolute comforts.
　　Penth. I touch what I deserve.[16]

16. The translation attempts to bring out some of the double meanings of these lines, on which see Lawrence J. Kepple, "The Broken Victim: Euripides' *Bacchae* 969–970,"

The line-by-line responsion of stichomythy here shortens to the half-line responses of *antilabē*. The language of the god now fully penetrates that of Pentheus, just as his personality penetrates and blends with the personality that Pentheus has kept repressed. The boundaries of their sentences become as fluid as the boundaries of their personalities. Dionysus' hypnotic power over Pentheus' mind takes the form of power over his language.

The overlapping of verbal expression on the level of syntax and versification parallels the overlapping and momentary coexistence of conscious and unconscious on the level of psychological meaning. Pentheus' speech loses its individual distinctness as he himself begins to become an extension of the god, now a Maenad worshiper and soon a beast-victim that takes the place of the god in the bacchic ritual of *sparagmos* and omophagy on the mountain (cf. the hints of devouring Pentheus in 1184, 1242, 1246f.). This scene shows the conscious self being submerged in the unconscious; the Agave-Cadmus scene shows conscious, ego-integrative functions reasserting themselves over the unconscious. But this process of anagnorisis (recognition) is fragmented between two different characters. Pentheus' momentary return to sanity is brief, pathetic, and ineffectual (1116–21), itself more like nightmare than reality (1122ff.).

In the *anderer Schauplatz* that the drama creates, visual appearances are doubled by the disguising of Dionysus as a Lydian youth and of Pentheus as a Maenad. This doubling has an equivalent in the realm of language. Just as there are two levels of visual representation, corresponding to the harsh and gentle sides of Dionysus (cf. 861), the smiling (1021) and the destructive god,[17] so there are two levels of verbal representation, corresponding to the conscious and unconscious self. Pentheus both sees and speaks double (cf. 920ff.). In the *Hippolytus* the confusion of appearance and reality by false speech—or, more precisely, by a doubling of language into written and spoken utterance—leads to the utopian wish that men might have "double voices" (*dissai phōnai*), one the true and "just" voice, the other "as it happened to be," so that there might be an infallible means of discerning the hidden reality of thoughts and feelings (*Hipp.* 925–32).

HSCP 80 (1976) 107–9; Segal, "Etymologies" (note 12) 88; and the commentaries of E. R. Dodds, *Euripides' Bacchae*, 2d ed. (Oxford 1960) and Roux (note 1) *ad loc.*

17. See Foley (note 8) 131–33.

Euripides

The language of the *Bacchae* in a sense carries out this project, but in a way very different from the rationalism envisaged in the *Hippolytus*.

The various forms of doubling effected by Dionysus create a mirror for language through which language seems to speak the words of the hidden Other, the unconscious that Dionysus brings to the surface by making visible on stage the self that Pentheus has repressed, the sensual and sexual self that he has held under the same constraints or binding as those with which he would constrain and imprison Dionysus.

Dionysus constitutes for Pentheus what Lacan calls a Discourse of the Other, the language of his repressed, unconscious self. This language reflects back to Pentheus an image where the important thing is what Pentheus cannot recognize, the self he refuses to know. "The unconscious is knowledge," Lacan remarks, "but it is a knowledge one cannot know one knows, a knowledge which cannot tolerate knowing it knows."[18] The language of Dionysus in his meetings with Pentheus follows the strategies of this language of the Other, both to reveal and to mask the unconscious, for it is in this way that the repressed contents of the unconscious can evade the censor and come to the surface as speech.

This Discourse of the Other, which Dionysus constitutes as Pentheus' repressed alter ego, is balanced at the end of the play in the discourse between Agave and Cadmus in the psychotherapy scene so ably analyzed by Devereux. We may perhaps call the language of that scene a Discourse of the Self.

In the first part of the play the initially definite, univocal, authoritarian language of Pentheus gradually fuses with the hidden purposes of his repressed other self, enacted on the stage in the person of the Lydian Stranger / Dionysus. In the last part of the play, language moves out of this (con)fusion to clarity and recognition. Visual appearances follow the same pattern. Covered with the dress and wig of a Maenad, Pentheus is led out of the ordered space of the city to the wild spaces of the god (and of the self) where his speech loses contact with the rest of reality, with everything that has constituted the defining structures of his life. At the end, to bring Agave back to those structures of her life, Cadmus reconstitutes her relations with

18. From unpublished remarks at a 1974 seminar by Lacan, quoted in Shoshana Felman, "Turning the Screw of Interpretation," *Yale French Studies* 55/56 (1977) 166.

the members of her *oikos* (household) and the reality of her role as wife and mother. He thereby returns her from the unbounded, wild spaces and from the dissolution of personal boundaries in the *thiasos* (sacred band) of the god to the defining frame of the oikos which makes language possible.[19] No longer laden with the double or triple meanings of madness or Dionysiac hallucination, language once more expresses a unified, common ground of shared experience.

In Pentheus' first meeting with Dionysus face to face, the god's disguise as a Lydian youth gives nearly every verse a hidden double meaning. In his later encounters with the god / Stranger, these double meanings come closer to expressing the two planes, conscious and unconscious, of Pentheus' self. The language of "hiding" and of "persuading," "obeying," and "suffering" (involving various plays on *paschein, peithein, Pentheus, penthos*) forms the most persistent group of double meanings;[20] and we have already seen how these reach their climax in Pentheus' total subjection of the god's spell in the antilabē of 966–70 as he exits for the last time.

Pentheus' experience of the other himself embodied in Dionysus develops in a progression, from Teiresias' descriptions of the god, to his own meeting with the god in the guise of the Lydian youth, and then on to his encounter with the god in his bull form, the culmination of the double visions that Dionysus opens before him (922). Each of these double visions also has a verbal equivalent in a doubling of language. Thus, to take one example, Pentheus' line, "You have become a bull" (τεταύρωσαι γὰρ οὖν, 922), also means, "You have treated me with the savagery of a bull."[21]

Richard Seaford has convincingly argued that the double meanings of Dionysus' language reflect the language of the Dionysiac Myste-

---

19. Devereux (note 1) 42.

20. See especially 367, 506ff., 787ff., 845f., 910–70. For further discussion see Segal, *Dionysiac Poetics* (note 9) 251–53, and "Etymologies" (note 12) 86. We may perhaps add 473, where Pentheus asks, ἔχει δ' ὄνησιν τοῖσι θύουσιν τίνα. The line means, "What help do [your rites] hold for those who do sacrifice?" But it might also be translated, "Do your rites hold any help for those sacrificing—whom?" or "Those to whom your rites bring help, whom do they sacrifice?" Line 357 holds a simpler form of double meaning. Pentheus threatens, "Bring him here to die seeing a bitter bacchanting in Thebes" (πίκραν βάκχευσιν ἐν Θήβαις ἰδών); but of course it is Dionysus who will convert what Pentheus sees as pleasurable into something bitter: cf. 634 and 815, and note the stress on seeing throughout (e.g., 624, 629f., 912ff., 1257ff., etc.).

21. See Segal, "Etymologies" (note 12) 88f.

ries, a language made deliberately obscure to the uninitiated but known to the initiates (472–74).[22] This hidden religious dimension of Dionysus' speech is paralleled by its hidden psychological dimension. The initiatory and the psychological functions of the double meanings are superimposed upon each other and are exactly symmetrical with each other. Both are different expressions of an aspect of reality which Pentheus denies. In both realms Dionysus is the god of the secret, other side of reality, the invisible world, whether of the self or of the gods, that remains in the shadow side of consciousness and of language.

This parallelism is particularly clear at the end of Pentheus' first encounter with the god, where the doubleness of meaning focuses on his most personal and most mysterious word, his name (506–8):

Dionysus. You do not know why you live, nor what you do, nor who you are.
Pentheus. Pentheus, Agave's son, my father Echion.
Dion. You are suited for misfortune in your name.

The play on the hidden meaning of the name of Pentheus as "grief" or "suffering" (*penthos*) echoes Teiresias' point at the end of the previous scene (367). The disguised god is now taking over the role of the prophet, Teiresias, in defending himself, Dionysus. But the lines that he speaks here also echo the lines spoken by another Teiresias to another tragic hero whose name conceals the hidden truths of his destiny and of his unknown self, the Oedipus of Sophocles' *Oedipus Tyrannus* (*OT* 412–14; cf. *OT* 367).

Teiresias' lines in the *Oedipus* constitute a vital element of intertextuality for this scene of the *Bacchae*. In both passages the hidden language of the self parallels the hidden language of the truth about the gods. Sophocles' Teiresias introduces Oedipus to the mystery of divine forces invisible behind the human actions of the foreground, and he simultaneously introduces him to the mystery of his identity hidden behind the surface of his official, public identity as the ruler of Thebes. The prophet (cf. *Ba.* 551) who takes over the role of Teiresias

22. See Richard Seaford, "Dionysiac Drama and the Dionysiac Mysteries," *CQ* n.s. 31 (1981) 252–75. Note the use of the term for riddles (double meanings of words) in Plato, *Phaedo* 69c when Socrates alludes to Orphic initiation and the different reception of initiated and uninitiated in Hades: πάλαι αἰνίττεσθαι.

in the *Bacchae* does the same for the ruler of Thebes, and in virtually the same words.[23] In Sophocles, however, the religious and philosophical aspect of this revelation of a hidden meaning behind words is paramount; in Euripides, the psychological meaning predominates, though the religious dimension, the covert references to the Dionysiac Mysteries, as Seaford has shown, is by no means negligible.

The two planes, the mystic and the psychological, remain intertwined throughout the *Bacchae*. What is "unspeakable" (*arrhēton*, 472) as the secret Bacchic Mysteries is also what is unspeakable as the Discourse of the Other, the problematical knowledge about the unconscious which remains at some level alienated from language. The mysterious light that blazes forth at the palace miracle marks both a religious mystery and the god's penetration of Pentheus' psychological defenses as he enters the well-guarded palace of the king.[24] The *theōria*, or sacred procession, in which Dionysus leads the maddened Pentheus out of the palace and the city to his doom on Mount Cithaeron (1043ff.) is both a mystic initiation that marks the revelation of Dionysus' full power as a god and simultaneously a revelation of the conflicts and contradictions within Pentheus which the god releases with a force that overwhelms Pentheus' ego and leaves him both physically and psychologically torn asunder.

The ambiguities of this procession on the ritual plane parallel its ambiguities on the psychological plane. Pentheus is both "lord" (*despotēs*, 1047) and passive victim, both human and beast, both hunter and quarry, both male and female, both preternaturally powerful (cf. 949ff.) and totally helpless, both sexually aggressive (cf. 957f.) and castrated or infantilized (1101ff., 1114ff.).[25] For the Dionysus of the *Bacchae*, even more than for the Aphrodite of the *Hippolytus*, the numinous power of the divine comprehends both the mysteries of the self and the mysteries of the god's presence among men.

This parallelism between the psychological and the mystical planes

---

23. It is another link between the stranger and the blind seer that *prophētēs* occurs only twice in the play, once of Teiresias (211) and once of Dionysus (551).

24. The identification of Pentheus' personal ego defenses with the physical defenses of his palace is implicit in what J. Wohlberg, "The Palace-Hero Equation in Euripides," *Acta Antiqua Academiae Hungaricae* 16 (1968) 149–55, calls "the palace-hero equation." Euripides' *Heracles* provides a close parallel.

25. On the implications of infantilization and castration in this scene see Segal, *Dionysiac Poetics* (note 9) especially chap. 6.

of action and language in the experience of Dionysus pervades nearly every aspect of the play. It is especially marked in the theme of *anankē*, "necessity." On the one hand anankē involves the psychological "constrictions" (inhibitions, rigidities) within Pentheus and their release or unloosing by Dionysus;[26] on the other hand it points to the supernatural "necessity" exercised by Dionysus as the executor of the will of Zeus (cf. 1349–51).

Directly after the encounter between Pentheus and Dionysus the chorus sings the second stasimon, which moves from the mystic themes of the birth and "revelation" of Dionysus (519–36) to the "revelation" (*anaphainei*, 538) of Pentheus' hidden monstrosity as the son of earth-born Echion, "a savage-visaged monster, not a mortal man, but like a murderous giant, opponent of the gods" (542–44). The chorus then expresses its fears that the king will imprison the Stranger, "hidden away in dark enclosures . . ., in the struggles of Necessity" (*en hamillais anankas*, 552). But the first sign of Pentheus' imminent defeat is his discovery, after the palace miracle, that "the stranger who had been constrained by the necessity of bonds [*desmois en katēnankasmenos*] has fled away" (642f.). Dionysus' kind of necessity will overcome Pentheus'. Later, the force of necessity will appear as the god's power not only to unloose the literal bonds of Pentheus' prison but to release the hidden desires of Pentheus' unconscious. Fully under the god's hypnotic spell in his last moments on stage, Pentheus delights in the thought of being "carried in his mother's arms" (968f.): "You compel me by necessity to be dissolute," he tells Dionysus (καὶ τρυφᾶν μ' ἀναγκάσεις, 969). The god's necessity is both an internal, psychological force (as in 969) and a divinely sanctioned, supernatural power (1349–51).

The two meanings are already implicitly interwoven in the second stasimon, for the phrase that describes the imprisonment of the Stranger "hidden in the dark enclosures" (σκοτίαις κρυπτὸν ἐν εἱρκταῖς, 549) is a close verbal and metrical echo of the mystic birth of Dionysus in the parode, "hidden from Hera by the golden pins" in the thigh of Zeus, from which he is to emerge into the light (περόναις κρυπτὸν ἀφ' Ἥρας, 98), just as he will emerge mysteriously

26. In 497f. Euripides alludes to the cult of Dionysus Lysios, the Unbinder. For the themes of constriction and release see also Segal, *Dionysiac Poetics* (note 9) 100–106, and "Etymologies" (note 12).

and mystically from the darkness into the light in the palace miracle (cf. 594–99, 608–11).[27]

The parallels between the two dimensions of the action go even deeper, for from Homer onward the anankē of the gods often takes the form of binding or otherwise immobilizing their foes. It is particularly the earth-born Giants or monstrous serpents that the gods have to subdue with the immobilizing Necessity of their force.[28] In the second stasimon the chorus explicitly refers to "earth-born Echion" and compares his son, Pentheus, to one of those dangerous Giants who fought against the gods (542–44).[29] When he is led off to his doom to find death in the ambiguously soft "necessity" of his mother's embrace (968f.), the chorus describes him as the offspring of Libyan Gorgons (989f.) and invokes Justice against this "godless, lawless, unjust earthborn offspring of Echion" (995f. = 1015f.).[30] Both passages make Pentheus a kind of primordial monster, defeated by divine Necessity in a great cosmogonic battle. This cosmic aspect of divine Necessity is parallel to the internal, psychological necessity of Dionysus, the power of the god to destroy Pentheus by releasing all the forms of his constrictions, the political authority of Pentheus' attempt to bind the god (cf. 504f.)[31] and the psychological constrictions of his tightly bound personality. Unbinding these, Dionysus also reveals the hidden monstrosity of Pentheus, the chaos beneath the orderly ruler, and the misfortune beneath his name and his origins (506–8).

The root *herk-*, "constrain," "hem in," recurs throughout the first part of the play to describe Pentheus' literal constriction of Dionysus by his political and military authority (e.g. 443, 497, 509, 549, 611,

---

27. See Segal, *Dionysiac Poetics* (note 9) 154–56. For the relation of light and darkness in 594ff. to the Dionysiac Mysteries, see Seaford (note 21) 256f.

28. On the gods' anankē in cosmogonic battle with Giants see Richard B. Onians, *The Origins of European Thought*, 2nd ed. (Cambridge 1954) 326ff.; Heinz Schreckenberg, *Ananke: Untersuchungen zur Geschichte des Wortgebrauchs*, "Zetemata" 36 (Munich 1964) 2–11, 40–42. Further discussion in Segal, *Dionysiac Poetics* (note 9) chap. 4 n.35.

29. See J. C. Kamerbeek, "On the Conception of *Theomachos* in Relation with Greek Tragedy," *Mnemosyne* ser. 4, vol. 1 (1948) 271–83, and Francis Vian, *Les origines de Thèbes: Cadmos et les spartes* (Paris 1963) 162ff.

30. On the chthonic aspects of Pentheus' "earth-born" ancestry see Segal, *Dionysiac Poetics* (note 9) chap. 5.

31. See Segal, *Dionysiac Poetics* (note 9) chap. 4 passim.

618). But as Dionysus uses his own very different kind of power to "release" (*lyein,* cf. 498), the same root marks the surfacing of Pentheus' repressed sexual fantasies as he imagines the Maenads "held like birds in a thicket in the dearest *enclosures* [*herkē*] of their *beds*" (957f.). The power to bring a sudden, mysterious flash of light into the dark, subterranean, enclosed places of Pentheus' heavily guarded interior domain applies to the religious epiphany of the god in his Bacchic Mysteries (594–611, 629–35) and also to his figurative epiphany as the "revealer" of what lies hidden within Pentheus (*anaphainein,* 538 and 528; cf. 501).

The cosmological and psychological significance of Dionysus' necessity forms a contrast as well as a complementation. Pentheus, after all, is not a monstrous Giant or a Gorgon-generated serpent to be defeated in a universal clash of elemental forces, as in the Titanomachy of Hesiod's *Theogony* or the battles between Zeus and Typhos in Hesiod or Pindar. For all his bluster, Pentheus is no mythic paradigm of *vis consili expers* but only a confused, immature young man.[32] The Greek divinities, however, are not forgiving. Pentheus' failure to integrate the Dionysiac in himself and his city is projected upon the plane of civic religion as well as of individual personality and then extended into the cosmological plane as a conflict of divine order and monstrous violence. This homology between the psychological and the religious necessity of Dionysus shows the power of the god as both an internal and an external force. But at another level the homology does not entirely fit. The discrepancy between Pentheus as a primordial Giant and Pentheus as a mortal sufferer becomes larger in the latter half of the play, as Euripides engages our sympathies for the human victim and reveals more of the ambiguous, problematical side of Dionysus.

If Dionysus as "looser" or "releaser" (*lysios*) liberates the repressed sexuality of Pentheus, he also liberates the repressed destructiveness and rage of his female victims, the women of Thebes. It is part of Pentheus' ironic misapprehension of everything about Dionysus that

---

32. For such cosmic conflicts between order and chaos, see Hesiod, *Theog.* 664ff.; Pindar, *Pyth.* 1.13ff. and *Pyth.* 8.12ff.; Aeschyl., *PV* 351ff.; Eur., *Ion* 205ff. In this last passage Dionysus has a major role in the struggle, as he does also on the Siphnian frieze at Delphi. See in general Francis Vian, *La guerre des géants* (Paris 1952). For the inappropriateness of such a schema for Pentheus, see D. J. Conacher, *Euripidean Drama: Myth, Theme and Structure* (Toronto 1967) 67f.

his Theban Maenads, so far from being sexually eager and submissive to males when released from the interior spaces of house and city (cf. 218–23, 957f.), turn against their submissive sexual role with unexpected and astonishing violence. After their defeat of the men who try to stop them from carrying off children and property (751–64), they fall upon a herd of cattle and tear apart with their bare hands both a "young cow full of milk" (*euthēlon porin*, 737) and bulls that toss their horns in both anger and sexual excitement (ὑβρισταὶ κἀς κέρας θυμούμενοι, 743). *Tauroi hybristai* in this verse almost certainly implies a sexual erection.[33] The Maenads here turn destructively against their own nurturant motherhood (the cow) and against the male procreative sexuality of the bull. Earlier they had nursed the young of wild animals at the breast (699–702) and caused the nourishing liquids of wine, milk, and honey to flow from the earth (702–13). But the other side of that promiscuous mothering of wild creatures is the symbolical destruction of their milk-giving capacities in rending the milch-cow. Its pendant is the tearing apart of the sexually aggressive bulls.

This double violence foreshadows Agave's rending of Pentheus, her own child, in a killing that is preceded by an act of symbolical castration as the Maenads uproot his fir tree (1104–10) and cast him down from his lofty perch to the earth below (1111f.). Both parts of this deed are prefigured symbolically in the rending of cow and bull (737–47). The destructive reaction against the motherhood of the cow reappears in the full release of maternal aggression in Agave's murderous rage against her own child. The revolt against the domination of male sexuality (of which the tumescent bull is the archetypal embodiment) takes the form of humiliating the phallic pride of Pentheus. In his madness he had delusions of lifting the mountain and of uprooting its peaks and valleys (945–50); but it is in fact the Maenads who have the superhuman strength to uproot the very tree to whose top Dionysus has shot him (1064–75), "upright into the upright sky" (1074).[34]

The power of Dionysus to release the repressed aggressiveness of

---

33. Cf. Pindar, *Pyth.* 10.36 and Xenophon, *Cyrop.* 7.5.62 ("*hybristai hippoi*, when castrated, cease from biting and from violent behavior," *hybrizein*). Roux (note 1) *ad* 743 cites the latter passage but does not draw the logical conclusion.

34. Note the verbal parallel between 949 and 1104 in the matter of "levers," *mochloi*.

the maternal figures as a complement to his release of the repressed sexuality of Pentheus is already implicit in the first description of the Maenads nursing baby fawns and wolves that they "hold in their arms' embrace" (ἀγκάλαισι . . . ἔχουσαι, 699f.). This phrase is the regular expression for carrying a baby, but it recurs near the end of the play when the hidden side of that motherhood has been fully revealed. What Agave then "holds in her arms' embrace" is the severed, bloody head of her son (ἐν ἀγκάλαις ἔχεις, 1277).[35] To this side of the maternal embrace corresponds the side of the maternal figure which the Dionysiac unloosing reveals, the imago of the terrible mother who glowers over the helpless, infantilized form of her son with foaming lips and rolling eyes (1114–24) before she tears his arm from its socket to commence the sparagmos (1125–36).

The landscape of the Maenad mothers' boundless generosity of milk, wine, and honey in the first scene (698–713) undergoes a corresponding reversal. That landscape of nourishing liquids reflects the life-giving functions of Dionysus as a god of the liquid vitality of nature and its fertility.[36] Several of the choral odes recreate this landscape of joyful abundance where water is the dominant element (cf. 141f., 154, 405–8, 419f., 519–22, 568–75, 865–76). But that liquid landscape, just like the nurturant motherhood that it symbolizes, shows its destructive other side when Dionysus releases the repressed rage of the Theban women. Then it becomes a strangling enclosure whose power to smother and obliterate lies just beneath the surface of quiet, shelter, and pleasure:

ἦν δ' ἄγκος ἀμφίκρημνον, ὕδασι διάβροχον,
πεύκαισι συσκιάζον, ἔνθα μαινάδες
καθῆντ' ἔχουσαι χεῖρας ἐν τερπνοῖς πόνοις.

There was a hollow vale, with crags around it, with water running through it, shaded over by pine trees, where the Maenads sat, holding their hands in pleasurable toils.

35. On the ambivalence of this embrace and related images of unfolding and strangulation see Segal, Dionysiac Poetics (note 9) 104, with n.35; also "Etymologies" (note 12) 91f.

36. On Dionysus as a god of fertility, especially of the liquid vegetative life of nature, see Plutarch, Isis and Osiris 35.365a; Eur. Phoen. 645–56. Further discussion in Segal, Dionysiac Poetics (note 9) 10f. and 149ff.

At first glance this valley is a sheltered *locus amoenus,* a watery pleasance. It has, perhaps, vaguely sexual implications as the hidden hollows of the female body that Pentheus, wishing "to see but not be seen" (1050), hopes to watch. But nearly every word of the description carries a sinister implication. The enclosure, marked by the three prepositions *amphi-, dia-,* and *syn-,* prepares for Pentheus' entrapment.[37] *Ankos,* "glade," contains the same root as the enfolding "embrace" (*ankalai*) of his doom (1277; cf. 699) and perhaps of the "necessity" (*anankē*) of his grim fate (969; cf. 1351). *Diabrochon* (1051), literally "with water flowing through it," also carries hints of smothering and certainly of the "noose" of death (*brochos thanasimon*) which the murderous "Maenad herd" (an aspect of cows very different from that of 737) will draw around him (1021–23).[38] George Devereux, citing parallels from Roheim's studies of the Australian aborigines, has plausibly suggested to me that the Maenads' "holding their hands in pleasurable toils" refers to ritualized group masturbation. If so, this "pleasurable effort" of the group rite soon changes to a nightmarish group ritual of the opposite kind, the destruction of a young male's sexuality and life by (symbolical?) castration and bloody dismemberment. In any case, the hands of these Maenads will be employed in "toils" or "efforts" that are far from "pleasurable" (1206f., 1209, 1280, 1286; cf. 969).[39] Fewer than fifty lines later the gentler qualities of this watery landscape fade entirely before its murderous side as the Maenads, "maddened by the god's breath upon them, leap through the valley's rushing torrents and the broken crags" (διὰ δὲ χειμάρρου νάπης / ἀγμῶν τ' ἐπήδων . . . , 1093f.).

On the level of psychological meaning, this landscape is a symbolical projection of the female body and particularly of the mysterious, hidden body of the mother which Pentheus hopes to see in its

37. Although Dodds (note 15) does not make this point explicitly, his translation (*ad* 1051f.) catches the tone of dangerous enclosure: "There lay a glen, cliff-bound, refreshed with waters, close-shadowing pines." Cf. *Phoen.* 1570–76; Theocr. *Id.* 26.3 and 11; André Motte, *Prairies et jardins de la Grèce antique* (Brussels 1973) 233ff. with n.4.
38. For the implications of *diabrochos* see Segal, *Dionysiac Poetics* (note 9) 104 with n. 35, and "Etymologies" (note 12) 89f.
39. For the importance of the theme of hands see Segal, *Dionysiac Poetics* (note 9) chap. 3. In contrast to the "pleasurable toils" of 1053, note the painful "efforts" (*mochthoi*) of 1105, 1228, 1279. On the reversals of pleasure and related words see Jacqueline de Romilly, "Le thème du bonheur dans les *Bacchantes,*" *REG* 76 (1963) 361–80.

secret places. But this landscape, like the figure of the mother itself, is also the object of nightmarish fantasies. The contrast of the two settings (1051–53 and 1093f.) exactly parallels the contrast of the two images of the maternal "embrace" (699f. and 1277). Dionysus' fusion of opposites collapses the two sides together in the ambiguities of 966–70. The power of Dionysus is the power to release both sides of these repressed images, each sliding into the other, each present in the other with a precarious balance that Euripides catches in the almost demonic ambiguity of his language (especially 968–70 but also 1051–53).

On the level of the play's religious meaning as a work about the place of Dionysus and the cults of Dionysus in the city, the ambiguities of these landscapes, shifting from joyful abandon to bloody horror, function as a microcosm of all the ambiguities surrounding this god. In writing his play about both aspects of Dionysus, Euripides reflects on the necessity for repression which makes the work of culture possible and also on the danger of those repressions for the individual and for the culture as a whole. As a psychological and religious drama simultaneously, the *Bacchae* explores the need and the capacity of man's cultural creations—the city, the family, religion, art—to absorb what most threatens those creations with dissolution. The classical polis had long made a place for Dionysus in its cults and festivals, among which were those at which such tragedies as the *Bacchae* were performed. In the *Bacchae* the attempt to exclude Dionysus from the individual personality and from the city as a whole ends in the violent dissolution of both the ruler and the community. Pentheus is literally dismembered; Thebes is left without a king; the remnants of the ruling family are scattered in exile (1352–60, 1379–87). But since everything that Euripides depicts as beautiful, lifegiving, and joyful about the god takes place in the wild, on the mountains, or at the fringes of the Greek world, we cannot conclude that he was optimistic about the city's capacity to incorporate into its ordered structures a force and a god that, by their very nature, call those structures into question.

IV /

TRANSFORMATIONS

CHAPTER 10

Boundary Violation and the Landscape of the Self in Senecan Tragedy

In Memoriam David S. Wiesen (1936–1982)

I

T. S. Eliot's remarks on self-dramatization in Seneca's tragedies anticipated and encouraged more recent attempts to revaluate the rhetorical texture of the plays.[1] Again and again, through a variety of rhetorical figures, the actor calls attention to the importance of his or her emotions. This technique, as Eliot pointed out, has contributed to Seneca's popularity at periods of cultural crisis and transition, like our own. *Medea superest* and "I am Antony still" are related by more than just literary influence.[2]

At periods when the traditional values are called into question and the social rewards and accepted marks of esteem are no longer felt as satisfying human needs and desires, men and women are likely to look inward and to define the meaning of life in terms of the self, in terms of internal and private rather than external and public things. The size and scale of the imperial bureaucracy (dwarfed, to be sure, by our own), the precariousness of public life under a Caligula, a

I thank the John Simon Guggenheim Memorial Foundation for a fellowship in 1981–82, during which this essay was written. I am grateful to Albrecht Dihle and Ernst A. Schmidt for helpful comments. I presented a version of this essay as the first David S. Wiesen Memorial Lecture at Brandeis University, December 9, 1982.

1. T. S. Eliot, "Shakespeare and the Stoicism of Seneca" (1927) in *Selected Essays,* new ed. (1950; New York 1960) 107–20, especially 112f. and 119. See also W. H. Owen, "Commonplace and Dramatic Symbol in Seneca's Tragedies," *TAPA* 99 (1968) 291–313, especially 292ff. and 312f.

2. Eliot (note 1) 113.

Nero, or a Domitian, the riskiness or illusoriness of freedom, all contributed to this inward focus. Tacitus' *Dialogus* sharply juxtaposes the traditional rewards of the Roman public man—power, influence, prestige, wealth, the gratifying crowd of clients at the door, the admiring finger pointing out the successful advocate in the forum—with the quasi-pastoral seclusion and quietude of the man of letters (*Dial.* 7–10 and 11–13). Seneca himself, in the *Thyestes,* dramatizes the disaster resulting from the protagonist's failure to follow his own good instincts and mistrust the "false names" of greatness in the world (*Thy.* 446f.). When these "great things" are perceived as delusory, men turn to the inner standards of value, ultimately to the value of the self alone. The wisdom, courage, and proudly won autonomy of the Stoic sage can then constitute the true index of personal worth. The external trappings of power and wealth are *adiaphora,* "indifferent things." "Stoicism," as Eliot remarks, "is the refuge for the individual in an indifferent or hostile world too big for him"; its theatrical equivalent (or "version of cheering oneself up," as Eliot calls it) is a self-dramatizing, rhetorically ostentatious individualism.[3]

Senecan "self-dramatization," for all its literary artifice, rests upon such a view of the importance of the self. It is, among other things, an expression of individual alienation from the central values of the culture. Seneca often dramatizes that alienation as the inflicting or suffering of physical violence, the most obvious form of violating the self. These are the terms that the last half-century has made all too familiar to our own age. The enormities and distortions of Senecan rhetoric no longer seem beyond the reach of our experience.

Stoicism is not the only response of Seneca's contemporaries to this condition of alienation; it is but one of several forms of individualism which develop out of the moral, social, and political crises in Roman society from the late Republic on. Seneca's stoicism seems to have provided him with a more or less consistent point of view, a stable intellectual basis suited to his rhetorical technique of projecting personal emotion into a cosmic frame. The Senecan dramatic assertion of the self takes two different but complementary forms. There is the I-statement of self-dramatizing emotion, like Phaedra's *me, me profundi saeve dominator freti / invade et in me monstra caerulei maris / emitte* ("Me,

---

3. Eliot (note 1) 112; both quotations come from this page.

me, make the object of your attack, cruel ruler of the deep sea, and against me send forth the monsters of the blue sea," *Pha.* 1159–61). And there is the involvement of the entire world in the hero's suffering, a responsive sympathy between individual and cosmos. The hero dramatizes his suffering through a bold network of imagistic correspondences between man and nature. These express, according to C. J. Herington, "a moral and physical unity from the depths of the universe to the individual human soul."[4] Thyestes calls to the sea and earth, to the gods of the lower and upper worlds, to listen to the atrocities inflicted on him (*Thy.* 1068ff.).[5] Jason sees Medea, murderess of their children, flying off into the aether and shouts that there, where she is going, there are no gods (*Med.* 1026f.). The Senecan hero places himself at the center of the world's stage and cries out, Look, my suffering is that of the entire universe. "Enwrap the whole world in fearful clouds," says Thyestes (*nubibus totum horridis / convolve mundum, Thy.* 1078f.). In himself alone, says Oedipus, Nature has overturned all her laws and so should devise equally unnatural modes of punishment for his guilt (*Oed.* 942–45).

This grandiose version of the pathetic fallacy is actually but an indirect or displaced form of the I-statement of self-dramatization described above. The hero's perception of the magnitude of his pain virtually causes the trees to turn pale, the waters to cease to flow, the air to thicken with mist, and so on (cf. *Ag.* 34ff., *Thy.* 197ff., 260ff.).

To this double strategy in the hero's assertion of his individual magnitude in suffering—I-statement and cosmic projection—correspond the two sides of the philosopher's wisdom. The Stoic sage abandons external power for the realm of the soul. To rule over the "evils of the heart" makes the true king (*Phoen.* 104ff., *Thy.* 348f., 380ff.; cf. *Nat. Quaest.* 6.32.4ff.). The sage also identifies himself with the world soul: he is the proper beneficiary of the gods' care and the appropriate spectator of the majesty and order of the universe (cf. *Ad Helv. de consol.* 8.3ff.; *De otio* 5; *De vita beata* 8.4ff.).[6] This latter

4. C. J. Herington, "Senecan Tragedy," *Arion* 5 (1966) 433; see also Owen (note 1) 300ff.

5. Cf. also the chorus of *Thy.* 789ff. on the turning of day to night; in general Otto Regenbogen, "Schmerz und Tod in den Tragödien Senecas," in *Vorträge der Bibliothek Warburg*, vol. 7, *Vorträge 1927–1928*, ed. Fritz Saxl (Leipzig and Berlin 1930) 204.

6. On the world soul and the wise man in Stoicism see J. M. Rist, *Stoic Philosophy* (Cambridge 1969) 209ff.; Max Pohlenz, *Die Stoa* (Göttingen 1948) 1.112ff., especially

attitude, as one would expect, is less suitable for tragedy, although the author of the *Octavia* has Seneca himself, as a dramatic character, discourse at length on this topic (385ff.).

Seneca's combination of the Silver Age rhetorical magnification of experience and the subjectivizing forms of expression in Roman poetic diction[7] creates a new vision of tragedy. The unbearable suffering possible in a world of uninhibited violence resonates with an intensity of personal agony which is comparatively rare in Greek tragedy. In the latter, formal structure and a fuller intellectual vocabulary help to contain the expression of suffering in more clearly demarcated limits. Euripides, for example, makes us hear the screams of the blinded Polymestor in the *Hecuba;* but how un-Senecan and how characteristically Euripidean is the subsiding into long rationalistic-historical debate (Eur., *Hec.* 1056–1254).

Senecan tragedy clearly does not create the towering heroic figures of Aeschylus or Sophocles. Such figures—Prometheus, Ajax, Antigone, Philoctetes—are so defined that their nature involves a hopeless struggle against the very conditions that are necessary to their existence; and in this struggle they are doomed by the greatness that they themselves possess, by their commitment to justice, nobility of nature, absolute values in a corrupt and imperfect world. In Seneca the tragic element operates in a struggle that is almost entirely inward, in a battle against the passions rather than in a head-on conflict with divine powers, universal moral principles, or an unyielding world order. Admittedly, this inward turning of the dramatic focus creates something that is often closer to the pathetic than to the genuinely tragic. Seneca's protagonists struggle much more with themselves than with essential laws of the universe or the basic conditions of life and society. But to the extent that such characters as

---

117f. In pointing to some links between Seneca's tragedies and Stoic philosophy, I do not mean to imply that a strictly Stoic interpretation exhausts the meanings of the plays or that their purpose was simply to illustrate Stoic doctrine. For a recent discussion and bibliography of this much discussed issue see A. L. Motto and J. R. Clark, "Art and Ethics in the Drama: Seneca's 'Pseudotragedy' Reconsidered," *ICS* 7 (1982) 125–40. Joachim Dingel, *Seneca und die Dichtung* (Heidelberg 1974) 97ff. and 116f., has suggested for Seneca a "negative Stoicism," like Lucan's (*Phars.* 7.445ff.), stressing the remoteness, incomprehensibility, and inhuman harshness of the divine powers and fate.

7. See, for example, Brooks Otis, *Virgil: A Study in Civilized Poetry* (Oxford 1963) chap. 3.

Phaedra, Medea, Clytaemnestra, Thyestes, or Hercules engage with
the evil and violence in themselves—and therefore potentially (if less
exaggeratedly) in us all—they do exemplify a quality of genuine
tragedy. They suffer guilt, take responsibility for their defeat by their
own uncontrolled emotions, and suffer the physical and moral consequences of their actions.[8]

In Seneca the ultimate truth of human character is revealed in
moments of tremendous violence, where even reason is pressed into
the service of intensifying every possible means of suffering, as in
Oedipus' self-torturing cry that he should use his "native cleverness"
in punishing himself (*utere ingenio, miser, Oed.* 947). Overwhelmed by
emotions beyond his control, the Senecan tragic hero becomes alienated from an aspect of his own humanity, from the rational moderation of desire, hatred, love, fear, hope, despair, and guilt.[9] No wonder our own age of decentered emotionality has rediscovered these
works.

Seneca's limitation of vocabulary, rhetorical figures, and concentration on the flow of emotional movement rather than on structures of action or events create a kind of artificial echo chamber where

8. For a good survey of discussions about the tragic element in Senecan drama and
a defense of the plays as tragedy, see Motto and Clark (note 6) passim, and Ilona
Opelt, "Senecas Konzeption des Tragischen," in E. Lefèvre, ed., *Senecas Tragödien,*
Wege der Forschung 310 (Darmstadt 1972) 92–128, especially 93f. In contrast to the
Greek tragedy of fate (*Schicksalstragödie*), Opelt argues, Seneca exemplifies a "tragedy
of evil" (*Tragödie des Bösen*), where the protagonist consciously, not blindly, takes
guilt upon himself (92). This form of tragedy, she believes, is foreshadowed in the
Xerxes of Aeschylus' *Persians* and in late Euripidean plays such as *Hecuba* and *Troades.*
Her analysis of *nefas,* however, does not really clarify "the tragic" in the plays. I
suggest that the tragic dimension lies in the conflict between good and evil in the
individual soul. In this conflict evil sometimes wins, and the hero is engulfed in his or
her own inner monstrosity (e.g. Medea, Clytaemnestra, Atreus, and momentarily
Hercules in both *HF* and *HO*), or after yielding to evil in the form of passion and
emotional violence turns against himself in remorse, retribution, and mental or physical self-punishment (Phaedra and the Hercules of *HF*), or suffers both physically and
emotionally as a result of an inadequate or mistaken moral decision (Agamemnon,
Thyestes, Oedipus). In all cases, however, as many have pointed out, Seneca's emphasis falls on the inner, emotional, and psychological dimension of the action and the
suffering.
9. On Oedipus' self-punishment see Regenbogen (note 5) 193. Compare Atreus'
helplessness before the obsession of limitless, inexhaustible vengeance in *Thy.* 255f.:
nil quod doloris capiat assueti modus; / nullum relinquam facinus et nullum est satis ("I am
plotting nothing which any moderation of ordinary resentment can contain; I shall
shun no crime, and none is enough").

human suffering, and all the emotional responses it involves, are magnified to a new level and therefore appear with a new pictorial expressiveness, what has been called a "psycho-plastic portrait of emotional affect."[10] Here the real action occurs in the spaceless and timeless realm of the emotional life.[11] The vast geographical hyperboles serve to set off that inner world as a distinctive reality of its own. Seneca's originality, as Otto Regenbogen has pointed out in a justly celebrated essay, lay not in the invention of new thematic material but in the vivid, imagistic depiction of this enclosed inner space of pathos, suffering, vehemence of feeling.[12]

The focus on character and emotional reactions rather than on events per se also creates an impression of staticity, of purely verbal happenings. The world of nature depicted in the tragedies is, in one sense, as artificial as the dramatic situations themselves. It exists less for its own sake than as a foil or objective correlative for the emotional reality of the protagonists. The forests of Hippolytus' hunting in the *Phaedra* or the remote seas of the *Argo*'s travels in the *Medea* are another form of this self-dramatization. They have their full existence in tension with an inner landscape of the soul. These expansive landscapes serve to set off the narrow, self-imposed limitation of hatred or vengeance in which an Atreus, a Hippolytus, or a Medea becomes enclosed.[13]

The two recurrent motifs of enclosure, entrapment, constriction on the one hand and all nature on the other are opposite but complementary poles of the sympathy that links microcosm and macrocosm. The *Oedipus* correlates the "inverted nature" (*natura versa est*, 371) of the entrails examined by Manto with the inverted nature made manifest in the hero's life (*leges ratas / Natura in uno vertit Oedipoda*, "Nature overturns her established laws in Oedipus alone," 942f.). Those laws are revealed to men in the microcosmic scrutiny of the viscera laid bare beneath the flesh as the priestess peers into the dark secrets of the sacrificed heifer's vitals and sees the monstrosity of

10. Regenbogen (note 5) 207. He goes on to remark that this emotional-rhetorical coloring is closer to Tacitus than to Greek tragedy.

11. See Owen (note 1) 312f.; Jo-Ann Shelton, *Seneca's Hercules Furens*, Hypomnemata 50 (Göttingen 1978) 30.

12. Regenbogen (note 5) passim, especially 204–14.

13. Cf., for example, the chorus of *Medea* 301–79, and contrast the death of Pelias through Medea's magic arts, *angustas vagus inter undas*, 668.

an unborn fetus "not in its rightful place, filling its parent" (*alieno in loco / implet parentem*, *Oed.* 374f.). But they are also revealed in the macrocosm through the "sympathetic" response of polluted air and parched earth (632ff.), which follow upon the horror of a "mother heavy once more in her accursed womb" (*utero rursus infausto gravis*, 637). The repetition of *gravis*, "heavy," from the account of the plague-bearing wind's "heavy breath" (*gravi flatu*) a few lines earlier (631) stresses the link between the interior pollutions of the incestuous womb and the deadly plague of the polluted natural world outside. The relation between the two is metaphorical or analogical as well as causal. From the corrupted liver to the irregular course of the stars, the message is the same.

Teiresias' unlocking of the enclosures of the "deep Styx" and the "Lethean lake" (*profundae claustra laxamus Stygis*, *Oed.* 401; *claustra Lethaei lacus*, 560) is the cognitive equivalent of Oedipus' revealing the hidden uterine secrets of the dark places from which he came and to which he has returned. Seneca deliberately exploits this interplay between the visceral horror of the entrails and the womb on the one hand and the havoc in nature wrought by the plague on the other. Teiresias' determination to "unloose the gates of deep Styx" (401, quoted above), stands in sharp contrast with the bacchic hymn that begins with the "sky's shining beauty" (*lucidum caeli decus*, 405). The tension is resolved when Oedipus accepts the dark horror of his begetting and expiates it by the self-imposed darkness of self-blinding (cf. 998–1003). He thereby restores vitality to the upper reaches of nature and brings back a "gentler condition of the sky" and "life-filled draughts of air" (*mitior caeli status*, 1054; *vividos haustos*, 1056), just as Laius' ghost had foretold.[14]

Here, as in the *Thyestes*, Seneca intensifies the sensation of physical suffering by playing off images of the open air against images of enclosing or penetrating the hidden cavities of the body. Thus the macrocosmic effect in the natural world of Oedipus' atonement is achieved through the visceral imagery of his self-blinding. He digs out (*scrutatur*) his eyes with "hooked fingers" (*Oed.* 965), tears them "from their furthest roots deep within" (966). His hand is "fixed

---

14. For other aspects of the finale of the Oedipus see C. Segal, "Sacral Kingship and Tragic Heroism in Five Oedipus Plays and *Hamlet*," *Helios* 5, no. 1 (1977) 5–7; Owen (note 1) 312.

deep inside" (*fixa penitus alte*, 968f.) and "tears the hollows and empty recesses" (*recessus . . . inanes sinus*, 969). The uterine and visceral associations of most of these words become unmistakable fewer than a hundred lines later when Jocasta atones for her unwitting crime by the grim poetic justice of penetrating with her incestuous husband's sword "the spacious womb which bore both sons and husband" (*uterum capacem qui virum et natos tulit*, 1039). Aside from the grim, even grotesque physical horror, Oedipus' language depicts the feelings of guilt, remorse, emotional suffering, the physical as well as the psychological wrench of anguish, through images of somatic violation, images of being trapped within himself and being pushed back within himself (952–79, 1024–41). The "rain that pours forth" and "waters" Oedipus' cheeks (*subitus en vultus gravat / profusus imber ac rigat fletu genas*, "Look, the sudden storm pours forth and makes heavy his face and with weeping waters his cheeks," 925f.; cf. 978) is the "eye's moisture" of his body (955); but it also foreshadows the healing macrocosmic effects at the end (1054ff.), restoring the parched and dying crops (50–52; cf. 649ff.).

   In the *Phoenissae*, Oedipus' self-dramatizing exaggeration of guilt goes further than the nails reaching into the eyes' hollow sockets: he would even reach through the eye into the brain itself (*nunc manum cerebro indue; / hac parte mortem perage qua coepi mori*; "now dip your hand into brain; complete your death in that part where I began to die," *Phoen.* 180f.). The physical gesture has a direct psychological correlate in Oedipus' sense of guilt as he reaches back into his prenatal existence in Jocasta's womb (*intra viscera materna, Phoen.* 249f.). He feels his place there as an already sinful penetration of his mother's body, into which "a god has driven him [*egit*], pushed back in concealment [*abstrusum, abditum*], doubtful of existence," the perpetrator of "an unspeakable crime" (*Phoen.* 251–53). When a few lines later he describes how "his father cast him away" (*abiecit pater*, 258) to die in Cithaeron's forests with its "wild beasts and savage birds" (255f.), he establishes a symbolic link between the cruelty of his fate both in the hiddenness of the womb and in the expulsion to the wild. The symmetry of accursed concealment within the womb of the mother and harsh expulsion by the father to a hostile mountain expresses the psychological meaning of Oedipus' crimes. He reenacts, as it were, the experience of losing the intimacy of womb / mother, which he regains by returning there as husband; he relives metaphorically the hatred of the father who "threw him forth" (*abiecit*), a deed he avenges by killing Laius.

The son's illicit penetration of the mother's womb even in being born (*Phoen.* 245–47) is answered by the father's penetration of the son's feet (*Phoen.* 254), an act of symbolic castration. The pattern of Oedipus' life is already present, quite literally, from the first beginnings: wrongful placement inside the mother followed by the physical violation and penetration of his own body.

The explicitness about the psychological dimension of Oedipus' suffering is Seneca's characteristic reinterpretation of the material of Sophocles' Oedipus plays. It is most marked, perhaps, in the apparition of Laius' ghost in the *Oedipus* (619–58). The ghastly apparition, surrounded by all the paraphernalia of subterranean horrors that are Seneca's hallmark (*Oed.* 559–98), is like the bad dream of a guilt-tormented mind. The murdered father has not a word of charity, compassion, or understanding for a son who acted in ignorance. He is virtually a foreshadowing of the Freudian superego, a harsh, demanding, guilt-raising father figure, a projection of the son's own conviction of his inherently evil nature. Through the eyes of this *tristis imago* (Virgil's phrase for another demanding father, *Aen.* 6.695), Oedipus sees himself as indelibly stained with the worst possible crimes of civilized humanity. He is a "bloody king" who holds both his scepter and the wife of his bedchamber as the rewards of the infamous double outrage of parricide and incest (*Oed.* 634–37):

> . . . rex cruentus, pretia qui saevae necis
> sceptra et nefandos occupat thalamos patris,
> invisa proles, sed tamen peior parens
> quam natus, utero rursus infausto gravis . . .

The *Medea* uses a different aspect of this relation between the macrocosm of nature and the microcosm of the individual's emotional and physical being. Medea's revenge dwarfs the vast reaches of sea and earth explored by the *Argo* (cf. 301–79) and cancels them out through the interior bonds of the womb, her weapon against the leader of the expedition. At the climax of her revenge she, like Oedipus, would reach into her vitals to extirpate in her womb the traces of motherhood that tie her to Jason (*in matre si quod pignus etiamnunc latet, / scrutabor ense viscera et ferro extraham,* "In the mother if any pledge still lies hidden, I will search my vitals with the sword and with iron draw it out," 1012f.). As *pignus* is a common term for the "child" who constitutes a "pledge" of love and fidelity between husband and wife, Medea's lines combine the literal and the metaphorical rooting out of her tie to Jason: she would excise the fetus that may be growing in her womb from their union and from the bond of love which should have insured its growth, safety, and birth. Medea soon uses that sword not on herself but on her remaining child; and the visceral imagery of 1012f. conveys the interior darkness of her insatiable vengeance. Lady Macbeth's "Unsex me here," with all the thickening of blood and change of milk to gall, spares us this uterine rooting out of motherhood.[15] In a reverse but complementary movement, Medea would make her fertility itself a symbol of her vengefulness. She envies Niobe, with fourteen children to sacrifice to vengeance (954–56), and complains that she has been "sterile in respect to [exacting] punishment" (*sterilis in poenas fui,* 956). "If this hand of mine," she goes on later, "could have been sated with single slaughter, it would have sought none; though I kill two, still is the number too narrow for my grief" (1009–11).

After this paradoxical interplay of fertility and sterility, Seneca opens out another contrast in moving from the enclosed space of womb and vitals to the "open path to the heavens" where her serpent-drawn chariot will carry her "among the winds" (1022, 1025). The violated interiority of her body and the violation of nature's limits in the *Argo*'s distant explorations and in the magic of Medea's aerial car are complementary aspects of the same theme, the pushing beyond limits, beyond civilized behavior, into the barbarian and the monstrous. At the frontiers of the civilized world where Medea's passion has its origins, we veer between the violated innocence of the Golden Age and the pitiless ferocity of inhuman savagery.[16] Calling

15. Shakespeare, *Macbeth* I.v.38–52; pallid too by contrast is the visceral imagery of Racine's Thésée who describes his paternal misgivings at condemning Hippolytus in these terms: "Malgré ton offense, / mes entrailles pour toi se troublent" (*Phèdre* IV.iii).

16. For the theme of the Golden Age in the *Medea,* see Gilbert Lawall, "Seneca's *Medea:* The Elusive Triumph of Civilization," in *Arktouros: Hellenic Studies Presented to B. M. W. Knox,* ed. G. Bowersock, W. Burkert, and M. Putnam (Berlin and New York 1979) 419–26; C. Segal, "Dissonant Sympathy: Song, Orpheus, and the Golden Age in Seneca's Tragedies," *Ramus* 12 (1983) 229–51.

up the primordial monsters of the earth's remotest places (674–704), Medea also releases her own interior monstrosity, suppressing the life-giving side of her motherhood and envisaging a Niobe-like fertility of death.[17]

II

This interaction between the enclosed depths of the soul and the expansive frame of nature obviously has its philosophical roots in the Stoic correspondence of macrocosm and microcosm and the ideal of living in harmony with the universe. But its literary effectiveness lies in another area, one where even Seneca's most grudging critics have acknowledged his power, namely his depiction of morbid states of the soul, anxiety, fear, obsession, vindictiveness, the lust for power. "La psychologie est peut-être ce qu'il y a de plus remarquable dans le théâtre de Sénèque," wrote Léon Herrmann sixty years ago, and few would disagree.[18] The powerful symbol of the underworld, corresponding to the darker hell of the soul, finds a place in nearly every Senecan tragedy.[19]

When Oedipus hears from the old shepherd the truth about himself in the simple four words, *coniuge est genitus tua* ("that child was born

17. Note, for example, the alliterative play on *Medea / malum* and *Medea / monstrum* (e.g. 362, 674f.) on the one hand and *Medea / mater* on the other (171, 289f., 933f., 950f.). See Alfonso Traina, "Due note a Seneca tragico," *Maia* 31 (1979) 273–75, and C. Segal, "*Nomen Sacrum:* Medea and Other Names in Senecan Tragedy," *Maia* 34 (1982) 241–46.

18. Léon Herrmann, *Le théâtre de Sénèque* (Paris 1924) 492. Good discussions of Seneca's psychological focus may also be found in Berthe Marti, "Seneca's Tragedies: A New Interpretation," *TAPA* 76 (1945) 222f. and 229–33; Norman T. Pratt, Jr., "The Stoic Base of Senecan Drama," *TAPA* 79 (1948) 10f.; Ettore Paratore, "Originalità del teatro di Seneca," *Dioniso* 20 (1957) 56ff.; Herington (note 4) 447f.; Jo-Ann Shelton, "The Dramatization of Inner Experience: The Opening Scene of Seneca's *Agamemnon*," *Ramus* 6 (1977) 33–43. On the other hand the attempt of Marc Rozelaar, *Seneca: Eine Gesamtdarstellung* (Amsterdam 1976) chaps. 2–4, to correlate the psychological concerns of the tragedies with Seneca's personal life, childhood experience, and private neuroses is, though interesting, most speculative.

19. E.g., Owen (note 1) 296f., 307, 311f.; Shelton (note 11) chap. 4: B. Walker and D. Henry, "The Futility of Action: A Study of Seneca's *Hercules Furens*," *CP* 60 (1965) 14f. and 21f.

of your wife," *Oed.* 867), he replies with a heavily alliterated invocation to Earth and the powers of the nether world (868–70):

> dehisce tellus, tuque tenebrarum potens,
> in Tartara ima, rector umbrarum rape
> retro reversas generis ac stirpis vices.

Yawn open, Earth, and you, powerful ruler of shades, carry back into the lowest depths of Tartarus these inverted exchanges of the race and its stock.

The "yawning of the earth" at the appearance of Laius' ghost earlier (*subito dehiscit terra,* 582; cf. *dehisce tellus,* 868) now changes from supernatural magic to emotional reality. It becomes an expressive indication of the horror in Oedipus' soul as he makes his terrifying discovery. Now the destructive darkness over the city which Oedipus described in the play's opening lines (1–5; cf. 44–49) is traced to its origin in himself.[20] With that revelation of the truth the earth really does seem to open beneath him, as it did in 582, and show the infernal realms of shades and darkness beneath the plants and trees (the mild agricultural metaphor of *stirps* in 870 is active here). The chiastic repetition *tenebrarum potens / rector umbrarum* ("ruler powerful of dark shadows") and the idea of "gaping" in *dehisce* provide a stylized but adequate verbal equivalent to Oedipus' split-second realization. At once he knows that his world is turned upside down, that the ground is no longer the same beneath his feet. The very nonrealism of the representation conveys the horror: the remote, fabled realm of Tartarus is the anguish that he is now living. Sophocles' Oedipus cries out *iou iou* and addresses the light that he sees for the last time (*OT* 1182–85); Seneca's Oedipus utters an initial word, *dehisce,* which suggests his open-mouthed speechlessness, and then addresses the darkness. The darkness of the lower world that opens before him (cf. 582f.) and the abyss of darkness within himself become visible, as it were, at the same time. This is an Oedipus who, in the course of minutes, is ready to call himself "the crime of the age" (*saeculi crimen,* 875). The sudden glimpse of the dark hell within in the

---

20. With this passage in *Oed.* compare *Phaedra* 1238–42: the figurative reopening of the lower world for Theseus corresponds to his recognition of the subterranean violence in himself, unleashed in his curse on his son. Cf. also *Tro.* 519f.

cry *dehisce, tellus* confirms in metaphorical terms the inner violence that the action has revealed in Oedipus' soul: his readiness to torture by fire and use "bloody ways" of interrogating (861f.), his acknowl-edged "savagery," and his loss of self-control (*si ferus videor tibi / et impotens* . . ., "if I seem to you savage and out of control," 865f.).

III

With his feeling for the emotive quality of visual scenes, Seneca often creates an objective correlative for these psychological events through images of place or landscape. The *locus horridus* of gloomy forest or strangling trees expresses the nightmare world of fear, anx-iety, despair.[21] Bruno Snell observes that Seneca "likes to surround his characters with what one could call a cloud of their milieu."[22] The power of that milieu, however, often derives from images that give a physical sense of helplessness in the face of emotions. "Anxiety" means, literally, the constriction of heart, diaphragm, and stomach when we encounter dread. Lucretius' *anxius angor* calls attention to the root meaning of the word and its physiological effects (cf. *DRN* 3.993).

Seneca, like many ancient writers, conveys the physiological con-creteness of emotions in metaphors like that of the mind "swelling" with anger or the "seething" of grief and pain (*tumet animus ira, fervet immensus dolor*, of Oedipus, *Phoen.* 352). But he often pushes this physiological correlate of emotion much further. In particular, he develops two complementary types of physiological sensations for

21. For the motif of enclosure in the *locus horridus* see Rosanna Mugellesi, "Il senso della natura in Seneca tragico," in *Argentea Aetas: In Memoriam E. V. Marmorale*, Pubbl. dell' Ist. di Filologia Classica di Genova 37 (Genoa 1973) 43ff., 63–66, who comments on "la nuova sensibilità pittorico-visiva di Seneca" (63). For this kind of "atmospheric" effect of landscape in Roman poetry, see also C. Segal, *Landscape in Ovid's Metamorphoses*, Hermes Einzelschrift 23 (Wiesbaden 1969) 5ff. The essay of Pierre Thévenaz, "L'interiorità in Seneca" (1944) in Alfonso Traina, ed., *Seneca, letture critiche* (Milan 1976) 91–96, is concerned not with spatial "interiority" but with the internalization of values, the importance of "the things under our control" in Seneca's philosophy.

22. Bruno Snell, *Scenes from Greek Drama*, Sather Classical Lectures 34 (Berkeley and Los Angeles 1964) 27.

emotional disturbance: entrapment, enclosure, engorgement, or im-
plosion on the one hand and dismemberment, invasion, penetration,
or mutilation on the other. In quite a literal sense his language grips
us in our vital places.

The "wide realm of Diana," as Snell describes the "cloud" of
Hippolytus' milieu at the opening of *Phaedra,* contrasts with Phaedra's image of herself as she enters immediately after. She is
"weighed on" by a "greater grief" (*maior incubat . . . dolor,* 99), has
an illness growing inside her, and feels her passion as the steam of a
volcano burning and seething within (101–3). As she describes her
condition of desperate, neurotically obsessive fixation on Hippolytus,
she uses other images of enclosure, the "dark house" of the Labyrinth
where Daedalus "shut in" the monstrous bull (*qui nostra caeca monstra
conclusit domo,* 122). The reference to the Minotaur locked in the
Cnossian Labyrinth suggests her own metaphorical entrapment in the
dark heredity of her mother, Pasiphae, of which Phaedra is painfully
aware (e.g., 127f., 242). Later the Nurse describes her love madness
(*furor*) as something burning inside, "shut up within" (*inclusus,* 362),
which, though concealed, is betrayed by her face and bursts forth as
fire from her eyes (360–64). Entrapment in an inner fire of uncontrollable passion as in a burning building is combined with another
image of radical alienation from the self: Phaedra's physiological sensation of the strangeness of her body as in a hopeless, feverish disease
(*spes nulla tantum posse leniri malum, / finisque flammis nullus insanis erit,*
"there is no hope that so great a suffering can be soothed; the wild
flames will have no check," 360f.).[23] Both images become more
powerful by the contrast with her fantasy wishes of the outdoors,
woods, hunting, the feeling of the wind in her hair (394–403).

Through such descriptions Seneca manipulates those anxieties,
present in all of us, which have to do with what psychologists call
primary boundary anxiety, the concern with the autonomy of our
physical being, our corporeal integrity in its most fundamental sense.
Such anxieties have their roots in the infant's first experiences, his
inchoate sense of his separateness from the mother, his fear of being
engulfed and swallowed. Such concerns surface in the language and

---

23. The modern reader may perhaps forget how real and present was the danger of
being trapped in a burning building in Imperial Rome: e.g., Juvenal 3. 197–202 and in
general A. G. McKay, *Houses, Villas, and Palaces in the Roman World* (Ithaca 1975) 85ff.

imagery of other Latin authors: Ovid and Ammianus Marcellinus, for example, have been fruitfully studied from this point of view.[24]

The spatial imagery of the *Phaedra* exploits both forms of boundary anxiety: Phaedra is entrapped in the cavernous hell of her hopeless desire, Hippolytus is dismembered. In both cases the self suffers a direct physical violation, an irreparable breach in ontological security. Phaedra, nurturing the evil within, becomes unrecognizable to herself. When the monster, called forth by Theseus' prayer to Neptune, emerges from the sea (1025ff.), Hippolytus initially holds out against panic (1066f.), but the nightmarish apparition cannot be checked by rational control (cf. the simile of the pilot, 1072–75) and soon overwhelms his hold on reality in the most elemental way, leaving him scattered in pieces over the woods that were once his secure and peaceful refuge from women and sexuality. By exaggerating the details of the monster in Euripides' play (*Hipp.* 1173–1248), Seneca shifts the event from the plane of mythical reality to the plane of nightmare fantasy, an externalization of a dream world of unconscious terrors. The Euripidean text, to be sure, already contains that element, but it is intensified by the secondary elaboration of Senecan rhetoric and artificiality. Seneca's play, in this respect, is a psychological reading of Euripides': the mythic and theological issues are reinterpreted as psychological states and symbols.

For Seneca's Hippolytus, as for his Oedipus, reality dissolves into nightmare. Oedipus' world opened to reveal the hellish depths in himself as *saeculi crimen*, "the criminal of the age" (the hero of the *Hercules Furens* undergoes a similar experience). Hippolytus' death turns him into exactly the opposite of what he has wanted to be, so that he is in a sense disintegrated from within as well as from without. Convicted of incestuous rape, he is mutilated and castrated (cf. 1099) by a creature that evokes both the castrating father imago (cf. 1046ff.) and his own neurotic distortions of the sexuality that he has repressed in himself.

In the *Phoenissae*, as I have remarked above, Oedipus images his guilt as a kind of uterine penetration of his mother's "entrails" (*intra*

---

24. Leo Curran, "Transformation and Anti-Augustanism in Ovid's *Metamorphoses*," *Arethusa* 5 (1972) 71–91, especially 78–82; R. F. Newbold, "Boundaries and Bodies in Late Antiquity," *Arethusa* 12 (1979) 93–114, with a bibliography of psychological literature; see also Bradford Lewis, "The Rape of Troy: Infantile Perspective in Book II of the *Aeneid*," *Arethusa* 7 (1974) 103–13.

viscera materna, 249f.) and also as entrapment in the guilty concealment of the womb: in its recesses he is "pushed back and hidden
away" (*abstrusum, abditum*, 251). That sense of being helplessly entrapped, enfolded, or compacted has its psychological dimension in
his feeling that it is not only the sky, gods, or crimes that he cannot
escape, but himself. His very body is a prison, a corporeal equivalent
of the confinement within his own guilt. "It is myself I flee," he says
(*me fugio*), "my breast [*pectus*], guilty of every crime, and this hand of
mine, and this sky and the gods and the dread crimes that I, though
innocent, performed" (*Phoen.* 216–18). The sensation of entrapment,
whether in the womb or in the corporeal / psychological prison of his
own body, depicts a self experienced as something that he wants to
escape but cannot. Correspondingly, he experiences his unremitting
burden of guilt as a boundary violation, the penetration or mutilation
of his body.[25] It is not enough, as in the *Oedipus*, that he digs his
fingers into his eyes; now he would reach through more "boldly"
into the brain (*nunc manum cerebro indue*, "now dip your hand into the
brain," *Phoen.* 180). In his next speech, as he traces his guilt to the
womb and to his birth, he uses an image of cruel penetration to
convey the malignancy of his fate: "With hot iron my father pierced
my tender feet" (*calidoque teneros transuit ferro pedes*, 254).[26]

Seneca's most effective manipulation of primary boundary anxiety
occurs, as one might expect, in the *Thyestes*. It is not so much the
imagery of eating and digestion which, in the last analysis, brings
home to us the horror of Atreus' revenge as the vivid sense of being
stuffed, crammed full, impacted. As Atreus unveils his triumph, he
seems to soar in the vast celestial spaces of boundless euphoria (885f.):
"I walk the equal to the stars and beyond all men, with my proud
head touching the lofty vault of heaven" (*aequalis astris gradior, et
cunctos super / altum superbo vertice attingens polum*). But images of his

25. The heavy emphasis on Oedipus' feelings of guilt that he can never escape in
Phoenissae (e.g., 216ff.) is one of the most interesting aspects of Senecan characterization and certainly underlies Oedipus' cries to the dead Laius, a figure who has virtually the status of an apparition (cf. 39ff. and 166ff.) and is treated almost explicitly as
a hallucination produced by neurotic anxiety.
26. Seneca has elaborated this detail from the description of the pierced feet in
Euripides' *Phoenissae* 26, *sphurōn sidēra kentra diapeiras mesōn* ("passing the iron spurs
through the midst of the ankles"). Sophocles' version leaves these details vague (*OT*
717–19, 1032–34, 1349–55). See in general P. G. Maxwell-Stuart, "The Interpretation of the Name Oedipus," *Maia* 27 (1975) 37–43, especially 38f.

own satiety follow almost at once, as he contemplates "filling the father full of the death of his sons" (890f.). When the vengeance comes, it pushes this fullness to the point of horror, in striking contrast with the free movement of Atreus' opening lines. The horror is quite literally visceral as Thyestes cries out (999–1001):

> quis hic tumultus viscera exagitat mea?
> quid tremuit intus? sentio impatiens onus
> meumque gemitu non meo pectus gemit.

What is the disturbance that tosses around my entrails? What trembles within? I feel a burden that will not endure me, and my breast groans with a groaning not my own.

The polyptoton *meum . . . non meo* ("mine . . . not mine") conveys the speaker's confusion of personal boundaries, his alienation from the physical substance of his own body. The situation is analogous to the sensation, in excruciating pain, of uttering a scream that one does not recognize as one's own.

It is fruitful to compare the scene in Sophocles' *Oedipus Tyrannus* where Oedipus, emerging blinded from the palace, cries, "Miserable that I am, where on earth am I carried, unhappy, where does my cry fly about me, borne aloft?" (1308–11). Comparison between the language of Seneca and Sophocles is instructive: Sophocles' language has none of Seneca's corporality. It is the lightness, the fluttering, that predominates (*diapōtatai phoradēn*, "the cry flutters carried around"). Aside from the Sophoclean hero's unobtrusive ethical dative, *moi*, in 1309, there are no personal pronouns. Far from being alienated from himself in the extremity of pain, Sophocles' Oedipus recovers a deepened sense of self as he plunges into a suffering of which he is the self-chosen agent, not the victim (*OT* 1331ff.).

Seneca's imagery of corporeal heaviness, the burden stuffed within, gains an added dimension of psychological suffering when Atreus reveals the truth. Thyestes says (1040–44):

> hoc est quod avidus capere non potuit pater.
> volvuntur intus viscera et clusum nefas
> sine exitu luctatur et quaerit fugam.
> da, frater, ensem (sanguinis multum mei
> habet ille); ferro liberis detur via.

This then is what the greedy father could not hold. My entrails roll around within; the closed in evil struggles, with no way out, and searches for escape. Give me a sword, brother (that sword of yours has much of my blood); with steel let a way out be given to my children.

This is the acme of the horror: Thyestes is trapped in the evil of his own body. The nightmare of the boundary violation is all the greater as the foreign matter, the source of evil (*clusum nefas*), is stuffed within himself as both alien and fearfully his own. The victim is bloated and distorted in his own flesh by being crammed full of a poisonous feast that he cannot disgorge and must assimilate. The scene's outrage works through its evocation of the primary processes over which we have no conscious control, the digestive absorption of alien substance converted into our very being.

Seeking to grasp and dramatize the horror, Thyestes reaches out to the remote geography of "the Caucasus' harsh rock" (1048) but cannot throw off the sensation of being "pressed down" (*premor*, 1050f.): *genitor en natos premo premorque natis* ("a father, I press down my sons, and by my sons I am pressed down"). The shift from the active to the passive form in *premo . . . premor* expresses the movement from outside to within, from an external to an internal heaviness.[27] This movement, in turn, is another aspect of that fundamental alienation from self conveyed by "mine . . . not mine" (1001f., quoted above).

As Thyestes calls to the seas to bear witness to the crime, he describes the waters too as "closed in" (*clausa litoribus vagis / audite maria*, "Hear me, you seas enclosed in your wandering shorelines," 1068f.), so that the inwardness of the "closed in evil" (*clusum nefas*, 1041) of the sons trapped in his belly colors his perception of the natural world as well. Atreus repeats the notion of constriction when he uses the verb *angit*, "chokes," metaphorically, of Thyestes' alleged bitterness that he did not prepare such a feast for Atreus first: "I know

27. Compare also Theseus' reabsorption into the dark hell of his own violence in *Phaedra* 1203: addressing Avernus and Tartarus he cries out, *(me) impium abdite atque mersum premite perpetuis malis* ("hide me, the evil one, away and press me down, submerged, in eternal suffering"). Here too, as in *Thy.* 1050f. and *Phoen.* 251f., the imagery of weight and oppression express feelings of overwhelming guilt and remorse. Theseus' language, however, does not develop the visceral equivalents of this heaviness, as in the passages discussed in the text.

332

why you are lamenting," Atreus tells his brother; "you grieve because I anticipated your crime; it chokes you not that you took in the unholy banquet [*nec quod nefandas hauseris angit dapes*], but that you did not prepare it" (1104–6). The alliteration and repetition in the play's last line, Atreus' *te puniendum liberis trado tuis* ("I give you over to be punished by your sons") continue the sense of entrapment in one's own flesh (*te . . . tuis*). The fresh pastoral woods that Thyestes reluctantly gave up to enter Atreus' palace (412ff.) are never more hopelessly distant.

This reduction of suffering to primary physical boundaries and to elemental digestive processes is more than just rhetorical sensationalism or the love of the grotesque. It corresponds to a large moral design. It is no accident that the ghost of Tantalus opens the play with his torment by the emptiness of hunger (1–6). His ever "greedy mouth" and "gaping hunger" are both a contrastive and a complementary image of the corruption of the house: such corruption will reduce men to their lowest and most basic functions. In his first appearance onstage Atreus contemplates his vengeance in images of fulness that anticipate the condition of Thyestes at the end. His lust for revenge takes the form of an insatiable hunger that makes him virtually a living Tantalus (252–54):

> non satis magno meum
> ardet furore pectus; impleri iuvat
> maiore monstro.

My breast burns with a madness that is not great enough. My joy is to be filled with a greater monstrosity.

When he unfolds his plot, he describes his breast again as "shaking" and "revolving deep within" by a "disturbance" that will be closely echoed in Thyestes' physical trouble later (260f.):

Atreus. tumultus pectora attonitus quatit penitusque volvit.

Trouble astonished shakes my breast and rolls it around deep within.

We may compare Thyestes at 999f.:

> quis hic tumultus viscera exagitat mea?
> quid tremuit intus?

What is this trouble that tosses my entrails? What has trembled within?

or at 1041:

volvuntur intus viscera.

My vitals are rolled around within.

A few lines later Atreus' growing lust for revenge is something in his mind (*animo*) that "swells" (*tumet*, 267f.) beyond normal limits.

In Thyestes' case the imagery of inward fullness, swollenness, turgidity shifts at the end from "breast" and "mind" (*pectus, animus*) to "entrails" (*viscera*). Yet the parallels show Atreus as already drawn into his victim's suffering, already as degraded spiritually as his victim is physically. His own malaise about the insatiability of his vengeance contrasts with the horrible satiety that he has brought to Thyestes (889–91): "It is well, it is abundant. Now it is enough even for me. But why enough? I shall go on, even though the father is filled up with the death of his children. . . ." And yet the very terms that he uses of his all-devouring vengefulness link him with his victim (cf. *satur est*, "he is sated," 913). His metaphorical ascent to the broad heavens at the culmination of his revenge (884–88) is soon enclosed in the narrow terms of satiety, filling, and constriction (889–900). The torturer is inextricably fused with the tortured and in his own way victimized by the very violation that he inflicts on the other. The monstrosity that swells in Atreus' soul (267f.) is more deeply corruptive than the monstrous food in his brother's stomach. Though physically defeated and degraded, Thyestes retains a dignity of spirit which eludes the successful and exuberant criminal, Atreus.[28]

This language of the body, especially of the viscera, functions in a manner analogous to metamorphosis in Ovid.[29] It is disturbing because it reminds us of our physicality, of our inevitable reduction to

28. On Thyestes' moral conflicts and superiority see Viktor Pöschl, "Bemerkungen zum Thyest des Seneca" (1977) in *Kunst und Wirklichkeitserfahrung in der Dichtung, Kleine Schriften* 1 (Heidelberg 1979) 311–19; J. P. Poe, "An Analysis of Seneca's *Thyestes*," *TAPA* 100 (1969) 369–76, and the references in 360 n.11.

29. See Irving Massey, *The Gaping Pig: Literature and Metamorphosis* (Berkeley and Los Angeles 1976) 22ff., especially 28.

being mere body. We are reduced to those primary bodily processes like digestion over which we have no conscious control but on which we nonetheless rely for our lives. By reminding us of our visceral physicality too, such descriptions indirectly evoke the inevitability of death. We are forced to see ourselves in the context of the corruptible entrails of animals. This ultimate reduction of our being to physical matter, to the fate that we share with all living (and dying) things, is profoundly disquieting.

Like the *Phaedra*, the *Thyestes* combines the internal boundary violations of the victim's imploded body with the external violation of the agent's delight in mutilation. When he has Thyestes before him stuffed with the impious banquet, Atreus gloats over the details of how he cut the sons limb from limb, chopping and breaking the individual members (1057–68).

Psychology aside, the sadistic violation of human flesh by mutilation, decapitation, and crucifixion was an all too familiar reality in the amphitheaters of Seneca's contemporaries. The anxiety reflected by the tragedies in this area of experience had a basis in fact. One does not witness such acts without some damage to the spirit; and Seneca's plays bear witness, if only indirectly, to the corruptive effect that torture has on those who permit or condone it.[30]

There is even archaeological evidence for the vivid impressions that the executions, gladiatorial games, and crucifixions left on more sensitive spectators. The Italian archaeologist Umberto Fasola describes a graffito on a shop wall near the amphitheater at Puteoli. The crude but gripping drawing is clearly the work of one who "was certainly a witness of such torture and was deeply impressed" by the suffering of the transfixed, dying man.[31] It is as if Seneca represses the knowledge of the actual tortures in the public spectacles of his day but allows the reality of their psychological effects and their emotional impact to surface in the remote, mythical, and bizarre violations of the human body depicted in his plays: the butchering of Thyestes' sons, the tearing out of Oedipus' eyes, the dismemberment of Hippolytus'

---

30. For some contemporary discussion see M. N. Nagler, *America without Violence* (Covelo, Calif. 1982) 17–30; Pierre Vidal-Naquet, *Torture, Cancer of Democracy* (Harmondsworth 1963) and *Les crimes de l'armée française* (Paris 1975).

31. Umberto M. Fasola, *Traces on Stone: Peter and Paul in Rome,* English trans. of *Ricordi archeologici di Pietro e Paolo a Roma* (Rome and Florence 1980) 107–14; the quotation comes from 111.

body. In Seneca, as in Lucan, Petronius, Tacitus, Juvenal, and other Silver Age writers, the proximity of violent death, torture, and help-less subjection to physical violation produces a corresponding ex-tremism of violence in the style.[32] The stylistic equivalents of the psychological impact of violence were, perhaps, one way to come to terms with experiences that, two millennia later, are no more easily assimilable to reality. However remote, stilted, and incredible Sene-ca's rhetoric of violence and violation may look, it has a modern descendant in the atmosphere of unreality and nightmare which per-vades the novels of Kafka, Canetti, and Wiesel and a still living cousin in the element of the surreal and the incredible that attaches to the (alas) nonfictional accounts of the tortured from Argentina to Al-geria, from Auschwitz to the Gulag.

32. See Regenbogen (note 5) 211ff., especially 215f., citing Seneca, *Ad Helv. matr. de consol.* 20.1–3.

Tragedy, Corporeality, and the Texture of Language: Matricide in the Three Electra Plays

I

In a famous passage in the tenth book of the *Republic,* Plato invokes the "ancient quarrel between poetry and philosophy" (607b). Tragedy, Plato argues, not only presents unseemly images of the gods but also feeds the irrational part of the soul and encourages us to indulge in these emotions—pity and fear, Aristotle will later specify—to the detriment of our rational faculties. The quarrel, however, has another dimension, implicit in Plato's argument but not fully developed by him, namely that the function of language in poetry is fundamentally different from its function in philosophy. Poetic language, unlike its philosophic counterpart, seeks not to define abstractly or to isolate conceptually but to connect imagistically. (Ironically, one of the great exceptions is Plato himself, in his own way as great a poet as Euripides.) Its peculiar strength, in fact, lies not in separating, strand by strand, the parts of an argument and examining each of the terms that constitute its underpinnings but in associations, in subtle relations, and above all in concrete detail. Hence the texture of the words in poetry is more important than or as important as the abstract lexical meanings; the connotations are as central as the denotations.

How separable, then, is the thought or meaning of tragedy from

This essay is based on a public lecture at Vassar College in February, 1984, sponsored by the departments of Classics and Philosophy. I thank the participants for helpful suggestions.

the texture of its language? To be sure, tragedy shares with moral philosophy a central concern with the great issues with which philosophers have traditionally concerned themselves: the meaning of life, the problem of death and suffering, the arguments for choosing one course of action over another, and so on.

Philosophers, of course, tend to approach these issues in the hope that rational definition and systematic logic can clarify, if not solve, the problems, whereas tragedians tend to approach the questions with a stronger sense of their unresolvability, the inherent irrationality of existence, the rootedness of suffering in the very essence of human life, and the ineradicability of the irrational, whether from man or from the world—social, moral, physical—in which he lives.

There are, of course, pessimistic philosophers like Schopenhauer and optimistic tragedies, or at least what the Greeks called tragedies, like the *Ion* of Euripides or (up to a point) the *Oresteia* of Aeschylus or even the *Oedipus Coloneus* and perhaps the *Philoctetes* of Sophocles. Pessimism or optimism, sad or happy ending, is not the issue. Philosophers nevertheless want, on the whole, to bring intellectual order into the world. They tend to believe in the inherently rational potentialities of language; the tragic poets do not deny that the world may be orderly (Aeschylus and Racine certainly believed in an underlying cosmic and political order), but they also make us feel the power that disorder exerts on everything around it. They explore the possibility that the irrational may irrupt into the most orderly life, that suffering—unexpected, undeserved, uncontrollable, and in some fundamental way inexplicable—does exist as a basic aspect of the human condition and that no rational explanation, no law of order or larger system, can account for that suffering.

The great tragedies show us the suffering of men and women whom we have come to value through an imaginative sympathy for them which the work creates. This experience of suffering, off the scale of correspondence with what they have done or what they are, leads us to question the familiar cultural, religious, and philosophical explanations of that suffering. Tragedy jolts us out of our complacency about life, bounces us out of the smooth, deadening effect of routine. If we attend responsively to *Lear* or *Oedipus Tyrannus* or less elevated contemporary tragedies, *The Iceman Cometh* or *Long Day's Journey into Night,* we experience something like the wrench of one those catastrophes—personal or communal—which we colloquially call a tragedy, the news that a loved one has been killed in an auto accident or has cancer, but of course without the reality.

Yet the effect of such works is not to leave us in despair. Why is this so? Aristotle thought that it was because we experience a cleansing or purgation of the pity and the fear that the tragedies aroused. Others have conjectured that it is because the experience of such suffering enhances our appreciation of the preciousness of life and thereby has a tonic effect. This central question of "the tragic paradox" is of the sort that will be answered and debated in countless ways. In approaching this paradox, I would like to return to the point I made earlier about language. The language of tragedy enables us to experience the pity and the terror in such a way that we feel a quality of greatness—what the Greeks called μεγαλοψυχία—in the suffering that the hero or heroine exhibits. "Great-souled" need not mean "good-souled." In fact, the hero is often close to being what we would consider morally bad (Clytaemnestra in the *Agamemnon*, Heracles in the *Trachiniae*, Ajax in *Ajax*). But the grandeur of language that surrounds the hero is an essential part of the tragic experience. In this respect Shakespeare is not, fundamentally, so very far from the Greeks. Consider Othello's

> Soft you; a word or two before you go.
> I have done the state some service, and they know't.
> No more of that.—I pray you in your letters,
> When you shall these unlucky deeds relate,
> Speak of me as I am; nothing extenuate,
> Nor set down aught in malice. (*Othello* V.ii.337–42)

or Lear's

> Poor naked wretches, wheresoe'er you are,
> That bide the pelting of this pitiless storm,
> How shall your houseless heads and unfed sides,
> Your loop'd and window'd raggedness, defend
> From seasons such as these? (*Lear* III.iv.28–32)

Such passages not only create in us the sense of tragic waste by depicting some quality of inner greatness, some valuable human quality, in the suffering hero, they also convince us of that greatness by enacting it in the grandeur of the poetry. The language, like the thought, rises to move us beyond the normal and carry us to the limits of the human experience. It puts us in touch with events and emotions that call forth extraordinary responses. I think of Medea's line, *pantes perissoi houn mesōi logoi* ("All the words in the middle are excessive," *Med.* 819) or Phaedra's line in Seneca, when she is about to make her fateful confession of love to Hippolytus: *curae leves loquuntur, ingentes stupent* ("Light cares are spoken; the great ones are silent," *Pha.* 607).

In this last passage the extraordinary moment of irrevocable and tragic decision is in fact enacted as a play of language: desires that must be kept repressed in silence break forth into speech, and the entire first part of the scene is in fact about speech and silence. Racine takes over from Seneca this technique of highlighting the moments when terrible secrets emerge from the muted and penumbral background of conversations restrained by the *bienséance* of the Racinian conventions. When translators ignore the dynamics of this chiaroscuro contrast, the results can be grotesque. Thus Racine is wonderfully delicate in handling the powerful erotic implications of the scene between Phaedra and Hippolytus which he took over from Seneca. Compare:

> Hippolyte, nunc me compotem voti facis;
> sanas furentem. maius hoc voto meo est,
> salvo ut pudore manibus immoriar tuis.

Hippolytus, you now make me fulfilled in my prayer; you heal me in my love-madness. This is greater than my prayer, that with my modesty intact I might die at your hands. (Seneca, *Pha.* 710–12)

> Voilà mon coeur. C'est là que ta main doit frapper.
> Frappe. Ou si tu le crois indigne de tes coups,
> Si ta haine m'envie un supplice si doux,
> Ou si d'un sang trop vil ta main seroit trempée,
> Au défaut de ton bras prête-moi ton épée.
> Donne. (Racine, *Phèdre* II.v, ad fin.)

But Robert Lowell destroys the subtlety by laying on a heavy hand of over-explicitness:

> Look, this monster, ravenous
> for her execution, will not flinch.
> I want your sword's spasmodic final inch.[1]

Essential to tragedy is the hero's recognition of himself as one caught in helplessness, error, destruction that he cannot reverse and of which he is in some way guilty. The tragedy brings together, in a single experience, the hero's greatness and his error, his strength and his weakness, his recognition of some truth about the human condition, and the self-recognition of himself as one who has committed, in error or folly, some crime against the world order or the social order or some other value important to him. But this coming together of strength and weakness is clothed in a language that convinces us of the importance of the suffering. It matters. And it matters, in part, because the hero matters. Even in the moment when he reveals the weakness, ignorance, or violence that has destroyed himself and others, the hero commands our respect and hence involves us in trying to understand why such a person had to undergo such a degree of suffering. Oedipus in the last scene of the *Tyrannus* says that no one else but him could bear these sufferings. Lear, foolish as he has been, still commands our respect, not only because he is still a king but because he is still kingly in his suffering. This is a suffering that implicates the world order and the social order. The king exposed to the brutal storm is quintessential man, "poor bare forked animal," poised between hell and bliss, simultaneously the figure whose absence from the kingship (literal and figurative) allows the chaos both within and without to surface from below and break through into soul, home, and kingdom.

In Euripides' *Heracles* the ruined hero, amid the shambles of his wrecked palace and his murdered children, refuses, like Job, to curse God and die. Instead he takes up his bow, accepts Theseus' offer of shelter in Athens, and says (*HF* 1351–57):

> ἐγκαρτερήσω βίοτον· εἶμι δ' ἐς πόλιν
> τὴν σήν, χάριν τε μυρίων δώρων ἔχω.
> ἀτὰρ πόνων δὴ μυρίων ἐγευσάμην·

---

1. Robert Lowell, *Phaedra and Figaro* (New York 1961) 45.

> ὧν οὔτ' ἀπεῖπον οὐδέν' οὔτ' ἀπ' ὀμμάτων
> ἔσταξα πηγάς, οὐδ' ἂν ᾠόμην ποτὲ
> ἐς τοῦθ' ἱκέσθαι, δάκρυ' ἀπ' ὀμμάτων βαλεῖν·
> νῦν δ' ὡς ἔοικε, τῇ τύχῃ δουλουτέον.

> I shall prevail against death. I shall go
> to your city. I accept your countless gifts.
> For countless were the labors I endured;
> never yet have I refused, never yet
> have I wept, and never did I think
> that I should come to this: tears in my eyes.
> But now, I see, I must serve necessity. (W. Arrowsmith's translation)

The strong simplicity of the lines expresses his new definition of a heroism of tragic suffering rather than of triumphant strength. We feel that the striking expression *egkartereō bioton,* "I shall endure my life," is worthy of Heracles, as are the parallelism of "gratitude for multitudinous gifts" / "tasting multitudinous toils" and the direct, matter-of-fact decisiveness of the next phrase, which even a first-year Greek student could translate, *eimi d' es polin ten sen.* Even as this hero of invincible strength has to acknowledge his dependency on a friend and his subjection, like a slave, to fortune, he does so in language that retains the spirit of heroism which has in fact called down on him the wrath of the gods and caused the reduced, miserable state in which he finds himself.

Or, to turn again to Shakespeare, Antony still possesses a stature worthy of Cleopatra even after his luxury and indecision have ruined both their lives. In her famous speech of commemoration, almost a funeral eulogy, the Egyptian queen looks back at what her dead Antony was and convinces us, through the grand hyperboles of her rhetoric, that with Antony's passing something great and irreplaceable is gone from among us:

> His legs bestrid the ocean: his reared arm
> Crested the world: his voice was propertied
> As all the tunèd spheres, and that to friends;
> But when he meant to quail and shake the orb,
> He was as rattling thunder. For his bounty,
> There was no winter in't: an autumn 'twas
> That grew the more by reaping. . . .(*Antony and Cleopatra* V.ii 82–88)

Such passages are of the essence of tragedy because they carry the conviction of the greatness of the loss that we experience. They show us the moving and disturbing spectacle of great men and women who, in and through their greatness as well as their weakness, are led to actions that destroy just what is valuable in them and those around them. This is not the only source of the tragic, but it is an important one; and A. C. Bradley seems to me right to emphasize the sense of waste as a basic component of the tragic.[2] Hamlet's death, for example, intensified for us by the contrast with Horatio's survival, enhances our sense of the waste in the loss of a man who could inspire so passionate and noble a friendship—friendship based on the recognition of innate nobility or *virtus,* after the Roman ideal of Cicero's *De Amicitia.* Horatio must not drain the cup of poisoned wine because, as Hamlet entreats him, he must live to indict the "harshness" of a world in which a Hamlet meets such a death ("in this harsh world draw thy breath in pain, / to tell my story," *Hamlet,* V.ii.362–63). This pain in "drawing breath" again recalls the basic bond of physical life, and its liability to suffering, which all mortals share. Hamlet's very words are made up out of the difficult, dying breath of a poisoned body.

Like a kind of personalized choral presence, Horatio also focuses our own gaze on the action. Through his eyes, we see and feel the death of the noble prince with grief and involvement. We are not only the hearers of the tale that Horatio will live to tell (Hamlet's dying, "to tell my story") but its spectators as it is (re-)created before our eyes. We, the audience, are the ones who will "look pale and tremble at this chance, / that are but mutes or audience to this act." And we are its spectators at the pure, intense origins of its telling, from the lips of the dying hero himself:

> Had I but time, as this fell sergeant Death
> Is strict in his arrest, O, I could tell you—
> But let it be. Horatio, I am dead:
> Thou livest; report me and my cause aright
> To the unsatisfied. (V.ii.350–54)

---

2. A. C. Bradley, "Hegel's Theory of Tragedy," *Oxford Lectures on Poetry* (London 1950) 69–95.

These words gain in authority and pathos from the fact that the speaker, a few seconds later, is only a spent, inert body on the stage.

II

We tend to think of the Greeks of the classical age as highly intellectual, formulating in their tragedies the conflicts of fate and free will, restraint and hybris, and society and individual with sculptural calm and marmoreal simplicity. This view of classical Greek literature and art doubtless owes much to Plato's influence and to his celebrated criticism of tragedy mentioned above. But the Platonic suspicions about the power of the emotions in works of art are a radical deviation from the main line of Greek thinking about poetry.

At the very beginnings of the literary tradition the strong, somatic response to the emotional quality of poetry is already firmly established as a possible, if disturbing, reaction: Homer's Odysseus weeps at the songs of Troy that Demodocus sings in the palace of Alcinous.[3] When Aristotle singles out the *pathēmata* of pity and fear as the central effects of tragedy, he is much more in the mainstream of classical Greek thought.

These emotions themselves are closely linked to the physical sensation of the body. Gorgias, for example, stresses the reactions of weeping and shuddering in a context related to aesthetic responses.[4] Plato himself provides important, if hostile, testimony to such affective responses when he has the rhapsode Ion describe his feelings as he recites Homer: "Whenever I recite anything that moves pity, my eyes fill with tears; and whenever I recite anything fearful or terrifying, my hair stands straight up in terror, and my heart pounds" (*Ion* 535c).

Such responses are encouraged by the works themselves. In the case of tragedy the critical issues are formulated in the most emo-

---

3. *Od.* 8.521–31. See George Walsh, *The Varieties of Enchantment* (Chapel Hill, N.C. 1984) 3ff., who suggests that the two responses embody fundamentally different types of audiences: an engaged audience that identifies with the narrated events on the one hand and a more disengaged, emotionally distanced, and pleasure-seeking audience on the other. "Odysseus' tears," he suggests, may "more accurately figure the norm for Homer's audience as well as for Aristotle's" (5).

4. Gorgias, *Helen* 9: poetry produces in its hearers "fearful shuddering and much-weeping pity" (φρίκη περίφοβος καὶ ἔλεος πολύδακρυς).

tional terms. And the basis of these emotions is more often than not corporeal rather than intellectual. Indeed, the sense of the body is one of the most powerful ways in which these tragic poets bring home to us the actuality of the suffering that is the subject of their plays. We must recall too that in drama the issues are quite literally embodied in the physical presence of solid, corporeal figures moving before us in three dimensions in the orchestra.

In the *Oresteia,* as elsewhere in Greek tragedy, the suffering of the body serves as a focal point, a microcosm, of the suffering caused by human cruelty, by the errors of judgment resulting from lust, ambition, and the passions generated by war. Thus we have the emphasis on the blow of the knife and the shedding of blood in the human sacrifices of Iphigeneia, Cassandra, and Agamemnon, or Aeschylus' bold metaphor of Ares the money-changer who sends the warriors back from Troy in their bronze vessels, transforming flesh into ashes (*Ag.* 437–55). In Euripides the sacrificed Polyxena and the broken body of Astyanax in the *Trojan Women* serve for all the innocents slaughtered in war. In its extraordinary ability to condense the impact of human suffering into carefully wrought, densely packed emblematic productions, Greek tragedy, like its rhetorically amplified Roman derivative so influential on Renaissance and French classical tragedy, uses this most fundamental of our modes of relating to the world. Much of the unique power of Greek tragedy lies in its directness of appeal to this basic level of our corporeal being.

While concentrating the suffering that they depict into these direct and tangible physical images, the ancient plays do not sacrifice the complex moral, theological, political, or psychological issues. They thus achieve a double effect: on the one hand, clarity and simplicity of focus, on the other, adequacy to the intellectual challenge of defining and describing a world order torn asunder by conflicting claims of justice or unexplained violence. They combine viscerally gripping actions (Oedipus blinding himself, Medea killing her children, Orestes' cutting down his mother) with poetic and sometimes philosophic language—a language that is both rich in the inherited images of its mythical material and supple enough to include the juridical terms of the law courts, the abstract reasoning of the Sophists, or the cosmological concepts of such physical philosophers as Anaxagoras. The poetry of the choral odes and the highly metaphorical language even of the iambic dialogues are not mere ornament but a mode of condensing, juxtaposing, and connecting the various forms of causality behind the events into richly suggestive patterns.

Medea's tragic conflict between her vengeful anger and her rational counsels, for example, has its sharpest focus when she feels the touch of her children's bodies (*Med.* 1074–80):

> ὦ γλυκεῖα προσβολή,
> ὦ μαλθακὸς χρὼς πνεῦμά θ' ἥδιστον τέκνων.
> χωρεῖτε χωρεῖτ' · οὐκέτ' εἰμὶ προσβλέπειν
> οἵα τε†πρὸς ὑμᾶς†, ἀλλὰ νικῶμαι κακοῖς.
> καὶ μανθάνω μὲν οἷα δρᾶν μέλλω κακά,
> θυμὸς δὲ κρείσσων τῶν ἐμῶν βουλευμάτων,
> ὅσπερ μεγίστων αἴτιος κακῶν βροτοῖς.

O sweet embrace, the soft skin and sweetest breath of children! Come to me, come. I am no longer able to look at you, but I am defeated by my evils. And I understand what evils I intend to do; but stronger than my reasoning counsels is my angry passion, the greatest cause to mortals of their evils.

Euripides attains his powerful depiction of Medea's terrible conflict through the emotional situation alone, expressed in the almost unadorned simplicity of her language, with its triple repetition of the general but important word *kaka*, "woes," "evils," "sufferings," in emphatic line-end positions. With superb restraint, he breaks the scene off at once and then has his chorus sing a low-keyed, straightforward ode on the tribulations of having children (1081–1115). Everything remains on the level of universal human experience. Even allowing for the elevation of the poetic vocabulary, Medea utters scarcely a word that is outside the familiar vocabulary of the emotions. The normality of her language is itself a reminder of the healthiness of the world around her; and this is reflected too in the everyday, prosaic considerations of the chorus that immediately follows her speech: "Those who have in their homes the sweet presence of children, / I see that their lives are all wasted away by their worries," and other words to that effect. The interplay of style and situation raises in its own way the essential question of tragedy: as Helen Gardner puts it, "What is it that lures men against their judgment and against their better nature to do what revolts them?"[5] Why, after careful deliberation, do they adopt a course of action repugnant to their instinctive feeling for the goodness of life and the value of right action?

Tragedy gives no final answer but makes us less able to deny the dark places from which such thoughts grow, the tangled undergrowth and dim forests of the soul. Not only does tragedy dramatize the razor's edge of that irreversible moment of action—that "terrible point" (*to deinon*) of hearing in *Oedipus Tyrannus*—but it also probes the places where the good and the evil have a common root. Medea's lines on her children's sweet bodies show her about to destroy something in herself that she values as inestimably precious; and it is the existence of this other Medea—not the Senecan monster but the Euripidean mother—which gives a tragic depth to what otherwise could be a passionate tale of savage vengeance only.

Shakespeare creates a similar union of contradictory emotions at the moment in which Lady Macbeth takes over from her husband the role of ruthless killer:

> I have given suck, and know
> How tender 'tis to love the babe that milks me:
> I would, while it was smiling in my face,
> Have pluck'd my nipple from his boneless gums
> And dash'd the brains out, had I so sworn as you
> Have done to this. (*Macbeth* I.vii.54–59)

And yet those tenderer feelings of which she is capable—the mother's love that she had denied even more drastically in the previous scene ("Come you spirits / That tend on mortal thoughts, unsex me here / . . . Come to my woman's breasts, / And take my milk for gall, you murdering ministers," I.v.41–49)—are ultimately of the same emotional stuff as the scruples that kept her from killing Duncan herself: "Had he not resembled / My father as he slept, I had done it" (II.ii.14–15). They return in another, darker form and on other nights to cause her death. Her choice of evil over good took the form, one could say, of blood over milk (Orestes has a similar choice in the

5. Helen Gardner, *Religion and Literature* (New York 1971) 85.

Choephoroe); but cutting out that essential part of her nature has its price, and the blood, quite literally, returns to haunt her:

> Yet who would have thought the old man to have had so much blood in him. . . . Here's the smell of the blood still: all the perfumes of Arabia will not sweeten this little hand. (V.i.42–44, 55–57)

The external success of a Medea or a Lady Macbeth, or an Electra or a Clytaemnestra, stands in the sharpest contrast with the internal defeat. Tragedy is here like philosophy in that it tries to strip away the externals and arrive at the essentials in our understanding of what constitutes goodness or happiness. What is the bottom line in pronouncing a man good or evil, a life happy or unhappy?

The task facing Socrates in Plato's *Republic* is not so very different: to answer Thrasymachus' challenge that the true test of the just man comes when he seems to be unjust, when he cannot even enjoy the *reputation* for justice in the eyes of his fellow men. Something similar happens in tragedy. Strip away from Antigone all those human ties which are the center of her life, isolate her from the bonds of love, affection, family devotion—all implied in the key word *philia*—and what is left of the essential Antigone? Strip away from Oedipus all the achievements of his life, all the defining and ennobling terms of his personal identity as king, husband, and father, and what is left? A man who can still say that he chose the punishment that he now shows to all, that he alone is able to bear these sufferings. And so for Euripides' Heracles, or Sophocles' Ajax and Philoctetes, or Shakespeare's Lear.

If the plays stirred only the corporeal dimension of immediate sympathy, Aristotle's pathēmata of pity and fear, they would perhaps resemble the Icelandic sagas—powerful, gripping, full of raw animal energy, sharp and jagged with hurt. But they would be limited in their range. One of Greek tragedy's strengths is the coexistence of the physicality with the intellectual questioning. In the *Bacchae,* for instance, the bloody dismembering of human and animal bodies described (and in part shown) is interwoven with Teiresias' rationalistic interpretation of Dionysus, the mystical choruses of the beginning, the recurrent concern with the meaning of "wisdom" and the relation between "nature" and "convention."

In most of Greek tragedy the strong emotional reactions produced

by the events are always pulled into the orbit of moral questioning
and raised to a level of poetical and sometimes philosophical refor-
mulation by the choral odes or by the reflections of the characters
either in soliloquies or in debate scenes. In Euripides we may recall
Hecuba's interpretation of Zeus as divine necessity, Theonoe's the-
orizing about the intellectual soul that survives after the death of the
body, or Clytaemnestra's belief that she incarnates the avenging spirit
or alastor of the house of Atreus. The stage of Aeschylus opens upon
the whole universe, and the first scene of the *Agamemnon,* for example, invites us to be spectators of the assembly of stars in the heavens;
the stage of an Ibsen or an O'Neill, by contrast, tends to open inwardly to the dark secrets of the individual heart. André Gide, in his
ironical version of the Oedipus story, has his Eteocles say that the old
monsters are dead; creatures like the Sphinx have all been killed by
our fathers, and now the monsters live only within our souls. In
Greek tragedy the impulses to personal vengeance, lust, ambition,
self-destructive egotism, and pride are counterbalanced by corresponding impulses to order, patterns of justice, meaning, and
coherence.

III

To take but one example of how Greek tragedy combines the
simplicity and directness of the physical with the poetic and mythic
evocations of its language, consider these lines of Cassandra spoken,
or rather sung, shortly before she enters the palace of Agamemnon to
be slaughtered next to her lord and captor (1146–49):

> ἰὼ ἰὼ λιγείας βίος ἀηδόνος·
> περέβαλον γάρ οἱ πτερόφορον δέμας
> θεοὶ γλυκύν τ' αἰῶνα κλαυμάτων ἄτερ·
> ἐμοὶ δὲ μίμνει σχισμὸς ἀμφήκει δορί.

Io, io for the life of the clear-singing nightingale; For around it the gods
have cast A body feather-borne And a sweet life, Without the cries of
woe. But for me there lies in wait The slash with sword of double edge.

The lines contrast the bird's song and the shrieks of murder soon to
follow, the flight of the winged creature and the prisoner's en-

trapment. But what adds special power to the passage is the simple lyricism of the second line, with its symmetrical sound pattern in πεϱέβαλον . . . πτεϱόφοϱον. The body of the frail bird is "covered," has something soft and buoyant "cast around" it, whereas the girl's soft body, there in Troy because of its tender beauty in love, will be "split" by a sharp weapon. I would not want to give the lines an importance out of proportion to their place in the action as a whole, but this vulnerable girl's longing for the "protection of feathers" that the gods have "thrown around" the bird of songful grief depicts the essence of Cassandra's tragic situation: her knowledge, her songlike prophetic power, and her nakedness when her god has withdrawn his protection.

It is not just that Aeschylus makes us feel the sensation of the slashing axe on the delicate body but also that the poetic imagery helps us view this wrenching physical violation against a large, ever-widening background of time and space: the gods' protection of the weak; the myths of the nightingale Procne-Itys and Tereus with its bloody killing and sexual violation within the family; and the questioning of world order ("the gods") that can permit or contain such violence. This passage is hauntingly suited to the brief but powerful appearance onstage of another innocent victim of the violence that spreads out from Atreus to Troy and back to Mycenae; but in its imagery of the animal world, of cutting, shouting, and singing, and of the loss of the "sweet life," it also points ahead to the death of Agamemnon, to Orestes' necessity to turn against the origin of his life, and to the eventual emergence of legal debate, holy persuasion, and at the end the celebratory ritual chant of joy from the death cries of the victims.

The physical violation of the body—cutting, chopping, piercing, dismembering, cooking, eating—is essential to the meaning of the *Oresteia*, but Aeschylus handles it with a poetic concentration and selection of detail which rivals Shakespeare. He refrains from elaborating the physical details of Iphigeneia's sacrifice, for example, but early in the trilogy he gives us another bloody event that stands in its place and widens its meaning, namely the omen of the twin eagles that symbolize the Atreid kings, Agamemnon and Menelaus (119f.):

βοσκομένω λαγίναν ἐρικύμονα φέρματι γένναν,
βλάψαντε λοισθίων δρόμων.

feeding on the birth of the hare that swells with her teeming burden, damaging her [it] in the last of her courses.

The dense style conveys an allusive picture of the pregnant animal, heavy with its young, trying unsuccessfully to escape the eagles. The phrase "in the last of her courses" can refer both to the grim end of her race with the predatory birds and to the nearness of birth—both courses that will remain unfinished. Aeschylus uses the same kind of allusive, metaphorical and symbolic style in describing the murder of Thyestes' children: the imagery of perverted sacrifice, hunting, and the butchery of meat is a powerful objective correlative for the physical horror of the torn and broken bodies.

Euripides pushes these physical details to their furthest, most explicit point. I have already mentioned Medea and her children's bodies. One can add, for example, the somatic response of Phaedra to the νόσος of her love sickness at the beginning of the *Hippolytus,* the contrast between Astyanax's shattered skull and the carefully cut lock of his hair set aside by his parents in the *Trojan Women* (1173–77), and of course the mangling of Pentheus in the *Bacchae.*

Orestes' killing of his mother, Clytaemnestra, is perhaps the most somatically powerful of all events on the ancient stage, and we have versions of the scene in all three dramatists. Euripides, as one would expect, focuses most sharply on the bodily aspect of the suffering. Yet Aeschylus, famous for his effects of ἔκπληξις, knocking you out of your senses (or your seat) by his theatrical effects, in his own way outdoes Euripides: he is the only surviving dramatist to have the matricide enacted onstage. His emphasis, however, is not so much on the details of the killing as on the principle of maternity as embodied in the physical realities of birth and nurture. This emphasis is in keeping with his tendency to displace the force of powerful physical detail from literal to symbolic meaning, to use it in the service of the larger order that the action implicates.

His Clytaemnestra is the only one of the three not to ask Orestes for pity. (It is unfortunate that the widely used Chicago translation by Richmond Lattimore mistranslates "revere this breast" as "pity this breast").[6] I quote *Choephoroe* 896–99:

6. Aeschylus probably had in mind the scene in *Il.* 22 in which Hecuba, baring her breast to Hector, asks for *both* "reverence" and "pity" (τάδε τ᾽ αἴδεο καί μ᾽ ἐλέησον,

—ἐπίσχες, ὦ παῖ, τόνδε δ' αἴδεσαι, τέκνον,
μαστόν, πρὸς ᾧ σὺ πολλὰ δὴ βρίζων ἅμα
οὔλοισιν ἐξήμελξας εὐτραφὲς γάλα.
—Πυλάδη, τί δράσω; μητέρ' αἰδεσθῶ κτανεῖν;

Clytaemnestra.	Hold off, my son, and show reverence, my child, for this breast, the breast at which you often dozed while you milked out with your gums the good-nurturing milk.
Orestes.	Pylades, what shall I do? Do I refrain in reverence from killing a mother?

In asking for reverence rather than pity, Clytaemnestra makes the breast and the milk symbols of a suprapersonal female principle in conflict with the male. At the same time, the specific details of the baby nursing at the breast and drawing milk with its gums (897f.) present the claims of motherhood as something more than a pallid abstraction. Aeschylus' physical details make us feel the physical and emotional reality of those ties which Orestes is now setting aside in favor of the male parent. The kernel of the *Oresteia's* tragic conflict is present in these graphic details: the contrast between the immediate, physical claims of the mother's birth and nurture and the more abstract, legalistic demands of paternity and of the kind of law and justice sponsored by the patriarchal Olympian and Athenian order.

In Aeschylus the physical meaning of the breast as nurture extends to the deepest emotional levels of the conflicts within the family. Clytaemnestra's display of the breast to Orestes builds upon earlier inversions or negations of the life-sustaining functions of the house. It reaches back to the enigma of the "breast-loving lion cub" nurtured "milkless" in the Trojan (but by implication also the Atreid) house: ἔθρεψεν δὲ λέοντος ἶνιν/δόμοις ἀγάλακτον . . . φιλόμαστον (*Ag.* 717ff.) and on to Clytaemnestra's terrifying dream of the serpent drawing blood from her breast in the *Choephoroe* (523ff.) and the

---

22.82). By late Euripides, the winning of "pity" (*eleos*) by showing the breast has become almost a stock motif. Orestes, defending himself against condemnation for matricide, generalizes from Clytaemnestra to all women and lists among their enormities that they "kill their husbands, taking refuge to their children, hunting for pity with their breasts" (μαστοῖς τὸν ἔλεον θηρώμεναι, 566–68).

Nurse's grief, in the episode before the matricide, at losing the child she once "nursed" (750, 754) and tended (748ff.). In the first case the mother's nocturnal fears in a sense come true, for the basic maternal bond of the breast proves unable to stay the son's murderous thrust that figuratively transforms the place of milk and tender care to the place of blood and wound. The Nurse's lament at the loss of one whom she "nurtured, receiving from his mother" (*Cho.* 750) does not prove that Clytaemnestra never gave Orestes the breast,[7] but it does remind us again of the mother's rejection of the child she bore and of the destruction of the closest bonds of blood in this family.

Sophocles plays down such physical details in favor of somewhat more distanced, less disturbing, less biologically immediate symbols of the bond between parents and children. He uses the cultural symbol of the burial urn, and he devises a brilliant stroke of pathos in having Orestes execute his mother as she is decking out his burial urn for the funerary ritual. But the urn has just been the primary mechanism by which Orestes has surrendered his plot to the irresistible force of the emotions inspired by seeing Electra's grief. When he reentered with the urn (following the plot he described in the prologue, 53ff.) to gain entrance to the palace, he met Electra; and he is unable to practice the deception on his sister as she laments over the supposed ashes of her brother. He breaks down and tells her the truth, even though it endangers the plot. But the plotter's surrender of his ruse to tender emotions in the case of the sister will not be repeated in the case of the mother. There the urn performs the purpose for which it was intended.

This matricide is not acted out on the stage, as in Aeschylus, but is reported to us by Electra, who has posted herself at the doorway of the palace. Thus we view the scene through the eyes of the embittered daughter who is also the central figure of Sophocles' play. When we hear Clytaemnestra's offstage cry, "My child, my child, pity the mother who bore you" (ὦ τέκνον τέκνον, / οἴκτιρε τὴν τεκοῦσαν, 1410f.), it is Electra, on the stage, who responds: "But he got no pity from you, nor did the father who sired him." Instead of the Aeschylean details of the breast or the milk, Sophocles empha-

---

7. So, for example, George Devereux, *Dreams in Greek Tragedy* (Berkeley and Los Angeles 1976) 183ff.; see *contra* Philip Vellacott, "Aeschylus' Orestes," *CW* 77 (1983–84) 154f.

sizes the complex relationship between this mother and daughter, here condensed brilliantly into a few vivid lines.

The detail of Clytaemnestra's ritual care of her son's supposed burial urn at the moment of his attack enriches the depth of her emotional life. It also throws another light on her ambivalence about Orestes' death when this was first announced (δεινὸν τὸ τίκτειν ἐστίν, "Terrible it is to give birth," 766ff.).

By introducing a long separation between Aegisthus' death and Clytaemnestra's, Euripides, in his *Electra,* sharpens the horror of the matricide: with Aegisthus dead, it appears as somewhat less necessary, particularly in the light of the weak character that he attributes to the queen. Orestes' gory invitation to Electra to impale the body of the slain Aegisthus (898f.) prepares us for the worst (compare the chopping off of a hand early in Fellini's *Satiricon*). His failure of nerve as the moment of the matricide approaches draws out our expectation of something horrible (963ff.). Now the motif of "pitying the mother who gave you birth" is not a last-ditch attempt of the mother who is trying to save her life. Rather, it is part of the son's premeditative reflection while Clytaemnestra is still in the distance (963ff.). Euripides closely follows the language of the Aeschylean scene (cf. *El.* 967 and *Cho.* 900f.) but refocuses its meaning. Instead of reverence for maternity, he explores the psychology of doubt, hesitation, and guilt in a forward-looking anticipation of the event. The long debate scene between mother and daughter then takes our attention away from Orestes' dilemma for some one hundred and fifty lines (*El.* 998–1146). We the spectators think that perhaps we may be spared the ultimate horror; and Euripides, in fact, for the moment mutes both the enactment and the report of the matricide.

But suddenly the choral song is shattered by Clytaemnestra's off-stage cry, "Children, in the gods' name, do not kill your mother" (ὦ τέκνα, πρὸς θεῶν, μὴ κτάνητε μητέρα, 1165). Her death cry, ἰώ μοί, μοι, follows almost at once. No cry for reverence or pity is here, only the bare address to children and the plea not to kill a mother.

The chorus pronounces the familiar claim of *dikē,* retributive justice (1169–71). These lines, through the familiar technique of rounding off a scene with gnomic moralizing, could have constituted a formal closure for the episode. Is Euripides, then, going to reduce the Aeschylean horror and the Sophoclean pathos to this single intense but austere moment? Will he outdo even Sophocles in restraint, con-

densing a thirteen-line scene into three verses (Soph. *El.* 1404–16 and
Eur. *El.* 1165–67)? As the doors of Electra's cottage open (probably
with the use of the eccyclema) to reveal the body, we realize that we
are not in fact going to get off so easily.

Orestes and Electra, standing over their mother's corpse, now
describe the bloody pollution they feel around them. Not only are we
far from the Sophoclean Orestes' cry of triumph (however ambiguous: Soph., *El.* 1424f.); we also experience the murder retrospectively
through the postmortem shock of the killers. Euripides has by no
means forgotten the Aeschylean effect of showing the breast, but he
uses the motif no longer as a stage gesture by Clytaemnestra (however managed by a male actor)[8] but as an indelible memory of the son
(1206–10):

> κατεῖδες, οἷον ἁ τάλαιν' ἔξω πέπλων
> ἔβαλεν, ἔδειξεν μαστὸν ἐν φοναῖσιν,
> ἰώ μοι, πρὸς πέδῳ
> τιθεῖσα γόνιμα μέλεα; τὰν κόμαν δ' ἐγὼ . . .

Did you see how she, miserable, from her robes put forth, showed
forth the breast in the midst of the slaughter—alas for me—on the
ground casting down the limbs that gave birth? And her hair I . . .

His added details, "the limbs that gave birth" and (if the text is right)
the hair, make us envision the scene of the killing through the eyes of
the son. Clytaemnestra's offstage cry for mercy earlier is close to the
Sophoclean treatment (cf. 1165 and Soph. *El.* 1410ff.). But Euripides
adds a new twist: it is the son who reports that cry, just as he was the
one to report her gesture of displaying the breast (βοὰν δ' ἔλασκε
τάνδε, 1214). To her verbal plea he adds the suppliant gesture: how
she put her hand on his beard and clung to his face (1214–17):

> πρὸς γένυν ἐμὰν
> τιθεῖσα χεῖρα· Τέκος ἐμόν, λιταίνω·
> παρήδων τ' ἐξ ἐμᾶν
> ἐκρίμναθ', ὥστε χέρας ἐμὰς λιπεῖν βέλος.

8. See Oliver Taplin, *Greek Tragedy in Action* (Berkeley and Los Angeles 1978) 61.

She shouted out this cry, putting her hand to my cheek: "I entreat you, my child!" And she hung from my cheeks so that my hands left the weapon.

These traditional gestures of the suppliant gain a new quality of pathetic tenderness because they are also the gestures of a mother touching the face of her son. And it is the son whose words convey to us the desperation of his mother. Orestes then tells how he covered his eyes with his cloak as he plunged the sword into his mother's throat. Electra adds that she urged him on, grasping his sword too (1221–26):

> Ορ. ἐγὼ μὲν ἐπιβαλὼν φάρη κόραις ἐμαῖς
> φασγάνῳ κατηρξάμην
> ματέρος ἔσω δέρας μεθείς.
> Ηλ. ἐγὼ δ' ἐπεγκέλευσά σοι
> ξίφους τ' ἐφηψάμαν ἅμα.
> Χο. δεινότατον παθέων ἔρεξας.

Orestes.   I raised my cloak before my eyes and with the sword made the sacrificial stroke, letting it within my mother's throat.
Electra.   And I urged you on and grasped hold of the sword along with you.
Chorus.   Most terrible the deeds of suffering that you have done.

The direct, brutal words "letting the sword go inside the mother's throat" (ματέρος ἔσω δέρας μεθείς, 1223) stands out in almost macabre contrast with the tenderness of Clytaemnestra's suppliant touch eight lines before (1216f.). The fact that Orestes is the one to describe both her touch and his murderous stroke focuses our attention on the emotional implications of the situation, Orestes' overpowering disgust and remorse as he holds together, in a single moment and in a single picture, this fearful contrast. The matricides linger on the scene a moment longer—before the arrival of the Dioscuri brings relief—covering the body. Here too Orestes again combines birth and killing: "You gave birth to killers for yourself" (φονέας ἔτικτες ἀρά σοι, 1229).

Sophocles hurries us from the scene of the matricide by the urgency of confronting and defeating Aegisthus. Aeschylus leads us into the next play, with its supernatural and suprapersonal dimensions of

the struggle, by introducing the Furies and with them the coun-
terclaims of the Justice between mother and father, the latter now
embodied in the commands of Apollo (*Cho.* 1021–39, 1055–64).

In place of Aeschylus' Erinyes, however, Euripides puts his deus ex
machina, the Dioscuri. Although they tie up some of the loose ends,
as the narrower compass of the single play requires, they render
Apollo's absolution ambiguous (cf. 1245–48). They further undercut
the Aeschylean resolution by transferring the founding of the court of
the Areopagus from Orestes' matricide to a remoter mythical event,
Ares' killing of Halirrhothius (1258–63). Euripides thus retains the
external frame of the Aeschylean events but completely transforms
their spirit. Remorse, horror, and an atmosphere of internal doubt,
guilt, self-pollution, and self-disgust replace Aeschylus' mood (ambiguous though it may be) of triumph, resolution, and cosmic justice.

To achieve this transformation, Euripides needed to change only a
few small details, notably the way in which the physical facts about
the matricide, about the body of Clytaemnestra, are reported. But as
we have seen, these small details are of so emotional a nature that
even a small alteration and a few words can produce the most devas-
tating effect.

Do such passages purify us of pity and fear? Do they, rather, as
Plato says, feed the irrational part of our souls? I am not going to
provide an answer but rather suggest that we think about the
Aeschylean Clytaemnestra claiming the reverence due to her breast
and her mother's milk, about the Sophoclean Clytaemnestra adorning her son's burial urn when he charges in with his sword at the
ready, and about the Euripidean Orestes describing his mother's suppliant touch on his face and the push of his sword into her throat.
There is something in the experience of the tragic moment which
defies description and analysis.

IV

I want to raise one final question as a consequence of what I have
been saying. This too is an old and famous question about tragedy. Is
it possible to speak, other than colloquially, of tragedy apart from the
literary form? Is there such a thing as "the tragic," or "a tragic sense
of life," or "a tragic conception of experience?" Our sense of the

tragic in life is probably molded by the literary form. Tragedy, that is, helps us to unify a mental and emotional field in which random acts of suffering fall into a pattern that creates in us an overpowering need to ask *Why?* and opens the way toward a probing of final meanings and ultimate questions.

One could certainly argue that there is something like a "tragic shape" to the human condition in this post-Orwellian year as we see before us every day the paradox that humankind, thanks to its intellectual capacity, has within reach the eradication of hunger, disease, poverty, and a good deal of material suffering and that humankind, thanks to its intellectual capacity, is also increasing rather diminishing the sum, real or potential, of violence, cruelty, and suffering on this planet. If the tragic involves a sense of the waste of greatness, whether of soul or body or both, a feeling of human helplessness in the face of the irrational, and the presence of evil working ineradicably beside the good as the lot of man or (if you wish) as part of the world order—then it is hard *not* to describe the situation of humanity today as tragic. We lack only someone to unfold this situation before us with the authority, intensity, and compelling intellectual and artistic coherence of (say) Thucydides' account of the disintegration of the brilliant Periclean age.

To close with a reply to Plato, we may ask whether the expulsion of the tragic poets from the *ideal* city only means that in the *real* city, tragic poetry is an absolute necessity. Human life itself, so far as our past can tell us, has a potentially tragic character, and it is the tragic poets who prevent us from forgetting this.

CHAPTER 12

Literature and Interpretation:
Conventions, History, and Universals

I

There are probably more people studying and (alas) writing about literature today than in the last five hundred years of Western history. Even for the modern literatures the volume of writings about literature far exceeds the corpus of the literature itself. This is a situation that the scholar working on Homer, Sophocles, Virgil, or Shakespeare has come to live with (in however uncomfortable a way), but it is a situation dismaying to students of Henry James or Proust or Joyce or even T. S. Eliot—authors whose books are scarcely decently cold and lack the moldy look of the texts we classicists poke around in.

As critics and teachers of literature, we swim in baffling currents and cross-currents of approaches, with their conflicting sources in ethics, epistemology, psychology, linguistics, political theory, anthropology, and so on. There is not one but several New Criticisms, to say nothing of the old New Criticism. The warring parties do not just exchange salvos between New Haven and Chicago, as in the good old days of the fifties, they have to deal with intercontinental missiles from Paris, Geneva, Constance, and even Tartu. The very boundaries of literature are being constantly redefined as the question of what constitutes a literary text becomes more acute. As literary study, in the wake of structuralism, has become more concerned with

This essay is based on a public lecture at Oberlin College, March 12, 1984. I thank my hosts, Nelson de Jesus, Nathan Greenberg, James Helm, and Thomas Van Nortwick for their hospitality, encouragement, and comments.

the problems of how discourse contructs meaning, it embraces a larger range of possible texts, from formal history and philosophy (always a sort of boundary area for literary criticism) to documents, letters, the writings of Freud (a favorite topic these days), or even literary criticism itself.

Literary study today is consequently less definitely literary than at any time in the past. It is extraordinarily hospitable to a wide range of extraliterary influences. Indeed, these are perhaps the most powerful determinants of current critical directions; for example, the Marxist and feminist approaches that call attention to the hidden ideological intent of works of art alongside the older and more established extraliterary movements, the anthropological or psychoanalytic.

Criticism, then, becomes necessarily hermeneutic, that is, it has to take account of the fact that there are different modes of reconstituting an apparently singular object. When a work is acknowledged to have a range of possibly divergent readings, in what sense can it be said to exist? What kinds of operations are valid for arriving at such readings? What kind of "truth" do these readings have, and indeed what kind of truth does the work itself have?

These are the problems that force themselves upon the scholar and teacher of literature, for, unlike the unsystematic reader, the critic is in the somewhat ambiguous position of treating an object of aesthetic experience as an object of knowledge. As a result, he or she has the unenviable task of relating this problematical object of knowledge to a problematical discipline and, whether liking it or not, has to confront the task of interpretation as itself a problem. Instead of the simple model of reader confronting work, he or she is aware of all the intermediary processes, processes that not only determine the nature of the critical activity but even to some extent determine the nature of the work itself. The literary critic lives, as we all do, in the post-Heisenberg era, knowing that the observation of a given phenomenon changes that phenomenon.

Those trained in the classical tradition probably find it congenial to view works of art as opening upon the external world rather than upon themselves. For this orientation the most powerful statement is still Longinus' famous comment on sublimity in literature (35.2):

What then was the vision which inspired those divine writers who disdained exactness of detail and aimed at the greatest prizes in literature? Above all else, it was the understanding that nature made man to be no humble or lowly creature, but brought him into life and into the universe as into a great festival, to be both a spectator and an enthusiastic contestant in its competitions. . . . The universe is not wide enough for the range of human speculation and intellect. Our thoughts often travel beyond the boundaries of our surroundings. If anyone wants to know what we were born for, let him look round at life and contemplate the splendor, grandeur, and beauty in which it everywhere abounds.[1]

Instead of this outwardly directed, ennobling contemplation of boundless horizons, the modern gaze is more inward, sees around the object, views both the inside and the outside simultaneously in a perspective that is steadily conscious of the aesthetic dimension, acutely aware of the viewer's eye and indeed of the eyes of a succession of viewers seeing the beloved object from multiple angles. With Longinus' magnificent vision to the limits of the universe, we may perhaps contrast Proust's Swann as he sits in Odette's apartment, enjoys the roseate glow of the lamps that she has placed before him in the winter twilight, and thinks of the view from outside, through the eyes of "some solitary lover wandering in the street below."[2] It is as if in the very moment in which it is being lived, the private, interior scene is self-consciously constructed as an aesthetic object with both an objective and a subjective dimension, a piece of rich artifice that can be seen and enjoyed from different perspectives of space (as here) or time (as often in the novel).

T. S. Eliot, writing about the difficulty of "trying to learn to use words," calls the effort "a raid on the inarticulate / With shabby equipment always deteriorating / In the general mess of imprecision of feeling, / Undisciplined squads of emotion" (East Coker, V). We still face the problem of imprecise feeling, but the critic's difficulty with words today is the opposite of Eliot's: not "deteriorating equipment" but an excess of fancy gadgets, a plethora of high-tech screens and buttons, and we are not always sure which ones to push, whether we should push them all, one only, or none.

1. Translation from D. A. Russell and M. Winterbottom, eds., *Ancient Literary Criticism* (Oxford 1972) 494.
2. M. Proust, *Remembrance of Things Past,* trans. M. K. Scott Moncrieff and T. Kilmartin (New York 1982) 1.241.

It is, then, natural to feel sympathy for a solution like that of Susan Sontag in the title essay of her *Against Interpretation:* cut the Gordian knot and simply reject interpretation as strangling literature. It would certainly uncomplicate our lives if we could go back to the texts and read them as if they, and we, existed in a total intellectual vacuum. The problem is that neither they nor we do so exist, and we have to take the texts with the problems of interpretation that they bring.

II

The appreciation of literature is both a moral *and* an aesthetic appreciation. The difficulty lies in the copula. One cannot detach the moral considerations inherent in meaning (that is, the questions about the ends and quality of life, the nature of human relationships, both personal and social, the questions of values and conduct, conflicts, emotions, crises of identity, and so on) from the experience of the language. This is among the most platitudinous truisms of literary study ("The medium is the message," in its most reduced form); and yet this relation between the content and the form of the discourse, between the signified and the signifier, is what makes criticism interesting, controversial, and problematical. In our current, poststructuralist interest in the signifier-signified nexus, we risk losing sight of the signified.

A recent issue of *New Literary History* proposes as its theme "Literature and/as Moral Philosophy."[3] One of the major texts discussed is Henry James's *The Golden Bowl.* One would hardly consider James a moralist, and yet his work is deeply moral: its endlessly and finely discriminating details are held in place by the moral seriousness of the central theme, the balance between our desire for perfection and integrity and the deceptions, concealments, and compromises that our complex emotional lives create and also can tolerate. This imperfection, of course, is among other things what the flaw in the Golden Bowl symbolizes.

Martha Nussbaum, in a valuable essay on the moral issues in *The Golden Bowl,* squarely faces the problem of the moral uses of literary works and asks: "Why, it may still be asked, do we need a text like

3. *New Literary History* 15, no. 1 (Autumn 1983).

this one for our work on these issues?"[4] Why, in other words, do we bother with a text that takes such a long, oblique, and indirect route to get to its admittedly important questions about honesty and dishonesty in personal relations? Nussbaum's answer, with which I agree, is that "this task cannot be accomplished by texts which speak in universal terms" or "with the hardness or plainness which moral philosophy has traditionally chosen for its style." Imaginative literature has a flexibility, a suppleness, a freedom to delve into the minute particulars of which so much of lived life is composed. Thus it enables us to enter the moral realm as an area of concrete emotional experience in ways that the more abstract language of philosophy or psychology would not permit.

If the reading of an author like Henry James shows us anything, it is that the moral experience of the work is mysteriously and inextricably fused with the experience of the style and the language: the puzzling and sometimes infuriating ellipses, the crucial nuances in phrases that seem to make a minimal statement but prove to be vital for the situation, the little pauses when a character at such a critical moment "hangs fire."

Like all great artists, James disciplines us to the demands of his language; and this disciplined following of meaning as it unfolds in a particular style, with a particular tempo, is one of the most important things that professors of literature have to teach their students to do. Good reading is a matter of paying attention, of observing the effects of adding one detail to another and of watching how the new details build on, qualify, refine, elaborate, or contradict what has gone before. The bold metaphors of Aeschylus, parodied in the first sustained piece of literary criticism in Western literature, or the hyperboles of Elizabethan drama, or the interminable convolutions in the sentences of Proust, these are not just a set of inconvenient obstacles to finding out what is going on: they are the substance of the work.

The strenuous participation in the verbal universe of the literary work, then, gives us an experiential grasp of an otherness that we assimilate as part of ourselves as we discover, recreate, and interpret in the act of reading. Georges Poulet tries to get at this paradoxical

4. Martha Nussbaum, "Flawed Crystals: James's *The Golden Bowl* and Literature as Moral Philolosophy," *New Literary History* 15, no. 1 (1983) 25–50. This quotation is from p. 39, the following quotation from p. 43.

combination of self-identification and self-alienation, the processes of assimilation and estrangement that go on in the responsive reading of literature, quoting Rimbaud's line, "Je est un autre."[5]

Poulet's work shows us how hard it is to define the mode of "knowledge" constituted by this experience. This is a form of knowledge different from the nuggets of factual information that a historical novel like Flaubert's *Salammbô* or George Eliot's *Romola* may contain. It is closely connected to the experience of rhythm and sound as well as sense. The ancient critics insist on the importance of individual syllables, clusters of consonants, sequences of vowels. In considering a passage of Demosthenes, Longinus experiments with rewriting the simile "like a cloud" in several different ways to show that the exact phrasing has a kind of inevitability and perfection to it.[6] We tolerate this microcosmic scrutiny of language for lyric poetry, rarely for other genres. But in prose too, of course, minor details of phrasing make a difference. Our view of the landscape, as it were, depends on the way in which we move over the terrain; and at times it is helpful to take a look at our feet. It makes a difference that the choral pronouncement awarding the crown of victory to the sick Philoctetes is in dactylic hexameters, the meter of epic and of oracles; or that Lady Macbeth's talk of blood changes from the pentameters in her speech of Act I to prose in her last utterances in Act V. Appreciation of the verbal texture of language is one of the most important objects of the teaching and study of literature. Nor is this merely a matter of stylistics in the narrow sense. Erich Auerbach's *Mimesis* shows how intimately language is bound up with thought, historical context, and intellectual history.

III

The emphasis on the synchronic over the diachronic dimension of the literary work during the past couple of decades—that is, the concern with structure and the process of signification rather than the historical filiations and origins—is probably one of those natural re-

5. Georges Poulet, "Criticism and the Experience of Interiority," in Jane P. Tompkins, ed., *Reader-Response Criticism* (Baltimore 1980) 45.
6. Longinus, *De Sublim.* 39.4; cf. also Aristot., *Poetics* 22.1458b20ff.

actions which take place as cultural styles and the paradigms of what constitutes knowledge shift from one phase to another.[7] But historical concerns have returned in a new way, informed by a new theoretical spirit. For example, when we study literary echoes, the imitation or quotation of one author by another, we are now likely to pose questions about source and influence less as problems of fact-finding in a positivistically conceived history than as issues that have to do with the nature of literary discourse, the universe of forms, traditions, conventions, and genres in which literature exists. The writer is not, like a Cynic philosopher, a naked wanderer who lives out of a barrel. He has his own intellectual capital, though this is not always fully evident or acknowledged.

Thanks to the work of Hans Robert Jauss and Wolfgang Iser and the *Rezeptionsästhetik* school, we are also more aware now that the reader too does not exist in a vacuum. The reader too is at the end of a long process of evolving tastes and judgments, as the canon of "classics" in any given period changes and the active genres expand, contract, or change boundaries. Jauss and his school are concerned to recognize the historical dimension of the aesthetic category. The development of a given genre at a particular time is not just a matter of the chronological priority of texts that were always there but also a function of what can be perceived and understood in a text as aesthetic horizons or expectations expand, contract, or alter direction. Why, for example, should Senecan tragedy have been rated so high in the Renaissance and so low in the nineteenth century, and why the recent interest in it? Why are Hesiod's *Theogony,* Euripides' later tragedies, Ovid's *Metamorphoses,* and the Greek Novel saying more to us now than to our predecessors of a century ago?

The concern with the place of the literary work in a long sequence of both literary production and literary consumption is a necessary corrective to the total isolation of the work from the historical process. At the same time, the hermeneutic emphasis on understanding how and why different works are judged differently at different times poses the question of changing tastes as a problem that can be approached with some degree of analytical rigor.[8] We neither have to

7. For the problem of classicists' resistance to such paradigm shifts in their discipline, see John Peradotto, "Texts and Unrefracted Facts: Philology, Hermeneutics and Semiotics," *Arethusa* 16 (1983) 15–33, especially 22ff.

8. See, for instance, Hans Robert Jauss, *Toward an Aesthetic of Reception,* trans. T.

hide such questions away in the closet nor see in them the bugbear of a relativistic subjectivism that condemns literary study as a matter of private indulgences and non-negotiable likes and dislikes.

For a variety of reasons, we have in the recent past come to a fresh awareness of the implicit value systems in the determination of literary values and literary canons. The revaluation of aesthetic categories and value judgments also brings a shift in the canon of accessible authors—something that makes some classicists uncomfortable. But in classical studies, as in other areas of literature, there are great rewards to be gained by sacrificing an absolutizing and idealizing aesthetic to a critical attitude that takes account of the contexts of production and considers the formation of literary conventions and the different needs that literary works satisfy both for their own time and for the times that preserve or enthrone them as classics.

Interpretation has to confront the ideologies masked by some of the greatest literary works—the patriarchal bias of Aeschylus' *Oresteia,* for example, or the aristocratic consciousness of property and inherited excellence in Pindar's Victory Odes. It has to consider too why some ideologies more than others are visible to us, or bother us, or interest us. If we have to acknowledge areas of narrowness and culture-bound ideology in Aeschylus or Plato or Virgil, we may discover other literary values that we have neglected. The gain in breadth of view and critical perspective which comes with freeing ourselves from a posture of defensive hostility to new movements and cultural change more than compensates for the recognition of flaws, limitations, and biases in our favored texts.

The reactions and counterreactions between historicist and universalizing or a-temporal approaches are probably a healthy situation, since every work of art exists both in its own well defined historical context and also, in a sense, out of time, as an artifact that can speak to men and women across the boundaries of specific historical moments. Certain forms seem to have a remarkable tenacity across the millennia. James Bond is a reincarnation of a very hoary type, fighting dragons and monsters that have vanquished all previous contestants, descending to underworld places, mixing war and love, and enjoying or combatting in turn helpful and sinister wizards, kindly

Bahti (Minneapolis 1982), especially "Literary History as a Challenge to Literary Theory," 3–45.

and deadly witches. Superman is a close cousin to Theseus, Perseus, Heracles, and others: he is raised by surrogate parents after mysterious separation from a quasi-divine realm of remote, godlike parents; he goes on a quest to a distant land to discover his real father, which he does through a token, weapon, or magical instrument; and he fights heroic battles against evil monsters to rid the world of disorder, and so on. Northrop Frye has accumulated long lists of generic continuities in romance and in other narrative forms that have strong mythic components.[9]

One side-benefit of taking a long view of continuities in literary forms is the realization that certain features of, say, narrative which we accept as a given are conventions that other periods may value less highly. As Alastair Fowler points out in an important article on literary canons, there are relatively few "active genres" at any one time; and the place of the novel's mimetic realism at the top of the generic hierarchy is a recent phenomenon in literary history.[10]

In Book 10 of the *Odyssey* Homer takes pains to show his hero's difficulty in carrying back to his men at the shore a deer that he has managed to shoot. But Virgil in *Aeneid* 1 can have his hero transport no less than seven deer from woods to shore. The beasts are no less heavy, and Aeneas is presumably not in that much better shape than Odysseus.[11] Commentators suggest various literalistic solutions.[12] We can perhaps better grasp the modification of Homer as due to a difference in the horizon of expectation that he and the norms of post-Hellenistic literature shape for his reader.[13] He uses a literary texture that does not necessarily give realism first place.

Genres themselves are not absolutes: they too change and evolve, and they have different definitions and demands at different times.

9. Northrop Frye, *The Secular Scripture: A Study of Romance* (Cambridge, Mass. 1976).

10. Alastair Fowler, "Genre and the Literary Canon," *New Literary History* 11 (1979) 97–119, especially 109f. *Critical Inquiry* 10, no. 1 (September 1983) is devoted to literary canons.

11. Homer, *Od.* 10.164ff.; Verg., *Aen.* 1.192ff.

12. See the note of John Conington *The Works of Virgil with a Commentary*, revised by Henry Nettleship, vol. 2 (London 1884) on *Aen.* 1.194, citing Forbiger. My remarks here owe much to the sensitive analysis of W. R. Johnson, *Darkness Visible* (Berkeley and Los Angeles 1976) 32ff.

13. The difference between the explicitness and continuity of oral style and the greater density and obliquity of written poetry obviously plays a role here.

They are not closed boxes or ideal forms but groupings based on "shared assumptions" between writer and audience, assumptions that have to do with a mental organization of reality deeply rooted in an entire culture.[14] For the Graeco-Roman literary world, for example, which is highly sensitive to formal classifications of meter and diction, pastoral poetry is a subspecies of epic.[15] Thus Theocritean pastoral at every point leans on Homeric diction and exploits the discrepancy between the heroic and the everyday, between the aristocratic warriors about whom much of this language was used and the lowly herdsmen who are, after all, slaves.[16] Virgilian pastoral exploits the discrepancy between the literariness of its Hellenistic model and the contemporary crisis of Rome. The generic leveling of pastoral, however, particularly through the influence of the sixteenth- and seventeenth-century norms, led to neglecting the political and historical dimension of Virgil's *Eclogues*—the confiscations and civil wars in the background of several of the poems—and to viewing their essential quality as a dreamy unreality, a golden haze of wistful contemplation, as in a Poussin or Claude Lorrain.

To take one example, the eighth seems of all the *Eclogues* perhaps the most literary and the most detached from political actualities. But any reading of the poem has to take account of the dissonance between the great "deeds" (*facta,* 8) accomplished in real places by the general addressed in the dedication (6–13) and the serenity of flocks and herdsmen in an idealized setting of magical song (1–5, 14–16). It has to take account too of the next poem's movement towards the violent urban world that disrupts the peaceful pursuits of pastoral life. In that perspective, *Eclogue* 8's wonder at song's power to suspend the movements of nature (1–5) appears as a precarious interlude. Its Orphic world is surrounded by forces that are not susceptible to the charm of shepherds' music. In such a case, generic expectations can blur what is unique and original in an author's handling of a tradi-

---

14. See Stephen Orgel, "Shakespeare and the Kinds of Drama," *Critical Inquiry* 6 (1979/80) 107–23, especially 115ff., 123. Of Renaissance drama he remarks, "Comedy and tragedy were not forms: they were shared assumptions" (123).

15. For some implications see John Van Sickle, "Theocritus and the Development of the Conception of the Bucolic Genre," *Ramus* 5 (1976) 19ff.

16. For some of these discrepancies see David Halperin, *Before Pastoral: Theocritus and the Ancient Tradition of Bucolic Poetry* (New Haven 1983) chap. 11, especially 236ff.

tional form. The label "pastoral" does not prepare us for Virgil's startling combination of Theocritus' elegant surface and the Roman concreteness of the political and historical moment.

IV

For the contemporary critic, there is no avoiding the problem of the hermeneutic circle. The problem is, as Martin Heidegger says, to come into it in the right way. Our understanding of the whole always depends on our view of the particulars, whether these are the individual lines of a text or a single work within the whole corpus of literature. And conversely, our ability to see and select the particulars—the felicitous adjective we find so powerful or the particular text we use as the basis of a revaluation of an author, a period, or a genre—will always depend on our view of the whole. Our literary evaluations have a basis in judgments, assumptions, theoretical and methodological choices, exclusions, rankings, preferences, and so on; and we need to be aware and explicit about these, both to ourselves and our students, as we go about the work of interpretation.

The deconstructive movement, from Jacques Derrida to Harold Bloom and the lamented Paul de Man, has helped to raise this critical self-awareness. It calls attention to the fact that all interpretation involves a process of supplementing the text studied and thereby producing another text in an infinite series of writings—disseminations and misreadings. Deconstruction has here a certain kinship with both Marxist and structuralist interpretation in pointing out the danger of merely replicating our own assumptions and thought processes when we think we are objectively reconstructing the text.

Here too we face the hermeneuticists' vicious circle: we can see the Other only through the lenses of ourself, through the knowledge, theories, and methodologies that we have assimilated in order to help us understand the otherness of the text. So we can no longer pretend that there is anything like a final, objective, impersonal criticism of literature. We need not, however, fall back into despairing solipsism. The problem may lie in the kind of truth we expect literature to give us and in the scientific model that we are accustomed to use as a criterion for that truth.

Transformations

Our reading of the text may indeed be a process of adding supplements from the outside; but those supplements are still brought to a definite text, and the features of the text should themselves suggest and direct us to the kind of supplements that we make. As David Hoy suggests, the deconstructive process may itself be a moment, a necessary and inevitable moment, in the hermeneutic process but not the whole of the process.[17] The process of interpretive understanding is a shifting movement between recognizing the text in its unassimilable otherness, its ultimate strangeness, and making the text in some sense our own, something to which we can assent on the basis of our experience of what the text signifies.

The fact that literary study involves personal choices and personal responses does not mean that it is totally subjective. The antithesis of "personal," as Charles Altieri points out in a 1978 essay on the question of literary indeterminacy, is not "subjective" but "impersonal."[18] That many meanings are possible for a given work does not mean that *any* meaning is possible. An interpretation still must have its grounding in a respectful accuracy about the details of the text. The absence of a transcendental signifier need not imply that there is no signified at all. Bellini, Canaletto, Turner, and this summer's tourist all have their pictures of Venice, and there are an infinite number of other such visions. But each of these, after all, still depends on an identifiable (if complex) entity many of whose features can be described with some degree of precision, objectivity, and unanimity.

The plurality of interpretations, incidentally, seems not to have tormented critics so much that in despair they stop interpreting. Stanley Fish, with a relish that some may find a bit grotesque, subtitles a chapter of a recent book, "How I Stopped Worrying and Learned to Love Interpretation."[19] To recognize the plurality of possible readings of a text is not to deny that some readings may be better than others: the "better" readings may have more insight, take

17. David C. Hoy, "Must We Say What We Mean," in S. Kresic, ed., *Contemporary Literary Hermeneutics and Interpretation of Classical Texts* (Ottawa 1981) 97.
18. Charles Altieri, "The Hermeneutics of Literary Indeterminacy," *New Literary History* 10 (1978) 71–99, especially 80f.
19. Stanley Fish, *Is There a Text in This Class?* (Cambridge, Mass. 1980) Introduction.

370

fuller account of the totality of the text and the author's *oeuvre*, range more widely over the implications, discriminate more keenly among the qualities of certain parts or certain characters, and so on.

The paradigm for teaching and criticizing literature is probably shifting from the notion of conveying "solid" nuggets of information in the tradition of a positivistic historicism to that of performing a score and teaching an art. We then have to stress, as Altieri does, the standards of competence which make for a good performance rather than the existence of objective, scientifically verifiable knowledge.

And of course a great deal of factual knowledge *is* necessary for the teaching and criticism of literature: philological knowledge, historical knowledge, knowledge of genres, conventions, formal expectations and their development in time and place. It goes without saying that the critic and teacher of literature should be continually trying to expand, enrich, and refine the bases of factual knowledge that he or she has to draw upon in interpreting a text. One can never know enough Greek to understand Aeschylus or Sophocles. The first step in any interpretation is to get the facts right; and someone has to know whether a given translation of a Greek tragedy or a Petrarcan sonnet is saying at a basic factual level what the original said.

Once these basic determinations of factual meaning are more or less satisfactorily settled (and sometimes that is not so easy, as students of early Greek literature know), we probably have to admit that we are dealing with texts rather than closed, sealed off "works"— that is, with complex structures that can be viewed in a very large number of ways, with many shifting perspectives.[20] We have to abandon a final, definitive interpretation for a process of endless interpreting. More important, we need to recognize that we are always interpreting. We perhaps need a more open definition of "the classic," and Frank Kermode seems to me to do rather well in his book of that name: the classics, he says, "possess intrinsic qualities that endure, but possess also an openness to accommodation which keeps them alive under endlessly varying dispositions."[21]

Every work of art, then, requires reinterpretation in the contempo-

20. See, for instance, Roland Barthes, "From Work to Text," in J. V. Harari, ed., *Textual Strategies* (Ithaca 1979) 73–81.
21. Frank Kermode, *The Classic* (London 1975) 44.

rary idiom and against the contemporary concerns of each generation. But each has also a meaning—or rather a complex of meanings—in its own time and place. I believe that it is both possible and necessary to determine those meanings as best we can, knowing full well that we can arrive at only an imperfect approximation. No full understanding of the *Iliad* is possible without knowing something about the central role of shame and honor in a warrior society, where the regard and esteem of one's peers form the central value. No full understanding of the *Divina Commedia* is possible without some grasp of the system-making, universe-ordering symmetries and hierarchies of the late medieval theologies. This effort at a historical as well as a contemporary understanding of the great literature of the past is important not just to satisfy our intellectual curiosity but also to help us understand ourselves by illuminating the gaps and the differences, as well as the similarities, between our condition of life, our attitudes to such fundamental things as social order and disorder, violence, war, love, and the conditions and attitudes of those who have preceded us and to some degree influenced us.

It is as important to appreciate the otherness that separates us from the past as well as the universal that unites us to it. Without the philological and historical work of determining basic factual matters, the interpretive activity is impossible. Without the interpretive effort to make the work somehow our possession, the work remains a captive of its own historical circumstances, "hermeneutically dead," so that, in its otherness, it would have no means of access or contact with us, in our otherness.

Classicists are so imbued with the historical approach that they often have to make a special effort to see literature in more general, more universalizing and synchronic terms. Yet this grounding in the historical dimension of literature is a very important part of all literary study, and classicists here have a major contribution to make. To flatten out the past into a great synchronic mush is like a perpetual diet of hamburger or noodle casserole—nourishing, but we should at least know that tournedos Rossini exist. Without the historical dimension, our sense of ourselves runs the risk of being thin and superficial. The philosopher George Santayana once wrote that he who is ignorant of history is compelled to repeat it. That dictum applies both to the past of the individual life and to the collective past of a whole culture.

V

Finally, for all of our fascination—and it is a healthy and just fascination—with the theoretical issues involved in the representation of reality by art and with the methodologies of structuralism, deconstruction, psychoanalysis, and affective stylistics which problematize in different ways the nature of literary discourse and the nature of our response to that discourse, we should not lose sight of the quality of pleasure which literature gives us, and we should not forget the naive delight in the experience of a text as it enlarges our sensibilities, widens our horizons, broadens the range of our emotions, and teaches or reminds us of what human life, for good or ill, is like. Plato has the rhapsode Ion thus describe his recitation of the Homeric poems: "Whenever I recite anything that moves pity, my eyes fill with tears; and whenever I recite anything fearful or terrifying, my hair stands straight up in terror, and my heart pounds" (535c).[22] A. E. Housman, in his 1933 lecture *The Name and Nature of Poetry,* describes a similarly physiological response to poetry:

Experience has taught me, when I am shaving of a morning, to keep watch over my thoughts, because if a line of poetry strays into my memory, my skin bristles so that the razor ceases to act. This particular symptom is accompanied by a shiver down the spine; there is another which consists in a constriction of the throat and a precipitation of water to the eyes.[23]

He continues with a third, located "in the pit of the stomach." Some of us, as teachers or as readers, would perhaps be content even with milder reactions; but these two practitioners of literature, two thousand three hundred years apart, will perhaps serve as an example of the peculiar and mysterious coinvolvement of both heart and head, feelings and thoughts, in the experience of literature and of every other art.

Do these responses to literary works make us better? The belief in the educative and improving force of literature persists through the

22. See also Gorgias, *Helen* 9: poetry produces in its hearers "fearful shuddering and much-weeping pity" (φρίκη περίφοβος καὶ ἔλεος πολύδακρυς).
23. A. E. Housman, *The Name and Nature of Poetry* (Cambridge 1933) 46.

centuries, from Aristophanes' *Frogs* to *Educating Rita*. Probably we can no longer assert this principle today with the same confidence. Housman, in his inaugural lecture as professor of Latin at University College London, delivered in 1892, observed wryly, against the Arnoldian tradition of high seriousness and moral improvement: "I never yet heard it maintained by the wildest enthusiast for Classics that the standard of morality or even amiability is higher among classical scholars than among men of science."[24] "The classics," he continues a little later, "cannot be said to have succeeded altogether in transforming and beautifying Milton's inner nature. They did not sweeten his naturally disagreeable temper; they did not enable him to conduct controversy with urbanity or even with decency." There are, of course, answers to Housman's rhetorical assertions. But in any case the idea that literature is only a toy or a leisure pastime on the one hand or a series of intellectual games—a kind of verbal chess—on the other is false to the content of literature as we survey the themes that have concerned the great writers, the meditations on death, suffering, war, love, and hope (to take but one cluster of themes) from Homer's *Iliad* to Saul Bellow's *The Dean's December*.

I end, as a Platonist might have begun, with a definition, a sort of operational definition of literature, a little old-fashioned perhaps, but still serviceable:

If it [literature] doesn't open up for you the inner life of at least one other human being, who may be either the author or one of his fictional creations; if it doesn't release you for a moment from your lonely island in the sea of the individual's isolation; if it doesn't inform you of some of the resources of the human spirit, of its triumphs and frustrations, or of its complexities, perversities, and incongruities; if it doesn't convince you that the inner world of the human spirit is as boundless and wonderful as the outer world of the seven seas and the starry heavens [one may think here of the passage I quoted from Longinus earlier]; if it doesn't indicate that the moral law is as important as the laws of thermodynamics; if it doesn't lead you toward an insighted understanding that, in spite of all outward and measurable differences, inwardly all human beings are akin—if it affects you in none of these ways, then no

24. A. E. Housman, *Introductory Lecture* (Cambridge 1937) 20. The following quotation appears on 21 (or in Housman, *Selected Prose*, ed. John Carter [Cambridge 1961] 9, 10).

matter how great its other merits of diction and form and style may be, what you have been reading is not literature.[25]

Or, from the poet's point of view, and more concisely,

> Que ton vers soit la bonne aventure
> Eparse au vent crispé du matin
> Qui va fleurant la menthe et le thym . . .
> Et tout le reste est littérature.[26]

25. Henry Alonzo Myers, "Literature, Science, and Democracy" (1954), in *Tragedy: A View of Life* (Ithaca 1956) 190f.
26. Paul Verlaine, "Art Poétique."

Index

Index

Index

Homer (*cont.*)
96, 108, 124, 324, 359, 367, 374. *See also* Iliad; Odyssey
Homeric Hymns, 52, 59, 63, 228; to Aphrodite, 59, 63
Hoplite, 57
Horatio, 343
Horse symbolism, in *Hippolytus*, 176, 200, 202, 279, 280, 281
Housman, A. E., 373–74
Hoy, David, 370
Humphreys, S. C., 22
Hunting, 52, 56, 151, 175, 185, 196, 239, 275, 276, 279–81, 283, 305
Hyacinthia, 252, 254
Hyacinthus, 252
Hydra, 27, 35, 44, 67, 275
Hyllus, 26, 27, 35, 58, 119
Hymenaios, 282
Hypsipolis, 148

Ibsen, 394
Ibycus, 230
Iceman Cometh, The, 338
Ida, Mount, 59
Iliad, 51, 53, 79, 93, 224, 230, 238, 372, 374
Initiation, 52, 252, 280, 305
Intertextuality, 304
Io, 85
Iole, 44, 58
Ion, 67, 373
Ion, 236, 242, 266, 338, 344
Iphigenia, 28, 45, 102–4, 345, 350
Iphigenia in Aulis, 95
Iphigenia among the Taurians, 95, 102–4, 173, 235, 236, 237, 260, 266, 272
Irony, 67
Iser, Wolfgang, 365
Ismene, 140, 143, 145, 151

Jakobson, Roman, 43
James, Henry, 359, 362
Jason, 317, 323, 324
Jauss, Hans Robert, 365
Job, 341
Jocasta, 30, 70, 71, 78, 97, 98, 115, 133, 322
Jones, John, 99
Joyce, James, 359
Jung, C. G., 21
Juvenal, 336

Kafka, Franz, 336
Kannicht, Richard, 258, 260
Kerdos, 141

Kermode, Frank, 371
King Lear, 338, 339. *See also* Lear
Kingship, 28, 29, 37, 38, 167, 272, 282, 287, 288, 293. *See also* Sacral Kingship
Kinship, 68
Kleos, 234, 241
Knox, Bernard, 21, 40, 209, 210
Kos, 228, 254
Kourotrophos, 276
Kratos, 283, 284
Kristeva, Julia, 64

Labyrinth, 328
Lacan, Jacques, 295, 302
Laius, 86, 97, 131, 133, 321, 326
Landscape: in *Bacchae*, 310–12; in Senecan Tragedy, 318–19, 327–29
Language (in tragedy), 24, 25, 36, 38, 43–45, 48, 49, 50, 53, 64, 65, 67, 68, 69, 87, 93, 295, 301–6, 337–43, 363
Langue, 53
Lanza, Diego, 76
Lattimore, Richmond, 351
Lear, 30, 339, 341, 348
Lenaea, 41, 77
Lessing, G. E., 76
Leucippus, 92
Leucothea, 229
Lévi-Strauss, Claude, 23, 26, 32, 49, 268, 269, 273, 293
Lichas, 119
Liminality, 31, 39, 64, 280, 285
Literacy, 73. *See also* Writing
Locus Amoenus, 230, 311
Logoi, 33, 93
Logos and *Ergon*, 93, 126, 238
Long Day's Journey into Night, 338
Longinus, 23, 285, 360, 361, 364
Lorrain, Claude, 368
Lowell, Robert, 340
Lucan, 336
Lucretius, 327
Lycus, 36
Lysistrata, 232, 242

Macbeth, 347. *See also* Macbeth, Lady
Macbeth, Lady, 324, 347–48
Maenads, 34, 37, 73, 283, 302, 309
Manto, 320
Marcellinus, Ammianus, 329
Marriage, 27, 36, 43, 44, 60, 63, 154, 275
Marxism, 65, 360, 369
Mask, 73, 105, 106, 127, 281
Mater Dolorosa, 40
Matricide, 130n.23, 351–52
Matthaei, L. E., 202

Index

Index

LIBRARY OF CONGRESS CATALOGING-IN-PUBLICATION DATA

Segal, Charles, 1936–
    Interpreting Greek tragedy.

    Includes index.
    1. Greek drama (Tragedy)—History and criticism. 2. Mythology, Greek, in literature. I. Title.
PA3131.S44 1986   882'.01'09   85-48266
ISBN 0-8014-1890-9
ISBN 0-8014-9362-5 (pbk.)